STRATEGY MAPS

STRATEGY MAPS

CONVERTING INTANGIBLE ASSETS
INTO TANGIBLE OUTCOMES

Robert S. Kaplan
David P. Norton

HARVARD BUSINESS SCHOOL PRESS
BOSTON, MASSACHUSETTS

978-1-59139-134-0 (ISBN 13)
Library of Congress Cataloging-in-Publication Data
Kaplan, Robert S.
  Strategy maps: converting intangible assets into tangible outcomes / Robert S.
Kaplan and David P. Norton
    p. cm.
  Includes index.
  ISBN 1-59139-134-2 (alk. paper)
  1.Strategic planning. 2. Intangible property—Management. 3. Human capital.
4. Management. I. Norton, David P., 1941- II. Title.
HD30.28.K35443 2004
658.4′012—dc22   2003024059

The paper used in this publication meets the requirements of the American National
Standard for Permanence of Paper for Publications and Documents in Libraries and
Archives Z39.48-1992.

This book is dedicated to the professionals, clients, and associates of the Balanced Scorecard Collaborative, who provided the wealth of the experience on which this work is based.

CONTENTS

PART V: THE CASE FILES

PREFACE

THE KAPLAN-NORTON COLLABORATION began in 1990 with a multi-company research project that explored new ways to measure organizational performance. We believed, at the time, that knowledge-based assets—primarily employees and information technology—were becoming increasingly important for companies' competitive success. But companies' primary measurement systems remained the financial accounting system, which treated investments in employee capabilities, databases, information systems, customer relationships, quality, responsive processes, and innovative products and services as expenses in the period in which they were incurred. Financial reporting systems provided no foundation for measuring and managing the value created by enhancing the capabilities of an organization's intangible assets.

We believed that executives and employees paid attention to what they measured, and that people could not manage well what they were not measuring. Consequently, executives' attention and effort were overly focused on influencing short-term financial measures, and insufficiently on investing in and managing the intangible assets that provided the foundation for future financial success. Without an improved performance measurement system, executives would not develop and mobilize their intangible assets effectively, and thereby would forfeit major opportunities for value creation.

From this one-year research project came the concept of a Balanced Scorecard of measurements.[1] We recommended that organizations retain financial measures, to summarize the results of actions previously taken, but that they should balance these outcome measures with nonfinancial measures in three additional perspectives—customer, internal processes, and learning and growth—that represented the drivers, the lead indicators, of future financial performance. This was the foundation of the Balanced Scorecard.

The article struck an immediate and responsive chord among executives. We began to work with several organizations to facilitate their implementation of the Balanced Scorecard. We soon learned that while executives appreciated a more comprehensive new performance measurement system, they wanted to use their new system in a more powerful application than we had originally envisioned. The executives wanted to apply the system to solve the more important problem they faced—how to implement new strategies. For not only was the nature of their internal value creation process shifting from tangible to intangible assets; the nature of competition in their external markets was shifting as well. Manufacturing companies, which formerly competed merely on production capabilities and product characteristics, discovered that success now required deep understanding of their markets and customers, and an ability to provide unique value propositions to their targeted customers. Newly deregulated service companies now faced vigorous competition from companies that had historically been outside their protected markets. Often entirely new companies had entered their industries based on effective deployment of advanced information technology. Even public-sector agencies and not-for-profit organizations were being asked to demonstrate how they created value for their constituents and stakeholders. So executives in all sectors and in all parts of the world were facing the dual challenges of how to mobilize their human capital and information resources and how to transform their organizations to new strategies, driven by informed and selective customers demanding outstanding performance.

Companies and public-sector and nonprofit organizations generally responded to the challenge by formulating new strategies and rededicating themselves—through inspirational new mission and vision statements—to deliver increased value to their customer segments and constituents. The deep problem that virtually all organizations encountered, however, was their inability to execute successfully on their new strategies. Employees could hear the words of the new mission, vision, and strategy statements, but they didn't understand what the words meant to them. How should they do their jobs differently or better to help the organization succeed with its new strategy? Various studies indicated that 70 percent to 90 percent of organizations failed to realize success from their strategies.

Executives implementing the Balanced Scorecard intuitively understood that a strategy-based measurement system could solve the problem of how to communicate and implement strategy. As we observed executives using the Balanced Scorecard, we could see them develop a new system for managing strategy. We described the elements of this new system in another *Harvard Business Review* article,[2] and our first book,[3] which consisted of two parts: Part I described the Balanced Scorecard as an enhanced performance *measurement* system, and Part II described how executives in early-adopting companies had embedded the Balanced Scorecard into a new strategic performance *management* system.

During the next four years, we tracked the performance of these adopting companies, and a new set of companies, some that we had assisted in the implementation and others that had implemented on their own. We learned that these companies were achieving breakthrough performance, and in relatively short periods of time—within two to three years of launching their BSC projects and their organizational transformations. When we asked the executives about the role of the BSC in their remarkable transformations, they responded typically with two words: *alignment* and *focus*. The BSC had enabled them to align all their organizational resources—executive teams, business units, support groups, information technology, and employee recruiting and training—to focus intensively on implementing their strategies. We documented the experiences and practices of these companies in our second book, *The Strategy-Focused Organization*.[4] This book expanded on the strategic management system we introduced in Part II of *The Balanced Scorecard*. It showed how successful adopters followed five management principles to become "strategy-focused":

- Translate strategy to operational terms
- Align the organization to the strategy
- Make strategy everyone's everyday job
- Make strategy a continual process
- Mobilize change through executive leadership

In addition to learning about the management principles to become strategy-focused, we also learned how to choose measurements that would be more meaningful to executives and employees. Our initial 1992 *HBR* article advocated using a broad set of measurements, organized by four perspectives, to improve performance. As we started to work with companies, we naturally had to address how to select the twenty to thirty measures in an organization's Balanced Scorecard. We soon realized that the measures should not be selected because they were already being used in the organization or because they could drive local continuous improvements. Our second *HBR* article described how the measurements should focus on what is most important for the organization: its strategy.[5] And because employees would pay much attention to the selected measures, we had to be careful that we were measuring the right things. As the saying goes, "Be careful what you wish for; you might get it." Measurement is a powerful motivator. Managers and employees strive to perform well on whatever measures get selected, particularly if the measures are tied to an incentive compensation plan. So before deciding what to measure, we had to ask executives what they were trying to accomplish: What were their objectives? This innocent question led to a seemingly small enhancement in our methodology that turned out to have far-reaching consequences.

We learned to start each engagement by getting executives to agree on word statements of their objectives in the four BSC perspectives. Once the executives agreed to the word statements of what they wanted to accomplish—how they wanted to describe success—the selection of measurements became much simpler. And, in an interesting twist, the selection of measures became somewhat less consequential. After all, when agreement existed about the objective to be achieved, even if the initial measurements for the objective turned out to be less than perfect, the executives could easily modify the measurements for subsequent periods, without having to redo their discussion about strategy. The objectives would likely remain the same even as the measurements of the objectives evolved with experience and new data sources.

The focus on objectives led to a breakthrough: *Objectives should be linked in cause-and-effect relationships.* Executives, as they listed objectives in the four perspectives, instinctively started to draw arrows to link the objectives. They could now articulate their strategy of how improving employee capabilities and skills in certain job positions, coupled with new technology, would enable a critical internal process to improve. The improved process would enhance the value proposition delivered to targeted customers, leading to increased customer satisfaction, retention, and growth in customers' businesses. The improved customer outcome measures would then lead to increased revenues and ultimately significantly higher shareholder value. Soon we were coaching all the executive teams to describe their strategy by explicit cause-and-effect relationships among the objectives in the four BSC perspectives. We named this diagram a *strategy map.* And while every organization's strategy map was different, reflecting their different industries and strategies, we could, after facilitating the development of hundreds of strategy maps, see a basic pattern emerge. We formulated a generic strategy map to serve as a starting point for any organization in any industry. We communicated the insights from strategy maps in our fourth HBR article,[6] and in the chapters on translating strategy into operational terms in *The Strategy-Focused Organization.*

The strategy map has turned out to be as important an innovation as the original Balanced Scorecard itself. Executives find the visual representation of strategy both natural and powerful. As one executive speaker exclaimed at the start of her talk at a conference, "I love strategy maps." When we post organizations' strategy maps on the walls of rooms where we hold conferences, delegates use their coffee breaks to study each diagram—even for organizations completely different from their own—often sketching the map and filling in some key objectives.

The realization of the importance of strategy maps motivated us to write this third book in the Balanced Scorecard series. The "equation" below positions this book relative to its two predecessors.

Successful execution of a strategy requires three components:

$$\{\text{Breakthrough results}\} = \{\text{Describe the strategy}\} + \\ \{\text{Measure the strategy}\} + \{\text{Manage the strategy}\}$$

The philosophy of the three components is simple:

- You can't manage (third component) what you can't measure (second component)
- You can't measure what you can't describe (first component)

Our first book, *The Balanced Scorecard,* addressed the second component by showing how to measure strategic objectives in multiple perspectives. It also presented the early ideas about the third component, how to manage the strategy. *The Strategy-Focused Organization* provided a more comprehensive approach for how to manage the strategy. It also introduced strategy maps for the first component, how to describe the strategy. The current book, *Strategy Maps,* goes into much more detail on this aspect, using linked objectives in strategy maps to describe and visualize the strategy.[7]

Thus we can rewrite the above equation as:

$$\text{Breakthrough results} = \{\text{Strategy Maps}\} + \{\text{Balanced Scorecard}\} + \\ \{\text{Strategy-Focused Organization}\}$$

This book introduces several important new contributions:

1. A template that describes the basic components of how value gets created in the internal and learning and growth perspectives
2. Themes, based on value-creating processes, that articulate the dynamics of a strategy
3. A new framework for describing, measuring, and aligning the three intangible assets in the learning and growth perspective— human capital, information capital, and organization capital—to strategic processes and objectives in the internal perspective

Templates, strategic themes, and intangible assets are the building blocks for understanding and executing strategy. They provide increased granularity for executives to describe and manage strategy at an operational level of detail.

ACKNOWLEDGMENTS

We could not have produced the work in this book without the great contributions made by our colleagues at Balanced Scorecard Collaborative (BSCol), their clients, and the other organizations that brought their work to us and shared their insights. We want to express special thanks to Cassandra Frangos for her commitment and dedication to building our understanding of human capital management.

We greatly appreciate the active support and contributions of the people identified below:

Organization	Organization Champion andlor Project Leader	Balanced Scorecard Collaborative Contributor
Amanco	Roberto Salas	Mathias Mangels, Carlos Graham
American Diabetes Association	John Graham, Tom Bognanno	Mario Bognanno
Bank of Tokyo-Mitsubishi HQA	Naotaka Obata, Takehiko Nagumo	Barnaby Donlon
Boise Office Solutions	David Goudge, Scott Williams	Randy Russell

Bonneville Power	Terry Esvelt	Cassandra Frangos
Boston Lyric Opera	Janice Mancini Del Sesto, Sue Dahling-Sullivan	Ellen Kaplan
Crown Castle International	John Kelly, Bob Paladino	Jan Koch
Datex-Ohmeda	Eero Hautaniemi, Mary Ann Worsman, Brant Sonzogni	Ann Nevius
Economic Development Administration (U.S. Department of Commerce)	Dr. David Sampson, Sandy Baruah, Danette Koebele	Mario Bognanno
Fulton County School System	Martha Taylor-Greenway	
Gray-Syracuse	Paul Smith	Cassandra Frangos
Handleman Company	Steve Strome, Rozanne Kokko, Gina Drewek	Geoff Fenwick, Dana Goldblatt, Mike Nagel
Ingersoll-Rand	Herb Henkel, Don Rice	Mike Clark
MDS	John Rogers, Bob Harris	Mike Nagel, Jay Weiser
Media General	Stewart Bryan, Bill McDonnell	Patricia Bush, Jan Koch
National City Corporation	Shelley Seifert	Cassandra Frangos
Northwestern Mutual	Ed Zore, Deborah Beck	Arun Dhingra
Royal Canadian Mounted Police	Commissioner G. Zaccardelli, Geoff Gruson	Andrew Pateman
Saatchi & Saatchi	Bill Cochrane, Paul Melter	Jan Koch, Patricia Bush

St. Mary's Duluth Clinic Health System	Dr. Peter Person, Barbara Possin	Ann Nevius, Judith Ross
Swiss Re	John Coomber, Rosemarie Dissler	Antosh Nirmul
Tata Auto Plastics	Rajiv Bakshi, Muhamed Muneer (Innovative Media)	
Teach for America	Jerry Hauser	
Thomson Financial	Dick Harrington, Dave Shaffer, Ro Pavlick	Barnaby Donlon, Rondo Moses
Thornton Oil	Rick Claes	Patricia Bush, Lauren Keller Johnson
T. Rowe Price	Pam McGinnis	Bob Gold
U.K. Ministry of Defence	Sir Kevin Tebbit, Commander Des Cook, Captain Mike Potter, Tracy Buckingham, Simon Howard	Gaelle Lamotte
United States Army	Strategic Readiness System Team	Patricia Bush, Laura Downing
University of California, Berkeley Administrative Services	Ron Coley, Claudia Covello, Beth Luke	Cassandra Frangos
Volvofinans	Björn Ingemanson, Marianne Söderberg	Carl-Frederik Helgegren

We also wish to acknowledge the contributions of Rob Howie and Michael Contrada, who manage the conference and consulting services of BSCol. These services provide the foundation to continuously develop our own intangible assets. In preparing the internal process chapters in Part II, we benefited from and summarized the work of several academic scholars. For the chapter on operations management, we used a risk management framework developed by Lisa Meulbroek of MIT; for the chapter on customer management processes, we drew upon work of Harvard

Business School faculty members Das Narandas, Rajiv Lal, Jim Heskett, and Robert Dolan; for the chapter on innovation processes, we drew on material produced by HBS faculty members Stephen Wheelwright, Kim Clark, Marco Iansiti, and Alan MacCormick, and benefited from the guidance of Stefan Thomke; and for the chapter on regulatory and social processes, we incorporated frameworks developed by HBS faculty members Forest Reinhart and Michael Porter, and benefited from the comments of Professor Marc Epstein of Rice University and Lester Lave of Carnegie-Mellon University. For the chapter on information capital, we built upon the work of Peter Weill of MIT and Marianne Broadbent of Gartner. Professor Arnoldo Hax of MIT helped us to understand the power of lock-in strategies. Professor Charles O'Reilly of Stanford provided valuable material and insights about culture and its measurement for the chapter on organization capital readiness. Michael Porter of HBS, of course, has provided the foundational work in strategy that has influenced and inspired our thinking. We are grateful for all their contributions and have attempted to integrate them faithfully within the strategy map framework.

We give special thanks to Rose LaPiana for preparing the manuscript and the graphics, coordinating the case studies, and keeping the project and us organized, and to David Porter of HBS for his administrative support.

We continue to value the enthusiasm and guidance of Carol Franco, president, and our editor, Hollis Heimbouch, at Harvard Business School Press, and the assistance of Jane Bonassar, manuscript editor, who guided us through the production process.

—Robert S. Kaplan and David P. Norton
Boston and Lincoln, Massachusetts, June 2003

NOTES

1. Robert S. Kaplan and David P. Norton, "The Balanced Scorecard: Measures That Drive Performance," *Harvard Business Review* (January–February 1992).
2. Robert S. Kaplan and David P. Norton, "Using the Balanced Scorecard as a Strategic Management System," *Harvard Business Review* (January–February 1996).
3. Robert S. Kaplan and David P. Norton, *The Balanced Scorecard: Translating Strategy into Action* (Boston: Harvard Business School Press, 1996).
4. Robert S. Kaplan and David P. Norton, *The Strategy-Focused Organization: How Balanced Scorecard Companies Thrive in the New Business Environment* (Boston: Harvard Business School Press, 2001).

5. Robert S. Kaplan and David P. Norton, "Putting the Balanced Scorecard to Work," *Harvard Business Review* (September–October 1993).

6. Robert S. Kaplan and David P. Norton, "Having Trouble with Your Strategy? Then Map It!" *Harvard Business Review* (January–February 2001).

7. *Strategy Maps* also extends our first book, by identifying specific measures for strategy map objectives, particularly in the internal and learning and growth perspectives.

PART ONE

Overview

CHAPTER ONE

INTRODUCTION

Even though we manage everyone's competencies, we had been biased toward the high-skill jobs. The identification of strategic job families brought something to the forefront that we wouldn't have seen otherwise. . . . It showed us an entry-level job that was just as important. The benefits of focusing on this job will be huge.

Paul Smith, director of human resources at Gray-Syracuse, was commenting on a new training program that would rapidly upgrade its thirty assemblypersons on a broad set of new competencies. Gray-Syracuse is a world-class producer of precision casting parts for highly engineered products used in aircraft engines, power generation equipment, and missiles. Senior management, after developing a Balanced Scorecard (BSC) and strategy map for its new strategy, had learned that the front end of the production process was a major opportunity to reduce rework and improve quality. The entry-level operators of this process, mold assemblypersons, had the greatest impact on reducing rework and decreasing the lead time from product idea to customer delivery. The company focused its limited training dollars on these critical few employees and cut the time to achieve strategic objectives in half.

The Gray-Syracuse example shows how companies can now focus their human capital investments and, more generally, their investments in all intangible assets to create distinctive and sustainable value. All organizations today create sustainable value from leveraging their intangible assets—human capital; databases and information systems; responsive, high-quality processes; customer relationships and brands; innovation capabilities; and culture. The trend away from a product-driven economy, based on tangible assets, to a knowledge and service economy, based on intangible assets, has been occurring for decades. Even after the bursting of the NASDAQ and dot-com bubbles, intangible assets—those not measured by a company's financial system—account for more than 75 percent of a company's value (see Figure 1-1). The average company's tangible assets—the net book value of assets less liabilities—represent less than 25 percent of market value.

What's true of companies is even truer for countries. Some countries, such as Venezuela and Saudi Arabia, have high physical resource endowments but have made poor investments in their people and systems. As a consequence, they produce far less output per person, and experience much slower growth rates, than countries such as Singapore and Taiwan that have few natural resources but invest heavily in human and information capital and effective internal systems.[1] At both the macroeconomic and microeconomic levels, intangible assets drive long-term value creation.

STRATEGY

An organization's strategy describes how it intends to create value for its shareholders, customers, and citizens. If an organization's intangible as-

Figure 1-1 The Increasing Importance of Intangible Assets

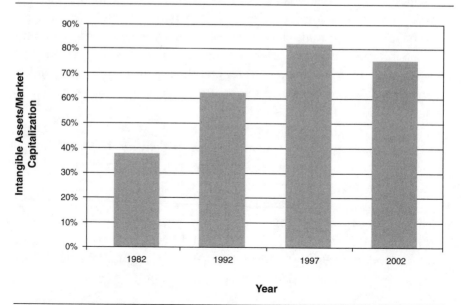

sets represent more than 75 percent of its value, then its strategy formulation and execution need to explicitly address the mobilization and alignment of intangible assets, the subject of this book.

We, and our colleagues, have worked with more than 300 organizations over the past dozen years, helping them to develop and implement Balanced Scorecards. We have learned that the Balanced Scorecard is a powerful management tool. A measurement system gets everyone's attention. For maximum impact, therefore, the measurement system should focus on the entity's *strategy*—how it expects to create future, sustainable value. In designing Balanced Scorecards, therefore, *an organization must measure the critical few parameters that represent its strategy for long-term value creation.*

In our practice, however, we observed that no two organizations thought about strategy in the same way. Some described strategy by their financial plans for revenue and profit growth, others by their products or services, others by targeted customers, others from a quality and process orientation, and still others from a human resources or learning perspective. These views were one-dimensional. This narrowness was further amplified by the background of the individuals on the executive team. CFOs viewed strategy from a financial perspective; sales and marketing executives took a customer perspective; operations people looked at quality, cycle time, and other process perspectives; human resources professionals focused on investments in people; and CIOs on information technology. Few had a holistic view of their organization.

We found little help on a holistic framework from the prevailing wisdom of management thought leaders. Strategic doctrines existed around shareholder value,[2] customer management,[3] process management,[4] quality,[5] core capabilities,[6] innovation,[7] human resources,[8] information technology,[9] organizational design,[10] and learning.[11] While each provides deep insights, none provides a comprehensive and integrated view for describing a strategy. Even Michael Porter's approach, based on positioning for competitive advantage, does not provide a general representation of strategy.[12] Executives who have successfully executed strategy—Lou Gerstner at IBM, Jack Welch at GE, Richard Teerlink at Harley-Davidson, and Larry Bossidy at GE, Allied Signal, and Honeywell—provide a wealth of experiential insights, but not a consistent way to represent strategy.[13] A generally accepted way to describe strategy did not exist.

Consider the consequences. Without a comprehensive description of strategy, executives cannot easily communicate the strategy among themselves or to their employees. Without a shared understanding of the strategy, executives cannot create alignment around it. And, without alignment, executives cannot implement their new strategies for the changed environment of global competition, deregulation, customer sovereignty, advanced technology, and competitive advantage derived from intangible assets, principally human and information capital.

In *The Strategy-Focused Organization,* we noted a study of failed strategies, which concluded, "in the majority of cases—we estimate 70 percent—the real problem isn't [bad strategy] . . . it's bad execution."[14] A more recent study by Bain & Company examined the performance of large companies (defined as companies earning revenues in excess of $500 million) in seven developed countries—the United States, Australia, the United Kingdom, France, Germany, Italy, and Japan— during the best ten years ever in economic history, 1988 to 1998. Only one out of eight of these companies enjoyed at least a 5.5 percent real cumulative annual growth rate in earnings while also earning shareholder returns above their cost of capital. More than two-thirds of these companies had strategic plans with targets calling for real growth in excess of 9 percent. Fewer than *10 percent* of these companies achieved this target.[15] Clearly, most companies don't succeed in implementing their strategies. In contrast to this bleak record, organizations that made the Balanced Scorecard the cornerstone of their management systems, as we described in *The Strategy-Focused Organization,* beat these odds. They implemented new strategies effectively and rapidly. They used the Balanced Scorecard to describe their strategies and then linked their management systems to the Balanced Scorecard and, hence, to their strategies. They demonstrated a fundamental principle underlying the Balanced Scorecard: "If you can measure it, you can manage it."

Describing Your Strategy

In order to build a measurement system that describes the strategy, we need a general model of strategy. Carl von Clausewitz, the great military strategist of the nineteenth century, stressed the importance of a framework to organize thinking about strategy.

> *The first task of any theory is to clarify terms and concepts that are confused. . . . Only after agreement has been reached regarding terms and concepts can we hope to consider the issues easily and clearly and expect to share the same viewpoint with the reader.*[16]

The Balanced Scorecard offers just such a framework for describing strategies for creating value. The BSC framework (see Figure 1-2) has several important elements.

- *Financial* performance, a lag indicator, provides the ultimate definition of an organization's success. Strategy describes how an organization intends to create sustainable growth in shareholder value.
- Success with targeted customers provides a principal component for improved financial performance. In addition to measuring the lagging outcome indicators of customer success, such as satisfaction, retention, and growth, the customer perspective defines the value proposition for targeted customer segments. Choosing the *customer value proposition* is the central element of strategy.
- Internal *processes* create and deliver the value proposition for customers. The performance of internal processes is a leading indicator of subsequent improvements in customer and financial outcomes.
- Intangible assets are the ultimate source of sustainable value creation. *Learning and growth* objectives describe how the people, technology, and organization climate combine to support the strategy. Improvements in learning and growth measures are lead indicators for internal process, customer, and financial performance.
- Objectives in the four perspectives link together in a chain of cause-and-effect relationships. Enhancing and aligning intangible assets leads to improved process performance, which, in turn, drives success for customers and shareholders.

The framework for value creation in public-sector and nonprofit organizations (see the right side of Figure 1-2) is similar to the private-sector framework described above, but with several important distinctions. First, the ultimate definition of success for public and nonprofit organizations is their performance in achieving their *mission*. Private-sector organizations, regardless of industry sector, can use a homogeneous financial perspective: Increase shareholder value. Public-sector and nonprofit organizations, however, span a broad and diverse set of missions and hence must define their social impact, their high-level objective, differently. Examples of missions include: "Improve the prospects of children growing up today in low-income communities" (Teach for America); "Ensure the long-term future of opera" (Boston Lyric Opera); and "Safe Homes, Safe Communities" (Royal Canadian Mounted Police).

Figure 1-2 Strategy Maps: The Simple Model of Value Creation

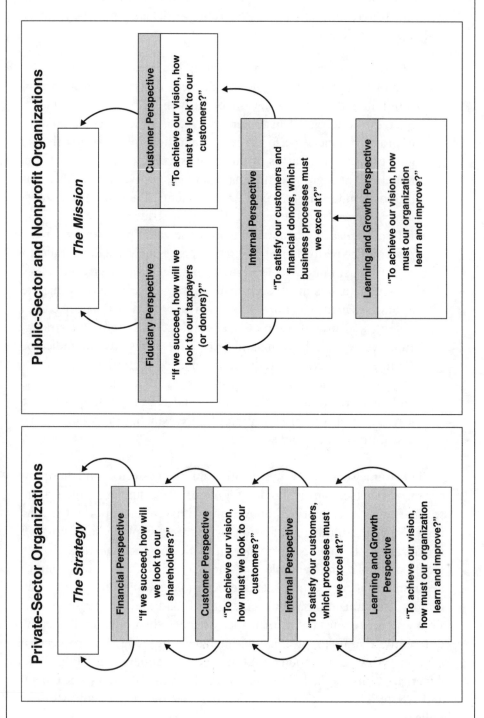

The mission for these organizations, as in the private-sector model, is achieved through meeting the needs of targeted *customers* (or constituents or stakeholders, as some of these organizations describe the people who benefit from their services). The organizations create success through internal *process* performance that is supported by their intangible assets (*learning and growth*). The *fiduciary* perspective, while not dominant, reflects the objectives of an important constituency—the taxpayers or donors who supply the funding. Satisfying both financial and customer stakeholders, consistent with the mission, creates a strategic architecture of efficiency and effectiveness themes that mirrors the productivity and revenue growth themes used by private-sector organizations.

STRATEGY MAPS: DESCRIBING HOW THE ORGANIZATION CREATES VALUE

Our work with more than 300 organizations has provided us with an extensive database of strategies, strategy maps, and Balanced Scorecards. In addition, we have studied the state of knowledge in diverse management fields, including shareholder value, business and corporate strategy, customer management, product development and innovation, operations management, environmental management, social investment, human resource management, information technology management, culture, and leadership. From this experience and knowledge, we have learned how the Balanced Scorecard, initially proposed to improve the measurement of an organization's intangible assets, can be a powerful tool for describing and implementing an organization's strategy. The four-perspective model for describing an organization's value-creating strategy provides a language that executive teams can use to discuss the direction and priorities of their enterprises. They can view their strategic measures, not as performance indicators in four independent perspectives, but as a series of cause-and-effect linkages among objectives in the four Balanced Scorecard perspectives. We facilitate the discussions among executives by creating a general representation of these linkages that we call a *strategy map*. We now realize that the strategy map, a visual representation of the cause-and-effect relationships among the components of an organization's strategy, is as big an insight to executives as the Balanced Scorecard itself.

The general strategy map, shown in Figure 1-3, evolved from the simple, four-perspective model of the Balanced Scorecard. The strategy map adds a second layer of detail that illustrates the time-based dynamics of a strategy; it also adds a level of granularity that improves clarity and focus. As we noted earlier, numerous approaches are used in practice to formulate strategy. Regardless of which approach is used, however, a strategy map provides a uniform and consistent way to describe that strategy, so that objectives and measures can be established and managed. The strategy map provides the missing link between strategy formulation and strategy execution.

The strategy map template described in Figure 1-3 also provides a normative checklist for a strategy's components and interrelationships. If a strategy is missing an element on the strategy map template, the strategy is likely flawed. For example, we frequently find that organizations have no connection between internal process measures and a customer value proposition, no objectives for innovation, and vague objectives for employee skills and motivation and for the role of information technology. Such omissions on a strategy map will generally lead to disappointing outcomes.

The strategy map is based on several principles:

Strategy balances contradictory forces. Investing in intangible assets for long-term revenue growth usually conflicts with cutting costs for short-term financial performance. The dominant objective for private-sector organizations is the creation of sustained growth in shareholder value. This implies a commitment to the long-term. At the same time, the organization must show improved results in the short-term. Short-term results can always be achieved by sacrificing long-term investments, frequently in an invisible way. Thus, the starting point in describing the strategy is to balance and articulate the short-term financial objective for cost reduction and productivity improvements with the long-term objective for profitable revenue growth.

Strategy is based on a differentiated customer value proposition. Satisfying customers is the source of sustainable value creation. Strategy requires a clear articulation of targeted customer segments and the value proposition required to please them. Clarity of this value proposition is the single most important dimension of strategy. In Chapter 2, and again in Chapter 11, we will discuss the four major value propositions and customer strategies that we have observed organizations using in practice: (1) low total cost, (2) product leadership, (3) complete customer solutions, and (4) system lock-in. Each of these value propositions clearly defines the attributes that must be delivered if the customer is to be satisfied.

Figure 1-3 A Strategy Map Represents How the Organization Creates Value

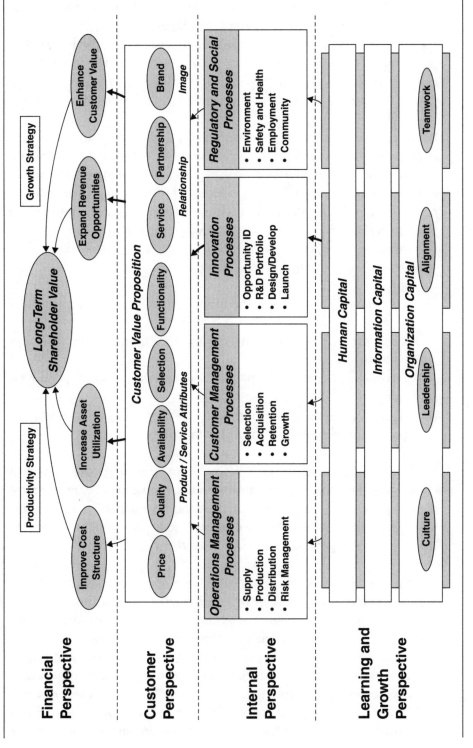

Value is created through internal business processes. The financial and customer perspectives in strategy maps and Balanced Scorecards describe the outcomes, that is, what the organization hopes to achieve: increases in shareholder value through revenue growth and productivity improvements; increases in the company's share of customers' spending through customer acquisition, satisfaction, retention, loyalty, and growth.

Processes in the internal and learning and growth perspectives drive the strategy; they describe how the organization will implement its strategy. Effective and aligned internal processes determine how value gets created and sustained. Companies must focus on the critical few internal processes that deliver the differentiating value proposition and that are most critical for enhancing productivity and maintaining the organization's franchise to operate. In Part II of this book, we introduce a taxonomy that classifies internal processes into four clusters:

- *Operations management:* Producing and delivering products and services to customers
- *Customer management:* Establishing and leveraging relationships with customers
- *Innovation:* Developing new products, services, processes, and relationships
- *Regulatory and social:* Conforming to regulations and societal expectations and building stronger communities

Each of these clusters can have literally hundreds of subprocesses that create value in some way. Executives practicing the art of strategy must identify the critical few processes that are the most important for creating and delivering the differentiating customer value proposition. We refer to these critical few processes as the *strategic themes.*

Strategy consists of simultaneous, complementary themes. Each cluster of internal processes delivers benefits at different points in time. Improvements in *operational processes* generally deliver short-term results through cost savings and quality enhancements. Benefits from an enhanced *customer relationship* start to phase in six to twelve months after the initial improvement in customer management processes. *Innovation* processes generally take even longer to produce higher customer revenues and operating margins, and the benefits from enhanced *regulatory and social* processes can occur further in the future as companies avoid litigation and enhance their reputations in the community. Strategies should be balanced, incorporating at least one strategic theme from each of the four internal clusters. By having strategic themes for enhancing processes in all four internal clusters, the organization realizes benefits that phase in over time, generating sustainable growth in shareholder value.

Strategic alignment determines the value of intangible assets. The fourth perspective of the Balanced Scorecard strategy map, *learning and growth*, describes the organization's intangible assets and their role in the strategy. Intangible assets can be classified into three categories:

- *Human capital:* Employees' skills, talent, and knowledge
- *Information capital:* Databases, information systems, networks, and technology infrastructure
- *Organization capital:* Culture, leadership, employee alignment, teamwork, and knowledge management

None of these intangible assets has value that can be measured separately or independently. The value of these intangible assets derives from their ability to help the organization implement its strategy. Our research studies show, however, that two-thirds of organizations do not create strong alignment between their strategies and their HR and IT programs.[17] The considerable investments, by these unaligned organizations, in HR and IT programs are off target. They do not facilitate the organizations' ability to execute their strategies. And these organizations are unlikely to generate a positive return on their HR and IT investments.

We have identified three targeted approaches for aligning intangible assets to strategy:

1. *Strategic job families* that align human capital to the strategic themes
2. The *strategic IT portfolio* that aligns information capital to the strategic themes
3. An *organization change agenda* that integrates and aligns organization capital for continued learning and improvement in the strategic themes

When all three components in the learning and growth perspective—human, information, and organization capital—are aligned with the strategy, the entity has a high degree of organization readiness: It has the *ability to mobilize and sustain the process of change required to execute its strategy*. Organization readiness is high when:

- Human capital capabilities in strategic job families are aligned closely to the strategic themes.
- Information capital provides the vital infrastructure and strategic IT applications that complement the human capital for promoting outstanding performance in the strategic themes.
- Culture, leadership, alignment, and teamwork reinforce the changes in organization climate required to execute the strategy.

In summary, the strategy map template, customized to the organization's particular strategy, describes how intangible assets drive performance enhancements to the organization's internal processes that have the maximum leverage for delivering value to customers, shareholders, and communities. Readers can get introduced to the use of strategy maps to align intangible assets to strategic themes by studying the two case studies following this chapter. The Bank of Tokyo case illustrates the design of a private-sector strategy map and scorecard. The American Diabetes Association case illustrates the nonprofit-sector approach.

BOOK STRUCTURE

In Chapter 2, we provide a primer on strategy maps. We explain the strategy map template (see Figure 1-3) and describe the selection of objectives in the four Balanced Scorecard perspectives. Part II of the book contains four chapters that explore in depth the objectives and measures for processes in the four internal perspective themes: operations management, customer management, innovation, and regulatory and social processes. Part III contains four chapters on aligning the learning and growth perspective to the strategic internal processes. Chapter 7 provides an overview for value creation from intangible assets. Chapters 8 through 10 provide in-depth descriptions of selecting objectives and measures for human capital, information capital, and organization capital. In Part IV, Chapter 11 applies the foundational material in Parts II and III to constructing strategy map templates for four generic differentiating strategies: low total cost, product leadership, total customer solutions, and lock-in. Chapter 12 provides the implementation road map by describing how stretch targets for organizational performance can be translated into subtargets for the major strategic themes in the map. The subtargets guide the selection of strategic initiatives and programs for driving the performance breakthroughs.

After each chapter in the book, and in Part V, we present brief excerpts from our case files. Each excerpt contains the context and strategy of the organization, its strategy map, and some results from managing with the strategy map. The organizations used the strategy map to clarify strategy at the executive level; communicate strategy to employees; align business units, departments, functions, and initiatives; and focus management processes. The implementing organizations include manufacturing and service companies, large for-profits and small nonprofits, and several public-sector agencies ranging from a school district to a national department of defense. They are drawn from experiences in North, Central, and South America and Europe and Asia. Collectively, these case excerpts represent the most comprehensive portfolio of strategy descriptions we have seen assembled. We hope that these illustrations of the principles articulated in our text will inspire many other organizations to exploit the power of strategy maps to develop and align their intangible assets for the journey to become strategy-focused organizations.

This book is directed toward managers who will be leading Balanced Scorecard projects. It provides them with a detailed conceptual framework to guide the important choices they must make—about the critical few internal processes at which they must excel for their strategy to succeed, and on the investments required in their human resources, information technology, and organizational culture and climate. Executives who wish to learn how to put their strategy maps and Balanced Scorecards into action may want to study the framework in our previous book, *The Strategy-Focused Organization*. Our goal in this book is to provide insights for practitioners and implementers—coming from strategic planning, quality, human resources, information technology, or finance—on how to build a comprehensive, integrated visual representation of their strategy, the first step to becoming a strategy-focused organization.

NOTES

1. GDP per Capita in Selected Resource-Poor and Resource-Rich Countries

Resource-Poor Countries	1970 GDP per Capita	1998 GDP per Capita
South Korea	1,954	12,152
Taiwan	2,987	15,012
Singapore	4,438	22,643
Hong Kong	5,695	20,193
Israel	8,102	15,152
Denmark	12,685	22,123

Resource-Rich Countries	1970 GDP per Capita	1998 GDP per Capita
Indonesia	1,194	3,070
Nigeria	1,233	1,232
Former USSR	5,569	3,893 (Russia)
Saudi Arabia	7,624	8,225
Venezuela	10,672	8,965

Source: A. Maddison, *The World Economy: A Millennial Perspective* (Paris: OECD, 2000). Numbers are in constant 1990 dollars.

2. G. Bennett Stewart, *The Quest for Value* (New York: HarperBusiness, 1991); A. Rappaport, *Creating Shareholder Value: A Guide for Managers and Investors* (New York: Free Press, 1997).

3. Don Peppers and Martha Rogers, *Enterprise One to One: Tools for Competing in the Interactive Age* (New York: Currency/Doubleday, 1997).

4. Michael Hammer and James Champy, *Reengineering the Corporation: A Manifesto for Business Revolution* (New York: HarperBusiness, 2001); Michael Hammer, *Beyond Reengineering: How the Process-Centered Organization Is Changing Our Work and Our Lives* (New York: HarperBusiness, 1996).

5. Peter S. Pande, Robert P. Neuman, and Roland R. Cavanagh, *The Six Sigma Way: How GE, Motorola, and Other Top Companies Are Honing Their Performance* (New York: McGraw-Hill, 2000); David Garvin, *Managing Quality: The Strategic and Competitive Edge* (New York: Free Press, 1988).

6. Gary Hamel and C. K. Prahalad, *Competing for the Future* (Boston: Harvard Business School Press, 1996); D. J. Collis and C. A. Montgomery, "Competing on Resources: Strategy in the 1990s," *Harvard Business Review* (July–August 1995): 118–128.

7. Gary Hamel, *Leading the Revolution* (Boston: Harvard Business School Press, 2000); Clayton Christensen, *The Innovator's Dilemma: When New Technologies Cause Great Firms to Fail* (Boston: Harvard Business School Press, 1997).

8. Dave Ulrich, *Human Resource Champions: The Next Agenda for Adding Value and Delivering Results* (Boston: Harvard Business School Press, 1996).

9. Peter Weill and Marianne Broadbent, *Leveraging the New Infrastructure: How Market Leaders Capitalize on Information Technology* (Boston: Harvard Business School Press, 1998).

10. Ronald N. Ashkenas, Steve Kerr, Dave Ulrich, and Todd Jick, *The Boundaryless Organization: Breaking the Chains of Organizational Structure,* rev. ed. (New York: Wiley, 2002); Michael Tushman and Charles A. O'Reilly III, *Winning*

Through Innovation: A Practical Guide to Leading Organizational Change and Renewal, rev. ed. (Boston: Harvard Business School Press, 2002).

11. Peter Senge, *The Fifth Discipline: The Art and Practice of the Learning Organization* (New York: Doubleday, 1994); David A. Garvin, *Learning in Action: A Guide to Putting the Learning Organization to Work* (Boston: Harvard Business School Press, 2000).

12. M. E. Porter, *Competitive Strategy: Techniques for Analyzing Industries and Competitors* (New York: Free Press, 1980); *Competitive Advantage: Creating and Sustaining Superior Performance* (New York: Free Press, 1985); and "What Is Strategy?" *Harvard Business Review* (November–December 1996).

13. Louis V. Gerstner Jr., *Who Says Elephants Can't Dance: Inside IBM's Historic Turnaround* (New York: HarperCollins, 2002); Jack Welch, *Jack: Straight from The Gut* (New York: Warner Books, 2001); Larry Bossidy and Ram Charan, *Execution: The Discipline of Getting Things Done* (New York: Crown, 2002); and Richard Teerlink and Lee Ozley, *More Than a Motorcycle: The Leadership Journey at Harley-Davidson* (Boston: Harvard Business School Press, 2000).

14. R. Charan and G. Colvin, "Why CEOs Fail," *Fortune,* 21 June 1999.

15. Chris Zook, *Profit from the Core: Growth Strategy in an Era of Turbulence* (Boston: Harvard Business School Press, 2001).

16. Tiha von Ghyczy, Bolko von Oetinger, and Christopher Bassford, *Clausewitz on Strategy: Inspiration and Insight from a Master Strategist* (New York: Wiley, 2001), 99.

17. SHRM/Balanced Scorecard Collaborative, Aligning HR with Organization Strategy Survey Research Study 62-17052 (Alexandria, VA: Society for Human Resource Management, 2002); "The Alignment Gap," *CIO Insight,* 1 July 2002.

CASE STUDIES

BANK OF TOKYO-MITSUBISHI HQA

Background

As one of the world's largest banks, the Bank of Tokyo-Mitsubishi (BTM) manages more than $608 billion in assets across more than 700 locations in Japan and throughout the world. BTMHQA, the bank's New York–based Americas headquarters, decides the offerings of its Americas operations—which commercial, investment, and trust banking products and services it will market to its multinational customers. BTMHQA's mission is "to be the number one foreign wholesale bank in the Americas."

In 2000, as part of a global initiative, BTM's Americas operations were reorganized into four independently managed business units (global corporate banking, investment banking, treasury, and corporate center), each reporting directly to its respective head office in Tokyo. As a result of these changes and changes in the regulatory environment, BTMHQA realized that it was no longer enough for strategy to be implicitly understood by top management. Its leaders needed to reinforce the strategic message throughout the organization.

The Situation

Japanese organizations are renowned for competing successfully without well-articulated strategies. That has never been a necessity in a society whose people are culturally so in tune with one another that business can practically run on *ishin-denshin* (mental telepathy). But as BTMHQA discovered, this practice has been losing its effectiveness in the global economy, where workforce diversity and the sheer speed of business require clear articulation of strategy for organizational success.

Unifying any workforce to a common set of strategic goals is daunting enough, but at BTM it was magnified by many cultural differences. Traditional Japanese ways of doing business prevailed; executive decisions were not routinely disclosed throughout the organization, and until recently, Japanese nationals dispatched from Tokyo occupied most leadership positions. Other common practices included rotating employees throughout functional areas (to foster cultural unity) and lifetime employment. And BTMHQA still relied upon seniority, instead of short-term performance, as the primary basis for promotion.

The Strategy

In 2001, with the Japanese banking industry still mired in recession and regulatory authorities increasing their risk-related oversight of financial institutions, BTMHQA began to question the effectiveness of its corporate governance, despite its stellar growth.[1]

Takehiko Nagumo, vice president for corporate planning, turned to the Balanced Scorecard because he felt it was the right vehicle to implement a common strategic platform, a needed risk-control framework, and, eventually, a new pay-for-performance system with coherence and synergy. "We knew that we would first have to articulate each unit's strategy before we could even determine the integrated regional strategy, and a bottom-up approach seemed to be an essential first step," says Hideo Yamamoto, senior vice president and group head of corporate planning. A task force of representatives from each business unit developed a worksheet for each group to complete, and the team crafted the integrated regional strategy from the collected responses.

The Strategy Map

In building its Americas-level scorecard, BTM first established a "strategic foundation," which defined broad categories and themes within the four perspectives of the Balanced Scorecard that each objective would be aligned to. Each objective was classified according to three types of objectives—*common, shared,* or *unique.*

a. *Common:* A mandatory bankwide objective, of which there were six in total. Example: "Enhance cost efficiency," required in the financial perspective of every scorecard.

b. *Shared:* An interdivisional objective shared by units that are expected to cooperate to achieve specific results. Examples: "Streamline credit-approval process," an internal process objective for operational excellence shared among the credit and lending units; "Enhance collaboration throughout the supply chain," shared among front, middle, and back offices; and "Close collaboration between relationship managers and product offices," meant to facilitate the offering of high-value products to targeted customers.

c. *Unique:* An intradivisional objective to be fulfilled independently by a given group. Example: "Maintain 'know your customer' files," an internal/risk management objective of the treasury office.

This classification system became the template for the bank's Americas scorecard as well as for each business unit's scorecard. Visually, employees could now easily see the juxtaposition of themes, categories, and shared objectives.

As an example of the type of strategy map that resulted, the Global Corporate Banking Business Unit (GCBU)-Americas strategy map reflects a strong emphasis on revenue growth, risk management, and productivity as follows (see Figure 1-4):

A. Financial
Setting "maximize net income after credit costs" as the ultimate goal, GCBU-Americas identified four core components in the financial perspective:

- Emphasize investment banking fee income rather than traditional interest income.
- Grow income from Japanese customers operating in the Americas and non-Japanese multinationals with whom BTM has a global relationship.
- Minimize credit costs, particularly in large U.S. corporate and Latin American segment.
- Adopt drastic cost reduction efforts on an enterprise-wide basis.

B. Customer
To be recognized as the best foreign bank operating in the Americas (particularly in the United States) by its core customers both in Japanese and non-Japanese segments, GCBU-Americas tries to differentiate its products and services on several key points: reliable lending capabilities, an extensive global network, and service quality that meets high standards for accuracy and speed.

C. Internal

Grow revenues: The GCBU-Americas revenue growth strategy consists of four major components: (1) Generating revenue by supporting Americas clients' business in Asia; (2) delivering highly customized products through collaboration between relationship managers and product managers; (3) clear customer segmentation based on profitability and risk appetite; and (4) clear definition of risk appetite and alignment to business strategy.

Figure 1-4 Bank of Tokyo-Mitsubishi Global Corporate Banking BU (Americas) Strategy Map

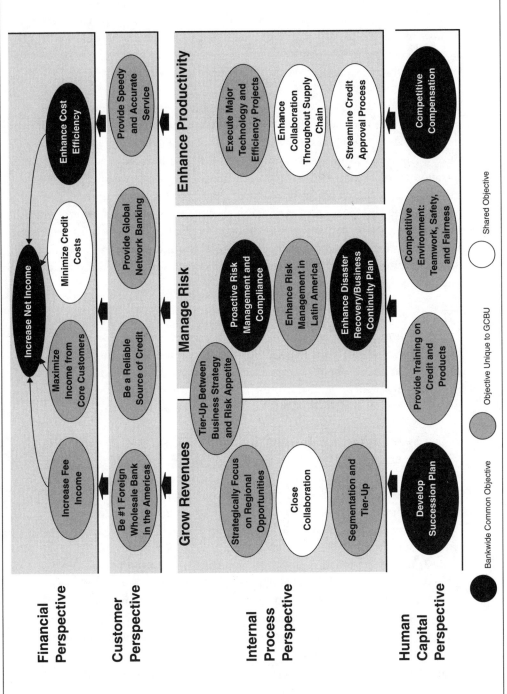

Manage risk: (1) Emphasis on proactiveness rather than reactiveness in identifying and mitigating risks in all areas of the bank; (2) minimization of transfer risks associated with credits in Latin America (where the business environment is often difficult); and (3) emphasizing the importance—especially after September 11—of disaster recovery and business continuity management as an integral part of bankwide risk management.

Enhance productivity: (1) Execute major technology and efficiency projects; for example, ensuring that the IT infrastructure can support operational competitiveness; (2) Enhance collaboration throughout the supply chain. To deliver customized products at desired speed, it is critical to optimize collaboration among front, middle, and back offices. The objective is applied to these offices as a shared objective; (3) Streamline credit approval process. The speed of credit approval enhances customer satisfaction as well as competitive advantage. As a shared objective among the front office (which prepares credit applications) and the credit division (which grants approval on the credit applications), GCBU-Americas tries to minimize the cycle time of credit delivery.

D. Human Capital

In a multicultural organization, it is critical to set clear standards in the management of human resources. Recognizing that people are the capital that most significantly influences BTM's competitiveness, GCBU-Americas adopted four objectives that are set as bankwide priorities in the human resources area. They represent an interesting blend of practices, both Japanese and local.

1. *Succession planning:* To maintain stability of operations by identifying key personnel well in advance and preparing succession plans for those people. Since Japanese staff rotate back to Japan every four to six years on average, and U.S. employees often change jobs or employers to elevate their careers (in contrast to the Japanese practice of lifetime employment), preparation of succession plans for all personnel is important for stable operations.

2. *Training:* To enhance credit risk management capabilities—a critical competency for all professionals in the banking business.

3. *Work environment:* To maintain a good *teamwork* orientation (a traditional Japanese organizational strength), *safety* where all basic standards are met, and *fairness* where no discrimination (race, sex, age, or nationality) of any kind exists.

4. *Pay-for-performance:* Blending Japanese seniority-based management style with the U.S. performance-based HR architecture, GCBU-Americas is working to establish a bankwide best practice in this area.

Anecdotes

Scarcely one year after adoption, changes were already visible. Strategy had started to become "everyone's job."

- Almost immediately after developing strategy maps, employees began talking about strategy for the first time because they knew what it was. The maps created a foundation for discussions at meetings. Also, BTM employees immediately recognized that performance against strategy needs to be measured—it's not just a conceptual exercise.
- Employees in support and oversight functions (such as HR, audit, and credit examination) became familiar with quantitative approaches to managing performance. They became more focused on the bottom line, and senior management had better control over their activities.
- Shared objectives helped to unify the back (processing), middle (risk assessment and review), and front (deal-making and customer-facing) offices. The bank's New Jersey–based operations unit met regularly with front and middle offices about how to improve collaboration along the supply chain and accelerate results for their shared measures.
- Internal BTM auditors explicitly recognized the Balanced Scorecard as an effective means of enhancing corporate governance.
- Risk managers now make regular presentations on the metrics in their scorecards. One powerful metric in the BTMHQA scorecards is "share of issues," which measures the percentage of issues identified through Committee of Sponsoring Organizations of the Treadway Commission (COSO)-based self-assessment out of all of the issues identified by other parties such as internal and external auditors and regulators.[2] The higher the percentage, the more proactively the bank's business lines are identifying risks. This metric had an immediate effect of making the business lines pinpoint risks they had previously ignored or waited to react to. The associated metric "share of issues closed during period" now forces a quicker resolution of risk issues. This metric reflects BTMHQA's efforts to emphasize the importance of being more risk sensitive, based on the assumption that a business is more aware of its own risk than anyone else. Waiting for third parties to identify risks is too reactive an attitude and is no longer tolerated at the bank. Linking COSO-based self-assessment to the BSC to enhance its effectiveness is perhaps the most creative aspect of BTMHQA's Scorecard initiative.

Mr. Naotaka Otaba, CEO of BTMHQA, commented:

As the regional head of a Japanese company operating in the Americas, I have been particularly interested in the synergy between Japanese business culture and U.S. best practices. It is in this context that we have developed a Balanced Scorecard initiative, which, in addition to becoming the core methodology for strategy management and performance measurement for our bank in the Americas, has also underlined the importance of teamwork in implementing the "Tone at the Top."

Our next challenge is the further development of business process improvement practice, such as those that have been successfully adopted by many Japanese manufacturers. We intend to enhance our Control Self-Assessment (CSA) methodology so that we can not only enhance our control environment for various business processes but also identify and remedy any defects in those processes. We plan to integrate this CSA methodology with the Balanced Scorecard initiative in order to foster improved governance.

Once fully integrated, we expect that these methodologies will form the basis for a successful integration of the best Japanese and U.S. business practices. If successful in the Americas, we would like to propose the initiative for implementation for our operations in Japan.

Case prepared by Barnaby Donlon of Balanced Scorecard Collaborative and Takehiko Nagumo of Bank of Tokyo-Mitsubishi. Our thanks to Mr. Naotaka Obata, CEO of BTMHQA, for sharing the BTMHQA experience with us.

NOTES

1. The 2000 Gramm-Leach-Bliley Act and other market developments have prompted U.S. regulators to focus increasingly on corporate governance as a critical factor in sound banking practice.
2. The Committee of Sponsoring Organizations of the Treadway Commission (COSO) is a voluntary private-sector organization dedicated to improving the quality of financial reporting through business ethics, effective internal controls, and corporate governance. Accoringly, BTM's COSO control self-assessment is a voluntary operational risk management program. See <http://www.coso.org>.

AMERICAN DIABETES ASSOCIATION

Background

The American Diabetes Association (ADA), one of America's largest non-profit health organizations, provides research, information, and advocacy on diabetes. Its operating revenues in fiscal year 2002 were $188 million. ADA is headquartered in Alexandria, Virginia, with offices in every state. It has a professional staff of 1,000 employees, tens of thousands of volunteers, and several million donors and members who annually offer their time and energy to ADA.

ADA's mission is to "prevent and cure diabetes and to improve the lives of all people affected by diabetes." Its vision is to "make an everyday difference in the lives of people affected by diabetes." Its goal, under CEO John H. Graham IV, is "by 2007 to be the leading diabetes organization by increasing income to $300 million to better support its efforts and programs of research, information, and advocacy."

The Situation

Although ADA merged fifty-seven separate corporate organizations in 1998, it was still not operating as a single organization with a defined organizational culture. The foundation elements were in place with a vision and corporate strategy; but it had little consensus on how to execute the strategy. The organization needed a way to measure success beyond raising money and managing expense ratios so that it could sustain future performance. Unlike many organizations, ADA decided to address the strategy execution issue while it was healthy—experiencing double-digit growth—instead of waiting until financial support stagnated or declined.

ADA used the Balanced Scorecard to bring business discipline to the execution of strategy. By balancing "growth" with "operational efficiency," it would create greater value for its stakeholders and constituents. This balanced approach allowed ADA to focus on a value proposition that would create sustainable excellence and not attempt to do all things for all people.

The Strategy Map

As shown in Figure 1-5, ADA's mission was to satisfy the needs of both stakeholders and constituents. Stakeholders include the board of directors, community volunteer leadership, and high-impact individuals who provide primary oversight for ADA's work. Constituents are the donors, corporations, diabetes professionals, diabetic individuals, high-risk individuals, and information seekers who receive value from ADA's products and services. These two groups share the same primary outcome: *progress toward prevention and a cure*. On the road to finding that cure, both groups want to *improve quality of life* for those people whose lives are affected by diabetes. A key input to improving quality of life is *improving quality of care*.

ADA must be economically viable to meet its stakeholder and constituent objectives. It wants to *increase net margin* growth by *growing revenues* while at the same time *operating efficiently*. ADA expects that this combination of

Figure 1-5 American Diabetes Association Strategy Map

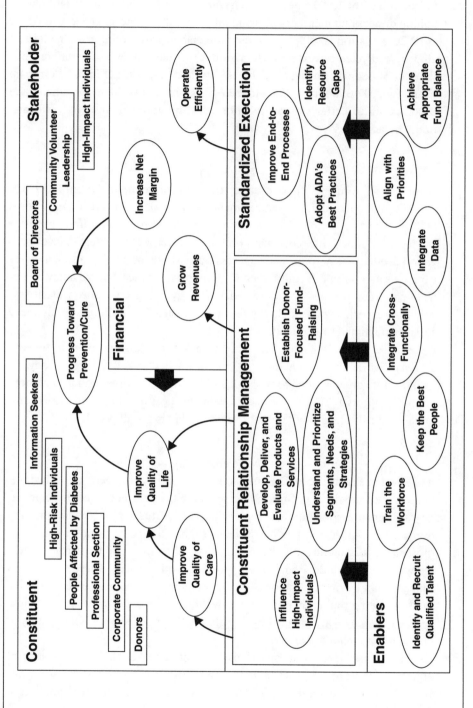

financial objectives will help it maintain its ability to serve stakeholders and constituents over the long run.

Stakeholder, constituent, and financial objectives will be achieved through two strategic themes: *constituent relationship management* and *standardized execution*. A driver of effective management of constituent relationships is to *understand and prioritize segments, needs, and strategies*. ADA will pick those groups and areas where it can have the most impact. This process objective will also enable ADA to *influence policy makers* with respect to more beneficial diabetes legislation. With priorities established for segment needs, ADA will be better able to *develop, deliver, and evaluate products and services* that meet its constituent and stakeholder needs. Finally, understanding segments ensures that it can *establish donor-focused fund-raising*. Fund-raising will become more donor-centric so that ADA can target the ways that its donors prefer to give versus how ADA thinks they should give.

The second strategic theme, *standardized execution,* requires *improving end-to-end processes*. ADA selected this theme because many of its existing internal processes were not well integrated or highly focused on providing internal or external value. Much of the targeted process improvement would come from *adopting ADA best practices,* capturing the best business practices that already existed within the organization. Additionally, *identifying resource gaps* would enable ADA to allocate incremental resources to important but currently underfunded processes.

The foundation of ADA's strategy is its human and organizational *enablers.* To have a talented workforce, both volunteers and staff, ADA must *identify and recruit qualified talent; train the workforce; and keep the best people*. People will stay with ADA if they experience an environment in which they feel valued. The drivers for this objective are an organization that *integrates cross-functionally, integrates data, and aligns with priorities.* In this way, people support one another's work and all work toward common ends. A final enabler for strategic success is to *achieve appropriate fund balance*. In summary, ADA's strategic linkages are that by focusing *human and organizational enablers* to support critical *internal capabilities,* the organization can better provide the desired value proposition to *constituents and stakeholders* in a *financially* responsible way.

Anecdotes

ADA's executive team reported that the process of building the strategy map was as valuable as the result, the map itself. But the process was not easy. The building of the ADA's strategy map and, subsequently, the Balanced Scorecard, brought a discipline and logic to the leadership team's strategic decision making that had not existed before. The strategic objectives on the map were debated until consensus was reached. The dialogue allowed ADA to clarify its stakeholders and constituents, define its deliverables, and describe its competitive capability. The end result provided a clear basis for internal and external communication on objectives and strategy. ADA could now explain "why it was doing some things and not others."

Case prepared by Mario Bognanno of Balanced Scorecard Collaborative and Tom Bognanno of ADA. Our thanks to John Graham and his colleagues for sharing the ADA experience.

CHAPTER TWO

STRATEGY MAPS

STRATEGY DESCRIBES how an organization intends to create sustained value for its shareholders.[1] In Chapter 1, we documented how organizations today must leverage their intangible assets for sustainable value creation. Creating value from intangible assets differs in several important ways from creating value by managing tangible physical and financial assets:

1. *Value creation is indirect.* Intangible assets such as knowledge and technology seldom have a direct impact on financial outcomes such as increased revenues, lowered costs, and higher profits. Improvements in intangible assets affect financial outcomes through chains of cause-and-effect relationships. For example, employee training in total quality management (TQM) and six sigma techniques can directly improve process quality. Such improvement can then be expected to lead to improved customer satisfaction, which, in turn, should increase customer loyalty. Ultimately, customer loyalty leads to improved sales and margins from long-term customer relationships.

2. *Value is contextual.* The value of an intangible asset depends on its alignment with the strategy. For example, training employees in TQM and six sigma techniques has greater value for organizations following a low total cost strategy than for one following a product leadership and innovation strategy.

3. *Value is potential.* The cost of investing in an intangible asset represents a poor estimate of its value to the organization. Intangible

assets, like employees trained in statistical quality control and root cause analysis, have potential value but not market value. Internal processes such as design, production, delivery, and customer service are required to transform the potential value of intangible assets into tangible value. If the internal processes are not directed at the customer value proposition or financial improvements, then the potential value of employee capabilities, and intangible assets in general, will not be realized.

4. *Assets are bundled.* Intangible assets seldom create value by themselves. They do not have a value that can be isolated from organizational context and strategy. The value from intangible assets arises when they are combined effectively with other assets, both tangible and intangible. For example, quality training is enhanced when employees have access to timely, detailed data from process-oriented information systems. Maximum value is created when all the organization's intangible assets are aligned with each other, with the organization's tangible assets, and with the strategy.

The Balanced Scorecard strategy map (see Figure 2-1), provides a framework to illustrate how strategy links intangible assets to value-creating processes. The *financial perspective* describes the tangible outcomes of the strategy in traditional financial terms. Measures such as ROI, shareholder value, profitability, revenue growth, and cost per unit are the lag indicators that show whether the organization's strategy is succeeding or failing. The *customer perspective* defines the value proposition for targeted customers. The value proposition provides the *context* for the intangible assets to create value. If customers value consistent quality and timely delivery, then the skills, systems, and processes that produce and deliver quality products and services are highly valuable to the organization. If the customer values innovation and high performance, then the skills, systems, and processes that create new products and services with superior functionality take on high value. Consistent alignment of actions and capabilities with the customer value proposition is the core of strategy execution.

The financial and customer perspectives describe the desired outcomes from the strategy. Both perspectives contain many lag indicators. How does the organization create these desired outcomes? The *internal process perspective* identifies the critical few processes that are expected to have the greatest impact on the strategy. For example, one organization may increase its internal R&D investments and reengineer its product

Figure 2-1 The Balanced Scorecard Framework

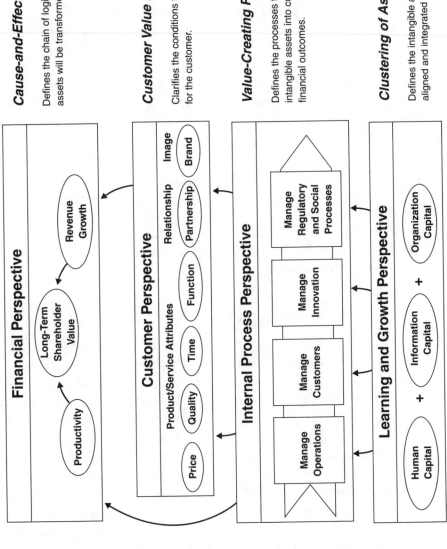

development processes so that it can develop high-performance, innovative products for its customers. Another organization, attempting to deliver the same value proposition, might choose to develop new products through joint-venture product partnerships.

The *learning and growth perspective* identifies the intangible assets that are most important to the strategy. The objectives in this perspective identify which jobs (the human capital), which systems (the information capital), and what kind of climate (the organization capital) are required to support the value-creating internal processes. These assets must be *bundled* together and aligned to the critical internal processes.

The objectives in the four perspectives are linked together by cause-and-effect relationships. Starting from the top is the hypothesis that financial outcomes can be achieved only if targeted customers are satisfied. The customer value proposition describes how to generate sales and loyalty from targeted customers. The internal processes create and deliver the customer value proposition. And intangible assets that support the internal processes provide the foundation for the strategy. Aligning objectives in these four perspectives is the key to value creation and, hence, to a focused and internally consistent strategy.

This architecture of cause and effect, linking the four perspectives, is the structure around which a strategy map is developed. Building a strategy map forces an organization to clarify the logic of how it will create value and for whom. In this chapter, we will describe the principles involved in building a strategy map.

STRATEGY IS A STEP IN A CONTINUUM

Strategy is not a stand-alone management process; it is one step in a logical continuum that moves an organization from a high-level mission statement to the work performed by frontline and back-office employees. Figure 2-2 presents a framework that we have found effective in practice.

The overarching *mission* of the organization provides the starting point by defining why the organization exists or how a business unit fits within a broader corporate architecture. The mission and the core *values* that accompany it remain fairly stable over time. The organization's *vision* paints a picture of the future that clarifies the organization's direction and helps individuals understand why and how they should support the organization. In addition, the vision sets the organization in motion, from the stability of the mission and core values to the dynamics of strategy, the next step in the continuum. *Strategy* is developed and evolves over

Figure 2-2 The Balanced Scorecard Is a Step in a Continuum That Describes What Value Is and How It Is Created

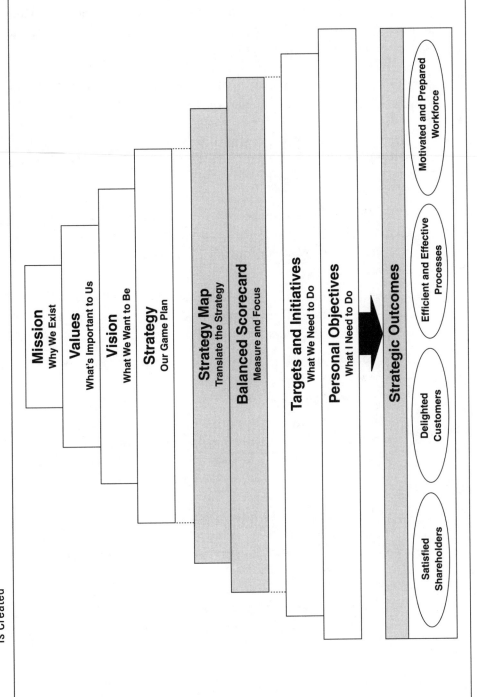

Mission
Why We Exist

Values
What's Important to Us

Vision
What We Want to Be

Strategy
Our Game Plan

Strategy Map
Translate the Strategy

Balanced Scorecard
Measure and Focus

Targets and Initiatives
What We Need to Do

Personal Objectives
What I Need to Do

Strategic Outcomes

Satisfied Shareholders

Delighted Customers

Efficient and Effective Processes

Motivated and Prepared Workforce

time to meet the changing conditions posed by the external environment and internal capabilities.

Most organizations already have mission and vision statements. While the exact definitions of mission and vision can vary, the following provide helpful guidelines:

Mission. A concise, internally focused statement of the reason for the organization's existence, the basic purpose toward which its activities are directed, and the values that guide employees' activities. The mission should also describe how the organization expects to compete and deliver value to customers. Below are examples of the mission statements of two quite different organizations:

Ben & Jerry's Mission Statement

Ben & Jerry's is dedicated to the creation and demonstration of a new corporate concept of linked prosperity. Our mission consists of three interrelated parts.

Product. *To make, distribute, and sell the finest quality, all-natural ice cream and related products in a wide variety of innovative flavors made from Vermont dairy products.*

Economic. *To operate the Company on a sound financial basis of profitable growth, increasing value for our shareholders, and creating career opportunities and financial rewards for our employees.*

Social. *To operate the Company in a way that actively recognizes the central role that business plays in the structure of society by initiating innovative ways to improve the quality of life of a broad community—local, national, and international.*

City of Charlotte Mission Statement

The mission of the City of Charlotte is to ensure the delivery of quality public services that promote the safety, health and quality of life of its citizens. Charlotte attempts to identify and respond to community needs and focus on the customer through:
- *Creating and maintaining effective partnerships*
- *Attracting and retaining skilled motivated employees*
- *Using strategic business planning*

Vision. A concise statement that defines the mid- to long-term (three- to ten-year) goals of the organization. The vision should be external and market-oriented and should express—often in colorful or "visionary" terms—how the organization wants to be perceived by the world.

City of Charlotte Vision

The City of Charlotte will be a model of excellence that puts its citizens first. Skilled, motivated employees will be known for providing quality and value in all areas of service. We will be a platform for vital economic activity that gives Charlotte a competitive edge in the marketplace. We will partner with citizens and businesses to make Charlotte a community of choice for living, working, and leisure activities.

Financial Service Company Vision

We will become the respected leader in financial services with a focus on seamless customer relationships and satisfaction, producing financial returns in the top quartile of the industry.

Mission and vision statements set the general goals and direction for the organization. They help shareholders, customers, and employees understand what the company is about and what it intends to achieve. But these statements are far too vague to guide day-to-day actions and resource allocation decisions. Companies make their mission and vision statements operational when they define a strategy for how the mission and vision will be achieved.

Strategy. The strategy literature is uncommonly diverse. Scholars and practitioners have very different frameworks for strategy and don't even agree on its definition.[2] While strategy maps and Balanced Scorecards can be developed for any strategic approach, we base our approach on the general framework articulated by Michael Porter, a founder and outstanding leader in the strategy field. Porter argues that strategy is about selecting the set of activities in which an organization will excel to create a sustainable difference in the marketplace. The sustainable difference can be to deliver greater value to customers than competitors, or to provide comparable value but at lower cost than competitors. He states, "Differentiation arises from both the choice of activities and how they are performed."[3] We will provide specific examples of such strategies when we discuss the value proposition the organization selects to deliver for its customers.

With this brief background on establishing high-level direction—mission, vision, and strategy—for the organization, we can now develop the role for the strategy map to provide the needed specificity for statements of high-level direction to become more meaningful and actionable for all employees. We start with the financial perspective of the strategy map and work successively through the customer, internal, and learning and growth perspectives.

Financial Perspective: Strategy Balances Contradictory Forces— Long-Term Versus Short-Term

The BSC retains the financial perspective as the ultimate objective for profit-maximizing companies.[4] Financial performance measures indicate whether the company's strategy, including its implementation and execution, are contributing to bottom-line improvement. Financial objectives typically relate to profitability—measured, for example, by operating income and return on investment. Basically, financial strategies are simple; companies can make more money by (1) selling more, and (2) spending less. Everything else is background music. Any program—customer intimacy, six sigma quality, knowledge management, disruptive technology, just-in-time—creates more value for the company only if it leads to selling more or spending less. Thus, the company's financial performance gets improved through two basic approaches—revenue growth and productivity (see Figure 2-3).

Companies can generate profitable revenue growth by deepening relationships with existing customers. This enables them to sell more of their existing product or service, or additional products and services. For example, banks can attempt to get their checking account customers to also use a credit card issued by the bank, and to borrow from the bank to purchase a home or car.

Companies can also generate revenue growth by selling entirely new products. For example, Amazon.com now sells CDs and electronic equipment in addition to books; Mobil encourages its customers to buy from its stations' convenience stores in addition to filling their cars with gasoline. Companies can also expand revenues by selling to customers in entirely new segments—for example, Staples now sells to small businesses as well as to retail customers—and in new markets, such as by expanding from domestic sales to international sales.

Productivity improvements, the second dimension of a financial strategy, also can occur in two ways. First, companies reduce costs by lowering direct and indirect expenses. Such cost reductions enable a company to produce the same quantity of outputs while spending less on people,

Figure 2-3 The Financial Perspective Provides the Tangible Definition of Value

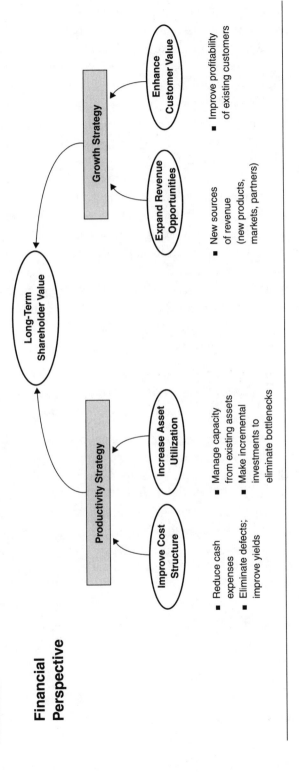

materials, energy, and supplies. Second, companies, by utilizing their financial and physical assets more efficiently, reduce the working and fixed capital needed to support a given level of business. For example, through just-in-time approaches, companies can support a given level of sales with less inventory. By reducing unscheduled downtime on equipment, companies can produce more without increasing their investments in plant and equipment.

The link to strategy in the financial perspective arises as organizations choose a balance between the often contradictory levers of growth and productivity. Actions to improve revenue growth generally take longer to create value than actions to improve productivity. Under the day-to-day pressure to show financial results to shareholders, the tendency is to favor the short term over the long term. Developing the first layer of the strategy map forces the organization to deal with this tension. The overarching financial objective is, and must be, to *sustain* growth in shareholder value. Thus, the financial component of the strategy must have *both* long-term (growth) and short-term (productivity) dimensions. The simultaneous balancing of these two forces is the organizing framework for the remainder of the strategy map.

Customer Perspective: Strategy Is Based on a Differentiated Value Proposition

The revenue growth strategy requires a specific value proposition, in the *customer* perspective, that describes how the organization will create differentiated, sustainable value to targeted segments. In the customer perspective of the strategy map, managers identify the targeted customer segments in which the business unit competes and the measures of the business unit's performance for customers in these targeted segments. The customer perspective typically includes several common measures of the successful outcomes from a well-formulated and implemented strategy (see Figure 2-4):

- Customer satisfaction
- Customer retention
- Customer acquisition
- Customer profitability
- Market share
- Account share[5]

Figure 2-4 Customer Perspective: Creating a Sustainable Differentiated Value Proposition Is the Heart of Strategy

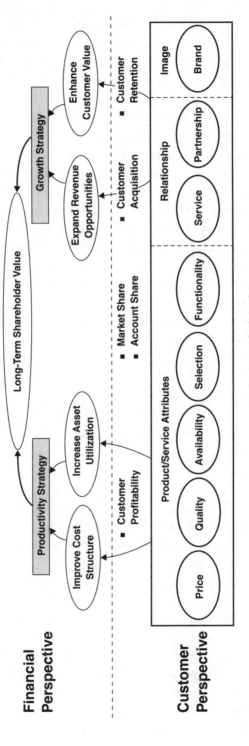

These common customer outcome measures can themselves be viewed in cause-and-effect relationships. For example, customer satisfaction generally leads to customer retention and, through word of mouth, the acquisition of new customers. By retaining customers, the company can increase the share of business—the account share—it does with its loyal customers. Combining customer acquisition and increased business done with existing customers, the company should increase its overall market share with targeted customers. Finally, retention of customers should lead to increases in customer profitability, since retaining a customer typically costs much less than acquiring new or replacement customers.

Virtually all organizations try to improve these common customer measures, but merely satisfying and retaining customers is hardly a strategy. A strategy should identify specific customer *segments* that the company is targeting for growth and profitability. For example, Southwest Airlines offers low prices to satisfy and retain price-sensitive customers. Neiman Marcus, on the other hand, targets customers with high disposable incomes who are willing to pay more for high-end merchandise. Companies should measure satisfaction, retention, and market share with their targeted customers. Price-sensitive customers with low disposable incomes are not likely to be very satisfied with the shopping experience at Neiman Marcus, and business travelers with generous expense accounts typically do not seek out a Southwest Airlines flight because of its long lines and lack of reserved seats and first-class cabins.

Once the company understands who its targeted customers are, it can identify the objectives and measures for the *value proposition* it intends to offer. The value proposition defines the company's strategy for the customer by describing the unique mix of product, price, service, relationship, and image that a company offers its targeted group of customers. The value proposition should communicate what the company expects to do for its customers *better* or *differently* than its competitors.

For example, companies as diverse as Southwest Airlines, Dell, Wal-Mart, McDonald's, and Toyota have been extremely successful by offering customers the *best buy* or *lowest total cost* in their categories. The objectives for a low total cost value proposition should emphasize attractive prices, excellent and consistent quality, short lead times, ease of purchase, and good selection (see the top row in Figure 2-5).

Another value proposition, followed by companies such as Sony, Mercedes, and Intel, emphasizes *product innovation and leadership*. These companies command high prices, above the average in their categories, because they offer products with superior functionality. The objectives

Figure 2-5 Customer Objectives for Different Value Propositions

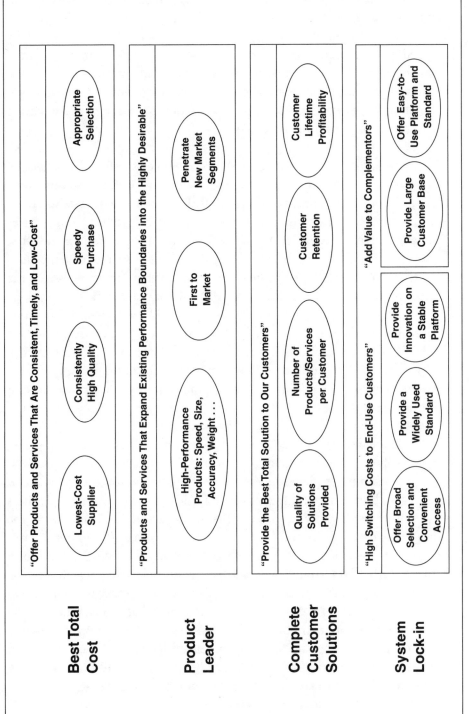

for their value propositions would emphasize the particular features and functionalities of the products that leading-edge customers value and are willing to pay more to receive. The objectives could be measured by speed, size, accuracy, power consumption, or other performance characteristics that exceed the performance of competing products and that are valued by customers. Being the first-to-market with new features and functionality is another objective for such product leadership companies (see the second row in Figure 2-5).

A third type of value proposition stresses the provision of *complete customer solutions*. Good examples of companies successfully delivering this value proposition are IBM and Goldman Sachs. For this value proposition, customers should feel that the company understands them and is capable of providing them with customized products and services tailored to their needs. IBM, when it dominated the computer industry, did not offer the lowest prices and only rarely delivered its new products on time. Nor were IBM's products the most advanced technologically, the most powerful, or the fastest. But IBM offered information technology executives, its targeted customers, complete solutions—hardware, software, installation, field service, training, education, and consulting—that were tailored to each organization's needs. Companies offering such a customer solutions value proposition stress objectives relating to the completeness of the solution (selling multiple, bundled products and services), exceptional service, both before and after the sale, and the quality of the relationship (see the third row in Figure 2-5).

A fourth generic strategy, called *lock-in*, arises when companies create high switching costs for their customers. Ideally, a proprietary product, such as a computer operating system or microchip hardware architecture, becomes the standard for the industry.[6] In this case both buyers and sellers want their products to be consistent with the standard to benefit from the large network of users and complementors who use it. Becoming a dominant exchange, such as eBay and the Yellow Pages, is another example of a successful lock-in strategy. Buyers will choose an exchange where the largest number of sellers offers their products or services; and sellers will offer their products and services on an exchange that exposes them to the largest number of potential buyers. In this situation, one or two companies will tend to be dominant suppliers of the exchange, and they will create large barriers to entry for other exchange providers and high switching costs to its buyers and sellers (see the bottom row in Figure 2-5).

The objectives and measures for a particular value proposition define an organization's strategy. By developing objectives and measures that are specific to its value proposition, the organization translates its strategy into tangible measures that all employees can understand and work toward improving.

Internal Perspective: Value Is Created Through Internal Business Processes

Objectives in the customer perspective describe the strategy—the targeted customers and value proposition—and the objectives in the financial perspective describe the economic consequences from a successful strategy—revenue and profit growth and productivity. Once an organization has a clear picture of these financial and customer objectives, the objectives in the internal and learning and growth perspectives describe how the strategy will be accomplished. The organization manages its internal processes and its development of human, information, and organization capital to deliver the differentiating value proposition of the strategy. Excellent performance in these two perspectives drives the strategy.

Internal processes accomplish two vital components of an organization's strategy: (1) they produce and deliver the value proposition for customers, and (2) they improve processes and reduce costs for the productivity component in the financial perspective. We group organizations' myriad internal processes into four clusters (see Figure 2-6):

1. Operations management processes
2. Customer management processes
3. Innovation processes
4. Regulatory and social processes

Operations Management Processes

Operations management processes are the basic, day-to-day processes by which companies produce their existing products and services and deliver them to customers. Operations management processes of manufacturing companies include the following:

- Acquire raw materials from suppliers
- Convert raw materials to finished goods
- Distribute finished goods to customers
- Manage risk

Operating processes for service companies produce and deliver the services used by customers.

Figure 2-6 Internal Processes Create Value for Customers and Shareholders

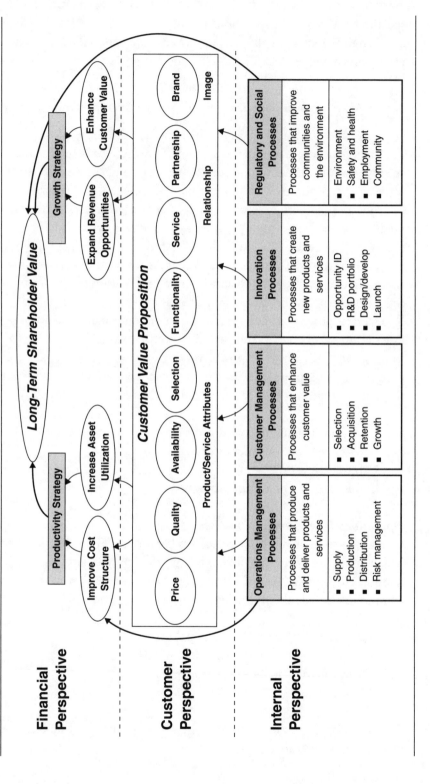

Customer Management Processes

Customer management processes expand and deepen relationships with targeted customers. We can identify four sets of customer management processes:

- Select targeted customers
- Acquire the targeted customers
- Retain customers
- Grow business with customers

Customer *selection* involves identifying the target populations for which the company's value proposition is most desirable. A customer selection process defines a set of customer characteristics that describes an attractive customer segment for the company. For consumer companies, segments can be defined by income, wealth, age, family size, and lifestyle; typical business customer segments are price-sensitive, early adopting, and technically sophisticated. Customer *acquisition* relates to generating leads, communicating to new potential customers, choosing entry-level products, pricing the products, and closing the sale. Customer *retention* is a result of excellent service and responsiveness to customer requests. Timely, knowledgeable service units are critical for maintaining customer loyalty and reducing the likelihood of customer defections. *Growing* a customer's business with the company involves managing the relationship effectively, cross-selling multiple products and services, and becoming known as a trusted adviser and supplier.

Innovation Processes

Innovation processes develop new products, processes, and services, often enabling the company to penetrate new markets and customer segments. Managing innovation includes four sets of processes:

- Identify opportunities for new products and services
- Manage the research and development portfolio
- Design and develop the new products and services
- Bring the new products and services to market

Product designers and managers generate new ideas by extending the capabilities of existing products and services, applying new discoveries and technologies, and learning from the suggestions of customers. Once ideas for new products and services have been generated, managers must decide which projects to fund and which will be developed entirely with internal resources, which done collaboratively in a joint venture, and which will be licensed from another organization or outsourced entirely. The design and development process, the core of product development, brings new concepts to market. A successful design and development process culminates in a product that has the desired functionality, is attractive to the targeted market, and can be produced with consistent quality and at a satisfactory profit margin. At the conclusion of the product development cycle, the project team brings the new product to market. The innovation process, for a particular project, concludes when the company achieves targeted levels of sales and production at specified levels of product functionality, quality, and cost.

Regulatory and Social Processes

Regulatory and social processes help organizations continually earn the right to operate in the communities and countries in which they produce and sell. National and local regulations—on the environment, on employee health and safety, and on hiring and employment practices—impose standards on companies' practices. Many companies, however, seek to go beyond complying with the minimal standards established by regulations. They wish to perform better than the regulatory constraints so that they develop a reputation as an employer of choice in every community in which they operate.

Companies manage and report their regulatory and social performance along a number of critical dimensions:

- Environment
- Safety and health
- Employment practices
- Community investment

Investing in the environment, health, safety, employment practices, and community development need not be for altruistic reasons alone. An excellent reputation for performance along regulatory and social dimensions assists companies in attracting and retaining high-quality employees, thereby making human resource processes more effective and efficient. Also, reducing environmental incidents and improving employee safety and health improves productivity and lowers operating costs. And last, companies with outstanding reputations generally enhance their images with customers and with socially conscious investors.

All these linkages—to enhanced human resource, operations, customer, and financial processes—illustrate how effective management of regulatory and community performance can drive long-term shareholder value creation.

STRATEGY CONSISTS OF SIMULTANEOUS COMPLEMENTARY THEMES

In developing the internal perspective of their strategy map, managers identify the processes that are the most important for their strategies. Companies following a product leadership strategy would stress excellence in their innovation processes; companies following a low total cost strategy must excel at operating processes; and companies following a customer solutions strategy will emphasize their customer management processes.

But even with an emphasis on one of the four clusters of internal processes, companies must still follow a "balanced" strategy and invest in improving processes in all four clusters. Typically, the financial benefits from improvements to the processes in the four internal perspective themes occur over different time periods (see Figure 2-7). Cost savings from improvements in operational processes deliver quick benefits (within six to twelve months). Revenue growth from enhancing customer relationships accrues in the intermediate term (twelve to twenty-four months). Innovation processes generally take longer to produce revenue and margin improvements (say, twenty-four to forty-eight months). The benefits from regulatory and social processes also typically take longer to capture as companies avoid litigation and shutdowns, and enhance their image as an employer and supplier of choice in every community in which they operate.

There are literally hundreds of processes taking place simultaneously in an organization, each creating value in some way. The art of strategy is to identify and excel at the critical few processes that are the most important to the customer value proposition. All processes should be managed well, but the few strategic processes must receive special attention and focus since these processes create the differentiation of the strategy. The selected strategic processes should also be drawn from all four clusters. Every strategy should identify one or more processes within operations management, customer management, innovation, and regulatory and social. In this way, the value creation process is balanced between the short and long term. This ensures that the growth in shareholder value will be sustained over time.

Figure 2-7 Internal Processes Deliver Value over Different Time Horizons

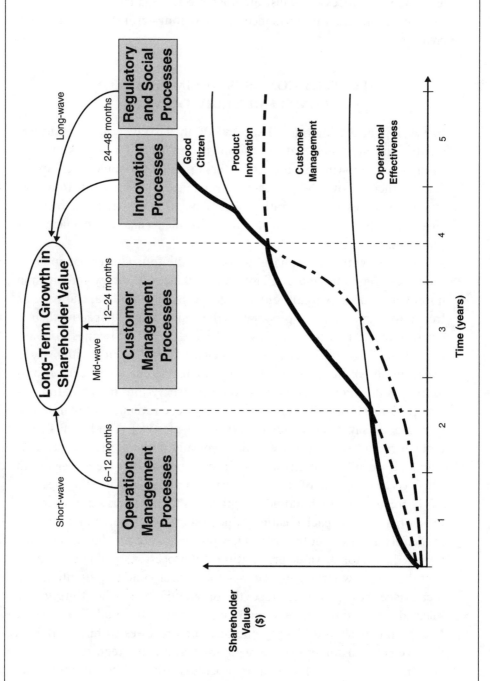

The critical few strategic processes are often organized as *strategic themes*. Strategic themes allow organizations to focus actions and to provide a structure for accountability. Strategic themes are the building blocks around which the execution of strategy occurs.

Figure 2-8 illustrates the seven strategic themes for a high-tech manufacturing company. Its strategy was to broaden the value proposition from a narrow product quality focus to one that delivered tailored product configurations capable of solving customer problems. At the heart of this strategy were two customer management themes—*solution selling* and *relationship management*. These themes provided the foundation of the new customer partnership. Two operations management themes—*just-in-time* production and *flexible manufacturing*—ensured that the products could be configured and delivered within the short time horizons required by the customer. Two innovation themes—*internal product development* and *technology partnerships*—provided two balanced sources of the technical know-how required to stay at the leading edge. The regulatory and social component of the strategy—*build the community*—reflected the company's desire, as the community's dominant employer, to help strengthen the institutions that influenced the quality of life of its employees. Thus, the company reduced the complexity of its strategy into seven strategic themes, each connected logically to the customer value proposition and financial outcomes.

Learning and Growth: Strategic Alignment of Intangible Assets

The fourth perspective of the Balanced Scorecard strategy map, learning and growth, describes the organization's intangible assets and their role in strategy. We organize intangible assets into three categories (see Figure 2-9):

Human capital: The availability of skills, talent, and know-how required to support the strategy

Information capital: The availability of information systems, networks, and infrastructure required to support the strategy

Organization capital: The ability of the organization to mobilize and sustain the process of change required to execute the strategy

Figure 2-8 Strategy Is Made Up of a Set of Themes Based on Value-Creating Processes

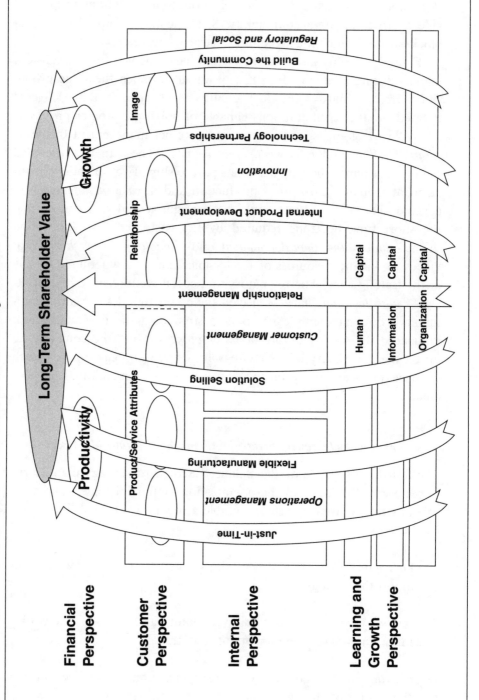

Figure 2-9 Intangible Assets Must Be Aligned with the Strategy to Create Value

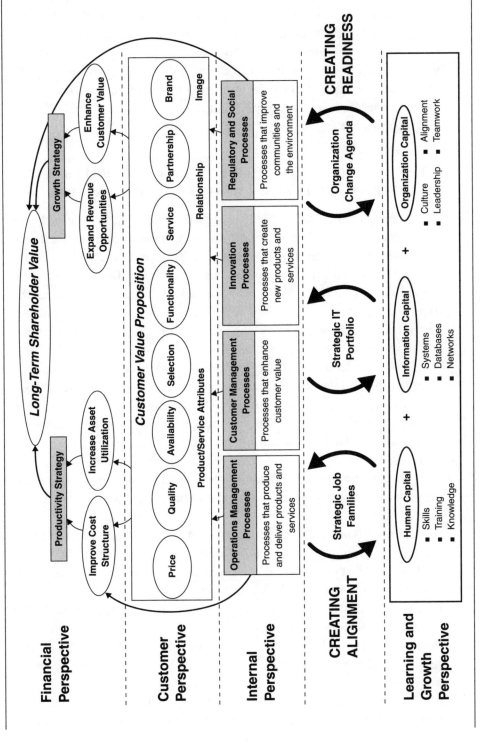

Whereas all organizations attempt to develop their people, technology, and culture, most do not align these intangible assets with their strategies. The key to creating this alignment is *granularity*—that is, to move beyond generalities such as "develop our people" or "live our core values" and focus on specific capabilities and attributes required by the critical internal processes of the strategy. The Balanced Scorecard strategy map enables executives to pinpoint the specific human, information, and organization capital required by the strategy.

THE BALANCED SCORECARD: MEASURES, TARGETS, AND INITIATIVES TRANSLATE STRATEGY INTO ACTION

The strategy map describes the logic of the strategy, showing clearly the objectives for the critical internal processes that create value and the intangible assets required to support them. The Balanced Scorecard translates the strategy map objectives into measures and targets. But objectives and targets will not be achieved simply because they have been identified; the organization must launch a set of action programs that will enable the targets for all the measures to be achieved. The organization must supply scarce resources—people, funding, and capacity—for each action program. We refer to these action programs as *strategic initiatives*. For each measure on the Balanced Scorecard, managers must identify the strategic initiatives needed to achieve the target. The initiatives create results. Hence, the execution of strategy is managed through the execution of initiatives.

The action plans that define and provide resources for the strategic initiatives must be *aligned* around the strategic themes, and must be viewed as an *integrated* bundle of investments instead of as a group of stand-alone projects. Each strategic theme should have a self-contained business case.

Figure 2-10 illustrates an action plan and business case for the "quick ground turnaround" theme of a low-cost airline. This theme was core to the low total cost customer value proposition. It would contribute to on-time departures and arrivals that would increase satisfaction among customers, leading to future revenue increases. It also would enable the company to reduce costs by operating with fewer planes and flight crews than competitive airlines, so that it could offer lower fares to attract price-sensitive customers while still earning profits and a return on investment above its cost of capital.

The figure shows the intangible assets required to enable the strategy: new skills for the ramp agent, an improved information system, and the

Figure 2-10 A Strategic Theme Defines the Process, Intangible Assets, Targets, and Initiatives Required to Execute a Piece of the Strategy

Strategy Map

Process: **Operations Management**
Theme: **Ground Turnaround**

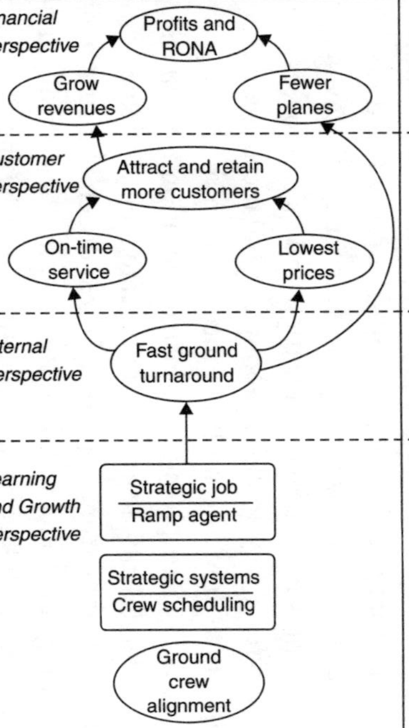

Profits and RONA
Grow revenues
Fewer planes
Attract and retain more customers
On-time service
Lowest prices
Fast ground turnaround
Strategic job
Ramp agent
Strategic systems
Crew scheduling
Ground crew alignment

Perspective	Strategy Map: Objectives	Balanced Scorecard: Measurement	Balanced Scorecard: Target	Action Plan: Initiative	Action Plan: Budget
Financial Perspective	■ Profitability ■ Grow revenues ■ Fewer planes	■ Market value ■ Seat revenue ■ Plane lease cost	■ 30% CAGR ■ 20% CAGR ■ 5% CAGR		
Customer Perspective	■ Attract and retain more customers ■ Flight is on time ■ Lowest prices	■ # repeat customers ■ # customers ■ FAA on-time arrival rating ■ Customer ranking	■ 70% ■ Increase 12% annually ■ #1 ■ #1	■ Implement CRM system ■ Quality management ■ Customer loyalty program	■ $XXX ■ $XXX ■ $XXX
Internal Perspective	■ Fast ground turnaround	■ On-ground time ■ On-time departure	■ 30 minutes ■ 90%	■ Cycle-time optimization	■ $XXX
Learning and Growth Perspective	■ Develop the necessary skills ■ Develop the support system ■ Ground crew aligned with strategy	■ Strategic job readiness ■ Info system availability ■ Strategic awareness ■ % ground crew stockholders	■ Yr. 1–70% Yr. 3–90% Yr. 5–100% ■ 100% ■ 100% ■ 100%	■ Ground crew training ■ Crew scheduling system rollout ■ Communications program ■ Employee Stock Ownership ■ Plan	■ $XXX ■ $XXX ■ $XXX ■ $XXX
				Total Budget	**$XXXX**

alignment of the ground crew to the strategy. The middle of the figure shows the Balanced Scorecard of measures and targets for the strategic objectives in the strategy map. The right side of the figure identifies the strategic initiatives and the costs required to achieve the targets established in the scorecard. The company has identified eight initiatives—each affecting one or two objectives—and all eight initiatives are necessary for the strategy to succeed. If one is deleted, a critical objective will be missed and the chain of cause-and-effect relationships will be broken. For example, ground crew training and a new crew scheduling system might be introduced, but if the ground crew does not understand how it fits in (communications program) or does not have incentives to improve organizational performance (employee stock ownership plan, or ESOP), then the strategy will fail. Thus, the figure shows how the strategic theme for fast ground turnaround requires aligned capabilities for intangible assets and a complete set of strategic initiatives.

BRINGING IT TOGETHER: THE STRATEGY MAP

We have now worked systematically through the four Balanced Scorecard perspectives to determine the objectives and measures that describe the strategy. A strategy map (see Figure 1-3) provides a visual representation of the strategy. It provides a single-page view of how objectives in the four perspectives integrate and combine to describe the strategy. Each company customizes the strategy map to its particular set of strategic objectives.

Typically, the objectives in the four perspectives of a strategy map lead to about twenty to thirty measures being required in the associated Balanced Scorecard. Some people have criticized the Balanced Scorecard, believing that people cannot focus on twenty-five different measures. If a scorecard is viewed as twenty-five independent measures, it will indeed be too complicated for an organization and its employees to absorb. But this is the wrong way to think about the Balanced Scorecard. The strategy map shows how the multiple measures on a properly constructed Balanced Scorecard provide the instrumentation for a *single* strategy. Companies can formulate and communicate their strategies with an integrated system of approximately two to three dozen measurements that identify the cause-and-effect relationships among the critical variables, including leads, lags, and feedback loops, that describe the trajectory, or the flight plan, of the strategy.

In the upcoming chapters, we will focus on the objectives and measures in the internal and learning and growth perspectives. The processes in the internal perspective create and deliver the value proposition for customers, the productivity improvements for the shareholders, and the societal performance for communities and nations. These are the processes that must be performed at an outstanding level, and in harmony with each other, if the company's strategy is to be achieved. The learning and growth objectives describe how the organization's intangible assets must be enhanced for performing and continually improving the critical internal processes. Organizations that can mobilize and sustain their intangible assets for the value-creating internal processes will be their industries' leaders.

SUMMARY

The strategy map provides the visual framework for integrating the organization's objectives in the four perspectives of a Balanced Scorecard. It illustrates the cause-and-effect relationships that link desired outcomes in the customer and financial perspectives to outstanding performance in critical internal processes—operations management, customer management, innovation, and regulatory and social processes. These critical processes create and deliver the organization's value proposition to targeted customers and also promote the organization's productivity objectives in the financial perspective. Further, the strategy map identifies the specific capabilities in the organization's intangible assets—human capital, information capital, and organization capital—that are required for delivering exceptional performance in the critical internal processes.

In the case study following this chapter, we discuss the strategy map of St. Mary's Duluth Clinics (SMDC), a regional health-care delivery system. SMDC provides an example of an organization with multiple customers—patients, physicians, and payers. Its strategy is to deliver a different value proposition to each customer: customer intimacy for patients, product leadership for physicians, and low total costs to payers.

NOTES

1. The strategies of public-sector and nonprofit organizations are designed to create sustainable value for their stakeholders and constituents.
2. See, for example, Henry Mintzberg, Bruce Ahlstrand, and Joseph Lampel, *Strategy Safari: A Guided Tour Through the Wilds of Strategic Management* (New York: Simon & Schuster, 1998), and P. Ghemaat, "Competition and Business Strategy in Historical Perspective," *Business History Review* (Spring 2002): 37–74.

3. Michael Porter, "What Is Strategy?" *Harvard Business Review* (November–
   December 1996): 61–78.
4. For nonprofit and public-sector organizations, the high-level objective is delivering value to constituents and citizens, not to shareholders. We discussed the
   modifications of the strategy map for nonprofit and public-sector organizations
   in Chapter 5, "Strategy Scorecard in Nonprofit, Government, and Health Care
   Organizations," in *The Strategy-Focused Organization* (Boston: Harvard Business School Press, 2001).
5. Market share refers to the percentage of company's sales to total industry sales.
   Account share measures the company's proportion of a given customer's or
   group of customers' purchases in a given category. For example, a retail clothing
   store can estimate that it supplies, on average, 13 percent of the clothing purchased by its customers. A fast-food outlet might supply 40 percent of a family's
   fast-food purchases or 2 percent of its total food consumption.
6. Carl Shapiro and Hal R. Varian, *Information Rules: A Strategic Guide to the
   Network Economy* (Boston: Harvard Business School Press, 1998); Arnoldo C.
   Hax and Dean L. Wilde, *The Delta Project: Discovering New Sources of Profitability in a Networked Economy* (New York: Palgrave Macmillan, 2001).

CASE STUDY

ST. MARY'S DULUTH CLINIC HEALTH SYSTEM

Background

An innovative leader in health care in northeastern Minnesota and Wisconsin, St. Mary's Duluth Clinic (SMDC) Health System encompasses twenty clinics, a 350-bed tertiary medical center, two community hospitals, and a specialty care facility. SMDC's medical team of more than 380 physicians and 200 allied health-care providers works with an experienced staff of more than 6,000 to provide primary care, specialty services, and medical technology to families in their own communities. SMDC's annual revenue is $650 million.

SMDC's goal is to provide residents of northeastern Minnesota and Wisconsin with a broad menu of health-care services close to their homes. Its mission states: "SMDC is a regional health-care system committed to enhancing the health status of the people we serve by:

- Promoting the personal health and total well-being of all people
- Providing expert medical services supported by compassionate care and innovation
- Creating value for our patients and customers through teamwork and continuous improvement
- Demonstrating leadership in medical education and research
- Regarding every person with dignity and respect"

The Situation

In January 1997, St. Mary's Hospital merged with Duluth Clinic, a large multispecialty clinic. Both St. Mary's Hospital and Duluth Clinic were financially sound at the time of the merger. The merger was expected to bring economic stability and strength by reducing duplication and enabling the new entity to compete better on quality and range of services. But the changes in medical coverage and cost reimbursement from the 1997 U.S. Balanced Budget Act, as well as unexpected financial burdens from the merger, put the new SMDC organization into deficit.

The Strategy Map

Realizing that the old "health-care formulation" strategy wasn't working, SMDC was ready for a new approach. When CEO Peter Person read *The Balanced Scorecard*, he believed he had found an approach that would help him accomplish two critical goals: to strengthen SMDC's margins and to better serve its patients. He informed the board of his intention to implement the Balanced Scorecard.

The process of implementing the BSC—and building the strategy map in particular—helped SMDC view itself as a business. The executive team targeted areas for growth that would help to support nongrowth areas. The cross-subsidy allowed SMDC to maintain its needed but less profitable services for patients. The BSC process also helped SMDC define three distinct sets of customers and identify the correct value proposition for each.

The SMDC strategy map, as with many health-care industry maps, begins with a clear articulation of the organization's vision and mission that provides a direct line of sight between the ultimate goals of the organization and the more tangible desired financial outcomes, both growth and efficiency (see Figure 2-11).

SMDC's strategy map articulates the values of its three sets of *customers*. Defining the value proposition for each customer group provides clarity to the strategy. For example, *primary care patients* require a "customer intimacy" strategy. "These patients need to know that they won't have to repeat their entire history every time they come to see us or call us," notes Mary Johnson, SMDC's chief operating officer. *Specialty care patients* and *referring providers and physicians* are grouped together because providers often refer specialty care patients to SMDC. "This group values clinical excellence and leading-edge technology and expertise," says Johnson. For that reason, SMDC approaches this group with a "product leadership" strategy.

SMDC's final customer group is *payers*, those who buy services from SMDC. This group wants low-cost service and innovative health-case coverage programs. They want to be able to offer to their employees and their customers the most value for their money. This translates into a "low total cost" strategy.

SMDC's internal process perspective articulates the processes that deliver the appropriate value proposition to each of the three customer groups. SMDC focuses on processes that "provide outstanding customer service" for its pri-

Figure 2-11 St. Mary's Duluth Clinic Health System's Strategy Map

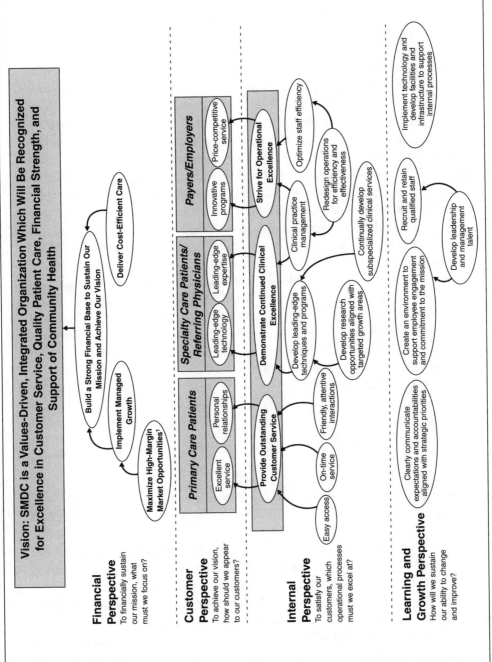

Vision: SMDC is a Values-Driven, Integrated Organization Which Will Be Recognized for Excellence in Customer Service, Quality Patient Care, Financial Strength, and Support of Community Health

Financial Perspective
To financially sustain our mission, what must we focus on?

Build a Strong Financial Base to Sustain Our Mission and Achieve Our Vision

Deliver Cost-Efficient Care

Implement Managed Growth

Maximize High-Margin Market Opportunities[1]

Customer Perspective
To achieve our vision, how should we appear to our customers?

Primary Care Patients

Provide Outstanding Customer Service

Excellent service

Personal relationships

On-time service

Easy access

Friendly, attentive interactions

Specialty Care Patients/ Referring Physicians

Demonstrate Continued Clinical Excellence

Leading-edge technology

Leading-edge expertise

Develop leading-edge techniques and programs

Develop research opportunities aligned with targeted growth areas

Payers/Employers

Strive for Operational Excellence

Innovative programs

Price-competitive service

Clinical practice management

Optimize staff efficiency

Redesign operations for efficiency and effectiveness

Continually develop subspecialized clinical services

Internal Perspective
To satisfy our customers, which operational processes must we excel at?

Learning and Growth Perspective
How will we sustain our ability to change and improve?

Clearly communicate expectations and accountabilities aligned with strategic priorities

Create an environment to support employee engagement and commitment to the mission

Recruit and retain qualified staff

Develop leadership and management talent

Implement technology and develop facilities and infrastructure to support internal processes

[1]Cardiothoracic, Orthopedics, Neurosurgery, Cancer, Gastroenterology, Surgery

mary care patients; processes that "continually develop subspecialized clinical services" for its specialty care patients and referring physicians; and processes that "strive for operational excellence" for its payers and employer customer. For example, whereas SMDC is now the largest provider in the Duluth area, it uses its internal process perspective to focus on processes that make primary care patients feel welcome and provide a small-town, local community feeling while taking advantage of scale benefits such as improved access and admissions technology. When it comes to processes that support the specialty care patient and referring physician, SMDC uses its internal process perspective to focus attention on the clinical technologies that both provide a competitive edge and appeal to physicians who use that technology every day. And the operational excellence portion of the strategy map forces SMDC to keep a clear focus on the operations processes that make clinical and administrative activities more efficient, such as staff scheduling and billing management, thereby reducing costs while creatively servicing payers and employers.

Finally, SMDC focuses on those learning and growth objectives that will optimize employee and organizational ability to change and improve. SMDC believes that the learning and growth perspective enables a two-way "contract" with all employees. SMDC pledges enabling support and expects increased commitment and performance in return. SMDC believes that only by clearly communicating its strategy and helping staff to understand their roles in the execution of that strategy can the organization optimize its performance while remaining a great place to work. The objectives within the learning and growth perspective serve as constant reminders of what is required to make the two-way contract possible. The objectives within the rest of the strategy map will be attainable only with appropriate investment in learning and growth. A clear understanding of and continuing dialogue about these objectives has energized the entire organization.

Anecdotes

After development and rollout of the corporate Scorecard and strategy map, SMDC cascaded the Balanced Scorecard across the organization, aligning all of the service lines (both growth and nongrowth areas), the community clinics, and key support departments. The BSC team implemented a strategic awareness campaign to communicate across the organization. SMDC has also linked strategy to the budgeting process, and has used the BSC to focus its monthly strategic operating review meetings. SMDC is now in its third year of BSC implementation, an ongoing, continually evolving process.

SMDC reviews and refreshes its strategy map each year at budget time. It readjusts the targets and initiatives for the next year and reaffirms that it is measuring the right things.

Three years after launching its BSC effort, SMDC has garnered significant results. In FY2001, it achieved:

- A $23 million increase in profitability, including an $18 million turn-around in the first year of implementation
- A stabilized cost per adjusted discharge and cost per encounter despite increased drug and salary costs
- A decrease of ten days in accounts receivable for clinics and eight days for hospitals
- A 13 percent improvement in appointment access availability for primary care clinics
- A 15 percent improvement in overall hospital patient satisfaction
- An 11 percent improvement in overall clinic patient satisfaction

According to Dr. Peter Person, CEO of SMDC:

Building the strategy map was a turning point for the executive team in fully understanding the organization as a business, defining our customers, and translating this into a clearly focused strategy. This resulted in a performance management tool to focus the entire health-care system. Our monthly scorecard review sessions are incredibly valuable to me as CEO. The scorecard enables us to easily scan and digest overall organizational performance and to identify any necessary course corrections. The balance of our discussion time has definitely shifted from day-to-day operations to strategic issue decision making.

St. Mary's Duluth Clinic Health System is a member of the Balanced Scorecard Hall of Fame.

Case prepared by Ann Nevius and Judith Ross of Balanced Scorecard Collaborative and Barbara Possin of SMDC. Our thanks to Dr. Peter Person and his colleagues for sharing the SMDC experience.

PART TWO

Value–Creating Processes

CHAPTER THREE

OPERATIONS MANAGEMENT PROCESSES

OPERATING PROCESSES PRODUCE and deliver goods and services to customers (see Figure 3-1). For a period in the late twentieth century, many scholars and companies believed that managing operations was the most critical component of any organization's strategy. Inspired by the remarkable results achieved by Japanese manufacturers in transportation, electronics, and optical industries, most companies placed a high priority on redesigning, reengineering, and continuously improving their critical operating processes.

Companies' efforts to achieve operational excellence were largely successful. Many enjoyed dramatic improvements in the quality, cost, and responsiveness of manufacturing and service delivery processes. While operational excellence alone is not the basis of a sustainable strategy, managing operations remains a priority for all organizations.[1] Without excellent operations, companies will find it difficult to execute strategies, even strategies that are not dependent on having the lowest cost structure in the industry.

FOUR OPERATIONS MANAGEMENT PROCESSES

Operations management can encompass up to four important processes (see Figure 3-2):

1. Develop and sustain supplier relationships
2. Produce products and services

Figure 3-1 Operations Management

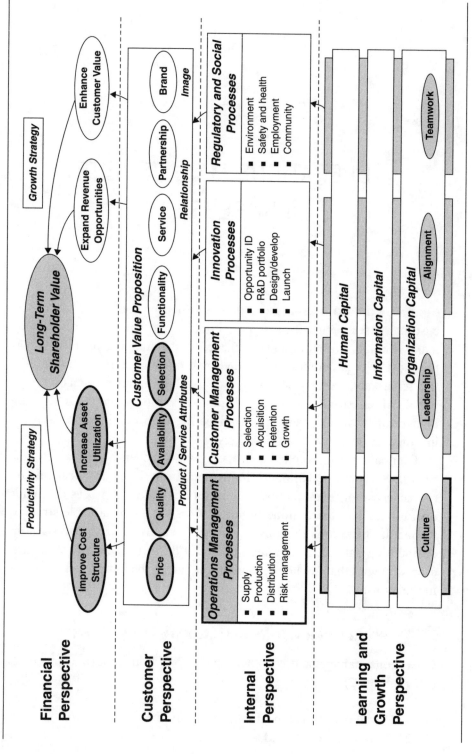

Figure 3-2 Operations Management Strategy Map Template

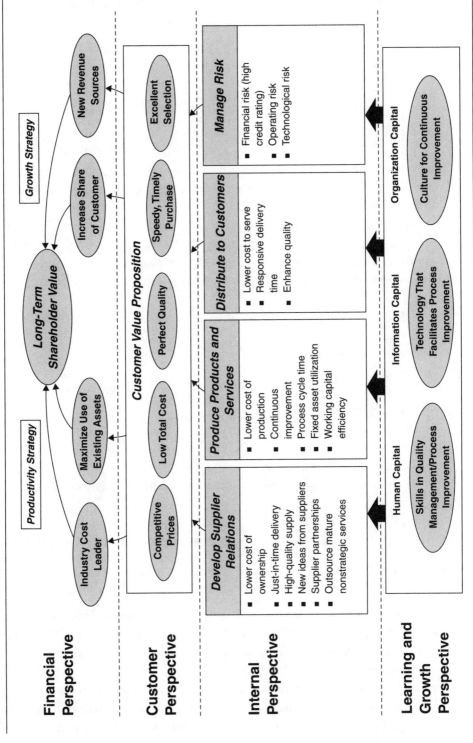

3. Distribute and deliver products and services to customers
4. Manage risk

We discuss each in turn.

1. Develop and Sustain Supplier Relationships

Companies, such as Toyota and Wal-Mart, depend on their suppliers to produce high-quality products on short notice and deliver them reliably to their point of use. These companies enjoy significant competitive advantages from their established networks of superb supplier relationships.

One objective for effective supplier relationships is to lower the total "cost of ownership." This objective represents the total cost of acquiring goods, materials, and services. In addition to purchase price, companies incur costs to perform the following activities when acquiring goods:

- Perform design and engineering work to determine materials specifications
- Order materials
- Receive materials
- Inspect materials
- Return materials
- Move materials
- Store materials
- Scrap obsolete materials
- Scrap and rework products because of (undetected) defective incoming materials
- Delay production because of late deliveries
- Expedite materials to avoid shutdowns because of late-arriving materials
- Pay for materials

The best suppliers are low-cost, not merely low-price. Purchase price is only one component of the total cost of acquiring materials. The *total cost of ownership* of acquiring goods or services from an individual supplier includes the purchase price plus the cost of performing all the procurement-related activities listed above for the items purchased from that supplier. Activity-based costing (ABC) enables companies to assign aggregate procurement costs to the procurement activities and then trace these activity costs to the goods and services acquired from individual suppliers.[2]

To lower the costs of acquiring products, companies strive to find suppliers that accept electronic orders (Internet or EDI) and that deliver products with no defects, requiring no inspection, just-in-time, and directly to the manufacturing process or point of use. Further, low-cost suppliers issue no invoices and accept automatic electronic payments.

Some companies have gone even further by eliminating their purchasing function for certain items entirely. Suppliers station their own person at the company's site and that person orders and manages the flow of incoming materials (including any local storage) before releasing the materials to the company's production process, as needed.

Other supplier objectives, beyond cost reduction, relate to the timeliness and quality of supplied goods and services. Many companies aggregate their supplier cost, time, and quality metrics into an overall supplier scorecard measure. For example, Visteon maintains a Web site on which suppliers can continually see their ratings on delivery and quality performance.

In recent years, many organizations have outsourced noncore functions, such as information technology, telecommunications, financial transaction processing, and plant maintenance, as well as the production of mature products and services. Such outsourcing enables the company to focus its resources and management time on the processes that provide differentiation, uniqueness, and competitive advantage. When extensive outsourcing is part of the organization's strategy, enhancing the performance (cost, quality, and response time) of outsourced services represents an important strategic objective for operations management.

Some companies depend on their suppliers for product innovation and design, freeing up internal engineering resources for advanced product development and systems integration. Others integrate their supplier products and services with their own to enhance the value proposition offered to customers. For example, financial service companies partner with their suppliers to provide customers with a single source for a broad range of financial products. In these situations, managing supplier relationships would include objectives for supplier innovation or the provision of value-adding services directly to the company's customers.

Once supplier relationships have been established, companies strive to lower the cost and time required to acquire materials and services from their suppliers and to eliminate errors. Drivers of efficient purchasing include the percentage of purchase transactions performed electronically, and the percentage of transactions done on a decentralized basis, say, by using a credit card with a specified upper limit, rather than through centrally approved purchase orders. Companies can explicitly measure the cost of operating the purchasing process with measures such as the (activity-based) cost per purchase order, and purchasing costs as a percentage of total purchases. The time required for purchases is measured by the elapsed time from when a request is made for an item until the item is delivered and ready for use. Of course, for organizations that have linked their operations to suppliers, replenishment can be continuous as suppliers track electronically the demands for their products and ship them without requiring an explicit purchase order. The quality of the purchasing process can be measured by the percentage of orders that arrive with the correct volume and mix of items at the correct time.

In summary, examples of objectives and measures for managing supplier relationships include the following:

Objectives	*Measures*
Lower the cost of ownership	• Activity-based cost of acquiring materials and services (includes cost of ordering, receiving, inspecting, storing, and coping with defects) • Cost of purchasing as percentage of total purchase price • Percent of purchases made electronically (EDI or Internet) • Supplier ratings: quality, delivery, cost
Achieve just-in-time supplier capability	• Lead time from order to receipt • On-time delivery percentage • Percent of late orders • Percent of orders delivered directly to production process by suppliers
Develop high-quality supplier capability	• Part-per-million or percent of defects, incoming orders • Percent of suppliers qualified to deliver without incoming inspection • Percent of perfect orders received
Use new ideas from suppliers	• Number of innovations from suppliers

Achieve supplier partnership	• Number of suppliers providing services directly to customers
Outsource mature, non-core products and service	• Number of outsourcing relationships • Benchmarked performance of outsourcing partners

2. Produce Products and Services

At the core of the operations management theme are the efficient, high-quality, and responsive operating processes that produce the goods and services used by the organization's customers. The books that have been written on improving process cost, quality, and cycle times could fill a library.[3] Initiatives such as reengineering, business process redesign, continuous improvement, activity-based management, total quality management, and time-based management are examples of the myriad programs that have been applied during the past quarter century to help employees improve process performance. We discuss the relevance of activity-based and total quality management later in this chapter.

Examples of objectives and measures for processes to be more efficient in the production of goods and services include the following:

Objectives	Measures
Lower the cost of producing products/services	• Activity-based cost of key operating processes • Cost per unit of output (for organizations producing homogeneous outputs) • Marketing, selling, distribution, and administrative expenses as percent of total costs
Continuously improve processes	• Number of processes with substantial improvements • Number of inefficient or non-value added processes eliminated • Part-per-million defect rates • Yield percentage • Scrap and waste percentage • Cost of inspection and testing • Total cost of quality (prevention, appraisal, internal failure, external failure)

Improve process respon-siveness	• Cycle time (from start of production until product completed) • Process time (time the product is actually being processed)[4] • Process efficiency (ratio of process time to cycle time)
Improve fixed asset utilization[5]	• Percent of capacity utilization • Equipment reliability (percent of time available for production) • Number and percent of breakdowns • Flexibility (range of products/services that processes can produce and deliver)
Improve working capital efficiency	• Days' inventory, inventory turnover • Days' sales in receivable • Percent of stockouts • Cash-to-cash cycle (days of accounts receivable plus days of inventory less days of payables)

3. Distribute Products and Services to Customers

The third process within the managing operations theme is delivering the product or service to the customer. This objective is really the downstream version of lowering the total cost of working with suppliers. As with the previous supplier and operating processes, the typical objectives for distribution processes encompass the company's cost, quality, and time performance as shown in the table below:

Objectives	*Measures*
Lower cost-to-serve	• ABC cost of storage and delivery to customers • Percent of customers reached via low-cost-to-serve channels; e.g., switching customers from manual and telephone transactions to electronic ones
Deliver responsively to customers	• Lead times, from order to delivery • Time from completion of product/service until ready for use by customer • On-time delivery percentage

Enhance quality
- Percent of items delivered with no defects
- Number and frequency of customer complaints

4. Risk Management

We have encountered, particularly in financial service companies, important objectives relating to managing risk, such as that arising from credit operations, interest rate movements, and foreign exchange fluctuations. For example, the Swiss Re strategy map (see Figure 3-3) includes two client (customer) objectives related to risk management:

- Long-term partner for risk and capital management
- The right risk and capital solutions

and several risk management objectives in the internal perspective:

- Leverage leadership in risk intelligence
- Comply with risk management processes
- Manage our book of risks

Of course, as a company offering risk management and diversification services to its customers, it is not surprising that Swiss Re has multiple risk management objectives in its strategy map.

Risk management should be about more than avoiding fluctuations in income and cash flow. A company's investors generally hold diversified portfolios that allow unsystematic variation in the outcome from any single company's performance to have minimum impact on their overall returns. Lisa Meulbroek describes five ways by which corporate-level risk management can create shareholder value in ways that investors cannot accomplish on their own:[6]

1. Reduce the costs associated with financial distress, such as bankruptcy
2. Moderate the risk faced by important nondiversified investors and stakeholders
3. Decrease taxes
4. Reduce monitoring costs
5. Lower the cost of capital

Figure 3-3 Swiss Re Strategy Map

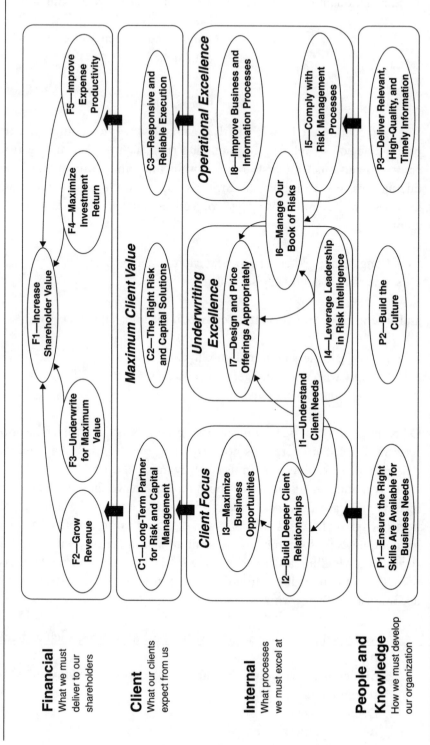

1. Reduce the Costs Associated with Financial Distress

Defaulting on debt covenants or working through bankruptcy proceedings incurs considerable costs to shareholders. The mere prospect of financial distress can cause important customers and suppliers to restrict their business with the company, or change the terms under which such business is conducted. Risk management processes that reduce the likelihood of such costly renegotiations can add value. Some companies hold large cash balances to reduce the likelihood of financial distress during an economic slowdown. For a somewhat extreme form of such risk management, Bill Gates, Microsoft founder and chairman, explained:

> *I wanted to have enough money in the bank to pay a year's worth of payroll, even if we didn't get any payments coming in. . . . We have about $10 billion now, which is pretty much enough for the next year.*[7]

2. Reduce Risk Faced by Key Undiversified Investors

Many managers and employees have a disproportionate share of their wealth, both financial and human capital, tied up in the company for which they work. This wealth concentration arises from stock option plans, employee retirement plans, and company-specific skills that would be worth far less were their employment with the company to cease. Effective risk-management policies reduce the risks faced by these undiversified employees and perhaps lower the total compensation that otherwise would have to be paid to employees to compensate for the high company-specific risks they bear.

3. Decrease Taxes

Corporations that face a graduated income tax have an incentive to smooth earnings to make maximum use of the lower tax rates on lower levels of income. Also, because of limits on tax loss carrybacks and carryforwards, companies that can shift income from good periods to loss periods can lower the total taxes paid over an economic cycle. Finally, if risk management reduces total firm risk, the company can increase its debt capacity and take greater advantage of the tax deduction for interest payments.

4. Reduce Monitoring Costs

Companies, especially financial service companies, can have risks that investors find difficult to assess. To the extent that outside investors and creditors have difficulty quantifying the risks of a company, they will demand higher returns to compensate them for their higher monitoring costs or the extra risk they feel they are absorbing. Therefore, a company could lower its cost of capital by implementing sophisticated risk management techniques that lower the unpredictability of its cash flows and earnings.

5. *Provide Internal Funds for Investment*

Companies should hedge against risks that would cause them to have inadequate funds to invest in positive net present value investments. For example, one group of risk management scholars concludes:

> *A risk-management program should . . . ensure that a company has the cash available to make value-enhancing investments. . . . A proper risk-management strategy ensures that companies have the cash when they need it for investment, but it does not seek to insulate them completely from risks of all kinds.*[8]

To accomplish the value-adding risk management objectives described above, a company can manage risk in three ways: Modify its operations, adjust its capital structure, and employ targeted financial instruments such as derivatives. Microsoft is an example of a company that uses an operating policy—to employ large numbers of temporary workers who can be laid off if business slows down—and a capital structure policy—a high stockpile of cash—to reduce its risk. Disney built its major theme parks in areas—Anaheim, California, and Orlando, Florida—where weather is generally pleasant and predictable. This lowers the volatility of its theme park revenues due to weather conditions. Additionally, companies take operating actions to reduce the risk that their products or services will be made technologically obsolete by competitors, or by actions taken by employees that can damage their brand and company reputations.

Choosing the appropriate level of debt clearly influences risk. Companies with high levels of debt, and low values of a key financial ratio—interest coverage, the ratio of earnings before interest, taxes, depreciation, and amortization (EBITDA) to interest expense—are more likely to encounter financial distress and be unable to fund positive net present value projects when they encounter business slowdowns. Conversely, high-debt companies reap benefits, when they are profitable, from the tax shield of interest payments and the leverage from earning high returns for share-holders using other people's (creditors') money. So lowering debt levels so that risk is totally avoided is not optimal.

Finally, by purchasing insurance and targeted financial instruments, such as futures, swaps, and options, companies can hedge their exposure risk to fluctuations in commodity prices, currency rates, interest rates, inflation, and stock market prices.

In summary, all companies should consider objectives for managing risk. Representative objectives and measures are shown in the table below:

Objectives	*Measures*[9]
Manage financial risk/ maintain high credit quality	• Bad debt percentage • Percent of uncollectible receivables • Exposure or losses from interest rate, foreign exchange, or commodity price fluctuations • Inventory obsolescence and spoilage • Debt-to-equity ratio • Interest coverage ratio • Months of payroll held in cash
Manage operating risk	• Order backlog • Percent of capacity from existing and backlogged orders
Manage technological risk	• Technology ranking of products and processes compared to competitors

LINKAGE TO CUSTOMER PERSPECTIVE OBJECTIVES

Managing operations for effectiveness and efficiency enables organizations to offer their customers important elements of an attractive value proposition (see Figure 3-2):

1. Competitive prices and low total cost of supply
2. Perfect quality
3. Speedy, timely purchase
4. Excellent selection

Competitive Prices, Low Total Cost of Supply

Efficient operations enable companies to earn a margin on sales sufficient to recover costs and earn a return on invested capital while still offering customers attractive prices. Companies that strive to be the low-cost producer and supplier would have an objective to be profitable at the lowest price point in the industry. As we discussed in the managing supplier relationships process above, an excellent supplier may be able to realize somewhat higher prices than competitors by becoming its customers' lowest-cost supplier. Such a company reduces its customers' internal costs by eliminating many activities formerly done by the customer. So an even better price measure is the total cost incurred by the customer to acquire the company's product or service. Of course, the customer must have a credible activity-based cost system to be able to attribute, and realize, the cost savings from having such a low-cost supplier.

Some companies' customers are distributors, wholesalers, or retailers who resell the company's product without changing its basic form. Such companies have an even more attractive value proposition for their customers. They would like to demonstrate that they are their customers' most *profitable* supplier. Again, the customer would require a good activity-based cost system to do such granular measurement, but if feasible, you can hardly find a more compelling value proposition than proving that your company's products make more profit for your customer than that made from any alternative supplier.

Perfect Quality

A company's operations should strive to have its customers experience zero defects with its products or services. This objective is straightforward. The ideal customer experience is a product that meets customer specifications and is suitable for immediate use by the customer.

Speedy, Timely Purchase

Customers value rapid, reliable delivery of goods and services. Reliable delivery means delivering on time based on the customer's expectation of the time window in which the delivery should occur. Most of us are unfortunately all too familiar with the quality of service from local monopolies, such as the telephone or cable company. Customers are told the serviceperson will arrive on a certain day, or, slightly better, in a four-hour time block (say, 8 A.M. to noon, or 1 P.M. to 5 P.M.). For people with full-time jobs or busy schedules, being forced to remain at home for several hours to a day waiting for a serviceperson to arrive is not a high-quality experience. Many manufacturers or retailers now expect their just-in-time deliveries from suppliers to arrive within a one-hour period, not a daily, or even four-hour, time block.

On-time delivery, by itself, may not be a sufficient indicator of timeliness. Companies can often improve their on-time delivery performance by quoting long lead times for the delivery of the product or service. Long lead times provide a comfortable buffer to produce the product or service. But most customers prefer receiving the product or service sooner rather than later. So measures, beyond on-time delivery, could include the lead time quoted by the company, and the difference between customer-requested lead time and the lead time quoted and committed to by the company.

From the customer perspective, the company must measure the lead time experienced by the customer, not how long it takes the company to produce the good or perform the service. Jack Welch describes how the GE engine repair business formerly measured its performance by the time taken to repair a customer's engine. The business took pride in having reduced this time from two days to one day. Welch challenged the business by asking how long the engine was out of service for the customer, the "wing-to-wing" time measured from the time the engine was taken off the plane to the time it was subsequently reattached. This total time was about thirty days. Looking at the issue from the customer's perspective led the engine repair business to expand its thinking beyond its own walls to incorporate improving the processes of external partners so that the entire process would be faster and more responsive to end-use customers.

Excellent Selection

A fourth dimension of a customer's value proposition relates to the range of products, merchandise, and services offered to customers. Some companies want to be like supermarkets, offering customers a full range of products and services. Other companies, especially those who wish to offer their customers some of the lowest prices in their industries, recognize that they may not be able to offer every possible product or service and still execute in a superb way. These companies exploit the empirical regularity of Pareto's Law, in which 20 percent of the possible variety will likely satisfy 80 percent of customers' demands. Excellent retailers, such as Wal-Mart and Costco, will typically offer less selection than full-line and more expensive retailers. But Wal-Mart and Costco know the top products and brands that most of its customers prefer, supplement these with a lower-price retailer-branded product line, and meet most of its customers' expectations for consistent quality, low-priced merchandise. Similarly, Southwest Airlines contributes to its low-cost strategy by avoiding congested, expensive airports like Logan Airport in Boston, La Guardia in New York, and Reagan National in Washington, DC. Instead, it offers customers nearby airports—Providence, Rhode Island, and Manchester, New Hampshire, for New England customers; Baltimore for the Washington, DC, area; and Islip, Long Island, for New York customers—that are less convenient for many customers but keep Southwest's costs down by so much that its lower prices still attract travelers from the high-density urban areas. Also, Southwest avoids the delays typical at congested urban airports, enabling it to offer more reliable departure and arrival times to its customers.

Customer objectives and measures for the value proposition offered by excellent operations management processes can be drawn from the following table:

Objectives	*Measures*
Lower the customer's cost; increase the customer's profit	• Price, relative to competitors • Customer's cost of ownership • Customer's profitability from own company's products and services
Deliver zero-defect products and services to customers	• Part-per-million (PPM) or percent of defect rates experienced by customers • Number and percent of customer complaints • Number of incidents of warranty and field service repairs
Deliver products on time	• Percent on-time delivery • Customer lead time (from order to delivery)

	• Percent of perfect orders (defect-free products and services delivered to the right location at the right time)
Offer excellent selection	• Index of product or service offerings measuring percent of customer needs covered
	• Percent of stockouts

FINANCIAL

Excellence in operations management has a direct connection to the productivity theme in the financial perspective, and an indirect link to the financial perspective's revenue growth theme (see Figure 3-2). Reductions in the cost of ownership and in the cost of operations and distribution processes should lead directly to improvements in the company's overall cost structure. Companies that sell relatively homogeneous products strive to have the lowest costs per unit in the industry. These companies typically benchmark their unit costs against competitors.

As companies improve their asset utilization—through better capacity planning, maintenance practices, and process improvements (which allow for more units to be produced with the same physical assets)—they reap benefits in asset productivity, the volume of throughput per unit of fixed asset capacity. Production planning and improved inventory management approaches, combined with optimized supply chains and distribution channels, enable companies to improve their inventory turnover working capital ratios.

The indirect link from improved operations to financial performance occurs as companies improve their price, quality, and delivery performance to customers. Such improvements should result in increased revenues from satisfied customers and opportunities to capture customers from competitors in price-sensitive and value-preferring market segments. A summary of the direct and indirect financial objectives and measures that can be influenced by excellent operations is shown below:

| *Objectives* | *Measures* |
| Become the industry cost leader | • Cost per unit, benchmarked against competitors |

	• Percent of annual reduction in costs per unit of output
	• Percent of cost budget variance
	• General, selling, and administrative expenses per unit of output or per location
Maximize use of existing assets	• Sales/asset ratio
	• Inventory turnover ratio
	• Free cash flow
	• Investment efficiency (NPV of new projects to total investment)
	• Product and development pipeline to capacity available
	• Percent of invoices paid on time
Increase account share with existing customers	• Percent of growth in existing customers' businesses
Increase revenue from new customers	• Dollar revenue from acquiring new customers

LEARNING AND GROWTH

Linking downward from internal processes to learning and growth objectives, we can identify the competencies, technologies, and organizational climates that foster excellence in managing operations.

Human Capital

Employee competencies in process improvement are foundational for improving operations. Especially important will be employee competencies in total quality management and six sigma. Objectives include increasing the percentage of employees who have achieved various competency levels of total quality management, including percentages that have achieved six sigma "green belt" and "black belt" status.

Information Capital

Technology plays a critical role in improving operational performance. Many repetitive, labor-intensive processes can be automated to provide lower-cost, more consistent quality and more rapid processing times. This is the traditional role for automation. But technology also plays a role in continuous process improvements. Employees need rapid feedback, including detailed, accurate measurements on the products and services they produce and the processes they control. Timely and understandable display of product and process information provides the foundation for more extensive data analysis, root cause analysis, and a whole range of other quality tools that lead to ongoing improvements in cost, quality, and process time.[10]

Offering customers the ability to track their order status improves the quality of customers' experiences with the company. FedEx and UPS use technology to continually track a package's position from the time it leaves a shipper's hands until it has been received and signed for by the customer. Customers can follow the progress of the package on the distributor's Web site. Measures on the availability of information for frontline employees about processes, products, services, and customers will be critical for an organization wishing to continuously improve cost, quality, lead time, and customer service.

Technology also lowers the company's cost of working with its suppliers and the customers' cost of working with the company. Supply-chain management software can contribute to an operations management objective to *reduce the cost of supplier relationships* and a customer objective to *lower customers' cost of acquiring products or services*.

Organization Capital

Teamwork and Learning
Organizations should not rely on each individual operating unit to devise its own ways of improving process cost, quality, time, and service. Many units throughout the organization generally work on similar problems every day. A critical learning and growth objective, therefore, is to identify innovations and best practices wherever they occur in the organization (or even outside the organization) and to disseminate the best practice rapidly to every organizational unit. Knowledge management systems should be key enablers of such best practice sharing throughout the organization. Measures such as number of new ideas posted or shared and number of new ideas adopted from other organizations will attest to the success of such a learning culture and the capability of the organization's knowledge management system.[11]

Culture

Employees must have an intense focus on continuous process improvement and consistent service delivery to customers. Periodic surveys should measure employees' understanding of the importance of operations management processes and how their daily actions are contributing to making processes better, faster, more responsive, and less expensive. The culture must encourage generating new ideas and solutions for process improvement, and sharing these ideas with other workgroups in the organization. And finally, the culture must overcome the typical "not-invented-here" syndrome that exists in most organizations. Employees must enthusiastically search for new process-improving, customer-service ideas, wherever these ideas arise, inside or outside the organization.

Objectives, measures, and programs in the learning and growth perspective that drive improvements in managing operations are summarized below:

Objectives	*Measures*
Develop skills in quality management and process improvement	• Percent of employees trained in quality management techniques • Number or percent of employees qualified at "black belt" six sigma quality level • Percent of employees with knowledge and training in activity-based management, just-in-time, and theory of constraints
Technology that facilitates process improvement and customer satisfaction	• Percent of employees who obtain immediate feedback from operations • Percent of customers who can track order status electronically
Culture for continuous improvement	• Employee survey on culture for continuous improvement and knowledge sharing • Number of new process improvement ideas generated • Percent of employee process improvement suggestions adopted

| Culture for continuous improvement (continued) | • Number of ideas for quality and process improvement shared across multiple organizational units |
| | • Performance improvement from employee suggestions and actions (cost savings, defect reduction, yield enhancement, process time reductions) |

INTEGRATION WITH INITIATIVES TO DRIVE OPERATIONAL EXCELLENCE

We have now described how to formulate objectives and measures for four operations management processes, and how these link upward to customer and financial objectives, and downward to learning and growth objectives. Activity-based management and total quality management are two important initiatives that help employees make fundamental improvements in operating processes.

Activity-Based Management

Activity-based costing (ABC) provides an analytic model that represents how individual products and customers use different quantities of the services supplied by indirect and support resources. In the first stage of an ABC model (see Figure 3-4), resource drivers link the expenses of resources supplied (as measured in a company's general ledger) to the activities and processes performed. Assigning resource expenses to activity and process costs illustrates a powerful link between ABC and the Balanced Scorecard. Cost, quality, and time usually define the performance of any process. Quality and time are relatively easy to measure, since they are based on physical measurements. Cost, however, is an analytic construct, not something tangible that can be measured by a stopwatch or a laser-gauging instrument. Only an ABC model can accurately trace organizational expenses to a procurement, manufacturing, distribution, or delivery process. So a properly constructed ABC model is central to measuring costs in the BSC's internal perspective.

But knowing the cost of a process is only the first step. Managers and employees must then act to improve the performance of the process. Activity-based management (ABM) encompasses actions that increase

Figure 3-4 Activity-Based Costing: From Expense Categories to Activities

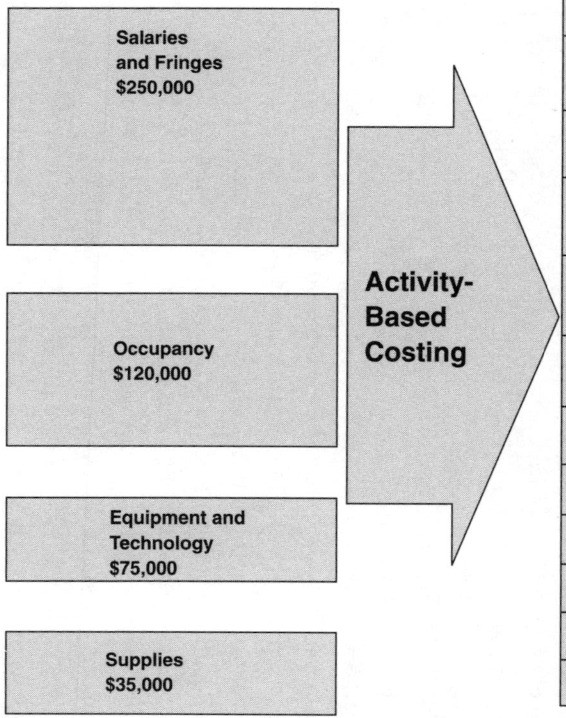

Activities	Salaries and Fringes	Occupancy	Equipment and Technology	Supplies	Total
Process customer orders					
Purchase materials					
Schedule production					
Move materials					
Set up machines					
Inspect items					
Maintain product information					
Perform engineering changes					
Expedite orders					
Introduce new products					
Resolve quality problems					

TOTAL $480,000

Salaries and Fringes $250,000

Occupancy $120,000

Equipment and Technology $75,000

Supplies $35,000

Activity-Based Costing

TOTAL $480,000

efficiency, lower costs, and enhance asset utilization. ABM strives to either increase capacity or lower spending, so that fewer physical, human, and working capital resources are required to generate the firm's products and services. The financial benefits from ABM can be measured by reduced costs, higher revenues (through better resource utilization), and cost avoidance (because the expanded capacity of existing resources obviates the need for additional investments in capital and people).

Activity-based management yields operational improvements through a five-step process:

1. Develop the business case
2. Establish priorities
3. Provide cost justification
4. Track the benefits
5. Measure performance for ongoing improvement

1. Develop the Business Case

Managers are often unaware of the many currently available opportunities for cost reduction and improved efficiency of activities and processes. Industrial engineers have focused for decades on improving frontline manufacturing and service operations within existing departments. But until recently, they have not been studying and attempting to improve support activities and processes, nor have they been improving cross-functional activities and business processes. When spending on support activities and processes was small relative to frontline operations, and operations and business processes were simple to understand, such a priority of effort was undoubtedly correct. In today's organizations, however, an increasing proportion of organizational expenses is associated with indirect and support activities, and the same activity or business process is affected by the actions taken in many different departments and functions. Until recently such activities and processes have not been subjected to process improvement activities.

Typically, collecting ABC process cost information on activities performed reveals to managers how much existing spending occurs in inefficient activities, and in defect-detection and correction activities. For managers who are still skeptical and suspicious about the potential benefits from process improvement, such as total quality management and six sigma programs, such information can provide them with the motivation to launch change initiatives. The activity data will show that while TQM and six sigma may be expensive programs to launch and sustain, the organization is already paying a high price, every day it operates, for inefficiencies and poor quality. To paraphrase an old Henry Ford axiom, "If you need quality process improvements and don't deploy them, you pay for them without getting them."

The ABC process cost information also provides the basis for benchmarking, both internally and externally. The use of a standard activity dictionary and data collection process across plants and companies enables the same activity to be compared across multiple organizational units. Awareness that activity costs are out of line with that of other organizational units provides visibility for where a unit should be focusing its process improvements.

In summary, the first benefit from an activity analysis occurs from classifying activity expenses by opportunities for cost improvement. The improvements get realized either by designing entirely new processes or by improving the quality and performance of existing processes. The activity classification enables managers to see how much of their current operating expenses occur in inefficient and low-quality processes. Used in this way, the ABC information provides the front-end insight and motivation for launching continuous and discontinuous improvement programs.

2. Establish Priorities

Many organizations already have the religion for process improvement programs. They therefore do not need the additional data about current spending on inefficient and low-quality activities, obtained during the first step of an ABM project, to become committed to continuous improvement programs. But without the information from an activity analysis effort, the managers may not focus their improvement programs on the activities and business processes with the highest potential payoff. As an example, many organizations have "empowered" their employees and work teams to do continuous improvement or reengineering of their processes. These decentralized employee work teams might accomplish remarkable improvements in their local processes, but without noticeable impact on total organizational spending. Making a process improvement of 50 percent or even 100 percent (by eliminating the need to ever perform the activity) in an activity that consumes less than 0.01 percent of organizational expenses will produce an imperceptible benefit to the organization's bottom line.

The scarcest resource in an organization is time. Rather than disperse employees' improvement initiatives across isolated and low-impact processes, managers can direct employees' efforts to improving activities and processes where the opportunity for substantial cost reduction is highest. The ABC model identifies where the largest opportunities for cost reduction exist. Managers can then use this information to set priorities for process improvement programs that, if successful, will deliver substantial and quantifiable financial benefits to the organization. The ABC information is not the ongoing operational tool for such improvement activities. For that, employees need direct feedback on quality, yield, and cycle time improvements. The ABC model provides the front-end guidance for deciding where process improvement initiatives should be launched.

3. Provide Cost Justification

In the early stages of the Total Quality Management movement, managers were told that "quality was free."[12] While initially skeptical that producing fewer defective items could be accomplished without increasing costs, the experience of both Japanese and U.S. companies with TQM programs soon convinced managers that they previously had been operating at highly inefficient production points. The early years of TQM implementation enabled lots of low-hanging fruit to be picked. Front-end TQM expenditures incurred by having employees focus on process improvement, robust product designs, and ongoing problem-solving and prevention activities were quickly and amply repaid with lower costs for appraisal, repair, rework, and scrap.

Once the early wins with low-hanging fruit have been achieved, however, then further improvements may not always come for free. That is, to get to pick the next level of fruit, someone may have to buy a ladder. Also, the original definition of quality for TQM programs was "conformance to specifications." Managers strived to produce each item and deliver each service in accordance with the specifications established for that product or service. Once operations and delivery processes had been stabilized so that they could produce consistent output in conformance with specifications, the quality stakes got raised. The definition of quality shifted from conforming to specifications to meeting customers' expectations. If targeted customers' expectations for product or service delivery performance exceeded previously established specifications, then the specifications would have to be raised. Even the most ardent TQM advocates would not argue that achieving higher levels of performance, versus adhering to conformance, could be achieved at zero cost.

And reengineering cannot deliver its promises for breakthrough improvements in cost and performance without substantial front-end investments. Reengineering programs are not inexpensive. Many organizations may be understandably reluctant to launch such major and expensive initiatives on faith alone. They will usually want to see a benefits case to justify the heavy commitments of time, energy, and financial resources required for a successful reengineering effort.

To summarize the ABM process, first, managers use the initial activity analysis to identify large amounts of spending in inefficient operations. They and employees can propose projects for which TQM, process improvement, or reengineering could have a major impact. Second, based on the opportunities for cost savings, the managers set priorities about which projects should be done first. Managers and employees have limited time for new initiatives. They should select projects that will have the largest impact and that can be implemented in the shortest time. And third, even though the most desirable projects often come with a hefty front-end price tag, managers can now see a rapid payback from documented cost savings from a process improvement project.

These first three aspects of ABM—identifying process improvement opportunities, setting priorities for these opportunities, and committing resources to realize these benefits—can be done quickly. These steps provide relatively easy, near-term, visible wins without involving people outside the production or operations organization (such as marketing, sales, or engineering).

4. Track the Benefits

Assume that ABM actions have been taken—TQM, process redesign or reengineering—based on the initial activity cost information, as described above. Many organizations, however, never fully realize the benefits from these actions. They improve or change processes, enabling the same output to be achieved with much fewer organizational resources, but they never redeploy or eliminate the resources no longer needed. So organizational expenses remain the same as before.

The ABC model provides information about resource elements—general ledger expense code, assets, and full-time equivalent (FTE) personnel—assigned to an activity. By periodically refreshing and updating the basic ABC model, the organization can reestimate the resources (expenses, assets, and FTEs) deployed for performing activities and business processes. In this way, it can verify whether the operational improvements are yielding actual benefits in terms of reducing resource capacity: fewer assets, fewer people, and lower spending required for the activity. The periodic ABC models provide tangible, documented feedback on whether benefits have been achieved from prior operational improvements, and signal when anticipated benefits have yet to be realized.

5. Measure Performance for Ongoing Improvement

The final aspect of operational ABM links to ongoing and continuous improvement. Managers can define process drivers that help to explain the quantity of resources, and hence the cost, required to perform an activity. For example, an activity such as processing materials through a machine might have, as a process driver, the quality of incoming materials. If incoming materials are out of specifications, or just inside specifications, more time and rework might be required to convert them to finished goods. Another process driver might be the training and skill levels of employees operating the process. Process drivers are local performance indicators that employees can track and improve every day. They are not the strategic measures on the unit's Balanced Scorecard; they are the operational indicators that measure, motivate, and evaluate daily improvement activities.

Summary

Activity-based management enables managers to get highly visible successes from a simple activity-based costing system. Opportunities for transformation, reengineering, and continuous process improvements get quickly identified and quantified. Learning the cost of each activity or process directs employee and manager attention and helps them to set priorities for attacking the most inefficient and least value-adding activities. The ABC model also provides the benefits case for launching the initiatives by revealing how much is spent each period by continuing to operate inefficiently. Many improvement projects turn out to be self-funding with even substantial front-end costs being rapidly repaid through much more efficient and responsive processes. Subsequent ABC models can track whether anticipated benefits have been achieved in the transformed processes. And process drivers can be defined to direct employees' attention for ongoing, continuous improvement of the transformed or reengineered process.

Total Quality Management

Many organizations already have well-functioning quality improvement programs.

Strategy maps provide a high-level, strategic context for these quality programs. Strategy maps focus quality programs and make them more effective by aligning them to the organization's strategic objectives. Let us explore the mutuality of benefits between strategy implementation and quality improvement programs.

Quality Measurement in Strategy Maps

Clearly, measures of process quality are important throughout operations management processes. Quality measures (such as PPM defects, yield, number of inspections) are used for several operations management objectives, such as purchasing, managing supplier relationships, producing goods and services, and distributing to customers. Quality measures also play a prominent role in the value proposition that excellent operating processes deliver to customers. Customer-detected defects, warranty and field service incidents, and on-time delivery all represent quality from the customer's point of view. So a well-functioning quality measurement program provides critical measurements to internal and customer objectives in most organizations' strategy maps.

A Strategy Map Enhances Quality Programs

We can identify four different ways in which strategy maps can provide significant value even to companies that are already far along in their TQM/six sigma journey.

1. The BSC provides explicit causal linkages through strategy maps and cascaded objectives. The outcomes from quality programs are often implicit and rarely tested. To build a Balanced Scorecard strategy map, the organization's strategy must be explicit. The process of building a strategy map—and associated objectives, measures, targets, and initiatives—engages the senior executive team in an intense process that creates consensus, clarity, and commitment to the strategy. The hypotheses underlying the strategy become explicit and testable as data accumulate over time and across similar organizational units.

Some organizations, however, fail to link their quality programs to explicit customer and financial objectives. As an example of a failure from a quality scorecard, consider a crude precursor to our strategy scorecards and strategy maps introduced at Analog Devices in the late 1980s.[13] In Analog's quality scorecard, the customer measures—on-time delivery, lead time, and customer-measured defects—all related to quality, and not to a differentiating value proposition. The Analog scorecard also did not include customer outcome metrics such as acquisition, retention, account share, or market share. The internal process measures focused only on manufacturing measures, and there were no measures relating to customer management and innovation processes. The failure on Analog's quality scorecard to link quality improvements to a customer value proposition or to any customer outcomes likely contributed to the 67 percent loss in shareholder value that occurred during the first three years that Analog used the scorecard. The disappointing initial results Analog experienced from its quality scorecard are in sharp contrast to the performance breakthroughs that companies have experienced when using a properly constructed strategy scorecard.[14]

Quality models can be local, tactical, and unlinked. The strategy map, in contrast, captures strategic objectives and only then identifies the initiatives and process improvements needed to support strategic objectives. As one executive has noted:

The BSC provided a unity and focus to our TQM efforts, and also to our annual and long-range planning. We had a lot of teams doing a lot of things, but the efforts were ad hoc. The BSC brought this all together into a unified systematic approach. Now when we assign responsibilities to departments, we do it within a framework.

2. The BSC establishes targets for breakthrough performance not merely to match existing best practices. Many quality programs evaluate their internal process performance against benchmarked best practice and focus as a result on continuous improvement. In contrast, target-setting with the Balanced Scorecard starts with aspirations for radical performance breakthroughs in financial and customer outcome measures. *Balanced Scorecard companies expect to become the benchmarks for others.* The targets for near-term performance are determined not by individual process benchmarks, but by what the organization must achieve in the short run to remain on a trajectory to longer-term performance breakthroughs. The targets for breakthrough financial and customer outcome performance get broken down into stretch targets for customer satisfaction and retention, internal process performance, and human resource and information technology capabilities and organizational alignment. Thus the targets for all BSC measures are linked together to drive breakthrough performance on high-level objectives. To be sure, quality programs' disciplined approach to benchmarking will be useful for BSC programs by helping organizations bring their substandard processes at least up to competitive levels.

3. The BSC often identifies entirely new processes that are critical for achieving strategic objectives. Quality models strive to improve existing organizational processes, making them better, faster, and cheaper. But applying the Balanced Scorecard principles, particularly when implementing a new strategy, often reveals entirely new processes at which an organization must excel. For example, one company was shifting from a low-cost strategy to a differentiated customer intimacy strategy. A critical process for the new strategy was to work closely with targeted customers to anticipate their future needs. The company had never done such a process before. With the previous strategy, it waited until the customer asked for a bid on a project and then responded. In a financial services company undergoing a similar shift in strategy, frontline employees had to be retrained from reactive transaction processors to proactive financial planners. With only a quality measurement model, employees could have scored high on performance related to speedy, responsive, and zero-defect processing of customer transactions. But this process, which would soon be automated, was no longer critical for the new customer relationship strategy. Instead, employees would have to excel at an entirely new set of processes: anticipating and understanding customers' emerging financial needs, developing deep knowledge of new financial products and services, and developing capabilities for customizing and selling financial products and services to individual customer needs. The BSC's high-level strategy deployment process easily identified the criticality of these new processes, and the reduced emphasis that should be placed on transaction processing. Once new strategically vital processes have been identified, quality programs can then be deployed to improve the performance of these processes.

4. The BSC sets strategic priorities for process enhancements. Even without the strategic need to introduce entirely new processes into the organization, companies still need to assess priorities. Some processes are more essential to strategic success than others. Benchmarking can provide an assessment of all an organization's processes by comparing them to industry best practice. Resources get committed to processes that have been identified as falling short of best practice. This allocation process, however, occurs independently of strategic priorities. The Balanced Scorecard, in contrast, identifies which processes must perform at or beyond current best practice levels, and which processes are less critical for strategic success. The BSC provides the guidance for organizations to redeploy their scarce resources of people and funds away from nonstrategic process improvements and toward those processes and initiatives most critical for implementing the strategy.

Of course, once organizations have identified their most critical and essential processes, they can apply quality management principles to enhance them. The self-assessment helps to identify the level of process investment required and the time required for the Balanced Scorecard to achieve targeted performance.

Reengineering: Discontinuous Process Improvement

Quality programs are often referred to as "continuous improvement" programs. Sometimes, however, existing processes are so inefficient or technologically obsolete that continuous improvements will not be sufficient to achieve the targeted performance. In these cases, organizations can sensibly abandon their traditional quality management tools and instead embark on a program of *reengineering* or discontinuous improvement.[15] The Balanced Scorecard enhances reengineering programs in the same manner as it does quality programs. It places reengineering programs in a strategic context linked to high-level organizational outcomes, it establishes performance targets (frequently nonfinancial ones) for the outputs from reengineering programs, and it sets priorities for where reengineered processes will have the highest impact on organizational performance.

Summary of Linkages Between Strategy Maps and Improvement Programs

A properly developed strategy map provides strategic focus to activity-based management and quality management programs. It embeds these improvement programs within a strategic framework that provides clear line-of-sight impact from process improvements to important organizational outcomes. We believe that each model—quality management and strategy maps—adds a useful dimension to the other. In using the two together, a management team leverages the knowledge and insights from each approach.

The continuous improvement from ABM and TQM programs helps organizations lower the cost of their processes and make these processes more consistent and more responsive. By avoiding defects, inefficiencies, and delays, organizations do things the right way. Strategy maps and the Balanced Scorecard focus an organization's improvement programs on the internal processes that will have the greatest impact on successful strategy execution. Strategy maps focus organizational processes to do the right things. Combining improvement programs with strategy maps enables companies to do the "right things right" (see Figure 3-5). Both sets of management tools clearly have their place for organizations wanting to achieve performance breakthroughs.

SUMMARY

In this chapter, we have reviewed the cluster of operations management processes that produce and deliver the organization's products and services. We have identified objectives and measures for operational excellence in processes that:

- Establish excellent supplier relationships and lower the total cost of purchasing goods and services
- Produce existing products and services for today's customers
- Distribute and deliver products and services to customers
- Manage operating and business risk

We have shown how important organizational improvement programs, such as activity-based management and quality management, are vital for

Figure 3-5 Business Excellence in Two Steps: Combining Business Excellence and Strategy-Focused Management Allows Organizations to Do the Right Things Right

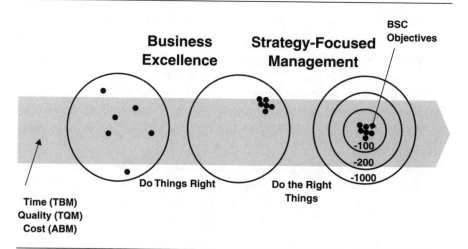

helping organizations to improve the cost, quality, and responsiveness of their critical operations management processes.

In the case study following this chapter, we discuss the strategy map of Thornton Oil. Thornton, which operates a chain of gasoline and convenience stores, used the development of a strategy map and Balanced Scorecard to drive dramatic improvements in operating processes so that it could become more competitive against recent entrants—including Wal-Mart, Meijer, Costco, and Kroger—to its business.

NOTES

1. Michael Porter, "What Is Strategy?" *Harvard Business Review* (November–December 1996): 61–64.
2. Robert S. Kaplan and Robin Cooper, *Cost and Effect: Using Integrated Cost Systems to Drive Profitability and Performance* (Boston: Harvard Business School Press, 1998), 203–210.
3. See the appendix to Chapter 5, "Internal Business Process Perspective," in Robert S. Kaplan and David P. Norton, *The Balanced Scorecard: Translating Strategy into Action* (Boston: Harvard Business School Press, 1996), 116–120, for a discussion of typical cost, quality, and cycle time measures for operating processes.
4. Cycle time is the total time required from the start of production to completion of outputs. Process time represents the time actually required for processing, excluding waiting, movement, and setup times. For example, the cycle time for mortgage approval could be twenty-eight days, but with only forty minutes of actual processing time during the twenty-eight-day time period.
5. Equipment utilization and reliability objectives are most critical for bottleneck resources. See Eliyahu M. Goldratt and Jeff Cox, *The Goal: A Process of Ongoing Improvement* (Croton-on-Hudson, NY: North River Press, 1986).
6. L. Meulbroek, "A Senior Manager's Guide to Integrated Risk Management," *Journal of Applied Corporate Finance* (Winter 2002): 56–70.
7. B. Schlender, "The Bill & Warren Show," *Fortune,* 20 July 1998.
8. K. Froot, D. Scharfstein, and J. Stein, "A Framework for Risk Management," *Harvard Business Review* (November–December 1994).
9. Targeted values for the managing financial risk measures are unlikely to be zero. Some amount of risk is desirable since hedging is expensive, and selling to only the most creditworthy customers will sacrifice much in potential sales.
10. See Robert S. Kaplan, "Texas Eastman Company," Case 9-190-039 (Boston: Harvard Business School, 1989) for an innovative example of how advanced information technology can drive daily process quality and cost improvements.
11. M. T. Hansen, N. Nohria, and T. Tierney, "What's Your Strategy for Managing Knowledge?" *Harvard Business Review* (March–April 1999): 106–116.
12. Philip B. Crosby, *Quality Is Free* (New York: McGraw-Hill, 1979).
13. Robert S. Kaplan, "Analog Devices: The Half-Life System," Case 9-190-061 (Boston: Harvard Business School, 1989).

14. Success stories from use of the Balanced Scorecard appear in Chapter 1 of Kaplan and Norton, *The Strategy-Focused Organization*. These experiences and others are documented in the Balanced Scorecard Hall of Fame, accessed at <http://www.bscol.com>.

15. Michael Hammer and James A. Champy, *Reengineering the Corporation: A Manifesto for Business Revolution* (New York: HarperBusiness, 1993).

CASE STUDY

THORNTON OIL CORPORATION

Background

Founded in 1971 by James H. Thornton, Kentucky-based Thornton Oil Corporation established a chain of convenience-store gas stations that ultimately grew to 140 units in nineteen states, and recorded annual revenues exceeding $700 million. Still family-owned, the company ranks among the five hundred largest privately held firms in the United States.

Things haven't always been so rosy for this mom-and-pop chain turned major enterprise. In 1998, the president and CEO left the company owing to a commodities trading scandal. Later that fall, the company named Rick Claes, a twelve-year veteran of Thornton's real-estate and construction division, the new chief executive. To meet his goal—aggressively growing the business—Claes knew that the company would have to address some big problems: a focus on short-term profitability; a lack of clear-cut strategy; a stifling command-and-control management style; and a poorly trained workforce plagued by internecine competition and lack of trust. Equally worrisome, Thornton faced stiffening *external* competition in the form of convenience-store gas stations launched by discount retail giants Wal-Mart, Kroger, and Costco. With rivals closing in, the new CEO was well aware that Thornton would have trouble maintaining its already slim gasoline profit margins. Clearly, something had to change.

The Strategy

The company decided to begin its transformation by clarifying its vision: to become a $1 billion company by 2005. Then it outlined a strategy for fulfilling this vision: Expand the convenience-store arm of the business, since profit margins from selling gasoline were notoriously meager. Expanding the convenience-store business, in turn, would hinge on customer intimacy: getting to know precisely who wandered into Thornton stores, what they bought, and what it would take to entice new customers into the fold. Thornton settled on a core theme of marketing excellence and growing its food franchise.

The Strategy Map

In the company's strategy map, the logic of Thornton's new strategy traveled inexorably through the four perspectives (see Figure 3-6). Some highlights from the map:

- *Customer perspective:* Success in growing the food franchise would lead directly to success in another key theme: making customers' lives easier. Five objectives related to providing customers with a low-cost shopping experience, including:
  - Low-price, quality gasoline
  - Basics: clean, safe, in stock
  - Quick in-out service
  - Friendly and knowledgeable store employees
  - Stores in locations easy for customers to access

  In addition, beyond providing these fundamentals, Thornton adopted a merchandising selection objective that would make its stores "destinations for signature food, products, and services." Simply put, the company wanted customers to head for Thornton's whenever they had a yen for a particular snack food, beverage, or other essential item. In the past, the firm had partnered with Dunkin' Donuts's parent company to install donut-and-coffee shops in many of its stores. Now it set out to develop its own brand items; for example, Thornton's coffee and pastries. Thus, Thornton wanted to excel at providing customers with the right selection and availability of differentiated food, products, and services.

- *Internal processes perspective:* Thornton had two themes for delivering a low-cost customer buying experience. The theme of *fuel supply-chain excellence* had three objectives related to lowering the cost of acquiring fuel to sell to customers. One of these was to "exploit B2B/B2C opportunities," which entailed using the Internet to buy and sell oil among smaller gas stations. The *operational excellence* theme stressed "excelling at the '5 C's' of store operations" (such as cleanliness, cus-

Figure 3-6 Thornton's: A Compelling Place to Work, Shop, and Invest

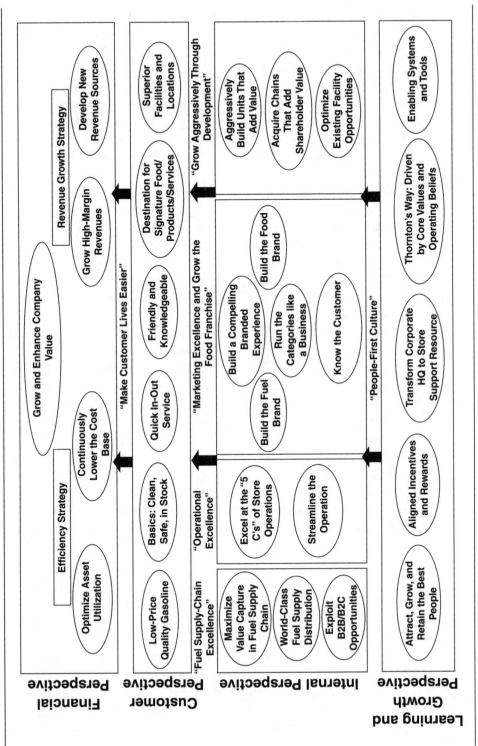

tomer service, and coaching) and improving store operating processes. In addition, finding new customers who would value the Thornton buying experience identified a theme of *growing the food franchise*. Internal processes included "knowing customers"—that is, identifying customer segments such as lunch-only shoppers, lunch-and-dinner buyers, gas-and-food customers, and finding ways to create new segments. Finally, the theme of *growing aggressively through development* included the objective to "optimize existing facility opportunities"; for example, improving selection by brainstorming new services to add to each store.

- *Learning and growth perspective:* To tap the intangible asset of employee knowledge and commitment essential to fulfilling its strategy, Thornton identified the key theme of establishing a "people-first culture." Related objectives included "transforming company headquarters from a command-and-control center to a support resource" for store managers and employees. In the past, headquarters had merely dictated decrees down to the stores. Now, it had to focus on understanding and meeting store personnel's needs.

  To further support the "people first" theme, the company defined the "Thornton's Way" objective—ensuring that the firm was "driven by core values and operating beliefs." Finally, to replace its antiquated communication systems, Thornton added the objective "enabling systems and tools," which sparked the adoption of a new, more efficient e-mail system that made it possible for employees and managers to communicate.

- *Financial perspective:* If all went according to plan in the preceding perspectives, Thornton expected to see hard-core financial results. This perspective's twin themes of efficiency and revenue growth were backed by four financial objectives: *optimize asset utilization, continuously lower the cost base, maximize high-margin revenues,* and *develop new revenue sources.*

Results

By clarifying, communicating, and evaluating progress toward its strategy through the Balanced Scorecard, Thornton achieved impressive results.[1] The company's emphasis on the customer perspective led to an increase of 44 percent in customer-service scores. Mystery-shopper scores—measures provided by secret shoppers hired to ask yes/no questions about store standards such as cleanliness—rose 14 percent. Total operating expenses were under or at budget every month. Thornton employees were clearly happier as well—as evidenced by a 48 percent reduction in total turnover and a 62 percent decrease in recruiting expenses.

Case prepared by Patricia Bush of Balanced Scorecard Collaborative, and Lauren Keller Johnson, a Balanced Scorecard Report contributor. Our thanks to Rick Claes and his colleagues for sharing the Thornton Oil Corporation experience.

NOTE

1. As a private company, Thornton Oil's actual financial results and improvement are unavailable.

CHAPTER FOUR

CUSTOMER MANAGEMENT PROCESSES

CUSTOMER MANAGEMENT reflects much of what is new in modern business strategy (see Figure 4-1). In the Industrial Era, strategies were product driven: "If we build it, they will come" was the underlying philosophy. Companies succeeded through efficient operations management processes and product innovation. Operating processes, focused on cost management, scale economies, and quality, enabled products to be delivered at prices that generated attractive profit margins while still being affordable to customers. Innovation processes produced a continual flow of new products that helped to grow market share and revenues. Customer management focused on transactions—promoting and selling the enterprise's products. Building customer relationships was not a priority.

The new economy has heightened the importance of customer relationships. Whereas innovation and operations management processes remain important for strategic success, the evolution of computer and communications technology, particularly the Internet and database software, has shifted the balance of power from producers to customers. Customers now launch transactions. They lead rather than reacting to marketing or sales calls. For example, customers of Dell and Levi Strauss can design their own product configurations using the companies' Web sites—Dell.com and IC3D.com (for blue jeans). Customer purchases, recorded at point-of-sale terminals at Wal-Mart, trigger production runs at vendor locations. Customers can find valid information about a company's products, including price, availability, features, and delivery times,

Figure 4-1 Customer Management

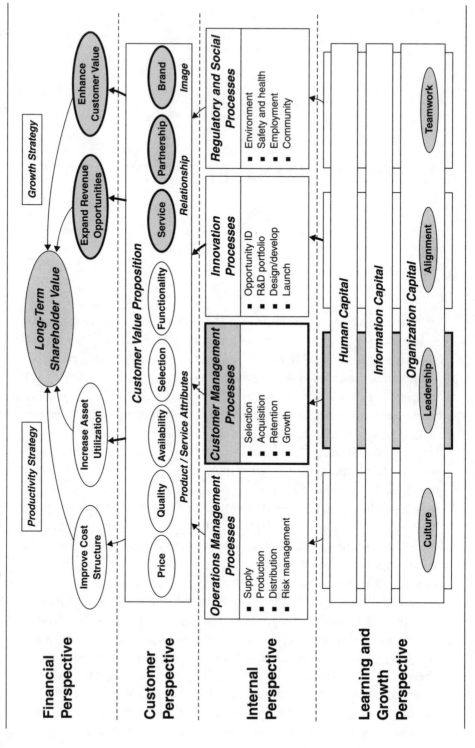

on the Web. Chat rooms provide testimonials from satisfied as well as dissatisfied customers.

Physical proximity of customers to the company is frequently not critical. Overnight shipping companies, such as FedEx, DHL, and UPS, allow products to be shipped to customers' places of business or homes from production sites scattered around the world. An organization can no longer define the success of its customer management process as merely generating a transaction, a sale. *Customer management processes* must help the company acquire, sustain, and grow long-term, profitable relationships with targeted customers.

FOUR CUSTOMER MANAGEMENT PROCESSES

Customer management consists of four generic processes (see Figure 4-2):

1. *Select customers:* Identify customer segments attractive to the enterprise, craft the value proposition to appeal to these segments, and create a brand image that attracts customers in these segments to the company's products and services.
2. *Acquire customers:* Communicate the message to the market, secure prospects, and convert prospects to customers.
3. *Retain customers:* Ensure quality, correct problems, and transform customers into highly satisfied "raving fans."
4. *Grow relationships with customers:* Get to know customers, build relationships with them, and increase the company's share of targeted customers' purchasing activity.

Customer management strategies should include execution along all four processes. Most organizations, acting without an explicit customer management strategy, do poorly on selection and retention processes (numbers 1 and 3). For example, Mobil pursued a confused pricing strategy for many years because it did not segment and target its vast market of potential consumers. Chemical Bank (now part of J. P. Morgan Chase) also lacked direction from a clear market segmentation strategy. It cultivated relationships with many unprofitable customers. Many organizations also pay too little attention to retaining customers. They treat sales as transactional events, avoid contact with their customers after the sale, and fail to measure whether they retain them for future business.

Figure 4-2 Customer Management Processes

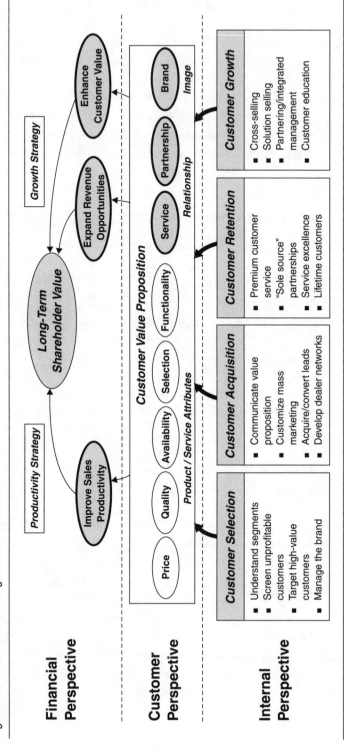

1. Customer Selection

The customer selection process starts with segmenting the market into niches, each with distinguishing characteristics and preferences.[1] The executive team selects *target segments* where the company can create a unique and defensible value proposition. Customer selection is not the same as order selection or pricing ("should we take this order?"; "at what price?"). Customers differ greatly in their profitability, and companies typically spend a great deal of money developing and nurturing customer relationships that can last for many years. To ensure that their marketing and sales investments are directed at the most profitable opportunities, executives should spend as much time and effort on selecting and investing in targeted customers as they do in selecting their investments in property, plant, and equipment. They should avoid the trap of trying to be the best supplier to all their possible customers.

Customer segmentation should ideally be done based on the customer value proposition, that is, the benefits customers desire from the product or service. Customers can be segmented by the benefits they seek or their relationship to the company, such as:

- *Use intensity:* Heavy, light, none
- *Benefits sought:* Price, service, performance, relationship, brand identity
- *Loyalty:* None, moderate, strong, committed
- *Attitude:* Dissatisfied, satisfied, delighted

In practice, especially in mass consumer markets, customer preferences can be difficult to observe directly, so segmentation is often done on more easily observable characteristics. For example, consumer segments can be defined by:

- *Demographic factors:* Age, income, wealth, gender, occupation, or ethnic identity
- *Geographic factors:* Nation, region, urban or rural setting
- *Lifestyle factors:* Value-oriented, luxury-oriented

Of course, segmentation on observable characteristics is valuable only if the characteristics correlate with the underlying preferences of customers. Advanced statistical techniques can be used for developing such valid segmentation in a heterogeneous population. These include cluster analysis for identifying homogenous customer segments, conjoint analysis for measuring customer preferences and needs, and discriminant analysis, for separating customers into distinct segments.

Once companies identify possible customer segments, they select targeted segments. A company's choice of customers can influence its capabilities, and, conversely, a company's resources, capabilities, and strategy can determine its best customers. For example, automobile component manufacturers for the "big three" U.S. automakers that subsequently became early suppliers to Japanese automakers (Honda, Toyota, and Nissan) became trained in Japanese total quality and just-in-time production processes. They soon became more differentiated suppliers and could compete on capabilities, not just price. As another example, a specialty, low-volume producer might get asked by a customer to produce a standard product in extremely high volumes. Such a customer order would begin the transformation of the company from a niche producer to a mass producer, with a very different cost structure.

In the more typical process, the company's strategy influences its choice of customers. Cigna Property and Casualty, as part of its turnaround strategy to become a specialist provider, would bid on business only when it judged its knowledge of the underwriting risks to be superior to the industry average. Dell Computer focused initially on sophisticated corporate customers who could provide local technical support for their installed base of personal computers. This focus on educated, corporate accounts enabled Dell to sell and ship directly to end-use customers, without requiring a retail or wholesale distribution channel. Dell also avoided the need to have an extensive technical support base for its customers. In this way, Dell could be the lowest-cost supplier of personal computers in the industry and soon became the industry leader.

Harrah's Entertainment, an operator of gambling casinos around the United States, targets the "low rollers," much like Southwest and other discount airlines target price-sensitive air travelers. Harrah's wants to be the casino of choice for couples on their evenings out to experience the "feelings of anticipation and exuberance" from small-stakes gambling that gives them a "momentary escape from the problems and pressures of their daily lives." Harrah's estimated that 26 percent of its players provided 82 percent of revenues, with avid players spending $2,000 annually. Such "avid experienced players," who could visit Harrah's casinos in multiple locations, became the company's targeted customers and removed it from direct competition with the high-cost luxury casinos operated by Mirage Resorts and Circus Enterprises.[2]

Marine Engineering's new strategy (see Figure 4-3) deemphasized a large customer segment that was highly price sensitive. It identified, for

Figure 4-3 Case: Marine Engineering

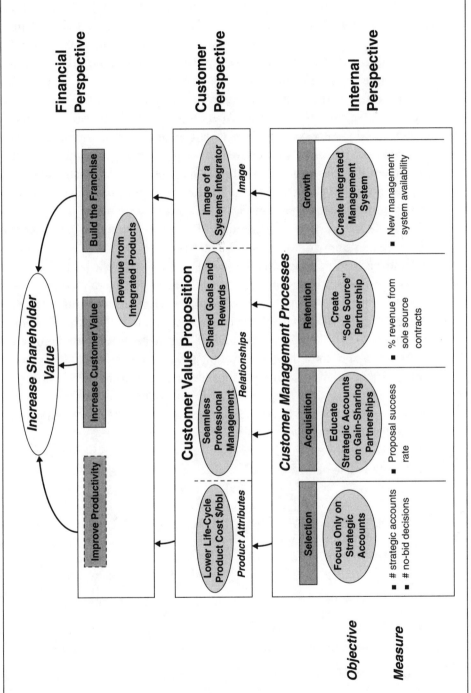

future growth and profitability, a market segment of customers that (1) valued long-term partnerships with suppliers, (2) wanted to outsource noncore services, and (3) asked suppliers to share in their risk and rewards from major projects. Marine Engineering would get paid more if its projects yielded higher returns for customers; its fees would be penalized when projects were late and above budgeted cost.

Marine Engineering chose a customer selection objective to "focus only on strategic accounts," those where business could be won by offering value-added services superior to those offered by competitors. It measured success for this objective by the number of customers whose business could be won based on superior services and relationships rather than low price. It also measured the frequency of not pursuing all potential business, particularly from customers who were seeking the lowest price bid. It used a measure—number of no-bids—to signal clearly that not every sales opportunity was to be pursued.

Some companies, especially in mature, commodity-type industries, do not see significant opportunities for growth through value-added services. The selection process for these companies focuses on avoiding unprofitable customers, those who use services costing more than the fees and revenues they generate. Metro Bank (see Figure 4-4) and Acme Chemicals (see Figure 4-5) both had significant but stable market shares. They chose an objective to "identify and then upgrade or exit unprofitable accounts." Using activity-based costing to measure profitability at the individual customer level, they measured their success in reducing the percentage of unprofitable customers.

Typical objectives and measures for customer selection processes are shown in the table below:

Customer Selection Objectives	*Measures*
Understand customer segments	• Profit contribution by segment • Market share in targeted segments
Screen unprofitable customers	• Percent of unprofitable customers
Target high-value customers	• Number of strategic accounts
Manage the brand	• Customer survey on brand awareness and preference

Figure 4-4 Case: Metro Bank

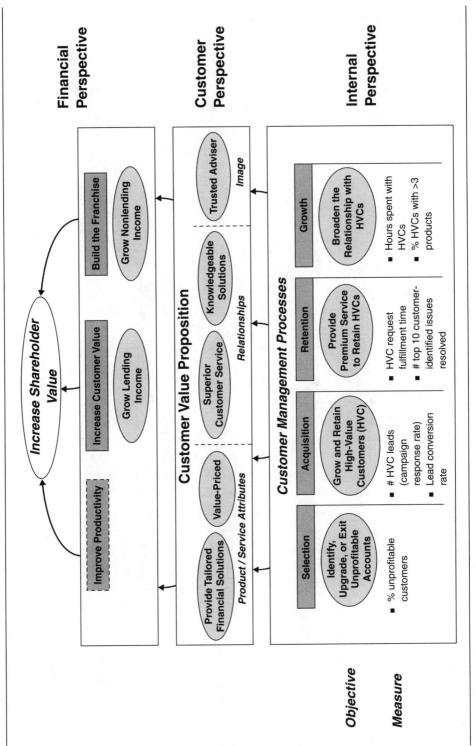

Figure 4-5 Case: Acme Chemicals

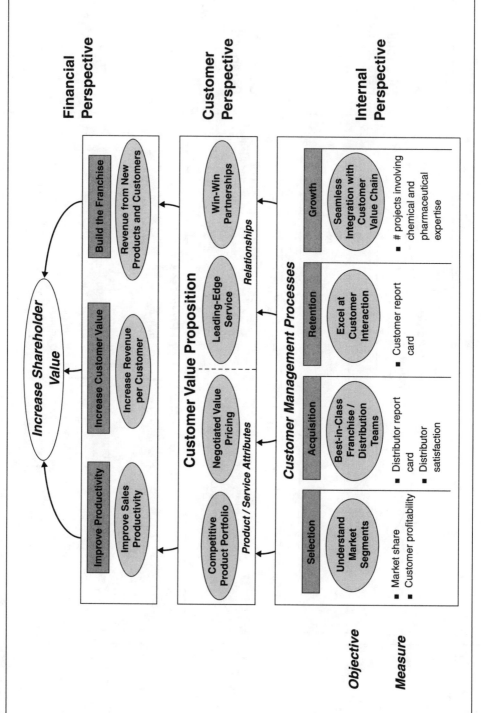

2. Customer Acquisition

Acquiring new customers is the most difficult and expensive customer management process. Companies must communicate their value propositions to new customers in the segments targeted by their customer selection processes. The company could initiate the relationship with an entry-level product that might be a loss leader, or a heavily discounted product. Ideally, an entry-level product should be inexpensive enough that the customer does not face much risk from purchasing it. The product should represent an important solution to the customer so that success makes a significant impression on the customer. The product's quality should be perfect so that the customer does not experience defects or failure with its initial purchase. And the performance of the product can be enhanced and complemented by additional products and services that can be sold to the customer in the future (using customer growth processes). For a financial service company, a checking account or a credit card represents an entry-level product with all these characteristics. For an insurance company, providing insurance on risks with high frequency of claims but low value per claim allows the customer to rapidly gain experience with the company's claim-handling processes and to build confidence in the company's ability to be a superior provider of insurance services.[3] Harrah's identified its targeted "low roller but loyal" customers with an extensive database marketing system. It sent special offers—such as $60 in chips—to attract its targeted customers for their initial visit to a Harrah's casino.[4]

Marine Engineering, dealing with a relatively small number of potential customers (twenty to thirty), developed an education program to show potential customers the benefits from gain-sharing partnerships. Marine measured its success rate on new proposals with these customers. Metro Bank launched a major sales campaign directed at the high-value customer (HVC) segment. It measured the number of leads generated by the program and its effectiveness in converting such leads into active customers (the lead conversion rate).

Acme Chemicals sold about half of its business through distributors. It monitored the quality of each dealer's customer acquisition performance through a periodic report card. It also received a feedback survey from dealers that evaluated, among other attributes, the quality of Acme's brand-building, advertising, and lead creation.

Typical objectives and measures for the customer acquisition process are shown below:

Customer Acquisition Objectives	*Measures*
Communicate value proposition	• Brand awareness (survey)
Customize mass marketing	• Customer response rate to campaigns • Number of customers using promotions to sample the product
Acquire new customers	• Percent of leads converted • Cost per new customer acquired • Lifetime value (estimated) of new customers acquired
Develop dealer/distributor relationships	• Dealer scorecard • Dealer survey feedback

3. Customer Retention

Companies recognize that it is far less expensive to retain customers than to continually add new ones to replace those who defect. Loyal customers value the quality and service of the company's products and are often willing to pay somewhat higher prices for the value provided. They are less likely to search for alternatives, thereby significantly raising the discounts that a potential competitor must offer to attract customers' attention.

Companies retain customers, in part, by consistently delivering on their primary value proposition, but also by ensuring service quality. Customers may defect from organizations that are not responsive to requests for information and problemsolving. Companies must develop capabilities, such as in customer service and call center units, to respond to requests about orders, deliveries, and problems. These units maintain customer loyalty and reduce the likelihood of customer defections. A company can measure its customer loyalty by whether customers are spending an increasing "share of their wallet" on repeat purchases.

The key to Harrah's success is its customer loyalty program. It issues its customers loyalty cards, called Total Gold cards, that enable the company to track customers' playing preferences, betting patterns, eating preferences, use of the hotel facilities, frequency of visits, and extent of play per visit. Harrah's runs experiments to learn how to increase loyalty and intensity of use of the company's facilities. It deploys direct marketing programs, such as a Total Rewards program, similar to an airlines' frequent flyer program, that provide rewards based on total business conducted at Harrah's locations. The rewards help in cross-marketing by encouraging loyal customers to earn and redeem rewards at any of Harrah's properties across the country. As CEO Gary Loveman noted, "The more we understand our customers, the more substantial are the switching costs that we put into place, and the farther ahead we are of our competitors' efforts."[5]

Even more valuable than customer loyalty is *customer commitment,* which occurs when customers tell others of their satisfaction with the company's products and services. Committed customers are also more likely to provide feedback to the company about problems and opportunities for improvement than to defect to competitors when dissatisfied. Companies can measure customer commitment by the number of suggestions made by customers, by the number of referrals existing customers make to new customers, and by the number of new customers acquired based on such referrals. *Customer apostles* are special cases of highly credible and authoritative committed customers. For example, Wal-Mart's recommendation that a supplier is reliable, high-quality, and responsive will carry considerably more weight than a comparable statement made by a local retailer. Being a qualified supplier to Toyota provides credible testimony to the company's ability to produce low-cost, zero-defect products and deliver reliably within a narrow time window. The highest form of loyalty occurs when customers take on ownership behavior for the company's products and services. *Customer owners* participate actively in the design of new products and supply recommendations on enhancements for service delivery. For example, Cisco Systems has followed recommendations from customers to acquire new capabilities through the purchase of other organizations. Frequent flyers of Southwest Airlines can participate in screening new cabin attendants. Customers who act as apostles or owners can provide far more lifetime value than a large number of merely loyal customers who maintain or even expand their purchasing behavior but do not recruit new customers or provide ideas for product and service improvements.[6]

Marine Engineering measured the strength of its customer partnership strategy by the number of sole-sourcing relationships, in which it won and retained business without submitting to competitive bids. Metro Bank monitored the service levels (request fulfillment time) for its high-value customers. It also surveyed key customers every six months to assess their satisfaction with the bank's performance in resolving their top issues of concern. Acme Chemicals introduced a Customer Report Card to gain feedback from its industrial customers. In each of these cases, the company's customer retention strategy consisted of providing superior service, actively soliciting and listening to customers' feedback, and building relationships that made it costly for customers to defect.

Typical objectives and measures for the customer retention process are shown in the table below:

Customer Retention Objectives	*Measures*
Provide premium customer service	• Number of premium customers • Quality ratings from premium customers • Time for customers to resolve concerns or complaints • Percent of customer queries not satisfied by initial respondent
Create value-added partnerships	• Dollars and percent of revenue from sole source contracts
Provide service excellence	• Service levels, by channel
Create highly loyal customers	• Account share (percent captured of customers' spending in category) • Number of referrals to new customers • Number of new customers acquired from referrals by existing customers • Number of testimonials from "apostle" customers • Number of suggestions for product and service enhancements from loyal customers

4. Customer Growth

Increasing the value of the company's customers is the ultimate objective of any customer management process. As already noted, acquiring new customers is difficult and expensive, and only makes sense if the size of the ensuing relationship exceeds the cost of acquisition. Acquiring new customers with entry-level products means that companies can expand their share of the customers' purchases by providing other, higher-margin products and services to them. Organizations should actively manage the lifetime values of their customers.

A company that can cross-sell and partner with customers expands its share of the customers' spending in the category. Increasing the depth and breadth of the relationship enhances the value of customers, and also increases the customers' cost of switching to alternative suppliers. One way to expand the relationship and also differentiate a basic product or service is to provide additional features and services after the sale. For example, companies can provide field service that performs remote monitoring of expensive equipment at the customer's location. Such monitoring enables the field service team to anticipate when unexpected failures are about to occur, and perform the maintenance that will prevent such failures and equipment downtime. The diagnostic monitoring and preventive maintenance adds considerable value to customers. It not only generates high customer retention; it also provides an attractive, high-margin revenue stream to the company. As another example, a commodity chemicals company was able to differentiate its basic product by providing a service that picked up used chemicals from customers so that it could reprocess the chemicals for disposal or reuse in an efficient process that conformed to environmental and safety regulations. This service relieved many small customers from expensive environmental processes and regulatory oversight.

Companies can partner with their customers, developing specific solutions for their targeted customer needs. For example, Marine Engineering attempted to lock targeted customers into sole-source partnerships by creating an integrated management system with them. Metro Bank measured success in its customer growth objective by the number of high-value customers who used more than three of the bank's services. It expected that establishing more personal, knowledgeable relationships, measured by the number of hours spent with customers by the relationship manager, was a driver of this desirable outcome. Acme Chemicals used a similar lock-in strategy by creating knowledgeable account managers who could work credibly and seamlessly with targeted customers. It measured the number of projects where such expertise could be leveraged into lock-in relationships.

Typical objectives and measures for customer growth are shown below:

Customer Growth Objectives	Measures
Cross-sell customers	• Number of products per customer • Cross-market revenues, revenues generated in markets or products beyond the entry-level product
Solution selling	• Number of jointly developed service agreements • Revenue/margin from post-sale services • Number of value-added services available to customers
Partner with customers	• Number of sole-source contracts • Number of gain-sharing agreements • Money earned from gain-sharing agreements • Number of hours spent with customers

CUSTOMER PERSPECTIVE LINKAGES

Customer management processes focus on the relationship and image dimensions of the basic customer value proposition (see Figure 4-2). Brand image helps both to select customers and to acquire them. Customer retention and customer growth processes build relationships with targeted customers. Our three general cases illustrate these points.

Marine Engineering's targeted customers had an overarching objective—engineering designs and construction projects that lowered their cost of recovering oil. Marine's *selection* and *acquisition* processes targeted customers who desired a partnership with suppliers. The processes paid less attention to customers whose sourcing decisions would be made mainly by price. Marine also wanted to build an image as a superb systems integrator, capable of managing across the life cycle of complex engineering projects: design, development, procurement, fabrication, installation, logistics, operations, and maintenance. Its *retention* and *growth* processes would deliver a seamless, integrated management process across these diverse projects and services, with a sharing of goals and rewards.

Metro Bank's value proposition was a relationship between an account representative and a client, enabling the bank to offer a portfolio of financial products and services tailored to individual client needs. The bank expected this value proposition to be attractive to a market segment of high-value customers (HVCs). Metro's *selection* process delivered a message to HVCs to establish the bank's image as a trusted financial adviser. Its *acquisition* process established relationships with clients who desired a knowledgeable adviser who could build customized financial solutions. Customers using more of the bank's solutions were the foundation for the *growth* process. And superior customer service would support the *retention* process.

Acme Chemicals competed in a mature market with a limited number of potential customers. Acquiring new customers was not a major objective. Acme's goal was to increase its account share with existing customers. The customer value proposition was to offer a portfolio of products and services at negotiated, but still competitive, prices. Its retention process focused on the customer's desire for leading-edge service, while its growth process focused on establishing win-win partnerships.

A typical set of objectives and measures for the customer perspective is shown below:

Customer Objectives	Measures
Increase customer satisfaction through an attractive value proposition	• Percent of customers highly satisfied
Increase customer loyalty	• Customer retention • Depth of relationship
Create raving fans	• Percent of business from customer referrals

FINANCIAL PERSPECTIVE LINKAGES

The financial outcomes from successful customer management processes show up primarily in revenue growth objectives (see Figure 4-2). Customer selection and acquisition provide *new revenue sources*, especially when companies are moving into new markets and adding new products and services. Financial measures include *sales from new products* and *revenue mix versus target*. Customer retention and customer growth processes should yield *increased customer value*. Desired outcomes from these processes included an increase in share of customers' wallet (spending) captured by the company and extent and length of relationship (lifetime customer value). In addition to these revenue growth objectives, however, effective customer management can contribute to a company's productivity objectives through the use of sales force automation and electronic marketing.

Typical financial objectives and measures for customer management processes are summarized in the table below:

Financial Objectives	*Measures*
Create new sources of revenue	• Revenue from new customers • Revenue from new products and services
Increase revenue per customer	• Account share (share of wallet)
Increase customer profitability	• Customer profitability (measured by ABC system) • Percent of unprofitable customers
Improve sales productivity	• Sales expense/total revenue • Cost per sale (by channel) • Percent of customer transactions done electronically

LEARNING AND GROWTH LINKAGES

Effective customer management processes require strong, enabling support from information technology, employee competencies, and culture and climate, as shown in Figure 4-6.

Human Capital

Advances in information technology and communication have generated the potential and, now, the expectation for heightened levels of customer marketing and services. This, in turn, has created a demand for new employee *competencies*. Employees with knowledge of database marketing, data mining, customer analytics, call centers, customer interaction centers, and Web page design now play a crucial role in customer management processes. Even the traditional salesperson has been transformed

Figure 4-6 Learning and Growth Strategies for Customer Management

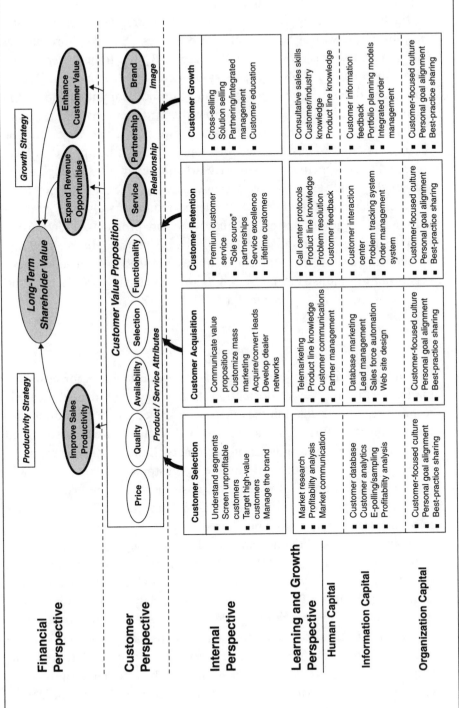

into a strategic partner who helps customers design the portfolio of solutions for their problems and needs.

Each of the strategic processes shown in Figure 4-6 requires a strategic job family, with a new set of competencies. (Strategic job families will be discussed in more detail in Chapter 8.) Customer *selection* requires the analytic skills typically associated with the marketing function. Customer *acquisition* is built around communication and negotiation skills. The ability to know the customer environment, understand customer needs, craft a value proposition, and close the sale are fundamental to customer acquisition. These can be applied in face-to-face discussions and through telemarketing channels. Managing service quality and delivery-level management are essential competencies for customer *retention*. Service excellence requires two-way communication and rapid resolution of questions and problems. Relationship management is the foundation for effective customer *growth*. Building an enduring customer partnership requires knowledge of the customer's organization, industry, and specific job. Excellent consultative and problem-solving skills are essential.

Information Capital

Information technology creates dramatic new possibilities for customer management processes. Information technology and related analytic techniques, such as data mining and activity-based customer profitability measurement, enable organizations to develop customized, personalized approaches even with millions of customers. Lands' End, for example, mails different catalogs to different customer segments. 1-800-Flowers.com automatically reminds customers of important dates. Amazon.com monitors individual sales and recommends books similar to prior purchases and those purchased by similar customers.

Many new capabilities are embedded within integrated customer relationship management (CRM) systems. Customer databases and related analytics permit better customer *selection* through cluster analysis from demographic data and customer profitability analysis. Database marketing supports the telemarketing process to improve customer *acquisition*. Operational CRM systems improve sales effectiveness through sales force automation and lead management. Customer service centers and self-help capabilities enhance customer *retention*. The Internet permits a new level of networking with customers that enhances education, collaboration, and customer growth.

Organization Capital

Customer management processes often require a new organization climate. One feature is creating a customer-centric *culture*. Take the example of a major oil company that had a long-standing marketing policy for its logo to appear on every product it sold. In the mid-1990s, this company, like Mobil, entered the convenience store business. It introduced a coffee island as part of its new retail space. For months, senior management insisted that coffee cups adhere to policy by bearing the company's familiar product logo. Only after expensive market research revealed that coffee drinkers prefer their coffee cups to display a recognized coffee brand, such as Starbucks, rather than a picture of an oil can, did senior management reluctantly change its policy. The culture of a product-driven company is deep-rooted, but must be overcome.

Customer management processes also demand a much higher degree of *teamwork*. Creating a lifetime customer means that many individuals must deal with the customer over time. The salesperson makes the initial transaction, the solutions engineer or relationship partner designs a portfolio of products and services, and the call-center help desk respondent provides follow-up. These diverse employees must all share the same base of information and work toward the same goals. *Alignment* to a common goal focuses all employees to work toward common, customer-based objectives. Team-based *incentive systems* and *knowledge sharing networks* reinforce the work of customer-focused teams, and reward all when the common customer objectives are achieved.

A typical set of learning and growth objectives and measures for customer management strategies is shown in the table below:

Learning and Growth Perspective	Objective	Measures
Human capital	• Develop strategic competencies • Attract and retain top talent	• Human capital readiness • Turnover of key personnel
Information capital	• Develop portfolio of customer management information and data systems • Increase knowledge sharing	• Customer application portfolio readiness • Extent of usage of knowledge management system

| Organization capital | • Create a customer-centric culture
• Create personal goal alignment | • Employee culture survey
• Percent of employee objectives linked to BSC customer process and outcome measures |

SUMMARY

Customer management processes in the internal perspective provide the capabilities for the organization to select, acquire, retain, and grow business with targeted customers. Understanding customers and the value proposition that attracts and retains them is fundamental to any strategy. Organizations whose internal process objectives focus only on quality, cost reduction, and efficiency are likely neglecting processes that would enable them to earn higher margins and grow their businesses. Figure 4-7 summarizes this chapter by showing a template of representative Balanced Scorecard objectives and measures for customer management processes.

In the case study following this chapter, we present the Handleman Company strategy map. Handleman, a large music merchandiser and distributor, used the strategy map to communicate and implement its new strategy based on forging long-term value-adding partnerships with its large retail customers, such as Wal-Mart and Best Buy.

NOTES

1. Helpful material on customer selection has been drawn from D. Narandas, "Note on Customer Management," Note 9-502-073 (Boston: Harvard Business School, 2002), and R. Dolan, "Note on Marketing Strategy," Note 9-598-061 (Boston: Harvard Business School, 2000).
2. R. Lal, "Harrah's Entertainment Inc.," Case 502-011 (Boston: Harvard Business School, 2002), 7, 9.
3. This discussion of entry-level products is drawn from the "foot-in-the-door" strategy described in D. Narandas, "Note on Customer Management."
4. Lal, "Harrah's Entertainment Inc.," 9.
5. Ibid.
6. The hierarchy of customer loyalty is due to J. Heskett, "Beyond Customer Loyalty," in *Managing Service Quality*, vol. 12 (Bradford, UK: MCB University Press, 2002).

Figure 4-7 Customer Management Scorecard Template

Perspective		Objective	Measure
Financial		• Create new scources of revenue • Increase revenue per customer • Increase customer profitability • Improve sales productivity	• Revenue from new customers • Share of wallet • Profits per customer (ABC) • Cost of sales (by channel)
Customer		• Increase customer satisfaction (with value proposition) • Increase customer loyalty • Create raving fans	• % customers highly satisfied • Customer retention • Depth of relationship • % business from customer referrals
Internal Process	Selection	• Understand segments • Screen unprofitable customers • Target high-value customers • Manage the brand	• Contribution by segment • % unprofitable customers • # strategic accounts • Brand awareness/preference
	Acquisition	• Communicate value proposition • Customize mass marketing • Acquire new customers • Develop dealer networks	• Brand awareness • Campaign response rate • # leads/conversion rate • Dealer quality rating
	Retention	• Provide premium customer service • Create sole source partnerships • Provide service excellence • Create lifetime customers	• # premium customers • % revenue from sole source • Service levels (by channel) • Customer lifetime value
	Growth	• Cross-selling • Solution selling • Partnering/integrated management • Customer education	• # products per customer • # jointly developed service agreements • #/$ from gain-sharing agreements • Hours with customer
Learning and Growth	Human Capital	• Develop strategic competencies • Attract and retain top talent	• Human capital readiness • Key employee turnover
	Information Capital	• Develop strategic CRM portfolio • Increase knowledge sharing	• Application portfolio readiness • # customer KMS hits/employee
	Organization Capital	• Create customer-focused culture • Create personal goal alignment	• Customer survey • Employee objectives linked to BSC

CASE STUDY

HANDLEMAN COMPANY

Background

Handleman Company (HDL) is one of the world's largest category managers and distributors of prerecorded music. HDL manages this category in more than 4,000 retail stores on three continents. Headquartered in Troy, Michigan, HDL generates $1.3 billion in annual sales and employs approximately 2,400 people worldwide, including 1,000 sales representatives. In the United States, HDL distributes more than 11 percent of all music sold. Its customers include mass merchant retailers, such as Wal-Mart and Kmart, as well as other large retailers such as Best Buy. HDL also owns Anchor Bay Entertainment, an independent home video label that markets a large collection of popular titles on DVD and VHS. Anchor Bay's library of titles ranges from children's classics to exercise to suspense and horror.

In calendar 2000, after several years of growth, sales in the music industry began to decline. Reasons for the decline include illegal file sharing over the Internet, competition for consumers' entertainment spending from DVDs and computer games, and the lack of hit records that sell millions of units within weeks of their release. To maintain its leadership position in category management and distribution, HDL focused on a strategy to increase shareholder value.

The Strategy

HDL formulated a three-year strategy to increase shareholder value by profitably growing its customer base, optimizing capital, and diversifying through strategic transactions. The strategy was based on HDL's continuing to provide leading value to its current customer base through operational performance and technology that was eighteen to twenty-four months ahead of competitors. By being more efficient and productive than other distributors and retailers could be on their own, HDL would remain an indispensable link between music suppliers and mass merchants. HDL would also offer a value proposition of providing flexible solutions to customers that would increase its share of current customers' business, enable it to capture and serve a greater number of retailers, and expand internationally. Strategic transactions would enable HDL to leverage its core competencies of category management and distribution into other product lines and markets.

The Strategy Map

HDL identified twenty-three key strategic objectives across the four perspectives of its corporate strategy map (see Figure 4-8):

Financial Perspective

F1: Increase long-term shareholder value by maximizing free cash flow was HDL's ultimate financial objective. This objective was motivated by external research that indicated a high correlation between free cash flow and stock price appreciation. HDL identified five financial sub-objectives expected to drive improvements in free cash flow.

F2: Grow profitable revenue. A primary driver of HDL's strategy was to generate growth in its current business. This objective signaled that HDL should seek revenue increases only when they would enhance profitability.

F3: Manage cost relative to growth. HDL would reduce selling, general, and administrative expenses as a percentage of revenue so that operating profits would increase as revenues increased.

F4: Optimize capital. HDL needed to manage its physical and financial capital effectively so that revenue and profit growth would also lead to shareholder value growth. By using assets wisely and balancing the mix between debt and equity, HDL would increase shareholder value.

F5: Grow via strategic transactions. HDL did not believe it could reach its objectives purely through internal growth with current businesses. HDL also needed to acquire or create new strategic partnerships that align with its core competencies of category management and distribution.

F6: Manage the multiple. HDL would increase its price earnings multiple by clearly communicating its strategy to analysts and investors, executing its

Figure 4-8 Handleman Corporate Strategy Map

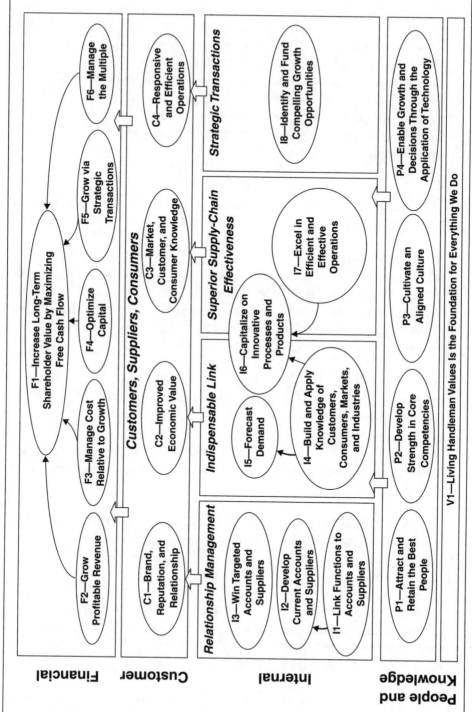

financial and operating strategy effectively, and attracting and retaining prestigious customers.

Customer Perspective

HDL would achieve its financial objectives by providing its retailer customers, suppliers, and end-use consumers with four key value propositions.

C1: Brand, reputation, and relationship. HDL's expertise at category management and its reputation for quality would create differentiation from competitors.

C2: Improved economic value. HDL's relationships and capabilities would produce better operating performance for its retailer customers than they could produce by themselves.

C3: Market, customer, and consumer knowledge. HDL's superior knowledge of markets and consumers would enable HDL to drive improved sales and profits for its customers.

C4: Responsive and efficient operations. HDL would satisfy customer objectives by being responsive to their needs and making the management of a complex business simple for them.

Internal Perspective

To deliver the four key value propositions in the customer perspective, HDL identified eight strategic objectives across four key internal process themes:

Relationship Management Theme

I1: Link functions to accounts and suppliers. To develop HDL's accounts with customers and suppliers, HDL would link its internal functions to all areas of customers' and suppliers' organizations. The linkages would also contribute to the second internal objective in this theme.

I2: Develop current accounts and suppliers. HDL would maximize sales for its current customers and suppliers by identifying growth opportunities.

I3: Win targeted accounts and suppliers. HDL would also develop its businesses and business models to win new customers and suppliers.

Indispensable Link Theme

I4: Build and apply knowledge of customers, consumers, markets, and industries. HDL would continually look to improve its understanding of consumers in order to provide each of its customers' stores with the best-selling music selections for that store. This capability would enable HDL to achieve another objective in this theme.

I5: Forecast demand. HDL would accurately forecast demand for its products through superior demographic and market knowledge, identification of market opportunities, and forecasting of industry trends and buying practices. Building and applying this knowledge would enable HDL to achieve its next objective.

I6: Capitalize on innovative processes and products. HDL would differentiate itself by creating and using innovative processes and products that competitors could not immediately duplicate.

Superior Supply-Chain Effectiveness Theme
I7: Excel in efficient and effective operations. In order to capitalize on innovative processes and products as well as to deliver continuous customer satisfaction, HDL would excel at core operating processes.

Strategic Transactions Theme
I8: Identify and fund compelling growth opportunities. HDL would work proactively to identify opportunities for strategic transactions, assess them wisely for financial and strategic benefits, and provide funding for the right opportunities.

People and Knowledge Perspective
To achieve the objectives of the prior three perspectives, HDL identified five objectives to equip the organization with the right people, competencies, culture, and technology.

P1: Attract and retain the best people. Employees who are aligned with HDL's strategy, values, and core competencies would drive the business forward and help secure HDL's success.

P2: Develop strength in core competencies. HDL would identify the critical core competencies that drive its strategy and then train or recruit employees who represent the highest levels of those core competencies.

P3: Cultivate an aligned culture. HDL's entire organization would be aligned to implement the strategy. Employees would understand how they contribute to the strategy and take accountability for achieving it.

P4: Enable growth and decisions through the application of technology. HDL's technology would differentiate it from the competition. HDL would continually look to better apply technology in its infrastructure, systems, and applications to enable growth and better decision making in all aspects of its business.

V1: Living Handleman values is the foundation of everything we do. Exhibiting HDL's values of honesty and integrity, accountability, continuous learning, and focus on stakeholders would drive the achievement of every other objective in HDL's strategy.

Anecdotes

After completing the corporate scorecard, HDL cascaded scorecards to its shared services units, subsidiaries, and departments, and created personal scorecards for its employees. Completion of its corporate strategy map provided HDL with the means to communicate strategy throughout the organization to help ensure successful strategy execution.

Case prepared by Geoff Fenwick, Mike Nagel, Paul Rosenstein, and Dana Goldblatt of Balanced Scorecard Collaborative. Our thanks to Steve Strome, Tom Braum, Rozanne Kokko, Gina Drewek, and their colleagues for sharing the Handleman experience.

CHAPTER FIVE

INNOVATION PROCESSES

SUSTAINING COMPETITIVE ADVANTAGE requires that organizations continually innovate to create new products, services, and processes (see Figure 5-1). Successful innovation drives customer acquisition and growth, margin enhancement, and customer loyalty. Without innovation, a company's value proposition can eventually be imitated, leading to competition solely on price for its now commoditized products and services.

Companies create considerable competitive advantages when they have the capability to bring innovative products—well-matched to targeted customers' needs and expectations—to the market fast and efficiently. Product innovation is a prerequisite for participation in some dynamic, technologically based industries, such as pharmaceuticals, semiconductors, and telecommunications. Exceptional innovation capabilities determine the industry leaders.[1]

FOUR INNOVATION PROCESSES

Managing innovation includes four important processes:

1. Identify opportunities for new products and services
2. Manage the research and development portfolio
3. Design and develop the new products and services
4. Bring the new products and services to market

Figure 5-2 summarizes the principal objectives in these four innovation processes. We discuss each below.

Figure 5-1 Managing Innovation

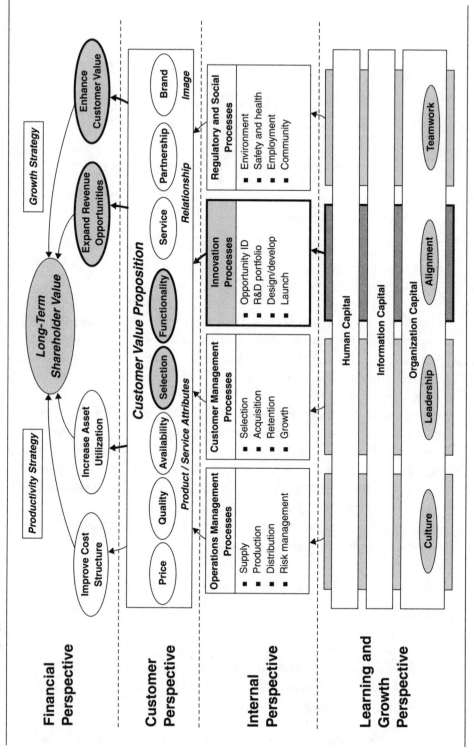

Figure 5-2 Innovation Management Strategy Map Template

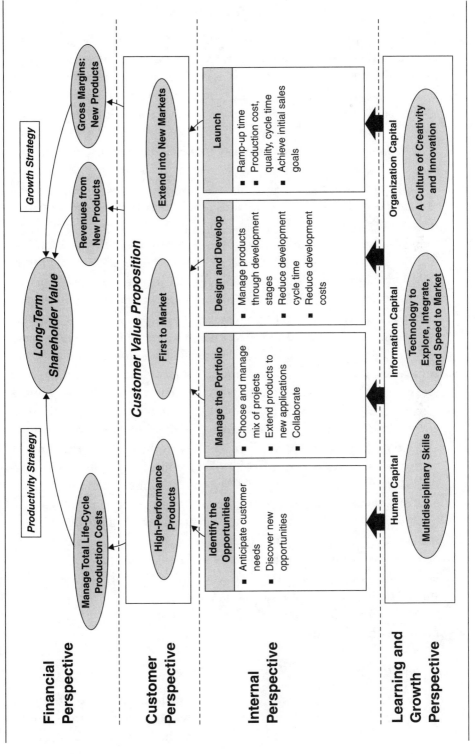

1. Identify Opportunities

Ideas for new products can arise from many sources. Typically, the research and development organization generates ideas based on the skills and technological understanding that it has accumulated from past product and process innovations. For example, the research labs of pharmaceutical companies screen and evaluate new compounds for their abilities to mitigate specific diseases. More recently, these labs have been applying the science of molecular biology to determine the characteristics of drugs that would affect specific biological targets, such as cell receptors and enzymes.

But organizations should not be too inwardly focused in their search for new ideas. They need to generate ideas from external sources, such as research laboratories, universities, and, especially, suppliers and customers. Companies that treat suppliers as strategic partners, rather than just as a source of low-priced materials and components, can benefit from suppliers' new product ideas and capabilities. Leading-edge customers are often a prime source of ideas for new products and new capabilities. For example, medical instrument companies continually speak with leading physicians around the world to learn about opportunities for new capabilities to make their care delivery more effective. Consumer electronics companies study how teenagers use newly introduced products to gain ideas for the next generation of products. A considerable body of literature (well beyond the scope of this book to summarize) describes the benefits and limitations of soliciting customer input for product innovation ideas. For example, Anthony Ulwick and Dorothy Leonard explain why companies should ask customers for the outcomes they want, not for particular features of new products.[2] Clayton Christensen describes the dangers of soliciting ideas solely from existing customers and missing the initially simpler needs of low-end consumers in rapidly growing customer segments.[3] W. Chan Kim and Renée Mauborgne's value innovation work describes how companies can customize the functionality of their products and services to meet the preferences of mass-market customers at substantially lower prices than competitors.[4]

Some typical objectives and measures for the idea and opportunity innovation process include:

Identify Opportunities Objectives	Measures
Anticipate future customer needs	• Time spent with key customers at targeted accounts learning about their future opportunities and needs

	• Number or percent of new projects launched based on client input
Discover and develop new, more effective, or safer products and services	• Number of new projects or concepts presented for development
	• Number of new value-added services identified

2. Manage the Research and Development Portfolio

Once ideas for new products and services have been generated, managers must decide which projects to fund, which to defer, and which to kill. Managers must determine whether a project should be done entirely with internal resources, done collaboratively in a joint venture, licensed from another organization, or outsourced. Even after a new project is funded, managers must continue to review, in light of new opportunities and resource constraints, whether to continue supporting the project at the current level of resources (money, capital equipment, and people), reduce resource commitments, or stop the project in light of limited progress made to date or more attractive opportunities that may have recently been identified. The output from the evaluation process is an aggregate project plan that defines the portfolio of projects the organization is investing in, the specific objectives to be achieved by the collection of projects, the resources required, and the mix between internal and external sources.

The research and development portfolio should include a mix of different types of projects drawn from the following categories:[5]

1. *Basic research and advanced development projects* create new science and technology knowledge that can subsequently be applied in commercial projects. Often such basic research is done in a separate organization.
2. *Breakthrough development projects* create entirely new products, based on applying science and technology in a new way. Typically, such projects establish a new product category or a new line of business for the company. The development of a lightweight, portable laptop computer in the late 1980s was a breakthrough product in the personal computer industry. Breakthrough product development projects typically extend over several years.

3. *Platform development projects* develop the next generation of products in a given category. The new platform defines the basic architecture for an extended set of products likely to be developed and launched for the next several years. Such projects may incorporate many technological features of the previous generation, but they also must introduce recent technological advances that offer significantly enhanced features and functionality. Platform projects generally require considerable resources since they deliver fundamental improvements in cost, quality, and performance over the previous generation of products.

4. *Derivative development projects* enhance particular features of the platform product to deliver a product targeted at a specific market segment. The modifications can lower the cost or enhance the functionality of an existing product. For example, a desktop computer product can offer one model with a faster processor for high-end users who require complex graphics or play interactive video games, as well as one with a slower processor for people who use their computer just for e-mail, simple spreadsheets, and word processing. Derivative development projects require far fewer resources than platform or breakthrough development projects since they leverage existing product and process capabilities.

5. *Alliance projects* enable a company to acquire a new product (or process) from another firm, either through licensing or through subcontracting. Companies turn to alliance projects when sufficient internal resources are not available for a desired project, when in-house development efforts fail to deliver desired results, or when smaller firms have already developed the basic capability for a new product or process, and purchasing this capability is less expensive than duplicating the development effort internally.

Consider the project portfolio for an automobile company. A basic research project could be the development of a fuel cell that would replace the gasoline-powered engine. A breakthrough development project would produce a hybrid car, capable of running on either batteries or gasoline. A platform product would be a new line of hybrid cars that the company would market over the next five to seven years. And derivative projects would develop the different models of the hybrid car—sedan, coupe, convertible—and options that would be offered to consumers. The derivative projects would also include annual enhancements to the basic hybrid platform. An alliance project occurs when the company has insufficient resources to design and develop all the car models it wants to market, so it turns to an independent company, such as Porsche, for design and product development of a particular car model or component.

The five types of projects have quite different resource requirements, project times, and risk profiles. The aggregate project plan determines the mix among the five project types and ensures that adequate resources are available for the selected project mix. The aggregate project plan links the various development projects to the business strategy, relates each project to specific product lines and markets served, allocates people, capacity, and financial resources to each project so that each has adequate resources to accomplish its objectives, and establishes a schedule for the sequencing of the projects within available resources.

Typical objectives and measures for managing the R&D portfolio process include the following:

Manage the R&D Portfolio Objectives	*Measures*
Actively manage the product/offer portfolio for superior innovation and customer positioning, performance, and profitability	• Actual versus desired mix of projects (advanced development, platform, derivative, and outsourced) • Actual versus desired spending on projects of each type • Technology ranking (independent peer review of current technology capabilities) • Net present value of products in project pipeline • Reach (customer feedback and revenue projections based on prototypes of products in pipeline) • Option value from project portfolio
Extend current product platforms into new and existing markets	• Number of projects leveraged from existing platforms that are targeted at new markets

| | • Number of life-cycle exten-
sion projects |
| Extend product portfolio through
collaboration | • Number of licensed prod-
ucts
• Number of joint projects in
new or emerging markets
• Number of technology or
product partners |

3. Design and Develop New Products and Services

The design and development process, the core of product development, brings new concepts to market.[6] A successful design and development process culminates in a product that has the desired functionality, is attractive to the targeted market, and can be produced with consistent quality and at a cost enabling satisfactory profit margins to be earned. In addition to these demanding specifications for the output it delivers, the development process has to meet its own targets for completion time and development cost.

The product development process is a complex set of activities that cut across multiple functions of a business. The process typically consists of a series of stages:

1. *Concept development:* The project team studies market research, competitive products, technology, and production capabilities to define the basic architecture for the new product. This stage starts with a conceptual design, including product functionality and attributes, and estimates of the target market, price, and production cost.

2. *Product planning:* The project team tests the product concept by model building, small scale testing, and initial investment and financial planning.

3. *Detailed product and process engineering:* The project team designs and produces working prototypes of the product. Simultaneously, the team undertakes the design of tools and equipment that will be used in large-scale production. Several design-build-test cycles can occur, in which the product design and the production process are modified to achieve the desired performance characteristics of functionality, cost, and quality.

Some authors have described the product development process as a *funnel* (see Figure 5-3) in which the wide opening at the beginning indicates the maximum flexibility for concepts, product design, and manufacturing processes. As the project evolves, the concepts, designs, and processes become better defined as options get discarded.

Many companies introduce a formal *stage-gate process* that specifically identifies a series of development stages through which a new product must pass as it moves from an initial concept to a fully defined product ready for release to large-scale production (see Figure 5-4).

The product development funnel and the stage-gate model give a structure for allocating resources among projects based on project experience to date and evolutions in technologies, customer preferences, competitors, and regulations. Each gate represents a go/no go decision, at which engineers and managers compare the project to others in the company's new product funnel that compete for the company's scarce development resources. A project can be deferred based on its performance to date, or because of new information about customers, technology, and competitor activity. The stage-gate model provides discipline to the often chaotic product development processes. It forces managers to periodically review every project in their pipeline and gives them the option to pull the plug on those projects that no longer seem promising, based on new information. Thinning the population of product development projects enables the company's development resources to be focused on the most promising opportunities.

Figure 5-3 The Product Development Funnel

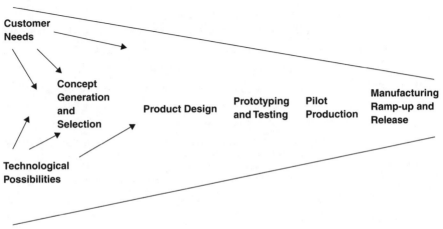

Figure 5-4 The Stage-Gate Model of New Product Development

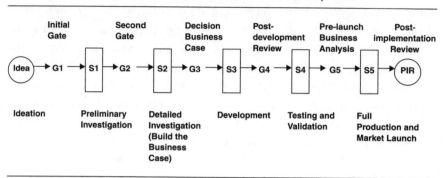

Pharmaceutical and biotechnology companies, of course, have different product development activities. Initially, scientists perform pre-clinical research involving laboratory and animal testing of new compounds. Promising drugs then require three phases of human clinical trials. Phase I trials are done on normal, healthy people (volunteers) to determine the safety, tolerability, and effective dosages of the drug. Phase II trials are performed on ill people to determine the clinical effects of the drug and to explore alternative dosage levels. Phase III trials are by far the most expensive, involving extensive testing of the drug against a control group receiving either a placebo or the best existing treatment to determine the benefits from the new drug, as well as knowledge of side effects. The cost of testing can be from $1 to $5 million in Phase I, from $10 to $20 million in Phase II, and from $20 to $70 million for each Phase III trial, which can last up to three years. At the end of Phase III, the drug is submitted for regulatory approval to be marketed and sold to the public. Even after the drug has been cleared for public use, companies often continue with Phase IV trials to look for rare adverse reactions and opportunities to decrease the dosage, and to extend the range of situations for which the drug can be prescribed. Thus, for pharmaceutical and biotechnology companies, managing the pipeline of drugs and the cost and time of each phase of development is perhaps their most important set of processes.

Software development companies follow routines similar to those used for developing traditional hardware products. For years, software companies followed a structured *waterfall process* (see Figure 5-5) in which one phase spilled into the next in a well-defined, sequential progression: concept design, product and feature specification, coding, and integration and testing. This process is used when customer requirements and requisite technology are well understood.

Figure 5-5 The Waterfall Model of Development

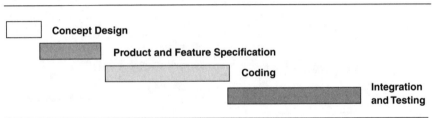

Recently, however, software companies have been doing their software development much more iteratively, enabling designers to incorporate changing customer requirements and evolving technologies into designs throughout the product development process. Following this evolutionary delivery model, companies post new beta versions of the software on the Internet for select, sophisticated users every few weeks, so that they can react quickly to feedback from users on capabilities and bugs and respond to new competitor products that may have just appeared on the market. The development process involves many "design-build-test" cycles, with each cycle incorporating and integrating more functionality into the high-level product.[7]

In developing the complex release of Office 2000, Microsoft used a flexible development process that exploited two key processes: Milestones and Daily Builds. For each software application, the project team broke the development work into several stages, each one encompassing the design, coding, and testing of a subset of the product's functionality (see Figure 5-6). The *milestone process* enabled engineers to test the functionality of the new product throughout the project rather than defer testing, as in the waterfall approach, until all the functionality had been coded into the final product. The project team established three development milestones several months apart, and allocated particular features to each milestone. If some features or functionality proved difficult to implement for the planned milestone, the feature was either deferred to a later milestone or eliminated entirely. In the milestone process, engineers must adhere to a targeted and inflexible final shipping date. They are allowed to reduce the planned functionality to adhere to the schedule. In contrast, the usual product development process allows the shipping date to be deferred until all the features have been incorporated, tested, and validated in the final product.

In the *daily build process* (see Figure 5-7), programmers check out a portion of the code to work on each day and submit their work at the end of the day. Special teams test the revised product overnight to

Figure 5-6 The Milestone Process

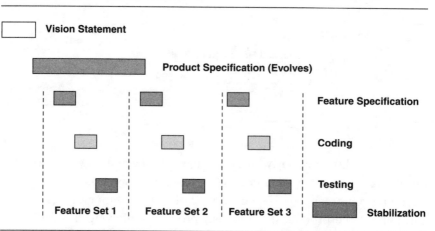

ensure that the additions worked well with the existing design, and to identify the bugs in the code for the programmers to work on in subsequent days. Revisions to the program are not accepted until a sufficiently low level of "bugginess" has been achieved, and the new code does not create problems elsewhere in the complete product. This process enables, in principle, a usable version of the final product to be available each day for testing and feedback by sophisticated users as the project evolved.[8]

With the considerable diversity in project management processes in different industries, companies need to develop their own customized

Figure 5-7 The Milestone Process with Daily Build

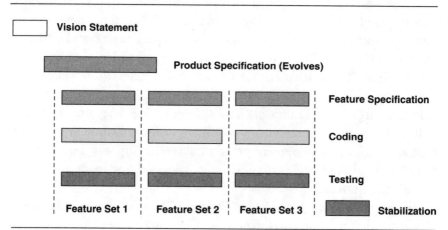

objectives and measures. Some ideas to stimulate thinking can be drawn from the following table:

Design and Development Objectives	Measures
Manage the project portfolio	• Number of patents; number of patent citations[9] • Project yield (percent of projects advancing from stage to stage) • Number of projects entering each phase of product development process • Number of projects reviewed using stage-gate analysis or other formal development review process
Reduce development cycle time	• Number of projects delivered on time • Average time spent by projects at the development, test, and launch stages of the development process • Total time (concept to market)
Manage development cycle cost	• Actual versus budgeted spending on projects at each development stage

4. Bring New Products to Market

At the conclusion of the product development cycle, the project team releases the product for initial ramp-up into commercial production. In this fourth process, the project team starts pilot production to finalize the specifications for the production process. The team builds all the components on the prototype production equipment and then assembles and tests the finished product. This process tests whether the new or modified manufacturing processes can produce the finished product at commercial volume levels that meet functional and quality standards. It also validates that all suppliers can deliver their materials and components within specifications, on-time, and at targeted costs.

In a final phase, the company starts commercial production at low volume levels to ensure that its production processes and those of suppliers can consistently produce and deliver the product. The marketing and sales organization also begins to sell the new product to customers. As customer orders increase and the supply and production processes stabilize, the production process ramps up further. Ultimately, the development project concludes when the company achieves targeted levels of sales and production, at specified levels of product functionality, quality, and cost.

Product Launch Objectives	*Measures*
Rapid launch of new products	• Time from start of pilot production until full volume capability achieved • Number of redesign cycles • Number of new products launched or commercialized
Effective production of new products	• Manufacturing cost of new products (actual versus targeted) • Manufacturing process yield for new products • Number of failures or returns from customers • Initial warranty and field service costs • Consumer satisfaction or complaints about new products launched • Number of safety incidents from new products • Number of environmental incidents from new processes
Effective marketing, distribution, and sales of new products	• Six-month revenues from new products (actual versus budgeted) • Stockouts or backorders for new products

INNOVATION LINKAGES TO OBJECTIVES IN THE
CUSTOMER PERSPECTIVE

Excellent innovation processes offer customers a value proposition consisting of two important components (see Figure 5-2). The first component represents the specific performance attributes of the company's products and services that describe how the performance of the new product or service dominates the performance of competitive offerings. By describing and communicating the most important functionality aspects of newly introduced products and services, all employees learn about the specific performance dimensions that the company must continually strive to enhance.

For example, in semiconductors, continual reductions in the size of the basic memory or processing chip generate advantages in the speed and functionality of the device. For displays, clarity, brightness, and power consumption are critical attributes. For pharmaceuticals, safety and relative product effectiveness for specific diseases and therapeutic categories generate competitive advantage. For medical devices and portable consumer electronics, customers desire reduced size and weight. For instruments, accuracy is an important performance attribute. Companies should identify the specific functionality that its innovation process produces for its customers. This functionality then becomes the basis for measuring the value proposition in the customer perspective of the strategy map.

The second component of the value proposition is the time at which the enhanced functionality becomes available to customers. Offering excellent functionality but getting to the market several months or years after competitors will not be the basis for high margins. Companies that excel at innovation and product leadership bring their superior products and services to the market faster than competitors. Being six months late in many product innovations may be far more costly to a company than incurring a cost overrun of 20 percent or more on the innovation process itself. Therefore an objective for being first-to-market with new products and services is an important source of revenue and margin growth for product leaders.

A third customer objective from the innovation process is to extend existing or new products into new markets. Pharmaceutical firms frequently discover that a new drug therapy is effective for diseases beyond the one initially targeted. Since the drug has already passed governmental approval for safety and toxicity, the approval process for applying the drug to new diseases is less onerous. Similarly, agricultural chemical companies can find that their treatments are effective on additional crops, pests, or diseases beyond the specific ones initially targeted and approved.

The core competency literature emphasizes how product excellence along a given functionality dimension can often be leveraged into many other applications and market segments.[10] For example, Honda's excellence in engine performance, originally developed for motorcycles and automobiles, has enabled it to enter such diverse segments as lawnmowers and backup engines for utilities. Canon's product leadership in optics for cameras has been leveraged into superb products for printers, copiers, and medical electronics. And eBay expanded its consumer auction capability into a powerful tool for selling used and reconditioned commercial equipment. The innovation process we described earlier in this chapter is very expensive. Companies should strive to get the maximum return from such investments by applying their leading products, services, and processes to applications well beyond the one initially targeted.

Customer objectives and measures for the output from an effective innovation process therefore encompass functionality, timeliness, and market innovation as shown in the table below:

Customer Objective	Measures
Offer enhanced product/service functionality to customers	• Specific performance attribute of new product/service (for example, size, accuracy, power consumption, heat generation, speed, brightness, storability, clarity, durability, ease-of-use, response time)
First-to-market with new product/service	• Lead time relative to competitors • Number of new products/services first-to-market • Percent of product launches on-time
Extend products/services to new segments	• Number of new applications from platform products • Revenue from new markets and segments

Financial

The financial objectives from innovation relate, of course, to revenue growth and enhanced margins from new products and services (see Figure 5-2). Products and services that offer distinct advantages over those of competitors and that are first-to-market should either command a price premium or generate sales growth that is faster than industry (and frequently both—higher prices *and* higher sales growth). The revenue and margin growth can occur with existing customers and markets as well as for entirely new customers and markets. Thus revenue and margin objectives can be developed for both existing and new customers. Also, the company should have an objective to get a return on the research and development spending it has done to develop new products and services.

Innovation is not often associated with productivity and cost reductions. Perhaps the main benefit from thinking about the relationship between innovation and cost management arises from the opportunity to manage costs over the entire life cycle of products. Companies may wish to have an objective to lower the cost of maintenance, repair, and disposal of their products. Product environmental issues are especially important in European countries where regulations require companies to internalize the cost of "put-back" for their products.

Financial Objective	*Measures*
Return on R&D investments	• Return on spending on technology • Actual versus targeted breakeven time (BET).[11] • Royalty and licensing income from patents
Revenue growth from existing customers	• Revenues and margins from existing customers from products released in last twelve months • Percent growth in sales to existing customers
Revenue growth from new customers	• Revenues and margins from new customers with new products
Manage life-cycle costs	• Maintenance costs as percent of total manufacturing costs • Disposal costs as percent of total manufacturing costs

Learning and Growth

Competencies, technologies, and organizational climate (see learning and growth perspective in Figure 5-2) are vital for fostering effective innovative processes.

Human Capital

Clearly, innovation would be impossible without deep expertise in the underlying science and technology for new products and processes. Innovative companies need scientists and engineers with the appropriate education and experience in the organization's fundamental technologies. The competency requirement can shift over time as new science is developed and new customer segments appear. In the pharmaceutical industry, for example, the scientific requirements in the search for new drugs have shifted from chemistry to molecular biology and computational genetics. In software, computer engineering skills that developed superb but highly proprietary architectures may be worth little as customer preferences shift to open architecture software. So companies must be continually alert to the mix of skills required to develop the next generation of products and services.

But deep competency in a given science or engineering field is unlikely to be successful by itself. Most important advances today require the integration of science and technology from several disciplines. Another key competency, therefore, is an employee's ability to work with scientists and engineers from other disciplines and backgrounds and to fuse the diverse knowledge bases into product performance breakthroughs.

Beyond the integration of technical expertise, all people in product development projects need to be able to interact effectively with employees from functions outside research and development, such as marketing, operations, and finance. Such integration enables development projects to meet their goals for functionality, launch time, quality, and manufacturing cost. Thus the competency theme that supports innovation processes encompasses having scientists and engineers with strong skills in all the underlying disciplines, and an ability to work effectively on multidisciplinary projects with multifunctional teams.

Information Capital

Information technology is increasingly a vital component for any important product development process. Project teams now use advanced three-dimensional simulation in lieu of physical mockups to experiment with and test alternative designs. Virtual prototyping is faster and less expensive, and allows more design cycles and learning than traditional prototyping with physical models. In pharmaceutical research, computational skills and capabilities have become as central to the research effort as biology and chemistry.[12]

Information technology also enhances the communication of knowledge and project experiences across functions, departments, and geographic units and fosters the sharing of best practices.

Beyond the use of technology for the innovation process itself, innovative companies can exploit information technology to achieve rapid introduction of new products to commercial production. Flexible manufacturing equipment enables new products to be introduced into production quickly and produced at commercial levels without having to acquire entirely new machines. The handoff from design to manufacturing is expedited considerably when project engineers' computer-aided-design (CAD) terminals interface with production's computer-aided-manufacturing (CAM) equipment.

Organization Capital

Teamwork. As we stated earlier, teamwork is critical for successful innovation projects. But beyond teaming with internal employees from other disciplines and functions, the people working on the innovation processes must also be actively involved with the external scientific and technological community. Not all inventions arise within the company's research laboratories. Company scientists and engineers should continually be engaged with scientific conferences, leading universities, and the scientific literature so that they stay alert for advances that can affect the company's products and services.

Culture. The organizational culture must emphasize innovation, disruption, and change as core values. The culture should also foster the acquisition of knowledge from outside the company and overcome the natural tendency, called the not-invented-here (NIH) syndrome, to derogate advances made by scientists and engineers outside the company, even if they work for competitive companies.

A summary of learning and growth objectives and measures appears below:

Learning and Growth Objectives	*Sample Measures*
Achieve deep functional expertise	• Strategic skill coverage in key R&D positions
Develop effective interdisciplinary and cross-functional teams	• Percent of R&D employees who work effectively in interdisciplinary and multifunctional product development teams • Percent of R&D employees capable of effective project management leadership
Deploy computer technology for simulation and virtual prototyping	• Percent of R&D employees with access to and knowledge of advanced modeling tools
Use technology for rapid product launch	• Percent of products launched with effective CAD/CAM integration
Capture leading knowledge from scientific and technological community	• Number of new ideas from external sources • Peer review of current scientific and technological capabilities
Foster a culture of innovation	• Number of suggestions for new products and capabilities • Employee culture survey for innovation and change

SUMMARY

Innovation processes can be the most important processes an organization performs to sustain competitive advantage. In this chapter we identify high-level objectives and associated measures for four innovation processes:

- Identify opportunities for new products and services
- Manage the research and development portfolio
- Design and develop the new products and services
- Bring the new products and services to market

Despite their importance, innovation processes often receive far less management attention than the more visible, repetitive, and predictable operating and customer management processes. All organizations, regardless of strategy, should strive to have at least one innovation objective on their strategy maps. And for companies following product leadership and system lock-in strategies, performance on innovation processes can be the most decisive for their success.

In the case study following this chapter, we describe the strategy map for Saatchi & Saatchi, a leading global advertising firm. Saatchi & Saatchi had adopted a new strategy based on its new vision for innovation, "to be revered as the hothouse for world-changing creative ideas that transform our clients' businesses, brands, and reputations." It wanted to excel at creating new advertising messages and vehicles that would provide breakthrough transformations in its clients' images.

NOTES

1. Steven C. Wheelwright and Kim B. Clark, *Revolutionizing Product Development: Quantum Leaps in Speed, Efficiency, and Quality* (New York: Free Press, 1992), 1.
2. A. W. Ulwick, "Turn Customer Input into Innovation," *Harvard Business Review* (January 2002): 91–97; D. Leonard, "The Limitations of Listening," *Harvard Business Review* (January 2002): 93.
3. Clayton Christensen, *The Innovator's Dilemma: When New Technologies Cause Great Firms to Fail* (Boston: Harvard Business School Press, 1997).
4. W. C. Kim and R. Mauborgne, "Value Innovation: The Strategic Logic of High Growth," *Harvard Business Review* (January–February 1997): 91–101; and "Creating New Market Space," *Harvard Business Review* (January–February 1999): 83–93.
5. Material in this section draws from S. C. Wheelwright, "The New Product Development Imperative," note 9-699-152, Harvard Business School, Boston, 1999.
6. Material in this section was drawn from Wheelwright and Clark, *Revolutionizing Product Development,* and M. Iansiti and T. Kosnik, "Product Development: A Customer-Driven Approach," note 9-695-016, Harvard Business School, Boston, 1995.
7. M. Iansiti and A. MacCormack, "Developing Products on Internet Time," *Harvard Business Review* (September–October 1997): 108–117; Tom Gilb, *Principles of Software Engineering Management* (Reading, MA: Addison-Wesley, 1988); A. MacCormack, "How Internet Companies Build Software," *Sloan Management Review* (Winter 2001): 75–84.
8. A. MacCormack, "Microsoft Office 2000," Case 9-600-097 (Boston: Harvard Business School, 2000).
9. The number of patents and patent citations has been identified in Baruch Lev, *Intangibles: Management, Measurement, and Reporting* (Washington, DC: Brookings Institution Press, 2001): 57–61, as a key indicator of research output.
10. C. K. Prahalad and Gary Hamel, "The Core Competence of the Corporation," *Harvard Business Review* (May–June 1990); and *Competing for the Future* (Boston: Harvard Business School Press, 1994).

11. BET is the elapsed time from the start of project until the company recovers its product development costs from the margins earned from commercial sales. See C. H. House and R. L. Price, "The Return Map: Tracking Product Teams," *Harvard Business Review* (January–February 1991): 92–100, and Robert S. Kaplan and David P. Norton, *The Balanced Scorecard: Translating Strategy into Action* (Boston: Harvard Business School Press, 1996), 102–103.

12. S. Thomke, *Experimentation Matters* (Boston: Harvard Business School Press, 2003).

CASE STUDY

SAATCHI & SAATCHI

Background

Saatchi & Saatchi, a wholly owned subsidiary of the French communications group Publicis Group S.A., is one of the world's leading advertising agency networks. It has annual billings of $7 billion from its 40 agencies and 138 offices in 82 countries, and serves 60 of the world's 100 top advertisers. Founded in 1970, Saatchi & Saatchi grew from a London boutique to a global giant through an ambitious series of acquisitions. With no unifying strategy, individual agencies operated as fiefdoms, unaware of the corporate bottom line. By the mid-1990s, Saatchi & Saatchi's explosive growth proved near fatal; only a de-merger in 1997 and a new leadership team saved it from probable bankruptcy. Amid mounting shareholder pressure, the company proclaimed its goal of growing its revenue base competitively, with bottom-line margins (on that incremental growth) of 30 percent, and doubling earnings per share. New CEO Kevin Roberts crafted a sweeping strategic plan, called "The Way Ahead." CFO Bill Cochrane introduced the BSC to help the firm achieve these ambitious targets. Both executives found the BSC unmatched for managing intan-gible assets—Saatchi & Saatchi's source of value creation. They saw that client retention, not necessarily new sales, was the best indicator of financial health (20 percent of the client base supported 80 percent of Saatchi & Saatchi's revenue). Hence the new strategy: *creating permanently infatuated clients (PICs)*. As a global advertising network, the greatest source of return would be to serve its global client base superlatively in every market.

The Strategy Map

As shown in Figure 5-8, the executive team defined three strategic themes:

- Operational excellence, including objectives for *financial discipline* and *working smarter across the network of worldwide agencies*
- Customer management, to *excel at account management* and *focus business development*
- Innovation, including objectives to *identify and implement appropriate communication services* and *win global fame for our idea leadership*

Saatchi & Saatchi chose, for simplicity's sake, not to overlay these themes on its strategy map, notes Paul Melter, director of strategy implementation. However, the firm's new vision—"To be revered as the hothouse for world-changing creative ideas that transform our clients' businesses, brands, and reputations"—is emblazoned across the top of the map.

Saatchi & Saatchi also reorganized from a geographic structure to one based on local mission. Each local agency was placed into one of three categories:

- Lead agency: One with the greatest potential for creating transformational ideas
- Drive agency: One that had excellent opportunities for profitable growth in its local market
- Prosper agency: A smaller agency with limited growth opportunities that would focus on optimizing near-term profits

Each agency type developed its own variation of the corporate strategy map.

Financial Perspective

Since December 1997, when Saatchi & Saatchi de-merged from Cordiant Communication, shareholder value has been the firm's top priority. Saatchi & Saatchi's financial targets remain aggressive. However, the executive team wanted to position financial performance as the result of pursuing excellence in the key themes and the client strategy, rather than as the explicit goal. Although the financial perspective appears at the top of the strategy map, Saatchi also uses an equation to emphasize the impact of the nonfinancial perspectives and their value as leading indicators:

$$A \text{ (People and Culture)} + B \text{ (Internal Processes)} + C \text{ (Client)} = D \text{ (Financial)}$$

Figure 5-8 Saatchi & Saatchi Strategy Map

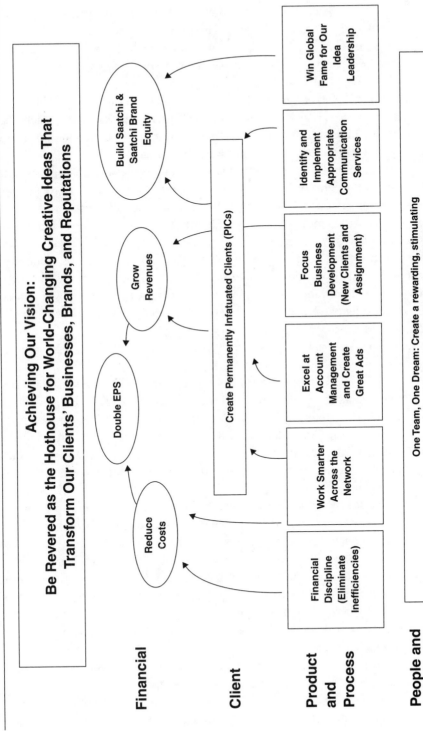

Client Perspective

Creating PICs is Saatchi & Saatchi's singular objective in the client perspective and the enterprise's overarching goal. This proposition crystallized the need to maximize the value of relationships with global clients. Creating PICs directly supports the objectives to *grow revenues* and *build brand equity*.

Product and Process (Internal Business Process)

To help achieve "financial discipline and eliminate inefficiencies," Cochrane created an annual health check each agency must undergo, in addition to the scorecard measures that help enforce fiscal accountability.

The major objective, "working smarter across the network," has broad impact on both operational excellence and client management. For example, today it is understood that putting your best copywriter on a network account helps make that client permanently infatuated (even if that account represents only 10 percent of your revenues). Working smarter also helps agencies to allocate resources better and, as explained by Paul Melter, to access Saatchi & Saatchi's vast organizational expertise—"getting support from the industry-savvy regional account directors, intelligence from a lead agency with major market experience for a client, or if necessary, going to another Publicis company for best-in-class thinking."

Additional internal process themes were:

- *Excel at account management and create great ads:* Within this theme lies one of Saatchi & Saatchi's core goals: creating "BFIs"—Big, Fabulous Ideas. More than just an ingenious ad concept, a BFI is a transformational idea; for example, a new product category (such as nonaspirin pain relievers, which Saatchi & Saatchi created for Tylenol), or a new product position (such as pitching Pepcid AC as a preventative, not just a relief, medicine).

  Another process objective within this theme was to revise the "ideas brief" process by which an agency advances a concept from proposal to end product. To conserve resources and prevent burnout, agencies now start with only the four key team leaders (account, planning, media, and creative) to meet and figure out the client challenge. Within twenty-four to forty-eight hours they craft a "challenge brief" defining the client's need. Only when the client approves the brief does the agency commit significant resources. This streamlined approach sharpened focus within Saatchi as well as within its client companies.

- *Focus business development:* Agency heads now must identify new business and new client opportunities—and demonstrate the greater payoff from investing to go after their business. This objective has forced a more strategic approach to business planning.

- *"Identify and implement appropriate communication services"*: This objective speaks to the innovation theme. "The best way to market isn't always traditional media like TV or print," notes Melter. "It might be event promotion or a direct-response insert in the phone bill."

People and Culture

The single inspirationally worded objective in this perspective—"One Team, One Dream"—reflects CEO Roberts's inspirational leadership. No arrows extend from this perspective, because the company considered this objective foundational to all other perspectives.

The value chain described by the strategy map has helped Saatchi executives achieve focus and make informed business decisions in accordance with their strategic mandates. This benefit is perhaps best exemplified by the new approach to what Melter considers the biggest "sticky" (Saatchi & Saatchi parlance for "issue"): How do we deliver first-rate creative content to the client, using existing resources?

By assigning pluses or minuses to each perspective, an agency head can see the long-term value of investing in, say, another copywriter, instead of making do with a junior one or spending freelance dollars. The salary cost is more than offset by the utilization gain ("working smarter") and faster speed to market (making the client happy)—both of which can generate more assignments from that client, thereby boosting revenue.

Results

Between the introduction of the new strategy and Balanced Scorecard (which Saatchi & Saatchi has renamed "Compass") in 1977 and Saatchi's acquisition by Publicis in September 2000, shareholder value quintupled, an increase of $2 billion. This dramatic performance earned Saatchi & Saatchi membership in the Balanced Scorecard Hall of Fame.

Case prepared by Patricia Bush and Jan Koch of Balanced Scorecard Collaborative and Paul Melter of Saatchi & Saatchi. Our thanks to Bill Cochrane for sharing the Saatchi & Saatchi experience.

CHAPTER SIX

REGULATORY AND SOCIAL PROCESSES

COMPANIES MUST CONTINUALLY earn the right to operate in the communities and countries in which they produce and sell (see Figure 6-1). National and local regulations—on the environment, on employee health and safety, and on hiring and employment practices—impose standards on companies' operations. At a minimum, to avoid shutdowns or expensive litigation, companies must comply with all these regulations on business practices.

Many companies, however, seek to go beyond complying with the minimal standards established by regulations. They wish to perform better than the regulatory constraints, so that they develop a reputation as an employer of choice in every community in which they operate. Marc Epstein and Bill Birchard have stressed the importance of integrating social and environmental accounting into a company's accountability reports to stakeholders.[1]

For example, see the following statement by Nova Chemicals:

At each of our plant sites, we have Responsible Care-based community initiatives that are designed to influence NOVA Chemicals' philosophy of being a neighbor of choice. That commitment means demonstrating outstanding performance concerning safety, health and environmental standards in the communities where we operate.

Our commitment to community is further enhanced with corporate sponsorships and donations. We are very proud of our commitment to sustainable development programs everywhere we are located.

Figure 6-1 Regulatory and Social Processes

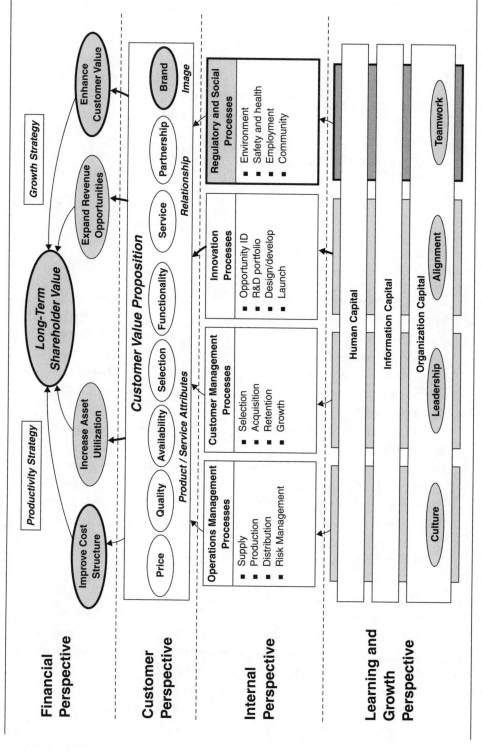

Highlighting regulatory and community performance in a strategy map and Balanced Scorecard is not a repackaging of the traditional stakeholder approach.[2] We recognize companies' responsibilities to employees, citizens, and their communities because failure to perform adequately on regulatory and social processes puts at risk the company's ability to operate, grow, and deliver future value to shareholders. Even more important, many companies believe that achieving excellence in such processes enhances long-term shareholder value.

An excellent reputation for performance along regulatory and social dimensions assists companies in attracting and retaining high-quality employees, thereby making their human resources processes more effective and efficient. For example, after benchmarking its HR practices against companies such as Apple Computer and Microsoft, BellSouth added benefits for domestic partners. This was not done specifically to attract gay candidates, but because the company had determined that the young people it wished to recruit wanted to work for a company that they deemed "progressive." It also added a diversity measure on HR department's scorecards to ensure that the company attracted and retained a good mix of employees from the communities in which it operated and served.[3]

Reducing environmental incidents and improving employee safety and health also improve productivity and lower operating costs. And finally, companies with outstanding reputations generally enhance their images with customers and with socially conscious investors. All these linkages—to enhanced human resource, operating, customer, and financial processes—illustrate how effective management of regulatory and community performance drives long-term shareholder value creation (see Figure 6-2).

Novartis, the Swiss-based pharmaceutical company, provides an annual Health, Safety, and Environment Report. Chairman and CEO Dr. Daniel Vasella states:

Because our business activities and our societal and environmental performance are integrally connected, we are publishing our Health, Safety and Environmental Report this year at the same time as our Operational Review. We are also responding to the increasing range of corporate responsibility in today's global economy by expanding our report to cover, in addition to the traditional HSE subjects, issues relating to sustainable development and its three principles of economic, social and environmental progress.

Figure 6-2 Regulatory and Social Strategy Map Template

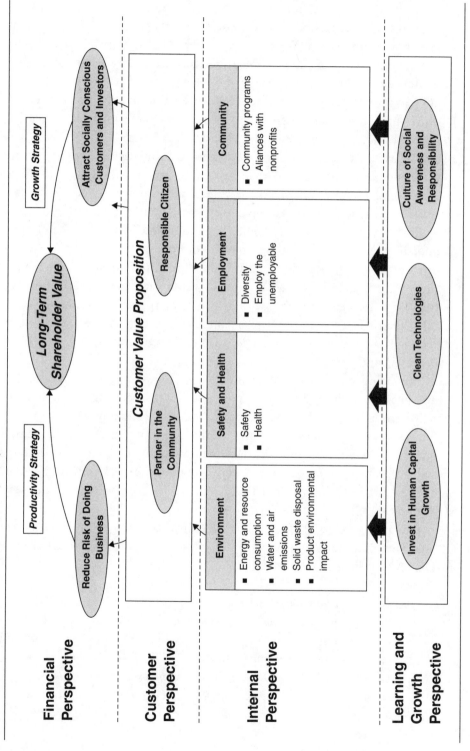

An important way for us to ensure top HSE performance is through our annual Sector Reviews by top management. The objective of the Sector Reviews is continuous improvement: we collect important data and information (e.g., data on emissions, waste, accident statistics, etc.) and use it to identify areas for improvement and to establish new priorities and targets.[4]

Coca-Cola asserts:

Stewardship takes us beyond compliance with laws and regulations to form alliances with those who seek solutions to environmental challenges. . . . [W]e explore and invest in stewardship initiatives ranging beyond the scope of our immediate business. . . . The Coca-Cola eKO system demands that we continually examine every aspect of our business for opportunities to reduce our consumption of resources and production of waste, while increasing the amount of recycled material in our packaging and other supplies.[5]

DuPont issues an extensive, well-documented annual Global Progress Report. The company asserts its commitment to "conduct our business with respect and care for the environment":

We will adhere to the highest standards for the safe operation of facilities and the protection of the environment, our employees, our customers and the people of the communities in which we do business.

We will strengthen our businesses by making safety, health and environmental issues an integral part of all business activities and by continuously striving to align our businesses with public expectations.[6]

These are just a few examples of how leading companies around the world pursue excellence in regulatory and social processes as an integral component of their long-term value creating strategies.

MANAGING REGULATORY AND SOCIAL PROCESSES

Companies manage and report their regulatory and social performance along several dimensions:

1. Environment
2. Safety and health

3. Employment practices
4. Community investment

Below, we provide examples of the measurements and disclosures companies currently use for each of these dimensions. We then discuss the links between strategy and regulatory and social performance.

1. Environmental Performance

Because of extensive regulation in developed nations, environmental performance is the most developed of the regulatory and social measurement systems for company reporting. In general, companies have several components to their environmental performance report:

A. Energy and resource consumption
B. Water emissions
C. Air emissions
D. Solid waste production and disposal
E. Product performance
F. Aggregate environmental measures

A. Energy and Resource Consumption
Energy consumption can be measured for all energy sources (total joules of energy consumed) or by type of energy, such as electricity and fuel. Companies typically report total energy consumption, compared to previous years, and also normalized for units of output (kilowatts or joules per pound [or barrel] produced). When a homogeneous measure of output is not available, because of the diversity of products and services produced, companies normalize by sales revenue or cost of goods sold (for example, joules per $1,000 cost of sales). See Figure 6-3 for an example of Bristol-Myers Squibb's disclosure of energy consumption.

In addition to measuring energy consumption, companies measure total and normalized consumption of other resources, principally water and materials. For example, Nokia gets considerable reduction in materials usage per unit by continually shrinking and lightening its core product, a cellular telephone.

Figure 6-3   Bristol-Myers Squibb Energy Consumption, 1999–2001

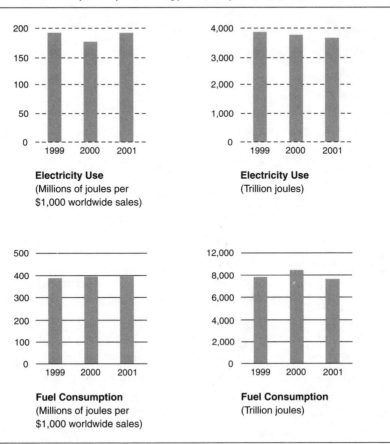

Source: Briston-Myers Squibb 2001 Sustainability Report.

B. Water Emissions

Clean water is a scarce resource. Companies are sensitive to their usage of clean water and their discharges back to water supplies. They measure the demands they make on clean water supplies and their total wastewater released (effluent discharges). See, for example, the disclosure by Novartis in its 2001/2002 Corporate Citizenship report, shown in Figure 6-4.

Figure 6-4 Novartis 2001/2002 Corporate Citizenship Report

Water Emissions	2001	2000	Change
Effluent discharge (thousand cubic meters)	2,100	1,960	7%
Suspended solids	627	609	3%
Chemical oxygen demand	4,220	4,110	3%
Total nitrogen	403	505	−20%
Phosphate	61.4	97.0	−37%
Soluble salts	20,200	20,800	−3%
Sum of heavy metals	0.46	0.32	43%

C. Air Emissions

Air pollution is a problem around the world. Companies report on their releases of toxic gases and air carcinogens. For example, DuPont provides data on air discharges in its Annual Global Report, shown in Figure 6-5.

With the concern about greenhouse gases as a potential cause of global warming, many companies report their releases of carbon dioxide (CO_2) gases. Similarly, the concern over acid rain motivates corporate reporting on nitrous oxide (NO) and sulphur dioxide (SO_2) gases. Chemical and other manufacturing companies commonly report on ozone depleting substances, such as chlorofluorocarbons (CFCs) and hydrochlorofluorocarbons (HCFCs). Air emissions are typically measured in kilograms of gas released, and normalized by output (kilograms/dollars of sales or kilograms/dollars of cost of goods sold).

Figure 6-5 Dupont Annual Report (Air Discharge Data)

U.S. Toxics Release Inventory Waste and Emissions

	1987	1991	1995	1997	1998	1999	2000
Total waste as generated	—	890	639	542	619	673	550
Deepwell disposal of hazardous waste	237	187	61	50	45	38	38

U.S. Toxics Release Inventory Waste and Emissions

	1987	1991	1995	1997	1998	1999	2000
Releases to air, water, and land	71	57	41	34	37	41	37

Millions of pounds. Data as reported to the U.S. EPA. 286 new chemicals added in 1995. Total waste as generated first reported in 1991. Reflects 38% reduction in total waste as generated, 84% reduction in deepwell disposal, and 48% reduction in releases to air, water, and land. Increase in total waste as generated in 1998 and 1999 reflects 143 MM lbs./yr. recycled on-site by two newly acquired facilities.

Global Air Toxics and Carcinogenic Air Emissions

	1987	1991	1992	1993	1995	1997	1998	1999	2000
Air toxics	68	53	41	29	32	26	24.5	18.8	16.1
Air carcinogens	9.1	5.7	4.7	3.6	2.0	1.6	1.2	1.4	1.2

D. Solid Waste Production and Disposal

Companies report on the production and disposal of both hazardous and nonhazardous waste. Bristol-Myers Squibb, for example, provides extensive data and descriptions of its solid waste reported (see Figure 6-6).

IBM reported that in 2000, despite increases in production, hazardous waste generation decreased by 15,703 metric tons (41.6 percent). Of hazardous waste generated, 61 percent was recycled. IBM also reduced the percentage of product-related scrap sent to landfill by 12.5 percent. Only 3.2 percent of material processed was sent to landfills in 2000.

E. Product Performance

Companies are increasingly sensitive to what happens to their products even after they have been sold to end-use consumers. Product leadership companies, such as Hewlett-Packard and Sony, continually introduce new products and therefore are concerned with the disposal and recycling of previous generations of products. Hewlett-Packard explicitly develops product end-of-life solutions, such as recycling technologies and infrastructures, to create reliable streams of recycled materials. Its engineers employ a design-for-environment perspective to optimize the environmentally related characteristics of a product, process, and facility. These

Figure 6-6 Bristol-Myers Squibb Materials Report

Nonproduct Output Returned to Process or Market

Each of our facilities worldwide is required to track its recycling of nonhazardous waste. We track data on plastic, cardboard, paper, and aluminum. As the chart indicates, nonhazardous waste recycling decreased 37 percent since 1997, with a significant drop in 2000 due primarily to increasing costs of recycling versus disposal. Bristol-Myers Squibb continues to promote recycling as a preferred alternative to disposal, although our ultimate goal is to reduce nonhazardous waste generation through source reduction. One of our Sustainability 2010 goals is to decrease non-hazardous waste generation, which should help drive change and increase our nonhazardous waste recycling.

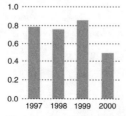

Nonhazardous Waste Recycled
(Kilograms per $1,000 worldwide sales)

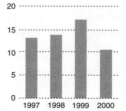

Nonhazardous Waste Recycled
(Millions of kilograms)

Nonproduct Output to Land

Nonhazardous waste disposal includes plastic, cardboard, paper, aluminum, off-specification or out-of-date product, chemicals not regulated as hazardous waste, general trash, and medical waste. Nonhazardous waste disposal has decreased 20 percent since 1997, in large measure due to source reduction.

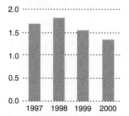

Nonhazardous Waste Disposal
(Kilograms per $1,000 worldwide sales)

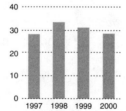

Nonhazardous Waste Disposal
(Millions of kilograms)

Hazardous Waste

We track hazardous waste sent off-site from our facilities worldwide. The chart shows the amount of hazardous waste (as defined by local requirements) sent off-site for disposal. The data do not include hazardous waste generated as a result of on-site remediation activities. The vast majority of hazardous waste is incinerated, with only the residual ash land disposed. As the chart indicates, hazardous waste disposal decreased 30 percent since 1997. The decrease from 1999 to 2000 was due, in part, to eliminating a process at one facility that had generated significant amounts of hazardous waste as well as increased treatment of waste on-site.

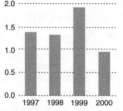

Hazardous Waste Disposal
(Kilograms per $1,000 worldwide sales)

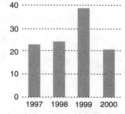

Hazardous Waste Disposal
(Millions of kilograms)

guidelines urge its product designers to consider the following issues when designing a new product:

- Identify design changes that reduce environmental impact throughout a product's life cycle
- Eliminate hazardous or toxic plastics and chemicals whenever possible
- Reduce the number and types of materials used, and standardize on types of plastic resins
- Use molded-in colors and finishes instead of paint, coatings, or platings whenever possible
- Help customers use resources responsibly by minimizing energy consumption of HP's printing, imaging, and computing products
- Increase use of pre- and post-consumer recycled materials in product packaging
- Minimize customer waste burdens by using fewer product or packaging materials overall
- Design for easy disassembly and recyclability

Each of HP's products includes environmental certifications, such as the absence of hazardous materials, for example cadmium and mercury, and of voluntary restricted materials (halogenated flame-retardants, halogenated plastics, and antimony trioxide), plus indications of features that conserve energy and other resources.

Sony similarly reports on the environmental impact of its products. For example:

When the entire life cycle of a product is considered, the greater part of energy consumption results from the use of electric power by customers when operating Sony products. The CO_2 generated over the whole lifetime of the products shipped during FY2000, for instance, is estimated at approximately 8.1 million tons. Sony is responding with efforts to reduce product power consumption and minimize CO_2 discharges through improved product design and the introduction of new types of products and services.

F. Aggregate Environmental Measures
Some companies want to provide an aggregate picture of their total environmental impact; see, for example, Sony's simple diagram (Figure 6-7) of

Figure 6-7   Sony Group's Total Environmental Impact

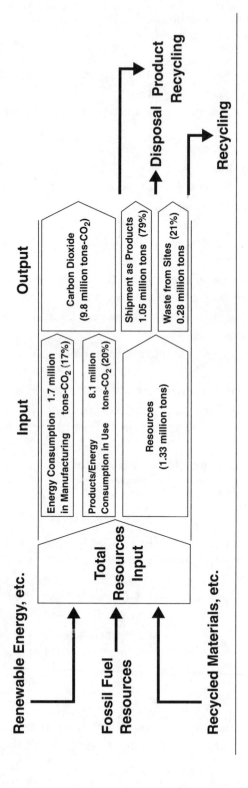

environmental impact, which is supplemented with detailed data for each aggregate measure shown.

Companies often create indexes of environmental incidents for their Balanced Scorecards. Company environmental experts develop strict definitions of what constitutes an environmental incident, such as an unexpected discharge of air, water, or solid waste. For example, Nova Chemicals, concerned about avoiding fires, started an initiative in 2000 to emphasize the triggering event for a process fire—the loss of process containment (LOPC). A team developed a definition of LOPC:

> *An unanticipated leak, spill or release of a process material in sufficient quantity or concentration to the air, water, land or work environment that resulted in, or could have resulted in, a process safety or environmental incident.*

Nova Chemicals was also concerned about product releases during transportation by rail, truck, and marine and pipeline routes. It developed a measure, Non-Accident Releases (NAR), to track any product release, in quantities as small as 250 milliliters, that is judged to have been preventable through maintenance or inspection.

Once environmental indexes have been defined, targets established, and systems installed for tracking the data, operating managers are then responsible for reporting (and the environmental group for auditing) all incidents. The environmental index alerts employees to the nature of incidents to be avoided, thereby affecting their behavior. It serves as a lead indicator on the scorecard for driving improvements in the company's environmental performance.

The International Organization for Standardization (ISO) develops voluntary technical standards for businesses around the world, helping to make "the development, manufacturing, and supply of products and services more efficient, safer, and cleaner." Starting in 1996, ISO has developed the 14000 family of standards for environmental management. To date, the family includes more than 350 specific standards for the monitoring of the quality of air, water, and soil, as well as standards for developing environmental management systems. Companies are beginning to report on compliance with the ISO 14000 family of international environmental standards on their environmental scorecards.

Other voluntary environmental standards have also arisen. In the United Kingdom, a group of companies established the Business in the Environment (BiE) Index of Corporate Environmental Engagement.

The BiE survey compares the extent to which participating companies engage in environmental management, and how they assess and manage their environmental performances. For example, Diageo, the U.K.-based wine and spirits company, provided the following information in its 2001 Environmental Report:

	BiE Index	
	1999	*2000*
Diageo score	63.8%	73.9%
Diageo overall ranking (184 participating companies)	n/a	74
Diageo ranking (industry segment)	10th/17	10th/23
Diageo ranking (FT100)	56	48

Acknowledging the need to improve in areas of weakness in suppliers, environmental management systems, transport, and biodiversity, Diageo pledged to improve environmental processes that would raise its performance in the future.

BT also participates in the BiE survey. In the BT 2001 report, "Better World: our commitment to society," the company disclosed:

In the BiE Index of Corporate Environmental Engagement (2000), BT was the top placed telecommunication company, and we were placed eight overall, out of the 78 FTSE 100 companies that participated. Our overall score was 96 percent compared with an industry average of 47 percent and a FTSE 100 companies average score of 68 percent.

At the end of 1999, Lloyds Register Quality Assurance awarded ISO14001 certification to BT's environmental management system covering all our UK operations.

The International Chamber of Commerce established the Business Charter for Sustainable Development. The charter articulates sixteen principles for environmental management, which it urges businesses to adopt and express public support for. But, to date, the charter offers no consistent quantitative way for companies to report their performance for each of the sixteen principles.

In summary, many companies already provide extensive quantitative information on their environmental performances. Most of these likely have such data to satisfy regulatory reporting requirements, and they repackage the regulatory data in supplementary reports, often called a Citizenship or Sustainability Report. For these measures to be relevant for a Balanced Scorecard, executives must identify those environmental measurements that are relevant and important to their strategy for long-term value creation. In the next section, we discuss how executives can think strategically about their environmental performance.

Linking Environmental Measures to Strategy

Forest Reinhardt has identified five ways in which companies can leverage their environmental capabilities to create shareholder value:[7]

1. Reduce cost
2. Differentiate products
3. Manage competitors
4. Redefine markets
5. Manage risk

1. Reduce cost. For some companies, improved environmental performance may constitute a rare instance of a "free lunch," much like the "quality is free" experience of early adopters of total quality management.[8] Michael Porter popularized the idea that companies could simultaneously cut costs and improve environmental performance.[9] While this is not a universal phenomenon, companies such as Xerox, with its Environmental Leadership Program, discovered that they could save substantial amounts in waste management (shipping waste to landfills) and raw materials purchasing by paying more attention to environmental impacts during the product design stage and by operating effective product take-back programs.

Activity-based cost systems can reveal total life cycle costs by assigning the costs of waste and disposal to individual processes and products. Such an analysis reveals which processes and products incur high environmental costs, and where opportunities exist for design and process improvements that will lower the total cost of producing and recycling products. Such cost reduction will be accompanied by a reduction in the company's environmental footprint.

2. Differentiate products. In the more usual circumstance, in which improved environmental performance does not come with more-than-offsetting cost-reduction benefits, companies can strive to recover their higher environmental costs by differentiating their products. Some customers are willing to pay higher prices or purchase more from companies known to have environmentally friendly products and processes. In some instances, the customers are not being altruistic; they may capture some of the benefits of the environmentally friendly product by having their own costs lowered.

Reinhardt points out the three necessary conditions for successful environmental product differentiation:

1. Customers are willing to pay more for an environmentally friendly product
2. Company has been able to communicate credibly its product's environmental (or cost reducing) benefits
3. Company can protect its environmental advantages from competitors

Shell and BP are actively trying such a differentiating strategy in the petroleum industry, and Patagonia, a manufacturer of recreational clothing, has developed a loyal base of customers who purchase its clothing for active outdoor sports, because of the company's well-publicized commitment to conservation.

3. Manage competitors. Chemical companies have worked through their industry associations to develop voluntary environmental and safety standards for all companies in the industry. In this way, the companies are more likely to have standards that are both effective and achievable in cost-efficient ways, rather than have punitive and cost-ineffective regulations imposed by governmental authorities. Also, by gaining agreement among all the major companies in the industry to adopt the voluntary standards, the industry reduces the cost to the public through reduced pollution but does not put any single company at a competitive disadvantage. All companies in the industry agree to comply with the new standards.

A variation of this strategy is available to a company that already exceeds existing regulatory requirements with its products and processes, but whose competitors don't (they are just complying with the requirement). The company can lobby the governmental regulatory agency to tighten the environmental standard to its current performance, thereby placing all competitors out of compliance and subject to costly remediation efforts.

4. Redefine markets. Some companies have redefined their business models in ways that lower their costs, increase customers' willingness to pay, and reduce environmental impact. Manufacturers of expensive electronic equipment, such as Xerox, HP, Canon, and IBM, now often require that customers return their used equipment when they purchase or lease new equipment. The customer avoids the costs—both out-of-pocket and environmental—of disposing of their obsolete equipment, and the manufacturer can disassemble and recycle many of the components from the used equipment into its new machines. In 1995, Xerox estimated that this change accomplished several objectives simultaneously:

- Saving several hundred million dollars in raw materials purchases by recycling parts from used machines
- Consuming significantly less natural resources in the manufacture of its products
- Lowering its customers' disposal costs

5. Manage environmental risk. Beyond benefits in higher revenues and lower costs, companies can enhance their overall risk management programs by improving their management of environmental risk. Environmental incidents can lead to heavy cleanup costs, litigation, consumer boycotts, and loss of reputation. Much like the management of foreign exchange, interest rate, and commodity price risks, companies may need to excel at managing their risk from environmental incidents. Companies can take several different steps to reduce their environmental risk exposure:

- Provide managers and employees with better information about how to avoid and mitigate environmental incidents
- Reduce the probability of environmental incidents through explicit prevention activities
- Reduce the total cost of an environmental incident should one occur through rapid response
- Transfer some of the risk through purchase of insurance policies

To summarize, companies should treat their environmental performance similarly to that of any important process. No company can expect to be the best across a broad range of environmental indicators.

Companies need to identify where enhanced environmental performance provides the greatest opportunity for them to lower costs, differentiate their products, and reduce risk. Some environmental monitoring and reporting will be diagnostic, not strategic. It will ensure that the company complies with the regulations where it operates and sells, but will not provide a basis for differentiation. The environmental objectives and measures chosen for a company's Balanced Scorecard should represent those areas in which environmental excellence can provide a synergy by simultaneously increasing shareholder value *and* reducing the company's environmental footprint.

2. Safety and Health Performance

Unlike the considerable diversity of environmental measures, companies tend to use relatively few and more standardized measures of employee safety and health performance. As with environmental measures, safety and health reporting is largely triggered by regulatory requirements. In the United States, such requirements come from the Occupational Safety and Health Administration (OSHA). A commonly used safety incidence measure is the number of OSHA recordable cases per 100 employees.[10] The effects of injuries and illnesses are summarized by lost workdays per 100 employees or per 200,000 hours worked (see Figure 6-8 for DuPont's injury and illness report in its 2001 Global Progress Report). The table below shows the statistics reported each year by Hewlett-Packard:

Region	Incidence Rate (OSHA recordable cases per 100 employees)			Lost Workday Case Rate (cases per 100 employees)		
	1999	2000	2001	1999	2000	2001
United States	2.53	1.71	1.54	0.47	0.25	0.24
EMEA	0.61	0.67	**	0.42	0.41	**
Asia Pacific	0.36	0.37	0.1	0.23	0.14	0.06
Canada	1.36	1.41	2.19	0.16	0.41	0.51
Latin America	0.26	0.11	0.23	0.17	0.09	0.16

*** 2001 EMEA data not yet available.*

Figure 6-8 DuPont Total Recordable Injuries and Illnesses (per 200,000 Hours Worked)

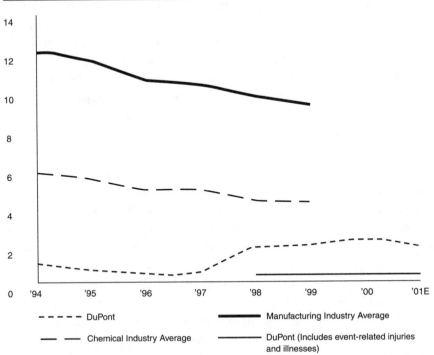

Royal Dutch/Shell reports health and safety performance using the Total Reportable Occupational Illness Frequency for illnesses per million hours worked, and Total Reportable Case Frequency for safety accidents and illnesses per million hours worked. DuPont goes one step further by including the incidence of employee off-job injuries, signaling that any injury to an employee, whether job-related or not, is costly to the individual, his or her family, and the company. Bristol-Myers Squibb measures employee exposure to hazardous compounds.

As with environmental measures, some companies develop definitions of safety-related incidents and track the frequency of such incidents.

3. Employment Practices

Much of the quantitative reporting about employment practices relates to increasing the diversity of employees. Companies attest to the ways in which increased diversity contributes to corporate success. For example, Siemens states:

*Diversity is for us an invaluable source of talent, creativity and experi-
ence. It comprises all the differences in culture, religion, nationality,
race, ethnicity, gender, age and social origin—in short, everything that
makes the individual singular and unique.*

*Diversity improves competitiveness by enlarging the potential for
ideas and innovation. Diverse teams addressing problems from varied
perspectives will be more productive and achieve better solutions. We
will benefit from the potential of diversity not only in a global context,
but also within countries, locations and teams. Diversity is a business imperative and part of our social responsibility as well.*

As a specific example, Siemens, in South Africa, established a target
that 70 percent of all new trainees must be from previously disadvantaged
communities, and that these employees should be increasingly represented at management levels. The initial target of 30 percent representation at middle and senior management levels was achieved eighteen
months ahead of schedule, and the target was revised upward to 46 percent representation over the next five years.

Quantitative representation of diversity is often presented by companies in tables that summarize the percentage of women and minorities by
type of employment: officials and managers, professionals, technicians,
marketing and sales, office and clerical, crafts, operatives, laborers, and
service workers. A global corporation, such as Royal Dutch/Shell, reports
on the percentage of country head positions held by people from that
country.

Benchmarking and rating organizations provide opportunities for
companies to demonstrate superior performance in their diversity programs. For example, Race for Opportunity, a U.K. national network of
business organizations, focuses on race and diversity as a business
agenda. It did a 2002 benchmarking study in corporate Britain covering
2.75 million U.K. employees in 99 private- and public-sector organizations (including 18 of the FTSE 100). BT could report that it ranked
number one among private sector organizations in its employment of
black and Asian managers. Opportunity Now, another component in the
U.K. Business in the Community organization, evaluates company performance on gender issues. In 2001, BT received a Gold Standard award
for its approach to gender issues.

The decision about which safety, health, and employment practice
measurements get incorporated into a company's Balanced Scorecard
should follow the same discipline as that articulated for environmental
measurements. Compliance with regulatory reporting standards is not a

sufficient rationale for such measurements to be incorporated. The Balanced Scorecard is not the only measurement and reporting system that a company needs. The BSC should represent those measures whose improvement will drive the company's strategy forward, in some explicit way, and ultimately lead to enhancements in shareholder value. Executives must determine those safety, health, and employment measurements that reinforce other aspects of the company's strategy through cost reductions, revenue and margin enhancement, and risk management.

4. Community Investment

Many companies provide extensive descriptions of the monetary contributions they make to community-based nonprofit organizations, and to the extensive volunteering done by company employees in communities. Most large corporations have established foundations by which money is systematically directed to worthy community-based organizations.

For example, Coca-Cola espouses, as one of its four core values:

Community

We will contribute our time, expertise and resources to help develop sustainable communities in partnership with local leaders. We will seek to improve the quality of life through locally relevant initiatives wherever we do business.

In its Citizen Report, Coca-Cola discloses:

The strongest communities are those that draw people together in common causes. We empower employees to support civic causes through volunteer programs designed together with community partners. We enhance their individual efforts by matching the donations to charitable organizations. Coca-Cola managers play key leadership roles on the boards of United Way, Big Brothers and Big Sisters, Boys & Girls Clubs of America, Special Olympics and other local, national and international nonprofit organizations.

Some companies provide specific quantitative information on their investment into communities. Bristol-Myers Squibb created "Secure the Future," a five-year, $115 million commitment to partner with the African nations of South Africa, Botswana, Namibia, Lesotho and Swaziland, Senegal, Côte d'Ivoire, Mali, and Burkina Faso, to find sustainable and relevant solutions for the management of HIV/AIDS in women and children, and to provide resources to improve community education and patient support. The Bristol-Myers Squibb Foundation provides extensive support on issues relating to women's health, health-care infrastructure in developing and transitioning economies, and science education and research.

Novartis established a Foundation for Sustainable Development that sponsors projects in the areas of health, social development, and emergency aid that will improve the quality of life to people living in poverty. Its Community Partnership Day gives its worldwide employees the opportunity to participate in social activities in the communities in which they live and work.

IBM has made education the top priority for its philanthropic efforts. Through its Reinventing Education program, IBM works with school partners throughout the world to develop and implement innovative technology solutions designed to enhance the education of disadvantaged children. For each grant site, IBM contributes money, researchers, educational consultants, and technology. In its KidSmart Early Learning program, IBM donates tens of thousands of Young Explorer computers to preschools in the United States and internationally to give computer access to millions of children, most from low-income families with little access to computers at home.

In April 2000, Nokia established the Make a Connection program, a global initiative with the International Youth Foundation to help young people connect with peers, families, and their communities. The program improves young peoples' educational opportunities and teaches them life skills through direct training, mentoring, and volunteering opportunities, and by training adults (teachers, youth workers). In the United States, Nokia initiated ClassLink, a project that equips thousands of classrooms with wireless technology, enabling students, teachers, and parents to connect more effectively, and VisionOne, providing tens of thousands of Native Americans with wireless phones.

Corporate Community Investment: The Dark Side

The preceding descriptions are just a small fraction of the quite extraordinary investments that companies are making in the communities in which they operate and in disadvantaged countries around the world. The extent of enlightened corporate philanthropy is remarkable. Unfortunately, there is a dark side to this picture. Companies reporting on their community investments describe only the inputs they provide— money, people, equipment, and expertise. Extensive reporting on these investment inputs can be found in the detailed annual reports of their corporate foundations. Missing from all these reports, however, is any measure of the outcomes achieved by such philanthropy.

Consider the reporting standards that companies use for their environmental, health, and safety reports, and contrast these with standards used to report on community investment. The company environmental, health, and safety reports documented earlier in this chapter provide quantitative evidence of the effectiveness of company investments. The reports contain detailed statistics and trends on reduction in water, air, and soil pollution, on reductions in energy and materials requirements per unit of output produced, and on reductions in days lost from accidents and illnesses. For employee hiring and promotion policies, companies provide detailed statistics of the number of women and minority employees who have achieved senior technical and managerial positions.

Company reporting on community investments, however, reveals only how much has been spent, how many employees have been involved in community activities, and which programs the company is supporting. While the reports often show pictures of committed employee volunteers and the happy and grateful recipients of this corporate largesse, we learn nothing systematic about the impact of companies' substantial investments. A Nokia statement, better than most, at least makes an attempt at output measures:

> *Altogether the Make a Connection program has already made a tangible difference in the lives of almost 20,000 young people, has trained almost 400 adults in reaching out to young people, and has indirectly benefited more than 1,000,000 young people and adults. Nokia has committed more than U.S.$11 million to the program.*

But even this disclosure falls far short of what company executives should expect to learn about the returns from their $11 million investment. What tangible difference has been made in the skills, capabilities, motivations, or successes of the 20,000 young people who have been reached by Make a Connection? What social return has Nokia realized from its investment?

Executives demand detailed justification for capital investments, and they expect tangible returns from spending on research and development, advertising, employee training, and quality. Yet these same executives put their analytic side to sleep when committing substantial financial, personnel, and equipment resources to community-based programs. Rather than being a constructive force for change, corporate executives acquiesce in the general lack of accountability and performance information from the nonprofit and NGO sectors.

Perhaps companies' community investments are in an early evolutionary stage, and company executives are not yet demanding quantitative performance data from these programs. But this complacency should not persist. Company executives should expect and demand performance data from any program in which they invest. The outcomes need not and likely should not be denominated in dollars, euros, or yen. But they should be denominated in measurable improvements in educational performance, women's opportunities, health, or whatever outcome the community-based program is expected to produce. Mechanisms for performance-based social investing do exist. Organizations like the innovative venture philanthropy fund New Profit, Inc., in Cambridge, Massachusetts, demand that the social enterprises in which they invest have a detailed performance model, based in fact on the Balanced Scorecard, to describe their strategy for success and to provide feedback on the outcomes achieved.[11] Companies need to demand output and outcome data from their foundation executives and from the executives of community-based programs that they support. The goal would be to have the quality of reporting from companies' community investments match that from their environmental, health, and safety programs.

Deriving Competitive Advantage from Community Investment

Michael Porter and Mark Kramer echo our view about the need for companies to think much more strategically about their philanthropic activities.[12] They argue that corporations should use their charitable efforts "to improve their *competitive* context—the quality of the business environment" in which they operate. For example, Cisco Systems invests in educational programs that train computer network administrators. The programs provide skills for an attractive job opportunity for high school graduates and simultaneously alleviates a potential constraint for expanded use of Cisco products. Porter and Kramer identify four elements of a competitive context that companies can influence through philanthropic activities:

1. *Input factor conditions:* A company's productivity and competitive position can be enhanced by increases in the supply of trained

workers, high-quality scientific and technological institutions, good physical infrastructure (such as roads and telecommunications in developing nations, and excellent arts organizations in developed regions and nations that attract mobile, talented employees), and transparent, honest governmental processes.

2. *Demand conditions:* Companies such as Digital Equipment Corporation in the 1960s and 1970s and Apple Computer donated their products to universities and schools. Upon graduation, students who had become computer literate with the donated equipment naturally preferred to purchase that equipment for their companies and their personal use.

3. *Rules for competition and rivalry:* Companies that compete based on superior products, processes, and services don't want to have their advantages undermined through theft of intellectual property and bribery and corruption activities by less able rivals. It is in the best interest of high-performing companies to compete on a level playing field. Companies can donate to organizations that improve the rule of law in countries where they produce and sell.

4. *Related and supporting industries:* Porter had previously described the competitive benefits in geographic clusters of suppliers, producers, and sophisticated consumers.[13] Companies can invest in suppliers and infrastructure that supports the industry in which it competes.

Porter and Kramer conclude:

The more tightly corporate philanthropy is aligned with a company's unique strategy—increasing skills, technology, or infrastructure on which the firm is especially reliant, say, or increasing demand within a specialized segment where the company is strongest—the more disproportionately the company will benefit through enhancing the context.[14]

They concur with us that companies must "rigorously track and evaluate results. Monitoring achievements is essential to continually improving the philanthropic strategy and its implementation."[15]

Company Strategic Alliances
Several companies have indeed moved beyond a pure "philanthropic but

no results" stage in their community investments to active involvement and partnerships in the community organizations they support. Research by Jim Austin of the Harvard Business School documents how companies' collaborations with nonprofits yield important benefits in:[16]

- *Strategy enrichment:* Generating business opportunities and promoting a positive and trusted image with customers (particularly important for retail service organizations), regulators, and legislators
- *Human resource management:* Attracting and retaining higher-quality employees; strengthening employee motivation and morale; developing leadership capabilities
- *Culture building:* Shaping and reinforcing the core values that elicit desired employee behavior
- *Business generation:* Enhancing a company's reputation, building goodwill, expanding networks of relationships, increasing access to key consumers, and providing a venue for testing innovations

The partnership between Timberland, the outdoor boot and apparel outfitter, and City Year, an urban youth service corps, provides an excellent example of such a strategic collaborative relationship. It took several years for this relationship to evolve from the philanthropic stage—giving money and in-kind donations (Timberland boots to City Year corps members); to the transactional stage—joint events, such as cause-related marketing, event sponsorships, licensing, and paid service arrangements; to the integrative stage—the company and the community organization have become an integrated joint venture that is central to both organizations' strategies. Value creation becomes a joint process, rather than two separate processes, one for the company and one for the community organization.

Georgia-Pacific and The Nature Conservancy (TNC) provide an example of a relationship that has evolved from confrontation to collaboration. TNC wanted to preserve land, untouched, and Georgia-Pacific wanted to use land intensively to harvest trees. The two organizations found common ground to jointly manage unique forested wetlands in ways that preserved biodiversity while also permitting commercial development. Other such integrative relationships include Starbucks and CARE; Bayer North America and the Bidwell Training Center in Pittsburgh; Reading is Fun and Visa, International; The College Fund (the largest minority educational assistance organization in the United States) and Merck; The National Science Resource Center (for improving the teaching of science in elementary and high school education) and Hewlett-Packard; Time to Read and Time Warner.

Successful collaborations generally occur when the community partner complements the company's core business or strategy. As a senior executive of Bayer emphasized:

> *You need to be invested in something that has to do with your business. . . . You need to be able to give and to get. We're a science-based company. It makes business sense for us to support science education. . . . It's not that we don't get good public relations from being involved, but we have a core reason to be involved.* [17]

When companies enter into such strategic collaborations, they can help to shape the value that will be created and the metrics that will be used to assess performance. The social value generated will arise from the mission of the nonprofit community organization. The challenge is for the company to assess the incremental or distinctive social value created by the collaboration. The company needs to measure how society is better off from its investment and its collaboration with the community organization.

As companies shift their community investments from the philanthropic stage to the integrative or collaborative stage, they will, like the New Profit, Inc. venture philanthropy fund, be able to exert more leverage for measurable performance data from the community organizations in which they invest. Even for their passive, philanthropic-stage investments, companies can restrict funding to those organizations that can document successful outcomes. Companies can then use such outcome data in their reports, rather than simply itemizing all the resources contributed to organizations.

With a performance-based model for community investments, the community organizations and the NGOs that are more successful in generating superior outcomes will attract higher and more stable funding. Those organizations that are unable to deliver measurable performance improvements will receive less and eventually wither away. This performance-based competitive dynamic will make the nonprofit/NGO "third sector" far more effective and much more efficient, thereby generating large aggregate benefits to society. But companies must take a lead role—through their foundations and through their voluntary contributions—in setting a standard that requires output and outcome measurement from their community investments. Continued simplistic reporting of money spent and programs supported, accompanied by pictures of grateful and happy recipients, should not be the preferred standard for companies' community investments, any more than disclosing money spent on environmental cleanup and an occasional picture of a smokeless exhaust tower and fish swimming in a nearby river would be considered adequate for environmental reporting.

SUMMARY

Many companies today recognize that achieving excellence in environmental, safety, health, employment, and community practices are part of long-term value-creating strategies. At a minimum, achieving good regulatory and social performance is a long-term objective that enables companies to maintain their franchises to operate in all communities where they wish to make, market, sell, and distribute their products and services. Beyond just complying with local regulations and expectations, however, companies that excel in critical regulatory and social processes can enhance their reputations among customers and investors, and also help to attract and retain valuable employees who take pride in their companies' roles in improving the environment, the workplace, and the community.

Companies should strive to identify the regulatory and social process objectives that will have the biggest impact for enhancing employee attraction and retention, the customer value proposition, and financial performance. In their investments in communities around the world, companies should seek opportunities that leverage their competencies and that enhance their strategic objectives. They should be as diligent and rigorous in assessing their returns from community investments as they are in evaluating the effectiveness of their investments in tangible and intangible assets.

Following this chapter is the case study and strategy map for Amanco, a Latin American company that is using the Balanced Scorecard to describe and implement its *triple-bottom line* strategy for simultaneously creating economic, social, and environmental value.

NOTES

1. M. Epstein and B. Birchard, *Counting What Counts: Turning Corporate Accountability to Competitive Advantage* (Reading, MA: Perseus Books, 1999), es-

pecially "The Figures of Social Responsibility," 130–140, and "A Social Accounting," 216–242.

2. Such (inaccurate) criticism has already appeared; see, for example, the statement, "The Balanced Scorecard is the managerial equivalent of stakeholder theory," in M. Jensen, "Value Maximization, Stakeholder Theory, and the Corporate Objective Function," *Journal of Applied Corporate Finance* (Fall 2001): 17.

3. "Diversity Lives at BellSouth," *Workforce* (January 2002): 18.

4. Novartis, "Innovation and Accountability: Health, Safety and Environment Report 2000."

5. Coca-Cola, "Keeping our Promise: Citizenship at Coca-Cola," 27.

6. DuPont, *Global Progress Report,* <http://www.dupont.com/corp/social/SHE/usa/us3.html>.

7. Forest Reinhardt, *Down to Earth: Applying Business Principles to Environmental Management* (Boston: Harvard Business School Press, 2000), and "Bridging the Gap: How Improved Information Can Help Companies Integrate Shareholder Value and Environmental Quality," in *Environmental Performance Measurement: The Global Report 2001–2002,* ed. D. Esty and P. Cornelius (New York: Oxford University Press, 2002).

8. See Philip B. Crosby, *Quality Is Free* (New York: McGraw Hill, 1979).

9. Michael E. Porter, "America's Green Strategy," *Scientific American* (April 1991): 168; and Michael E. Porter and C. van der Linde, "Green and Competitive: Ending the Stalemate," *Harvard Business Review* (September–October 1995).

10. OSHA Regulation 1904.7 states: "*Basic requirement.* You must consider an injury or illness to meet the general recording criteria, and therefore to be recordable, if it results in any of the following: death, days away from work, restricted work or transfer to another job, medical treatment beyond first aid, or loss of consciousness. You must also consider a case to meet the general recording criteria if it involves a significant injury or illness diagnosed by a physician or other licensed health care professional, even if it does not result in death, days away from work, restricted work or job transfer, medical treatment beyond first aid, or loss of consciousness."

11. See Robert S. Kaplan, "New Profit, Inc.: Governing the Nonprofit Enterprise," Case 9-100-052 (Boston: Harvard Business School, 2000).

12. Michael E. Porter and Mark R. Kramer, "The Competitive Advantage of Corporate Philanthropy," *Harvard Business Review* (December 2002): 57–78.

13. Michael E. Porter, *The Competitive Advantage of Nations* (New York: Free Press, 1990).

14. Porter and Kramer, "The Competitive Advantage of Corporate Philanthropy," 63.

15. Ibid., 68.

16. James E. Austin, *The Collaboration Challenge: How Nonprofits and Businesses Succeed Through Strategic Alliances* (San Francisco: Jossey-Bass, 2000).

17. Ibid., 67.

CASE STUDY

AMANCO

Background

Amanco is a leading company in Latin America in the production and marketing of plastic pipes and fittings for fluid transportation, with solutions for buildings, infrastructure, irrigation, and environmental engineering. Amanco's mission is to profitably produce and sell complete, innovative, world-class solutions for the transportation and control of fluids. The corporate vision is "to be recognized as a leading industrial group in Latin America, operating in a framework of ethics, eco-efficiency, and social responsibility, that generates economic value and improves our neighbors' and our region's quality of life."

Amanco is part of Grupo Nueva, a privately owned group that consists of several business divisions and is supervised by a board of directors. Amanco is present in all major countries in Latin America including Mexico, Central America, Panama, and the Andean and Mercosur regions.

The Situation

The company introduced a sustainability scorecard in 2000 as its integrated management system, and to report on its activities based on the global reporting initiative. Julio Moura, president and CEO of GrupoNuevo, stated that "Customers want products that improve the society in which they exist, that protect its environment, and that team up with its people." In 2002, Amanco revised its sustainability scorecard to align better with the Balanced Scorecard framework. The revision process ended in early December 2002. Strategy meetings, with the goal of managing Scorecard effectiveness and results, have been held from that date on. The company is also revising the sustainability scorecard of its regional operational units.

The Strategy Map

Amanco's strategy map shows the "triple bottom-line" results and the strategy it is following to achieve those results (see Figure 6-9).

The top of the strategy map shows Amanco's commitment to triple bottom-line performance:

1. Create economic value sustainably in the long run
2. Generate value through a system of corporate social responsibility
3. Generate value through environmental management

The financial dimension has an objective for sustainable profitable growth with targets of 10 percent annual sales increases and return on net assets of 24 percent. Amanco also wants to "operate efficiently," and includes an objective to reduce working capital.

The customer dimension encompasses three objectives. The brand management objective describes the four Amanco brand attributes—integrity, innovation, solutions, and reliability—that would lead Amanco to be viewed as the number one pipe system supplier in Latin America. Innovation and high-margin products enable Amanco to offer differentiated solutions to its customers. Customer satisfaction measures relate to on-time delivery, first-pass yields for complete and accurate deliveries to its more than 35,000 customers, order lead time, and overall customer perception of satisfaction.

The process and technology dimension emphasizes effective product creation processes to produce environmentally friendly, innovative products that are reliable and long-lasting. The product development process includes a screening phase to evaluate the potential effects of all new products on health and the environment. It uses a cradle-to-grave approach that includes raw materials, production processes and equipment, use of finished goods, packaging, and final disposal. This dimension also includes initiatives in customer relationship management (CRM) and e-business to create a deeper knowledge of customers' needs and expectations. A pilot CRM project in Mexico focuses on improving logistics processes, leading to more accurate orders, compliance with time and quality delivery commitments, and freight cost reductions.

Amanco's special emphasis on social responsibility and eco-efficiency has led to a fifth dimension: environmental and social. In this dimension, Amanco measures health and safety performance by lost-time injury frequency. Its environmental performance objective, based on eco-efficiency concepts, is to reduce the per-unit inputs and wastes from its products and processes. It measures

Figure 6-9 Amanco Triple Bottom-Line Strategy Map

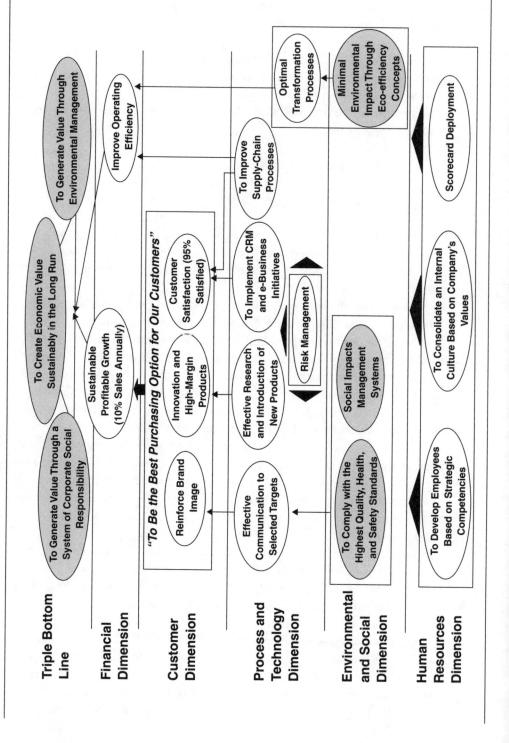

per-unit energy and water consumption and raw materials waste and scrap. In addition to contributing to lower costs, Amanco believes its eco-efficiency will add value to its products; it expects to attract more customers through the environmental and social responsibility embedded in its company branding and logo. Its social impacts objectives relate to community development projects throughout Latin America. Each operating company must have at least one project implemented, in collaboration with a nongovernmenal organization (NGO), in a local community. Amanco wants to add value where others are not taking action, particularly in areas related to its core businesses, such as housing, water, and sanitation.

The human resources dimension includes measures of job satisfaction with the working environment, job turnover, and skills and competencies of employees. This dimension also includes measures of a healthy mix of youth and seniority, and availability of good employment opportunities for young workers.

Anecdotes

The company has been able to communicate the strategy in a more objective and clear way, helping executives and employees understand strategic goals and initiatives. The sustainability effect, with its triple bottom-line results, has been better understood and managed.

Amanco has scheduled and implemented quarterly meetings to manage and learn from the current strategy. A strategy management committee was created for these activities, and a yearly strategic planning process will ensure strategy updates when needed. Roberto Salas, Amanco's CEO, states that "the Balanced Scorecard, in this new version, is a very powerful tool to align our people to the strategy and monitor the advances in our strategic goals."

Mathias Mangels and Carlos Graham of Symnetics, the Latin American affiliate of the Balanced Scorecard Collaborative, helped to prepare this case study. Our thanks to Mr. Roberto Salas, CEO, for sharing the Amanco experience.

PART THREE

Intangible Assets

CHAPTER SEVEN

ALIGNING INTANGIBLE ASSETS TO ENTERPRISE STRATEGY

WE DISCUSSED IN CHAPTER I how intangible assets have become decisive for sustainable value creation. The dictionary definition of intangible, "incapable of being realized or defined," points to the difficulty that an organization has in managing these assets. How can it manage what can't be defined?

The learning and growth perspective of the Balanced Scorecard highlights the role for aligning the organization's intangible assets to its strategy (see Figure 7-1). This perspective contains the objectives and measures for three components of intangible assets essential for implementing any strategy:

1. Human capital
2. Information capital
3. Organization capital

The objectives in these three components must be *aligned* with the objectives for the internal processes and *integrated* with each other. Intangible assets should build upon the capabilities created in other intangible and tangible assets, rather than create independent capabilities with no synergies among them.

Figure 7-1 Intangible Assets Must Be Aligned with the Strategy to Create Value

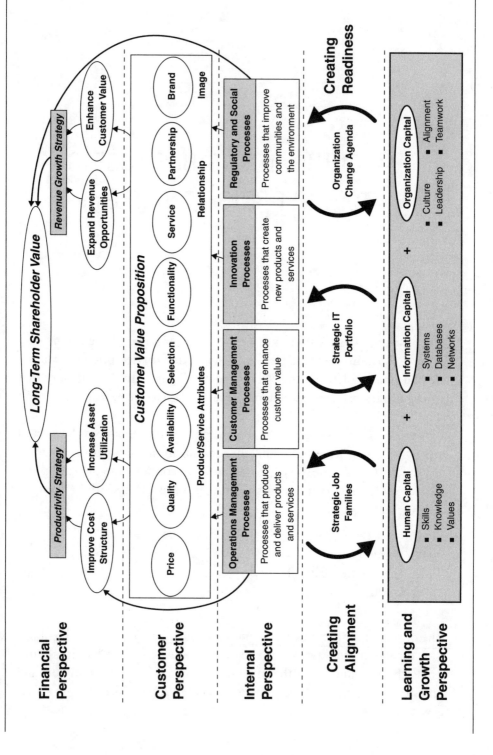

1. ALIGNMENT.
The Intangible Assets Must Be Aligned with the Strategy, in Order to Create Value.

Intangible assets take on value only in the context of strategy, what they are expected to help the organization accomplish. For example, assume an organization wants to invest in staff training. Assume further that it has two choices—a training program on total quality management (TQM) or a program on customer relationship management (CRM). Which program has the greatest value? Clearly the answer to this question depends on the organization's strategy. A company following a low total cost strategy, such as Dell and McDonald's, that needs to continually improve its operating processes would get higher value from TQM training. A company such as Goldman Sachs or IBM Consulting, however, that follows a total customer solution strategy, would benefit most from CRM training. The same investment in training creates dramatically higher returns when it is aligned with the organization's strategy. *Strategic alignment* is the dominant principle in creating value from intangible assets.

2. INTEGRATION.
The Strategic Role of Intangible Assets Cannot Be Addressed on a Stand-Alone Basis. An Integrated Program Is Required to Support the Enhancement of All the Organization's Intangible Assets.

When an organization groups its activities around functions, such as HR and IT, it often creates silos of specialization. People in the separate functional departments look to professional models within their disciplines as points of reference or benchmarks. Such specialization is obviously beneficial for creating deep functional excellence in each department. But, in practice, the different functional units strive for excellence in isolation from each other. Each department competes for the organization's scarce resources; one argues to increase employee training while the other urges an expansion of technology capabilities. Solutions are sought in isolation and the results are usually disappointing.

Investments in IT have no value unless complemented with HR training and incentive programs. HR training programs have little value unless complemented with modern technology tools. HR and IT investments must be integrated if the organization is to realize the full potential benefits.

Alignment and integration provide the conceptual building blocks for developing objectives for human capital, information capital, and organization capital in the learning and growth perspective. Few organizations, however, exploit the potential competitive advantages from aligning and integrating their intangible assets. We conducted two surveys of HR and IT executives, to better understand their approaches to strategic alignment (see Figure 7-2). Only one-third of the organizations reported strong alignment of HR and IT priorities with enterprise strategy. Why the misalignment? Fundamental management processes designed to create alignment were not being used as intended. Few HR and IT organizations integrated planning with strategy, assigned relationship managers, or linked budgets to strategy.

Executives do not dispute the need to align and integrate their intangible assets. Until now, however, they lacked a method for alignment and integration. In this part of the book, we build upon the internal process objectives developed in Part II to describe how the strategy map and Balanced Scorecard enable organizations to accomplish the following:

- Describe intangible assets
- Align and integrate intangible assets to the strategy
- Measure intangible assets and their alignment

DESCRIBE INTANGIBLE ASSETS

Intangible assets have been described as "knowledge that exists in an organization to create differential advantage"[1] or "the capabilities of the

Figure 7-2   Summary of Alignment Practices of HR and IT Groups

Survey Says ...	IT Survey[1]	HR Survey[2]
About the HR/IT Alignment with Enterprise Strategy		
1 Alignment of functional priorities to enterprise strategy	34%	33%
2 Viewed as a "strategic partner"	28%	34%
About Alignment Techniques		
3 Integrated planning process used to determine strategic priorities of HR/IT	32%	23%
4 Relationship managers assigned to business unit	33%	43%
5 Alignment of functional priorities to budget	29%	17%

[1]Conducted by Balanced Scorecard Collaborative and *CIO Insight*, 2002 (634 participants)
[2]Conducted by Balanced Scorecard Collaborative and Society for HR Management (1,266 participants)

company's employees to satisfy customer needs."[2] Intangible assets encompass such diverse items as patents, copyrights, workforce knowledge, leadership, information systems, and work processes. We have examined the learning and growth perspective of several hundred strategy maps and Balanced Scorecards. Six objectives consistently appeared:

Human Capital

1. *Strategic competencies:* The availability of skills, talent, and know-how to perform activities required by the strategy. (About 80 percent of the scorecards included such an objective.)

Information Capital

2. *Strategic information:* The availability of information systems and knowledge applications and infrastructure required to support the strategy (included in 80 percent of scorecards).

Organization Capital

3. *Culture:* Awareness and internalization of the shared mission, vision, and values needed to execute the strategy (included in 90 percent of scorecards).
4. *Leadership:* The availability of qualified leaders at all levels to mobilize the organizations toward their strategies (included in 90 percent of scorecards).
5. *Alignment:* Alignment of goals and incentives with the strategy at all organization levels (included in 70 percent of scorecards).
6. *Teamwork:* The sharing of knowledge and staff assets with strategic potential (included in 60 percent of scorecards).

These objectives describe important intangible assets and provide a powerful framework for aligning and integrating them to the organization's strategy.

Take, for example, the learning and growth objectives in Datex-Ohmeda's strategy map (see Figure 7-3). The largest division of Instrumentarium Corporation, Datex-Ohmeda is based in Helsinki, Finland, and has manufacturing operations in Finland, Sweden, and the United States. The company has been making a wide range of machinery used in acute care since the 1900s. The company has a history of world firsts, beginning with its development in 1924 of the first four-gas anesthesia machine in collaboration with the Mayo Clinic. The company also created the first post–iron lung ventilator. Today, Datex-Ohmeda's product line includes patient monitors and networked systems for anesthesia,

Figure 7-3 Datex-Ohmeda Strategy Map

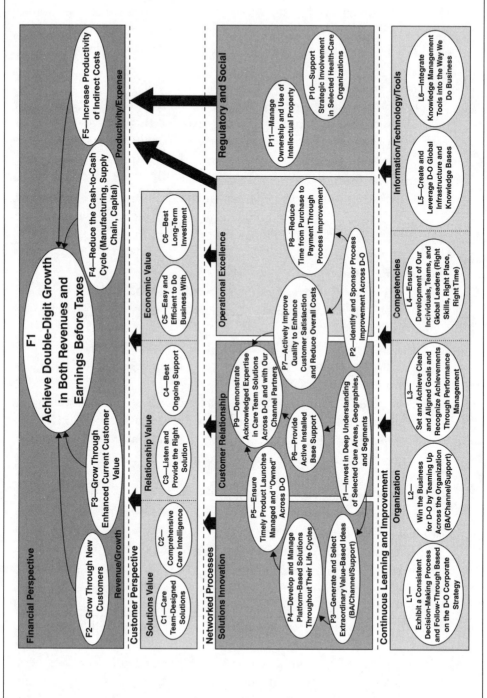

intensive-care units, and subacute care, as well as anesthesia machines, ventilators, drug delivery systems, pulse oximeters, and supplies and accessories.

Its legacy of product innovation worked well for Datex-Ohmeda, but in recent years, as the company faced toughening competition from companies such as Philips, Siemens, and Drager, it needed to offer its customers something more. Datex-Ohmeda realized that developing and maintaining long-term customer relationships—something it had always naturally excelled at—needed to become the key to its future success.

Organizational alignment, always difficult in a global enterprise, was a particular challenge for Datex-Ohmeda because most of the company's factories and business units had been acquired through mergers, and already had established ways of doing things. Historically, Datex-Ohmeda operated a collection of fairly independent business units and sales channels. The goals of these different entities often conflicted or diverged. In the summer of 2001, Datex-Ohmeda executives finalized their strategy, using the strategy map to crystallize their thinking. Their planning sessions confirmed the wisdom of the company's transition from a strategy based on innovation to one focused on customer relationships. Datex-Ohmeda's new value proposition was to provide the right solutions for customers based on thoroughly understanding their needs. This also meant focusing on ongoing support and the ease of doing business through customer-focused processes. The strategy map describes these new directions.

The *financial* perspective of Figure 7-3 shows two revenue growth objectives: acquiring new customers (F2) and expanding relations with existing customers (F3). Datex-Ohmeda would achieve the F3 objective by delivering "team-designed solutions" (C1) based on the breadth of its product line. Objectives for two internal processes describe how this value proposition will be created and delivered: A customer management objective (P9) defines the process of teamwork across Datex-Ohmeda, as well as with its channel partners; objective P4 defines the innovation required to "develop and manage platform-based solutions throughout their life cycles." These two internal process objectives, in turn, create the demand for organizational capabilities and culture that would promote the development of new human and informational capital, and strong networking and teamwork across lines of business and national boundaries.

Datex-Ohmeda's learning and growth objectives, organized under the heading "Continuous Learning and Improvement," align the intangible assets with the strategic priorities. Objectives L1, L2, and L3 describe the organization capital required for implementing the new strategy. Objective L1 identifies the need for consistency in decision-making processes required for a platform product strategy. Objective L2 defines the need for teamwork required by the team-solutions strategy. Objective L3 focuses on the process of alignment with the strategy at the individual level. The strategy map addresses the human capital needs ("right skills, right place, right time") of the new strategy in objective L4. The details of these requirements will be described in lower-level human resources plans. Objectives L5 and L6 focus on the information capital requirements, with particular emphasis on knowledge sharing across the organization.

Thus, by using strategy maps, the groups that manage the organization's most important intangible assets become tightly aligned to the organization's strategy. The strategy map provides the framework for aligning human, information, and organization capital to the strategy, with sufficient specific detail to be meaningful, measurable, and actionable.

ALIGN AND INTEGRATE INTANGIBLE ASSETS

In *The Strategy-Focused Organization*, we described the case of a global bank that attempted to implement a new strategy.[3] The bank's differentiation strategy was to offer innovative and sophisticated financial products and services to global customers (corporations) that could be accessed seamlessly from any location around the world. The strategy failed when the complex information technology required to implement this strategy was not deployed in a timely or effective fashion. When questioned about the performance of the information services (IS) business unit, however, the CEO replied that this unit was performing well, according to its Balanced Scorecard. But the IS unit had built its scorecard by benchmarking the performance of the IS units it believed were the best in the world. It adopted the metrics used by "high-performing" information services groups. According to these metrics, the bank's IS unit was now "world class," performing comparably to its top-tier benchmarked peer group. The IS unit, however, while performing well against externally determined metrics, had failed miserably to deliver the services vitally needed for the bank's new strategy. Because of this lack of alignment, the business unit and the bank's strategy could not be implemented and eventually failed. The bank's experience is a classic lesson on the consequences from not aligning a functional unit's strategy and scorecard to entity objectives.

The strategy map (see Figure 7-1) creates alignment and integration by providing a common point of reference for the enterprise strategy. The internal perspective of the map identifies the critical few processes that create desired outcomes for customers and shareholders. The intangible assets must be aligned to these value-creating internal processes. We have used three alignment techniques to establish a bridge between the strategy map and intangible assets.

- *Strategic job families:* For each strategic process, one or two job families will have the greatest impact on the strategy. By identifying these job families, defining their competencies, and ensuring their development, we can accelerate strategic results.
- *Strategic IT portfolio:* For each strategic process, specific IT systems and infrastructure support implementation. These systems represent a portfolio of technology investments that should receive priority in funding and other resources.
- *Organization change agenda:* The strategy requires changes in cultural values, both internally focused (for example, teamwork) as well as external (for example, customer focus). An agenda of cultural change, derived from the strategy, helps shape the development of the new culture and climate.

Companies, by developing, aligning, and integrating their human, information, and organization capital to the critical few strategic processes, create the greatest returns from their intangible assets.

Take the example of Consumer Bank (see Figure 7-4). Its strategy map defines seven strategic themes, one of which is "Cross-sell the Product Line." The human resources executive at Consumer Bank owns the process for developing the *human capital* required to support the strategy. Human resources and line executives, at a planning workshop, identified the "financial planner" as the job most important to the cross-selling process. The workshop further identified four competencies as fundamental to this job—solution selling skills, relationship management, product line knowledge, and professional certification.

Similar work with Consumer Bank's information technology executive led to specific objectives for the *information capital* (networks, data, and knowledge) to support the strategy. Information technology and line executives identified four technology priorities—a financial self-planning model, a customer profitability system, an integrated customer file, and Web-enabled access by customers.

Figure 7-4 Linking Intangible Assets to the Strategy at Consumer Bank

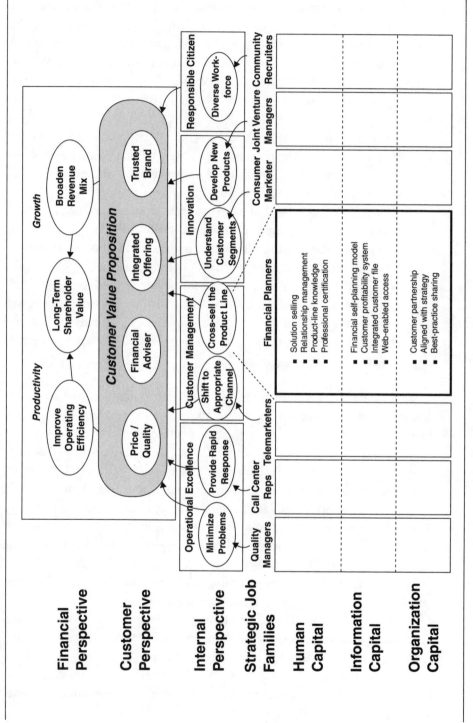

Finally, Consumer's executive team established three priorities for *organization capital*: a culture based on partnerships with customers, alignment of employees' personal objectives to the strategy, and improved teamwork to promote best-practice sharing.

By using the strategy map as its point of reference, the HR and IT executives at Consumer Bank narrowed the focus of their activities to a small number of processes (seven) that were decisive for the success of the strategy. Each of these constitutes a *strategic theme*. They could now identify a focused set of strategic jobs and information systems that would drive performance of the critical processes. This focus became the link between their functional responsibilities and the strategy of the enterprise. And the clear focus and alignment to the strategy simplified their jobs. They could now work intensively on the "critical few" instead of reacting broadly and diffusely to the generic multitude of issues that bombarded them on a daily basis.

The seven *strategic themes* provide the building blocks for the strategy and describe how the strategy will be implemented. If each of these themes is executed, the bank should create sustained value for its shareholders. A new customer base will be created, new products launched, a solutions-selling interface installed, improved quality perfected, and a diverse workforce developed that reflects community values. The seven strategic themes cross organizational boundaries and force an integrated approach to strategy. Responsibility and accountability for the strategy get organized around these strategic themes, not around traditional departmental or functional objectives.

Figure 7-5 describes the plan for the "cross-selling" theme. Successful cross-selling requires an increased level of customer confidence in the bank's financial advice. If a customer's confidence increases, the bank should get an increased share of the customer's business, which generates greater revenue growth and a broader revenue mix. The cross-selling process depends on its intangible assets—strategic skills, information, and alignment. For each of these interrelated objectives, the plan identifies the measure, the target, the initiatives required to achieve the target, and the investment required to perform the initiative.

This plan has all the information required to execute the strategic theme. Most important, it defines the combination of intangible assets required to support the strategy and create value. Human resources, information technology, and organizational incentive programs are aligned to the strategy, and the desired integration among them is specified. Economic justification of these strategic investments can be performed, but

Figure 7-5 Action Planning for a Strategic Theme at Consumer Bank

Strategic Theme: Cross-sell the Product Line

Strategic Objectives	Measure	Target	Initiatives	Budget
Financial Perspective — Broaden Revenue Mix	▪ Revenue mix ▪ Revenue growth	▪ New = +10% ▪ +25%		
Customer Perspective — Increase Customer Confidence in Our Financial Advice	▪ Share of segment ▪ Share of wallet ▪ Customer satisfaction	▪ 25% ▪ 50% ▪ 90%	▪ Segmentation initiative ▪ Satisfaction survey	$ XXX $ XXX
Internal Perspective — Cross-sell the Product Line	▪ Cross-sell ratio ▪ Hours with customer	▪ 2.5 ▪ 1hr/Q	▪ Financial planning initiative ▪ Integrated product offering	$ XXX $ XXX
Learning and Growth Perspective — Develop Strategic Skills / Access to Strategic Info / Align Personal Goals	▪ Human capital readiness ▪ Strategic application readiness ▪ Goals linked to BSC	▪ 100% ▪ 100% ▪ 100%	▪ Relationship management ▪ Certified financial planner ▪ Integrated customer file ▪ Portfolio planning application ▪ MBO update ▪ Incentive compensation	$ XXX $ XXX $ XXX $ XXX $ XXX $ XXX
			Total Budget	**$ XXX**

not in traditional ways. The common approach is on a stand-alone basis: "Show the ROI of the new IT application," or "Demonstrate the payback from the HR training program." The strategic program plan in Figure 7-5 shows how all IT and HR programs combine to create a collective financial payoff—revenue growth of 25 percent—from the strategy. Specific human capital, information capital, and organization capital initiatives, each requiring investments in people and cash, are needed to achieve this revenue growth. But each investment or initiative is only one ingredient in the bigger recipe. Each is necessary, but not sufficient. Economic justification is determined by evaluating the return from the entire portfolio of investments in intangible assets that will deliver the ROI from enhancing the cross-selling process.

MEASURE INTANGIBLE ASSETS

At first glance, it seems daunting to measure assets—employee capabilities and alignment, information technology, and organizational climate and culture—that are defined by their intangibility, but some measurement principles seem clear. Intangible assets should not be measured by how much money was spent to develop them, nor should their value be determined by independent appraisals of the capabilities and value of HR and IT assets. The value of intangible assets comes from how well they align to the strategic priorities of the enterprise, not by how much it costs to create them or how much they are worth on a freestanding basis. If the intangible assets are closely aligned to the strategy, they will have greater value to the organization. The converse is also true; intangible assets that are not aligned to the strategy will not create much value, even if large amounts of money have been spent on them.

For measuring intangible assets, perhaps we can learn from the principles used in a company's balance sheet to measure the organization's tangible and financial assets. Accountants organize the asset side of the balance sheet by categories, such as cash, accounts receivable, inventory, property, plant, and equipment, and long-term investments. Assets are ordered hierarchically, by their degree of *liquidity*, the ease with which the asset can be converted to cash (see Figure 7-6). Accounts receivable is more liquid (quicker conversion to cash) than inventory, and both accounts receivable and inventory are classified as short-term assets since they typically convert to cash within twelve months. Long-term assets, as their name suggests, take longer to return the amount invested in them back to cash. For example, property, plant, and equipment (PP&E)

Figure 7-6 Framework for Measuring Intangible Assets

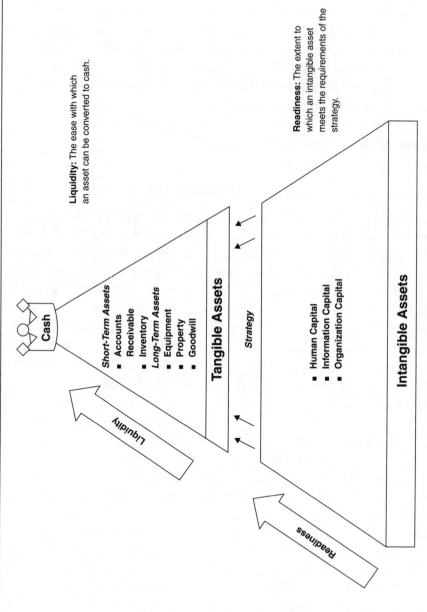

provide a capability for converting raw materials to finished goods inventory, which gets sold, becomes accounts receivable and, eventually, cash. But many cycles of such conversion are required before the initial investment in PP&E is recovered.

The strategy map framework enables human, information, and organization capital to be represented as assets that eventually get converted into cash, the ultimate liquid asset, through higher sales and lower spending. We introduce the concept of *strategic readiness* to describe the status of intangible assets to support the organization's strategy. Strategic readiness is analogous to liquidity—the higher the state of readiness, the faster intangible assets contribute to generating cash.

Strategic readiness gets converted into tangible value only when internal processes create increased levels of revenue and profit. An organization cannot possibly assign a meaningful financial value to an intangible factor like a "motivated and prepared workforce" because tangible value can be derived only in the context of the strategy. It is possible from the financial perspective of the strategy map to state that successful execution of the strategy is worth some amount in revenue growth and another amount in shareholder value. A workforce that has achieved satisfactory levels of strategic readiness is one, but only one, of the factors that enable such revenue growth or shareholder value creation to be achieved. Thus, the readiness of the human capital intangible asset is a necessary but not sufficient condition for strategic success.

For example, in Figure 7-4, Consumer Bank identified four specific competencies for its financial planners to support the strategic internal process "Cross-sell the Product Line":

- Solution selling
- Relationship management
- Product-line knowledge
- Certification as a licensed financial planner

Consumer Bank needed to measure the readiness of its existing staff of financial planners for this internal process. Assume that 100 financial planners are required to execute this strategy. Consumer Bank used rigorous testing to determine that as a result of targeted hiring, training, and development programs, forty of its financial planners have reached a level of proficiency sufficient to execute the cross-selling objective (see Figure 7-7). Since 100 individuals are required to execute the strategy, the bank's human capital readiness for this piece of the strategy is only 40 percent.

Figure 7-7 Measuring the Strategic Readiness of Human Capital

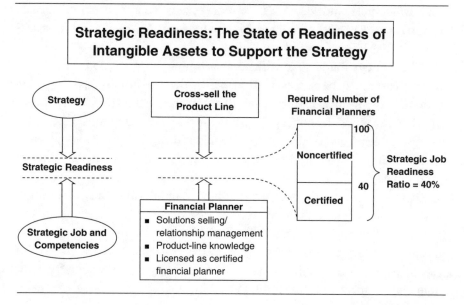

The measurement of intangible assets can use a cascading model, similar to that used in a balance sheet for the organization's tangible and financial assets. The top level, the balance sheet (level 1), describes the different classes of assets, ranked by liquidity; for example, cash, accounts receivable, inventory, property, plant, and equipment. The next level (level 2) describes the portfolio of assets within a specific class. For example, the accounts receivable asset consists of several subcategories, such as:

- Current (less than thirty days)
- Overdue (thirty to sixty days)
- Overdue (sixty to ninety days)
- Overdue (more than ninety days)

Similarly, the inventory account can be broken into subcategories of raw materials, work in process, and finished goods. The assets in each of the subcategories have a different degree of risk. Finally, a third level describes specific assets (for example, John Smith owes $5,290 and is thirty to sixty days overdue; the company owns $6,000 worth of a particular purchased item or grade of steel).

Extending this balance sheet model to intangible assets, level 1 provides aggregate information on three categories: human capital, information capital, and organization capital. Level 2 describes information on how each intangible asset relates to its targeted internal processes, and level 3 describes characteristics of individual intangible assets.

These ideas are illustrated in Figure 7-8, which shows the level 2 detail for human capital assets at Consumer Bank. The figure provides a comprehensive view of the state of readiness of Consumer Bank's human resources to deliver on its new complex strategy. The company has identified the specific job families expected to drive performance improvements for each strategic internal process. For example, the financial planner is the most important job category for the cross-selling process, while the call center representative is most important for the rapid response process. Consumer Bank needs to ensure that it has a sufficient number of people, within each of the seven strategic job families, with the right skills to support the associated internal process. As shown in Figure 7-8, the bank is in good shape for its two operations management processes (100 percent and 90 percent readiness), but deficient in its human capital capabilities for the two customer management processes (only 40 percent and 50 percent readiness) and one of the innovation processes (20 percent readiness). The level 1 aggregate measure of 65 percent human capital readiness (in the red zone) is a weighted average of readiness across the seven strategic job families.

Level 3 measures identify the capabilities of specific individuals— their qualifications for their strategic roles. Individual capabilities, compared to the category requirement, are the basic building blocks for measuring the organization's human resources assets. Individuals' capabilities get aggregated into level 2 and level 1 descriptions to produce a broader portfolio picture of the strategic readiness of all the organization's human resources assets.

A similar decomposition can be done for the three levels of the organization's information capital and organization capital. Figure 7-9 provides a sample Strategic Readiness Report, which gives a consolidated snapshot of the ability of each class of intangible asset to fulfill its strategic role. Just as a military organization constantly assesses the availability of trained manpower, equipment, ammunition, intelligence, and logistics relative to requirements as a measure of mission readiness, organizations must assess the status of the six intangible assets in Figure 7-9 as their indicators of strategic readiness. The organization illustrated in the figure has major deficiencies in the readiness of its IT systems to support the strategy. The education and incentives for the workforce to orient the culture in new directions are also lagging. These would both present formidable barriers to the execution of strategy.

Figure 7-8 Human Capital Readiness: The Portfolio View

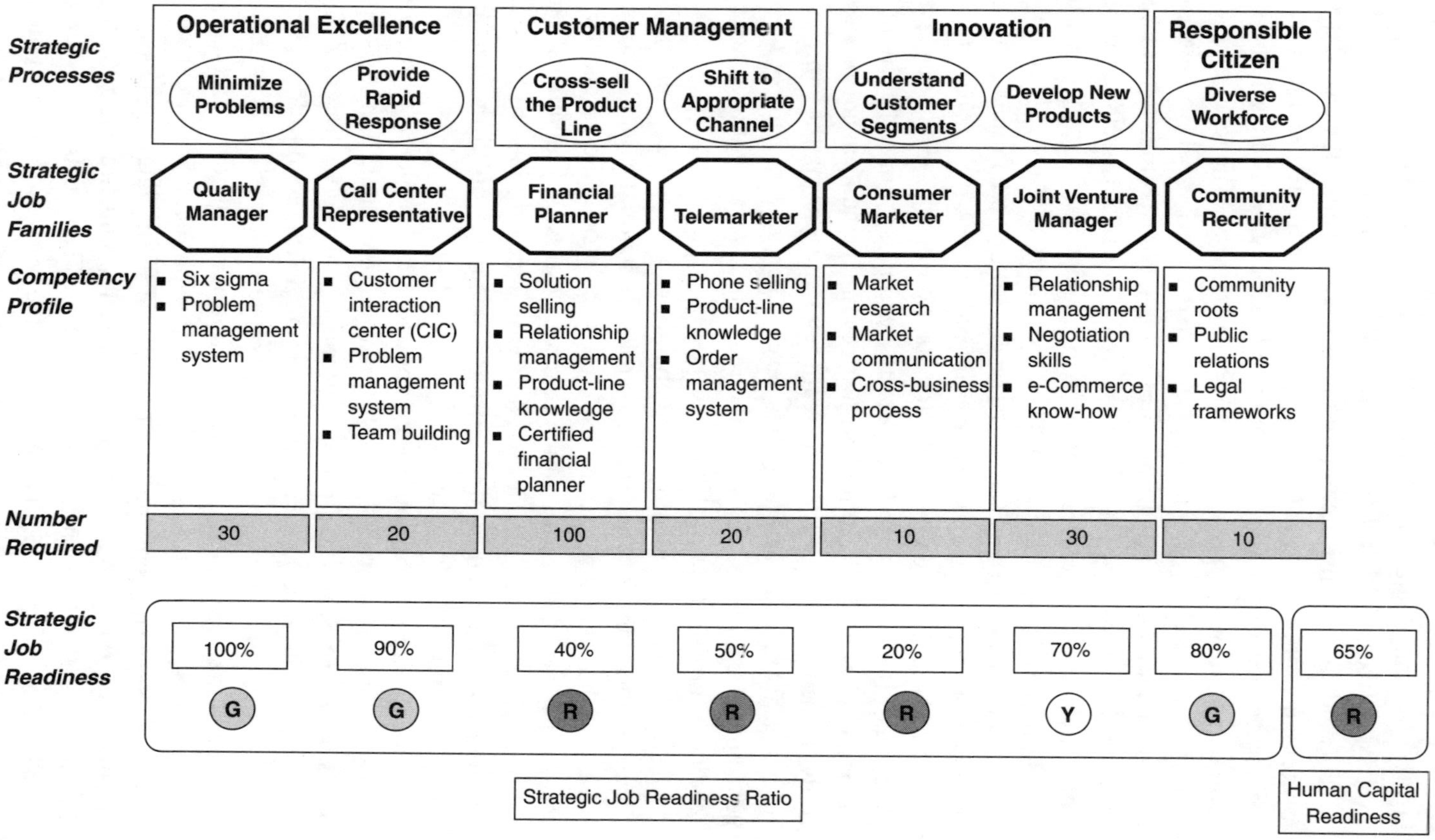

Strategic Processes	Operational Excellence		Customer Management		Innovation		Responsible Citizen
	Minimize Problems	Provide Rapid Response	Cross-sell the Product Line	Shift to Appropriate Channel	Understand Customer Segments	Develop New Products	Diverse Workforce
Strategic Job Families	Quality Manager	Call Center Representative	Financial Planner	Telemarketer	Consumer Marketer	Joint Venture Manager	Community Recruiter
Competency Profile	■ Six sigma ■ Problem management system	■ Customer interaction center (CIC) ■ Problem management system ■ Team building	■ Solution selling ■ Relationship management ■ Product-line knowledge ■ Certified financial planner	■ Phone selling ■ Product-line knowledge ■ Order management system	■ Market research ■ Market communication ■ Cross-business process	■ Relationship management ■ Negotiation skills ■ e-Commerce know-how	■ Community roots ■ Public relations ■ Legal frameworks
Number Required	30	20	100	20	10	30	10
Strategic Job Readiness	100% G	90% G	40% R	50% R	20% R	70% Y	80% G

Strategic Job Readiness Ratio

65% R

Human Capital Readiness

Figure 7-9 Strategic Readiness Report

Learning and Growth Perspective	Human Capital	Organization Capital			Information Capital
	Human Capital Portfolio	Culture	Leadership	Alignment Teamwork	Information Capital Portfolio

Strategic Readiness Report

Asset	Objective	Measure	Target	Actual
Human Capital	**Human Capital Portfolio:** Understand and eliminate the gaps between available and required competencies in strategic job families	■ Strategic Job Readiness	75%	65% Y
Organization Capital	**Leadership:** Build a cadre of leaders at all levels required to mobilize the organization toward its strategy	■ Leadership Gap	90%	92% G
	Culture: Develop the awareness and internalization of the mission, vision, and core values needed to execute the strategy	■ Core Values Achieved	80%	52% R
	Alignment: Ensure the alignment of goals and incentives with the strategy at all organization levels	■ Strategic Awareness	80%	75% Y
	Teamwork: Ensure the sharing of knowledge and staff assets with strategic potential	■ Best-Practice Sharing	75%	80% G
Information Capital	**Information Capital Portfolio:** Provide the full portfolio of IT applications required of the strategy	■ Information Portfolio Readiness	95%	70% R

SUMMARY

The Strategic Readiness Report consolidates the essential elements of our approach to managing intangible assets:

- Define the asset
- Align it to the strategy
- Measure the degree of readiness

In the remaining chapters of this part, we describe approaches to defining and measuring the readiness of the three sets of intangible assets— human capital, information capital, and organization capital. The case study following this chapter describes the situation faced by Crown Castle, in which the company had to change the culture from a collection of independent acquisitions to an integrated company that gained synergy from leveraging capabilities from its multiple properties.

NOTES

1. Thomas A. Stewart, "Brainpower," *Fortune*, 3 June 1991, 44.
2. Thomas A. Stewart, *Intellectual Capital: The New Wealth of Organizations* (New York: Doubleday, 1998), 67.
3. Robert S. Kaplan and David P. Norton, *The Strategy-Focused Organization: How Balanced Scorecard Companies Thrive in the New Business Environment* (Boston: Harvard Business School Press, 2001), 163, 165.

CASE STUDY

CROWN CASTLE INTERNATIONAL, INC.

Background

Crown Castle International is a leading global provider of shared wireless communications and broadcast infrastructure. It rents towers, leases antenna space, and provides broadcast transmission service and related services to a "who's who" of wireless providers and broadcasters, including British Telecom, Verizon, Cingular, Vodafone, T Mobile (Deutsche Telekom), and the British Broadcasting Service (BBC), for whom the company provides full television transmission services. Crown Castle serves more than two-thirds of the U.S. markets and more than 90 percent of the British and Australian populations. Total revenues for 2002 were $901.5 million.

The Situation

Crown Castle's growth paralleled the wireless digital boom of the mid-1990s; from 127 towers and 700 employees in 1995, the company today has grown to more than 15,000 towers and 2,000 employees. When Crown Castle went public in 1998, its strategy was simple: an intensified "land grab." By acquiring strategically located towers for lease and offering outsourced services, the company could help its telecom customers achieve speed to market. Once it met its fixed costs, revenues would become pure cash flow. Early on, this formula produced successful results; but when the capital markets began to tighten and the predicted 75 percent margins didn't materialize, the executive team realized that the growth-through-acquisitions strategy had run its course.

The Strategy

In June 2001, Crown Castle rolled out a new strategy—operational excellence—along with its Balanced Scorecard initiative. The company now sought to maximize return on existing assets, realize greater efficiencies, and reap economies of scale by offering such value-added services as equipment maintenance. John Kelly, who became CEO in August 2001, led the company through its transformation, fully aware that in an industry as fluid as telecommunications, Crown Castle would have to adapt its strategy, and thus its scorecard, periodically. In 2002, the company decentralized its management structure to produce more detailed data and knowledge about its core assets, transmission towers. The increased knowledge would be the key to achieving operational excellence across three continents.

Strategy Map

Though operational excellence was present in Crown Castle's initial strategy map, the map still represented its former acquisitions strategy. By early 2003, the company had revised the map, with input from district-level employees, to better reflect its operational excellence strategy and new, decentralized approach. The team sharpened objectives in the internal perspective, cleansed the map of vague "corporate-speak," and reconfigured cause-and-effect relationships. The result: a more granular, unambiguous strategy map that would guide Crown Castle's far-flung workforce in executing strateg (see Figure 7-10).

Financial Perspective

Crown Castle would achieve revenue growth through two objectives aimed at boosting returns from existing assets: *increase recurring revenue,* the annuity income from leases, and *increase installation margin,* a source of higher-margin revenue. On the productivity side, the company sharpened its asset utilization objective to *reduce accounts receivable (A/R), unbilled revenue, and work-in-progress (WIP).*

Customer Perspective

Crown Castle has two types of customers: wireless operators and broadcasters. Anticipating no new customer segments and few new marketplace entrants, the company identified partnership as its customer value proposition. "If the customer has to roll out 1,000 sites this year, they want to know they have a business partner with the right infrastructure and time-to-market capability," notes Robert Paladino, senior vice president of global performance. Customer research revealed that *speed to market* should replace an earlier objective, *good to do business with. Quality,* another added objective, referred not only to the general concept but also to regulatory compliance (for example, number of on-time minutes of transmitter time). For the BBC, its primary broadcast

Figure 7-10 Crown Castle Strategy Map

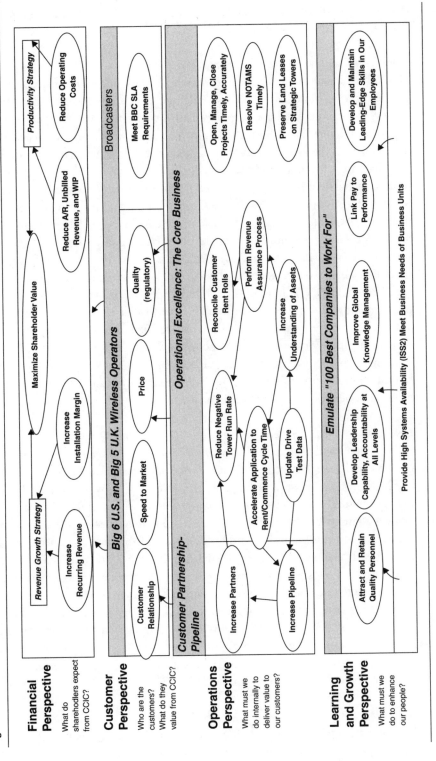

customer, the objective for fulfilling customer needs became *meet site license agreements (SLA) requirements.*

Operations (Internal Process) Perspective

"By knowing our assets better and making better process improvements, we can better serve our customers," says Paladino, explaining the crux of the company's operational excellence strategy and the rationale for this perspective's supporting theme, customer partnership. *Increase understanding of assets* was a foundation of the new strategy. The company could better serve its customers and maximize tower performance by having more and better data about its towers, such as available space, engineering specifications, and customer usage. Several objectives within this perspective were modified from high-level statements (such as *establish/improve core capabilities and support processes to maximize efficiencies*) to more actionable objectives, such as *resolve NOTAMS [trouble tickets] in a timely way.* Paladino noted that "selected, specific processes we must measure are now on the strategy map." This heightened specificity helped to standardize operational procedures throughout the company, making the strategy map more useful to district managers. Similarly, *amaze customers in each interaction* became clarified as *accelerate application to rent/commence cycle-time.* The new objective was more specific and addressed customers' main concern. The new objective supported *reduce negative tower run rate* (lower-performing towers) as well as *increase the pipeline* (the number of new applications for potential tenants).

Learning and Growth Perspective

In its theme *emulate* Fortune *magazine's "100 Best Companies to Work For,"* Crown Castle sought to create a superior working environment for its employees. Most notable of the learning and growth objectives was the central objective to *improve global knowledge management.* Early in 2003, Crown Castle made a giant stride by launching a knowledge management system that would become a repository of best practices and performance standards for key processes. It delineated processes, such as site inspections, at the task level through video clips and documentation. The knowledge management system was a direct outcome of Crown Castle's BSC. Paladino stated, "We moved from getting data, to understanding information, to gaining knowledge that we could act upon." Supporting the entire learning and growth perspective was the *information systems and services* objective; instead of focusing solely on the latest e-business system, the company now gave equal weight to the service and solution aspects of enabling technologies.

Results

Paladino credits Crown Castle's Scorecard and strategy map with helping the company thrive in a market environment so punishing that two of its four competitors declared bankruptcy. Indeed, its aggressive management of expenses and capital—the essence of its productivity strategy—propelled cash flow from negative to positive, representing improvements of several hundred million dollars. These financial gains have allowed Crown Castle to undertake major initiatives with confidence: fulfilling the U.K. government's mandate to convert television transmission to digital; and establishing Freeview, a joint venture providing free digital television with thirty new channels throughout the United Kingdom. Crown Castle is a member of the Balanced Scorecard Hall of Fame.

Case prepared by Janice Koch of Balanced Scorecard Collaborative and Robert Paladino of Crown Castle. Our thanks to John Kelly for sharing the Crown Castle experience.

CHAPTER EIGHT

HUMAN CAPITAL READINESS

IN THIS CHAPTER, we describe how organizations develop a measure of human capital (HC) readiness (see Figure 8-1). This measure represents the availability of employee skills, talent, and know-how to perform the internal processes critical to the strategy's success. We introduce a framework that enables organizations to identify HC requirements for the strategy, estimate the gap between the HC requirements and current employee readiness, and build programs to close the gap between requirements and current readiness.

The process of measuring human capital readiness starts with identifying the competencies required by individuals performing each of the critical internal processes in the organization's strategy map (see Figure 8-2). *Strategic job families* are the positions in which employees with these competencies can have the biggest impact on enhancing these critical internal processes. *Competency profiles* describe these job requirements in considerable detail. An *assessment* process defines the current capabilities of the organization in each of the job families along dimensions established in the competency profiles. The difference between the requirements and the current capabilities represents a "competency gap" that defines the human capital readiness of the organization. The organization launches human capital development programs to eliminate the gap.

Figure 8-1   Framework for Describing Human Capital Readiness

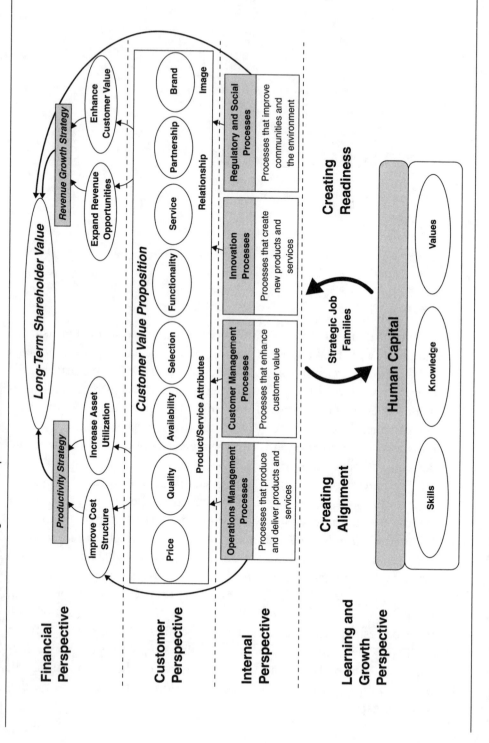

Figure 8-2 The Human Capital Readiness Model

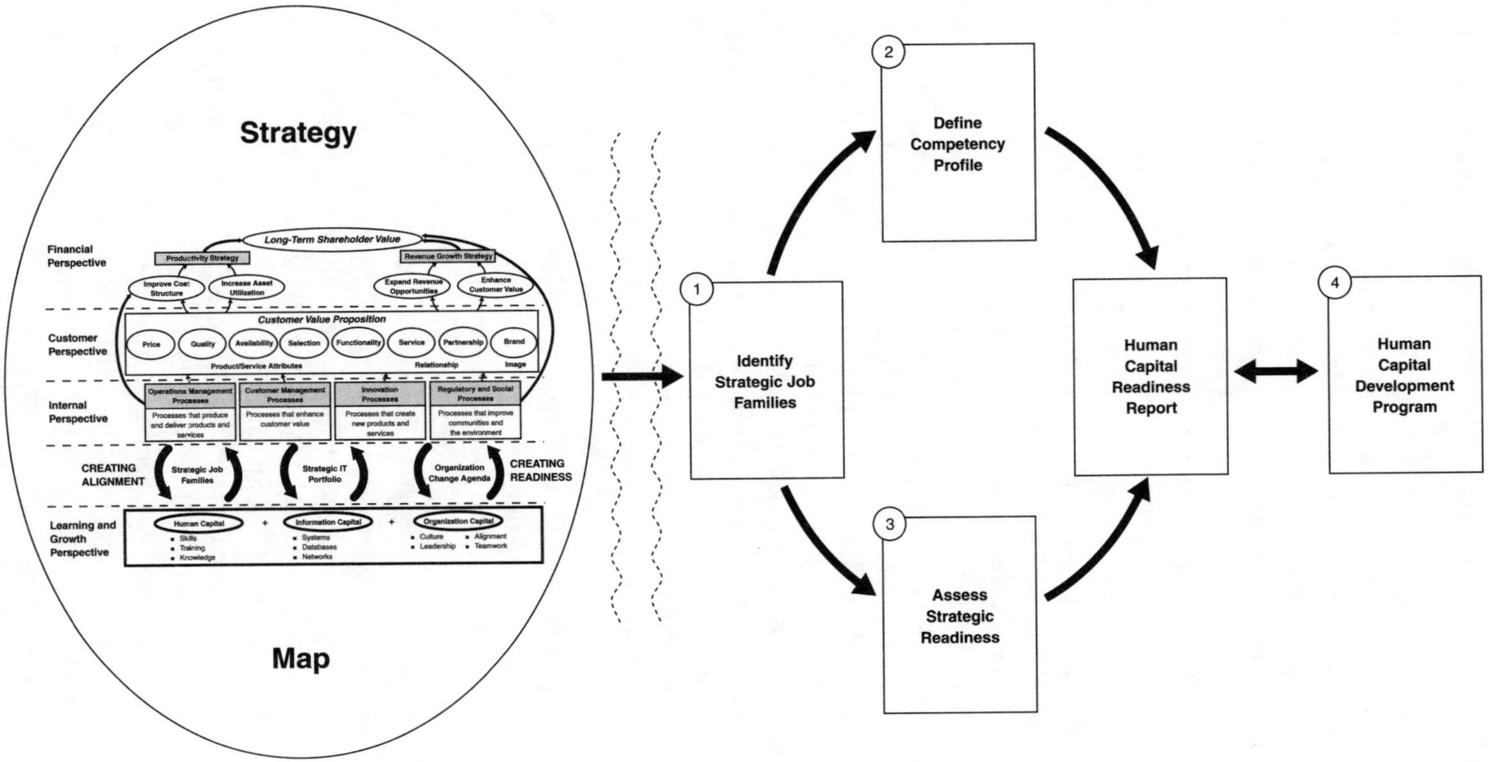

STEP 1: IDENTIFY STRATEGIC JOB FAMILIES

All jobs are important to the organization; otherwise it wouldn't hire and pay people to perform them. Many jobs, however, provide basic capabilities and requirements, but not distinctive ones that create differentiation. Organizations may require truck drivers, computer operators, custodians, receptionists, and call center operators, and make it clear that contributions from all these employees will improve organizational performance. But while managers must develop the potential of everyone in the organization, they must also recognize that some jobs have a much greater impact on the strategy than others. The strategic human capital management process must identify and focus on the critical few jobs that have the greatest impact on the strategy. John Bronson, vice president of human resources at Williams-Sonoma, estimated that people in only five job families determine 80 percent of his company's strategic priorities.[1]

Work with several organizations in our human resources research programs corroborates Bronson's observation. Consider UNICCO, a large integrated facilities service management company that offers services ranging from simple cleaning to maintaining complex machinery. Its customer solutions strategy strives for growth by customizing and expanding the range of services offered to each account. The strategy starts by demonstrating outstanding capabilities in the quality, consistency, and reliability of the basic services initially delivered to the client. This success establishes credibility that UNICCO subsequently leverages to expand service into new areas. UNICCO employs more than 6,000 people. Kimberlee Williams, UNICCO's vice president of human resources, stated that three job families provide the key leverage points for the strategy: *project managers,* who oversee the operations in specific accounts; *operations directors,* who broaden the relationships within existing accounts; and *business development executives,* who help acquire new accounts. These three job families employ only 215 people, less than 4 percent of the workforce. By focusing human capital development activities on these critical few individuals, UNICCO obtains great focus and leverage from its human capital investments.[2]

As another and more comprehensive example, Figure 8-3 shows the strategic job families for Chemico, Inc., a manufacturer of leading-edge specialty chemicals. Chemico delivers a customer solutions strategy by having its engineers build personal and technical relationships with the engineers employed by its key customers. Chemico's engineers generate innovative solutions to customers' problems through tight linkage of engineering and new product development.

Figure 8-3 Chemico, Inc. Strategy Map

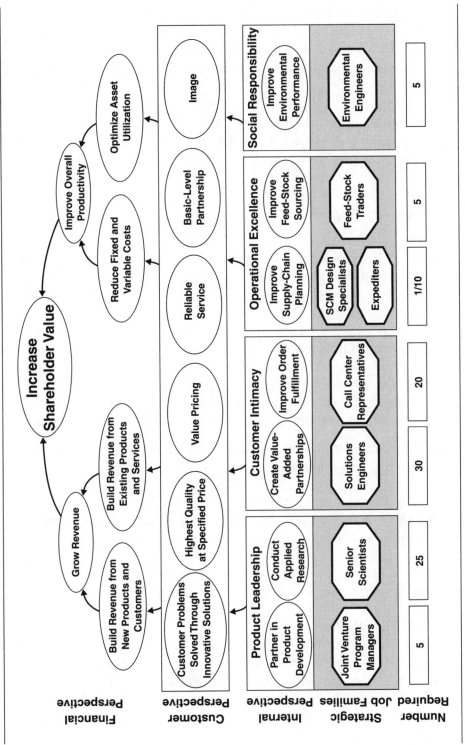

Chemico's innovation theme has two strategic processes: *partnering* to improve the diversity and speed of new product development, and *applied research* to ensure a steady flow of proprietary new products. Chemico's executives identified a strategic job family for each strategic innovation process:

Product Development Partnering Process
Joint venture program managers: Individuals who effectively manage the complexities of multicompany joint ventures[3]

Applied Research Process
Senior scientists: Individuals with mastery of narrow technical domains who develop new product applications

Chemico's customer management theme had two strategic processes, each with an associated strategic job family.

Customer Partnering Process
Solutions engineers: Engineers who work as consultants, applying Chemico's products to solve customer needs

Order Fulfillment Process
Call center representatives: Specialists who work in partnership with solutions engineers to ensure the quality and timeliness of product deliveries

The operations management theme consisted of two strategic processes and three strategic job families.

Supply-Chain Planning Process
Supply-chain management design specialists: Individuals who could lead Chemico's major reengineering of the supply-chain process

Expediters: Individuals who worked with suppliers and customers to co-ordinate scheduling throughout the supply chain.

Feed-Stock Program
Feed-stock traders: Specialists who would work in a newly established energy trading office to achieve significant cost reductions by working continually on the spot market to secure necessary feed stock

The social responsibility theme had one strategic process and an associated job family.

Environmental Performance Program

Environmental engineers: A set of specialists who have mastered clean air and clean water requirements, and the approaches required to satisfy the requirements

In summary, based on Chemico's strategy map, the executive team identified eight strategic job families. These families employed approximately 100 (7 percent) of the total employment of 1,500 staff. Thus, the success of the organization strategy would be determined by how well the company developed competencies in less than 10 percent of the workforce. This is the essence of strategic focus.

STEP 2: BUILD THE COMPETENCY PROFILE

In step 1, the organization identifies the job families that determine strategic success. In step 2, it defines the requirements of these jobs in considerable detail, a task often referred to as *job profiling* or *competency profiling*. A competency profile describes the knowledge, skills, and values required by successful occupants in a position. Human resources departments have a variety of methods for creating such profiles, such as interviewing an individual who best understands the job requirements. The competency profile provides the reference point that the HR department can use when recruiting, hiring, training, and developing people for that position.

Chemico, Inc. used a simple diagram (see Figure 8-4) to illustrate the three components in its competency profile:

Knowledge: The general background knowledge required to perform the job. This includes job-specific knowledge (for example, a "subject matter expert"), as well as surrounding knowledge (for example, "know the customer") that tailors the job-specific knowledge to the environment and context of the job.

Skills: The skills required to complement the general knowledge base; for example, negotiating, consulting, or project management skills.

Values: The set of characteristics or behaviors that produce outstanding performance in a given job. Some jobs require teamwork, while others are built around a customer focus. Matching the values to the job is essential.

Figure 8-4 Competency Profile Model Used at Chemico, Inc.

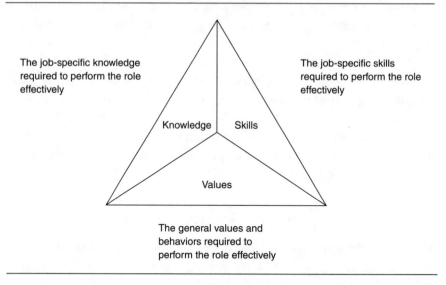

The job-specific knowledge required to perform the role effectively

The job-specific skills required to perform the role effectively

Knowledge | Skills

Values

The general values and behaviors required to perform the role effectively

Figure 8-5 shows a simplified competency profile for seven of Chemico's strategic job families. As one example, solutions engineers function as consultants in their direct work with customers. They use their knowledge of Chemico's products to solve customers' problems. The general *knowledge* requirements for their job include a sound understanding of a customer's industry and business model, and a similar understanding of Chemico's product line and how the customer could best use these products. The solutions engineer requires consulting skills, including problem solving, project management, and change management, and relationship management skills. The solution engineer's dominant value is to create enduring, trusting customer partnerships.

STEP 3: ASSESS HUMAN CAPITAL READINESS

In step 3, organizations assess the current capabilities and competencies of the employees in the strategic job families. Assessors can draw from a broad range of approaches to evaluate an individual's performance and potential. At one extreme, each employee performs a self-assessment relative to job requirements that he or she then discusses with a mentor or career manager. Alternatively, an assessor solicits 360-degree feedback from peers, superiors, and subordinates on various topics related to the employee's performance. The feedback, again, serves as the basis for a career development dialogue. These assessments provide individuals with

Figure 8-5 Strategic Jobs and Competencies at Chemico, Inc.

Strategic Processes	Innovation		Customer Management		Operations Management		Social Responsibility
	Partner in Product Development	Conduct Applied Research	Create Value-Added Partnerships	Improve Order Fulfillment	Improve Supply-Chain Planning	Improve Feed-Stock Sourcing	Improve Environmental Performance
Strategic Job Families	Joint Venture Program Managers	Senior Scientists	Solutions Engineers	Call Center Representatives	SCM Design Specialists	Feed-Stock Traders	Environmental Engineers
Competency Profile							
Knowledge	■ Industry knowledge	■ Subject matter expertise ■ Customer knowledge	■ Customer knowledge ■ Product knowledge	■ Customer knowledge ■ CRM system mastery	■ Acknowledged SCM expertise	■ Subject matter expertise ■ Company knowledge	■ Subject matter expertise ■ Company knowledge
Skills	■ Contracting skills ■ Negotiation skills ■ Relationship management skills	■ Business acumen ■ Project management skills	■ Consulting skills ■ Relationship management skills		■ Consulting skills ■ Project management skills ■ Change management skills	■ Negotiating skills	■ Project management skills ■ Change management skills
Values	■ Results-oriented	■ Team player	■ Customer partnership	■ Results-oriented	■ Results-oriented	■ Results-oriented	■ Team player
Number Required	5	25	30	20	1	5	5
Qualified	2	15	15	15	0	1	2
Human Capital Readiness	40% R	60% Y	50% R	75% Y	0% R	20% R	40% R

a clear understanding of their objectives, meaningful feedback on their current competencies and performance, and a practical approach for future personal development. Because of its importance, assessing strategic readiness of employees in strategic job families should be treated differently from the routine performance management process used elsewhere in the organization.

For many organizations, clearly articulating their strategies through the structured discipline of a strategy map is a new experience. The strategy, focusing on major areas of change and development within the organization, often reveals that several strategic job families don't currently exist in the organization. At Chemico, for example, four of the eight strategic job families were new to the organization. The joint venture managers and environmental engineers had been introduced in the past year, and hiring individuals for the supply-chain and feed-stock processes was just beginning.[4]

Chemico's HR executive chose a manager to lead an initiative to fill these positions. The manager created job profiles based on the competencies required for the new processes. The manager, along with the HR executive, performed the assessment of the readiness of current staff to fill these newly defined roles. As illustrated in the lower portion of Figure 8-5, strategic readiness in these jobs (senior scientists, solutions engineers, and call center representatives) was currently between 40 percent and 75 percent. The manager launched a human capital development program to close the gap. She linked this program to the performance management program, so that the new competency profiles became part of the employees' personal objectives and development plans.

STEP 4: THE HUMAN CAPITAL DEVELOPMENT PROGRAM

The strategy map adds focus to human resources programs—recruiting, training, and career planning—that develop the organization's human capital. Without the guidance of a strategy map, most HR development programs attempt to meet the needs of all employees, and therefore underinvest in the jobs that really make a difference. By focusing human capital investments and development programs on the relatively small number (often less than 10 percent) of employees in strategic jobs, organizations can achieve breakthrough performance faster and less expensively than by diffuse HR spending.

Two different operational approaches, summarized in Figure 8-6, can be used to create strategic alignment. Under the *strategic job family*

Figure 8-6 Models for Strategic Human Capital Development

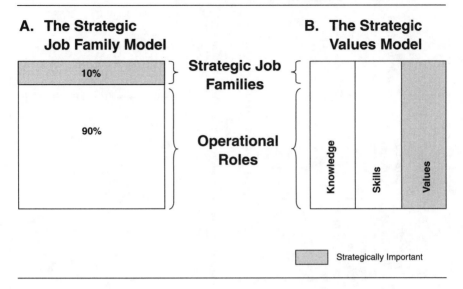

**A. The Strategic
   Job Family Model**

**B. The Strategic
   Values Model**

model, the organization concentrates its HR programs on the critical few jobs that are pivotal to the strategy. This focus contributes to speed of action and efficient spending. But this approach implies that up to 90 percent of the workforce is nonstrategic and thus that companies could ignore their legitimate needs for development. The *strategic values model* begins with the premise that strategy is everyone's job—that strategy involves a set of values and priorities that should be incorporated into everyone's objectives and actions. Clearly, both of these models are legitimate and are necessary for success, and both fit our definition of focus and have been used successfully in practice. But in our experience, they cannot be run as one integrated program. The programs to develop competencies of individuals in strategic job families should be segregated and funded separately, just as capital investments are funded and managed separately from annual operational spending programs. Progress in closing the competency gaps in strategic job families should be the basis for reporting on strategic human capital readiness. On the other hand, the strategic values model provides the basis for a revised performance management program for setting objectives for the entire workforce.

Figure 8-7 illustrates the human capital development program for Chemico, Inc. Based on the strategic job family model, the company wanted to achieve human capital readiness above 90 percent in all eight

Figure 8-7 Human Capital Development Program at Chemico, Inc.

Human Capital Readiness Report

Human Capital Objective	Measure	Target
Develop Strategic Competencies	■ Human Capital Readiness	> 90%

Human Capital Development Program

Strategic Initiatives	Strategic Budget	Lead Indicators
■ Recruiting ■ Training ■ Development ■ Peer Communities	$XXX $XXX $XXX $XXX	■ Fill Rate (% Open) ■ Hours of Training (Strategic Focus) ■ Peer Community Involvement

Human Capital Readiness (Detail)

Strategic Theme	Strategic Job Family	Number Required	Human Capital Readiness
Product Partnering	■ Joint Venture Program Managers	5	40%
Applied Research	■ Senior Scientists	25	60%
Customer Partnering	■ Solutions Engineers	30	50%
Order Fulfillment	■ Call Center Reps	20	75%
Supply Chain	■ SCM Design Specialists	1	0
	■ Expediters	10	70%
Feed Stock	■ Feed-Stock Traders	5	20%
Environmental Performance	■ Environmental Engineers	5	40%

Strategic Initiatives (Detail)

Recruiting	Training	On-Job Development	Peer Communities
R1	T1		PC1
R2		OJ1	PC2
	T2	OJ2	PC3
R3	T3	OJ3	PC4
R4			PC5
R5		OJ4	PC6
R6		OJ5	PC7

strategic job families. The HR organization developed and managed the initiatives required to achieve this objective. Chemico's HR strategy team, assigned to support this process, selected four strategic initiatives—a new employee recruiting initiative, a formal training initiative, an on-the-job development initiative, and a network of peer groups to exchange best-practice experience. The HR strategy team tailored each of these initiatives to achieve the strategic readiness target for the specific job families. The executives accountable for each strategic theme (see the left column in lower panel of Figure 8-7) served as the customers for the initiatives, providing funding and evaluating their performance. Chemico's human capital development program was now focused and aligned with its enterprise strategy.

Strategic Job Families at Gray-Syracuse

Gray-Syracuse (GS), the precision casting company described at the beginning of Chapter 1, provides another example of a human capital development program based on the strategic job family approach. Its employees design castings and select alloys to meet customers' demanding performance requirements. Additional components in the value proposition include high-quality precision products, timely delivery, and competitive prices. Workforce competencies encompass computer modeling using complex dimensional integration software, metallurgical specialties, and foundry operations. One of its operations management processes focused on delivering high quality to the customer by reducing rework (see Figure 8-8). GS had historically used flexible manufacturing at the back end of the production process, where the molded parts were finished. The new strategy identified the front end of the process as a major opportunity to reduce rework. This meant bringing flexible management approaches to the mold assembly process, in which employees assembled wax patterns produced by an injection-molding machine before converting them into the metallic alloys. The strategy map analysis identified the mold assemblyperson, an entry-level position, as the *strategic job family* for this process. Thirty individuals, selected based on their manual dexterity in the assembly process, were currently employed in this position.

The strategy of bringing flexible manufacturing to the front-end mold assembly process would require a broad new set of competencies. As outlined in box 2 of Figure 8-8, the process had eight distinct configurations of activities (known as cells) to produce different types of products. For

Figure 8-8 The Gray-Syracuse Human Capital Readiness Program

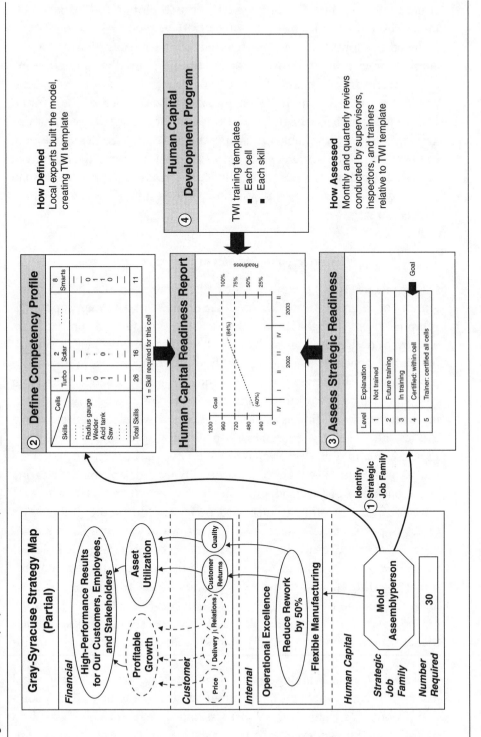

example, one cell might require the use of welding equipment, an acid tank, an X-ray, and a hot knife, whereas another cell required shellacking and gauging, as well as welding and X-ray. The simplest cell required eleven different activities, while the most complex cell required twenty-seven. Using a Japanese manufacturing technique known as Training Within Industry (TWI), experienced GS experts developed activity and competency profiles for each cell, summarized in a TWI template. All thirty current assemblypersons would have to master the activities required by each cell. The template would guide their training and evaluation. Box 3 in the figure describes the five-level scale used to measure the strategic readiness of assemblypersons.

The supervisor, the quality inspector, and/or the trainer used the TWI template to evaluate each of the thirty assemblypersons monthly and quarterly. They had a target to bring all assemblypersons to level 3 ("in training") as soon as possible, and then quickly to level 4 ("certified: within cell").

GS constructed its strategic readiness measure by adding together the ratings of each assemblyperson at each cell:

Readiness Level = Σ [Personal rating (for each assembler and each cell)]

As shown in the human capital readiness report, the readiness level was 400, an average level of 1.6 per person per cell, when the program was introduced in 2001. This level was only 40 percent of the phase 2 objective. One year later, the readiness level had risen to 810, an average level of 3.3 and 84 percent of the phase 2 objective. Paul Smith, the director of human resources at Gray-Syracuse, attributed the speed with which the competency levels rose to the TWI program. Smith stated that Gray-Syracuse is the first U.S.-owned company to successfully import the TWI program from Japan. He estimated that the TWI program cut the time to achieve strategic readiness in half. Rework dropped by 76 percent during this period, creating dramatic economic benefits.

Strategic Values Model at BAS

The University of California, Berkeley's Administrative Services group (BAS) provides a good example of the strategic values model (see Figure 8-9).[5] BAS delivers the full range of administrative services that support the school's academic mission and campus priorities. The departments in BAS include physical plant, public safety, health and counseling, human

Figure 8-9 The UC Berkeley Administrative Services (BAS) Strategy Map

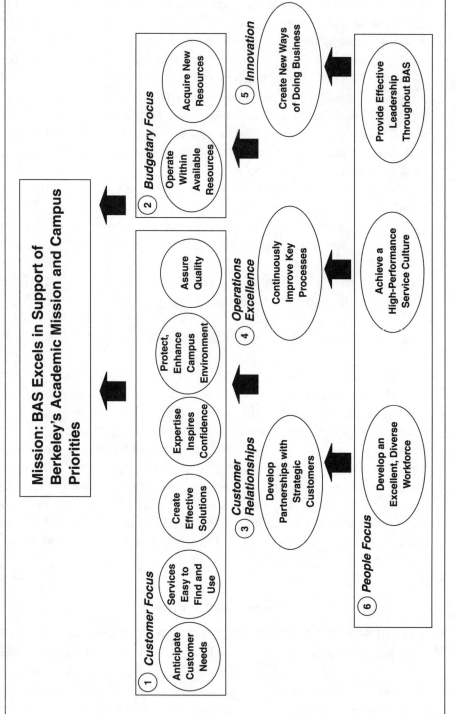

Mission: BAS Excels in Support of Berkeley's Academic Mission and Campus Priorities

1 *Customer Focus*

- Anticipate Customer Needs
- Services Easy to Find and Use
- Create Effective Solutions
- Expertise Inspires Confidence
- Protect, Enhance Campus Environment
- Assure Quality

2 *Budgetary Focus*

- Operate Within Available Resources
- Acquire New Resources

3 *Customer Relationships*

- Develop Partnerships with Strategic Customers

4 *Operations Excellence*

- Continuously Improve Key Processes

5 *Innovation*

- Create New Ways of Doing Business

6 *People Focus*

- Develop an Excellent, Diverse Workforce
- Achieve a High-Performance Service Culture
- Provide Effective Leadership Throughout BAS

resources, printing, and recreation. In effect, BAS manages the equivalent of a small city.

As a support organization, BAS pursues a customer solution strategy. The customer value proposition emphasizes characteristics of effective partnerships such as "anticipate customer needs," "create effective solutions," and "expertise inspires confidence." Financial objectives reflect the realities of performing within the constraints of academic budgets. BAS selected three strategic themes for its internal perspective themes:

Strategic Theme	Process
Develop customer partnerships	Customer relationships
Continuously improve key processes	Operations excellence
Create new ways of doing business	Innovation

The BAS learning and growth perspective, referred to as "people focus," had three strategic objectives:

- Develop an excellent, diverse workforce
- Achieve a high-performance service culture
- Provide effective leadership throughout BAS

BAS's human resource team translated the six customer focus objectives from its strategy map into profiles of the strategic values required to support each objective (see Figure 8-10). For each value, the project team defined a more detailed set of objectives. "Assure quality," for example, implies that the individual "follows through on commitments," "holds self accountable," "concentrates on problem solving—not blame," and "ensures the highest quality." Having defined these strategic values at the executive level, BAS used a cascading process to communicate the values to the next level of management. Discussing, clarifying, and internalizing the new values began the process of transforming BAS's traditional administrative approach and service culture. Once assimilated at managerial levels, the strategic values will be communicated and incorporated into individual goals and performance plans at every level. This will provide a point of reference for 360-degree feedback and strategic readiness reporting.

Figure 8-10 The BAS Strategic Readiness Report

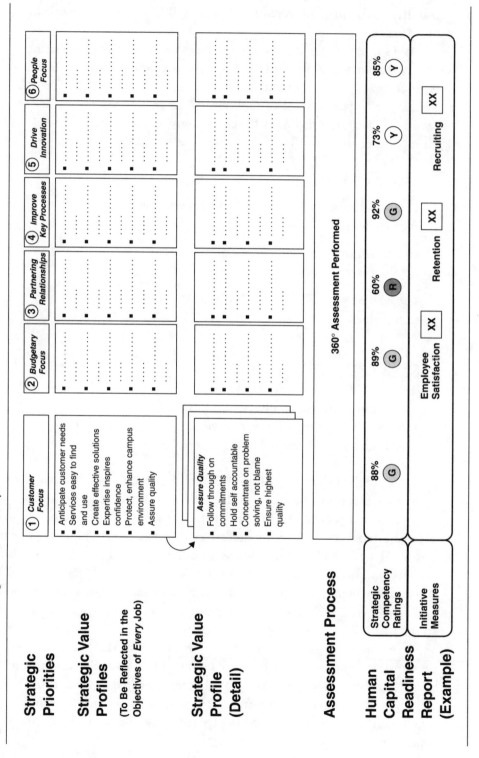

Strategic Priorities

| ① Customer Focus | ② Budgetary Focus | ③ Partnering Relationships | ④ Improve Key Processes | ⑤ Drive Innovation | ⑥ People Focus |

Strategic Value Profiles

(To Be Reflected in the Objectives of *Every* Job)

Strategic Value Profile (Detail)

Customer Focus
- Anticipate customer needs
- Services easy to find and use
- Create effective solutions
- Expertise inspires confidence
- Protect, enhance campus environment
- Assure quality

Assure Quality
- Follow through on commitments
- Hold self accountable
- Concentrate on problem solving, not blame
- Ensure highest quality

Assessment Process

360° Assessment Performed

Human Capital Readiness Report (Example)

	Customer Focus	Budgetary Focus	Partnering Relationships	Improve Key Processes	Drive Innovation	People Focus
Strategic Competency Ratings	88% Ⓖ	89% Ⓖ	60% Ⓡ	92% Ⓖ	73% Ⓨ	85% Ⓨ

Initiative Measures				
	Employee Satisfaction XX	Retention XX		Recruiting XX

SUMMARY

Human capital must be aligned to the strategy if the organization is to gain value from its employee competencies. The strategy map identifies the critical few internal processes that create differentiation for the strategy. These processes determine the focused set of strategic job families that enable the critical internal processes to be performed at an exceptional level. HR executives can then develop competency profiles for the strategic job families and apply standard assessment approaches to measure human capital readiness and strategic competency gaps. The gaps set the agenda for human capital development programs that will increase the organization's strategic human capital readiness.

The approach used by Gray-Syracuse and Chemico focused on investments in employees in the critical few strategic job families. Several of these job families were entirely new to the companies, having been identified while the companies developed the learning and growth perspective for their strategy maps. The strategic values approach used at Berkeley Administrative Services communicates the new customer-focused strategy to the entire workforce, clarifies the new values required for the strategy, and integrates the new values into the performance management process used throughout the organization. Organizations should attempt to build their human capital development programs using both the strategic job family approach for managing strategic human capital development programs in a focused and urgent manner, and the strategic values approach, for making strategy everyone's job.

The case study following this chapter discusses National City Corporation, a bank that had to transform and align its employees to become customer champions if its new customer-focused strategy were to succeed.

NOTES

1. John Bronson, speaking at the Balanced Scorecard Collaborative Conference on Human Capital, Naples, Florida, 27 February 2002.
2. Reported by Kimberlee Williams, Balanced Scorecard Collaborative Human Capital Working Group, 10 September 2002.
3. Several other job families supported this process, but the joint venture program manager had the greatest impact on its success or failure.
4. The remaining three programs (applied research, value-added customer partnerships, and order fulfillment) were extensions of mature processes that were being refocused and refined.
5. As the strategy maps of BAS evolves, the "people focus" will also change, ensuring that human capital will remain aligned with the overall strategy. To view the most current BAS strategy map, see <http://bas.chance.berkeley.edu/BASexcels/index.htm>.

CASE STUDY

NATIONAL CITY CORPORATION

Background

Founded in 1845, National City is the ninth-largest bank in the United States, employing more than 33,000 people. The company is headquartered in Cleveland, Ohio, and operates in Ohio, Pennsylvania, Indiana, Kentucky, Illinois, and Michigan. With more than 1,200 retail branches, its primary businesses include commercial and retail banking, consumer finance, asset management, mortgage financing and servicing, and card processing. It is a $100 billion financial holding company. In 2001, National City's earnings per share were the highest in its history. National City has been profitable every year, frequently reflecting double-digit return on equity.

The Strategy

National City was going through a culture shift as an organization, putting more emphasis on the needs of its customers. It was also focusing on service quality, revenue generation, and cost control. To bring more focus to its customers, National City created its "customer champion" brand promise, which states: "National City cares about doing what's right for our customers."

The human resource organization had a unique opportunity to address brand in terms of both corporate support and establishing brand standards to its internal customers. National City's HR organization faced the challenge that many HR organizations face: how to align the HR organization's strategy with the enterprise-wide business strategy. The Balanced Scorecard was selected as a tool that the HR organization would use to articulate its strategy and measure its performance. The company wanted to start its Balanced Scorecard effort in HR because of the priority to ensure the strategic readiness of the workforce to execute the brand promise.

The Strategy Map

A core team was formed to work in partnership with the HR leadership team to translate the strategic plan into a strategy map (see Figure 8-11). The team found many different perceptions and expectations of the HR strategy. With more than 300 people in HR, it was critical to have a consistent way of describing the human resource organization's strategy. For HR to be a strategic partner with the business units, it needed to proactively address business unit needs. Shelley Seifert, executive vice president of human resources, stated that HR was transforming itself from a transaction-oriented, reactive mode to a value driven, proactive one.

Historically HR has not always been at the forefront of thinking about the organization's *financial results*. At the top of National City's HR strategy map is the objective to increase National City's shareholder value. HR is only one of many contributors to shareholder value, but Seifert wanted all HR professionals to have this financial objective clearly in their minds. In order to achieve this objective, HR needs to be more efficient and effective to deliver financial results. The supporting objectives are to enable net income growth and maximize the return on investment in people. The philosophy is that by strategically investing in human capital, financial returns will follow.

From a *customer perspective,* the team wanted to reach out to the internal customers of HR. The customer value proposition articulated in the strategy map reflects the views of customers from a bank teller to a senior vice president. The customer perspective is divided into two customer segments: business partners and employees. These two customers have different needs, and HR needs to provide a different service to each. For example, a business partner needs HR to be a trusted partner and adviser, and an employee is looking for quality service.

The *internal process* objectives are organized in four strategic themes:

- Recruit the best and brightest
- Drive a high-performance culture that enables success
- Deliver customer-centric communication
- Provide consistent high-quality service

"Recruit the best and the brightest" is a core part of National City's customer champion brand promise. A key strategic objective for HR is to hire

Figure 8-11 National City HR Strategy Map

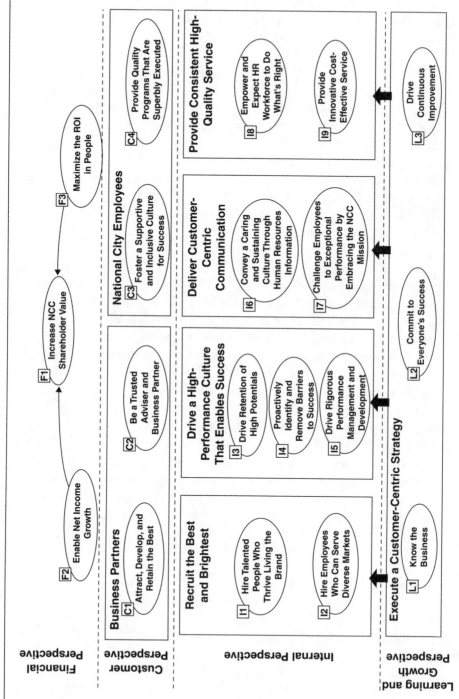

Financial Perspective

F2 Enable Net Income Growth

F1 Increase NCC Shareholder Value

F3 Maximize the ROI in People

Customer Perspective

Business Partners

C1 Attract, Develop, and Retain the Best

C2 Be a Trusted Adviser and Business Partner

National City Employees

C3 Foster a Supportive and Inclusive Culture for Success

C4 Provide Quality Programs That Are Superbly Executed

Internal Perspective

Recruit the Best and Brightest

I1 Hire Talented People Who Thrive Living the Brand

I2 Hire Employees Who Can Serve Diverse Markets

Drive a High-Performance Culture That Enables Success

I3 Drive Retention of High Potentials

I4 Proactively Identify and Remove Barriers to Success

I5 Drive Rigorous Performance Management and Development

Deliver Customer-Centric Communication

I6 Convey a Caring and Sustaining Culture Through Human Resources Information

I7 Challenge Employees to Exceptional Performance by Embracing the NCC Mission

Provide Consistent High-Quality Service

I8 Empower and Expect HR Workforce to Do What's Right

I9 Provide Innovative Cost-Effective Service

Learning and Growth Perspective

L1 Know the Business

Execute a Customer-Centric Strategy

L2 Commit to Everyone's Success

L3 Drive Continuous Improvement

talented people who thrive living the brand. HR is taking the leadership role in ensuring that the right people are being hired for a customer-focused culture. The second theme, to drive a high-performance culture that enables success, is essential to drive retention of employees. This strategic theme also addresses the need for rigorous performance management and the need to focus on developing employees. Delivering customer-centric communication will be a key differentiator for HR. Corporate communications, a part of the HR organization, must shape the way employees view National City's culture. The communications team is helping to communicate the direction of the organization and HR's role in executing National City's strategy. The final theme addresses the need for consistent high-quality service, which is at the core of any good HR strategy. Many HR organizations realize that getting the basics done right will go a long way when you are shifting to become a strategic partner. Business partners and employees expect high-quality service from HR.

The *learning and growth perspective* has an overall theme for HR employees to execute a customer-centric strategy. The three key objectives are: know the business, commit to everyone's success, and drive continuous improvement.

Anecdote

Following the development of the strategy map, National City began collecting measurement data that communicate the performance of its Balanced Scorecard. National City reports on its HR Balanced Scorecard monthly; the leadership team meets to discuss the results and make strategic decisions based on the results.

The Balanced Scorecard process has also provided a new platform for communicating within HR. National City implemented a multipronged communication strategy, in which the executive team conducted town hall meetings and quarterly video conferences and developed an intranet site. They called their communication campaign the "Road to Bestville." During this time they not only communicated HR's Balanced Scorecard initiatives, but they also engaged all 350 HR employees to identify their own personal objectives that tie to the strategy map.

According to Seifert:

All HR employees now have a direct line of sight between their responsibilities and corporate goals. This improved clarity provides a unifying focus and strengthens the ability of the HR organization to add measurable value to the corporation. We believe that HR plays a critical role in maximizing the value of human capital at National City, and the Balanced Scorecard provides us with a useful tool to fulfill that mission.

Further amplifying National City's experience, Paul Clark, executive vice president of institutional management, states:

> *A critical ingredient in this effort has been the development of metrics, the Scorecard, to identify issues to resolve and to measure progress in our HR effort. The Scorecard provides numbers that create a common language for our leadership to communicate. The Scorecard helps us measure output, which, after all, is what it's all about. The Scorecard for HR is a lot like any line of business's P&L—you shouldn't manage HR without a Scorecard.*

Case prepared by Cassandra Frangos of Balanced Scorecard Collaborative. Our thanks to Shelley Seifert for sharing the National City experience.

CHAPTER NINE

INFORMATION CAPITAL READINESS

INFORMATION CAPITAL (IC) IS the raw material for creating value in the new economy (see Figure 9-1). Information capital, consisting of systems, databases, libraries, and networks, makes information and knowledge available to the organization. Information capital, like human capital, has value only in the context of the strategy. An organization pursuing a low total cost strategy gets the highest returns from information systems that focus on quality, process improvement, and workforce productivity. A customer solutions strategy benefits most from information systems that reveal knowledge about customer preferences and behavior, and that enhance customer contact, service, and retention. And a product leadership strategy requires information capital to enhance the product design and development process through tools such as three-dimensional modeling, virtual prototyping, and CAD/CAM. Thus, information capital, like human capital, must be managed to *align with the strategy*. We use the general framework previously introduced for intangible capital to organize this chapter:

1. Describe information capital
2. Align information capital to the strategy
3. Measure information capital readiness

Figure 9-1 Framework for Describing Information Capital Readiness

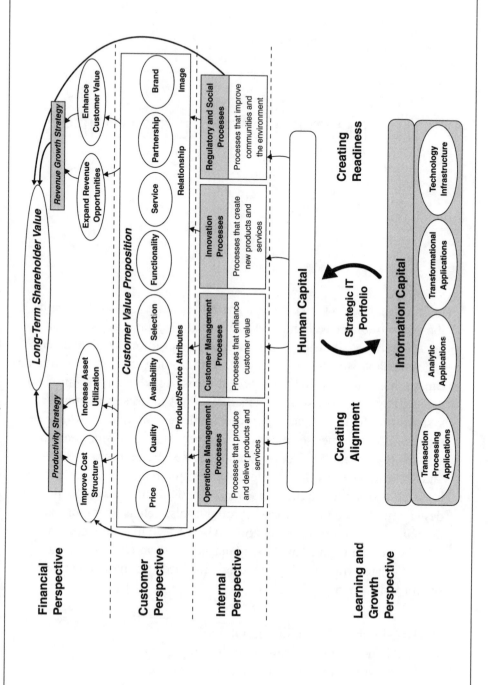

DESCRIBE INFORMATION CAPITAL

The four-level framework, summarized in Figure 9-2, provides a useful taxonomy for describing information capital.[1] Information capital consists of two components: technology infrastructure and information capital applications. Technology infrastructure includes both technology, such as central mainframes and communication networks, and managerial expertise, such as standards, disaster planning, and security, required to enable effective delivery and use of information capital applications. An information capital application, a package of information, knowledge, and technology, builds upon the technology infrastructure to support the organization's key internal processes for innovation, customer management, operations management, and regulatory and social.

We have identified three categories of information capital applications. A *transaction processing application,* such as an ERP system, automates the basic repetitive transactions of the enterprise. *Analytic applications* promote analysis, interpretation, and sharing of information and knowledge. *Transformational applications* change the prevailing business model of the enterprise. Transformational applications can themselves be either transactional, such as the interactive system used by Levi Strauss to custom tailor jeans to the individual customer, or analytic,

Figure 9-2 Describing Information Capital

Information Capital Category	Description
Transformational Applications	Systems and networks that change the prevailing business model of the enterprise
Analytic Applications	Systems and networks that promote analysis, interpretation, and sharing of information/knowledge
Technology Infrastructure	The shared technology and managerial expertise required to enable effective delivery and use of Information Capital applications
Transaction Processing Applications	Systems that automate the basic repetitive transactions of the enterprise

such as the real-time system used by the Home Shopping Network to measure the "profits per second" being generated by merchandise. Transformational applications are distinguished by their significant potential impact on strategic objectives and the degree of organization change they require for the benefits to be delivered.

Taken together, technology infrastructure and information capital applications make up the *information capital portfolio*. Executives must understand how to plan, set priorities for, and manage an information capital portfolio that supports their strategy.

As with objectives for human capital, the strategy map provides the point of reference for information capital objectives. Take the example illustrated in Figure 9-3. The internal perspective of a strategy map identifies strategic objectives for innovation, customer management, and operations management processes.[2]

The information capital portfolio to support *innovation* processes might include (1) transactional level CAD/CAM and product development pipeline management systems, (2) an analytic level knowledge management system (KMS) for sharing best-practice information among product designers, and (3) a transformation-level interactive system that allows customers to directly design their own products (for example, Dell's customer interface). This entire portfolio of technology applications supports innovation processes.

The information capital portfolio to support *customer management* processes typically begins at the transactional level with a customer relationship management (CRM) system. CRM software provides a range of applications, including sales force automation, order processing, and call center management. Analytic level applications provide customer profitability measurement and data mining capabilities for customer segmentation. A transformational application could be call center sales support protocols such as those used by Lands' End to identify customer buying patterns and to assist call center operators in their sales processes.

Supply-chain management (SCM) and manufacturing requirements planning (MRP) are typical of the transactional systems that support *operations management processes*. These applications integrate a range of systems such as inventory control, order processing, purchasing, and capacity planning which were previously fragmented. Analytic level applications might include systems to analyze product and process quality, activity and product costs, lead and cycle times, and complaint analysis.

Figure 9-3 Typical Information Capital Portfolio Applications

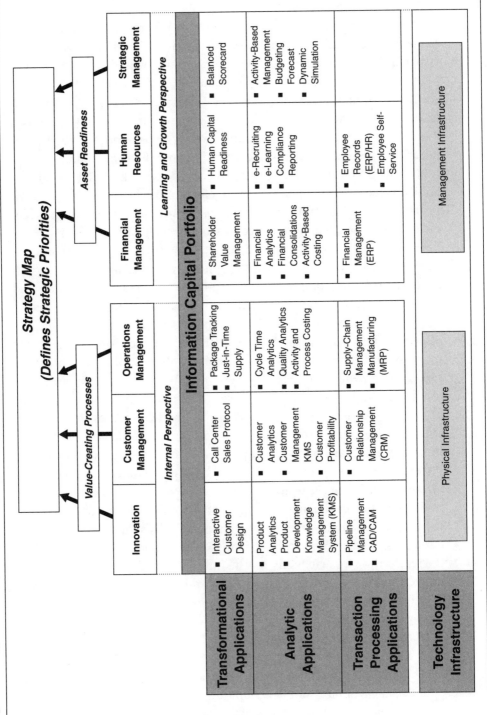

Package tracking applications, like those introduced by UPS and FedEx, have been transformational.

The staff groups that manage the strategic readiness of other intangible assets, and the organization's tangible and financial assets, also require information capital. These groups would include finance, human resources, and strategic planning. New levels of potential effectiveness have been introduced to financial management through the transaction-level ERP systems introduced in most organizations during the 1990s. These transaction-level systems support analytic applications such as activity-based costing and financial analysis, and transformational financial management frameworks such as shareholder value and value-based management. The introduction of ERP systems has had a similar positive impact on human resource management, streamlining employee records and benefits management. Web-based HR systems permit direct employee control of parts of their benefits programs. The ERP systems also permit analytic applications, such as compliance reporting to regulatory agencies, and Web-based recruiting. A major strategic application involves tailored e-learning programs to develop the competencies in strategic job families discussed in Chapter 8. Transformational applications include the program for managing human capital readiness. Strategic planning processes rely on the transaction systems of other processes, integrated through a data warehouse. A host of analytic applications such as activity-based management, forecasting models, scenario planning, and dynamic simulations greatly enhance strategic planning processes. Balanced Scorecard software, embedded in new management reporting systems and providing a strategic agenda for strategic management meetings, is proving transformational.

Information capital applications function only if supported by a foundation of *technology infrastructure* that is typically shared across multiple applications. Peter Weill and Marianne Broadbent have provided much of the recent thought leadership on this subject. Based on their research on more than 100 businesses around the world, they identify ten categories of infrastructure that must be actively managed by the enterprise (see Figure 9-4).[3]

Physical infrastructure includes:

- *Applications infrastructure* (shared applications such as e-mail, Internet capability, mobile computing)
- *Communications management* (broadband networks, intranets)

Figure 9-4 Components of IT Infrastructure: The Weill/Broadbent Model

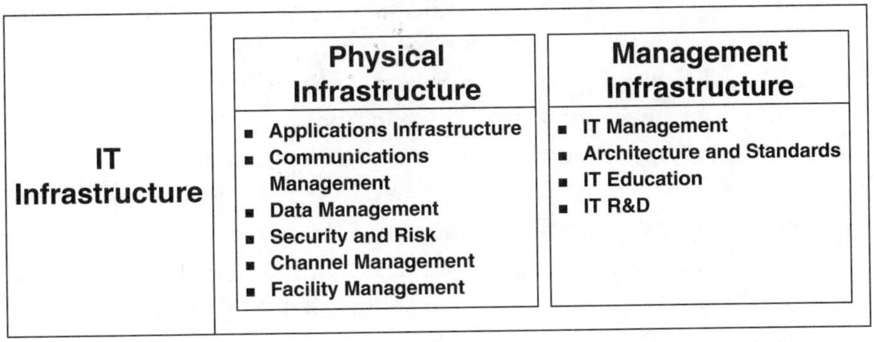

IT Infrastructure	Physical Infrastructure	Management Infrastructure
	■ Applications Infrastructure ■ Communications Management ■ Data Management ■ Security and Risk ■ Channel Management ■ Facility Management	■ IT Management ■ Architecture and Standards ■ IT Education ■ IT R&D

- *Data management* (centralized data warehouses)
- *Security and risk* (security policies, disaster planning, firewalls)
- *Channel management* (Web sites, call centers)
- *Facility management* (large-scale mainframes, server farms, LANs)

The *management infrastructure* includes:

- *IT management* (IS planning, service-level agreements, supplier negotiations)
- *Architecture and standards* (for data, communication, technology, and so on)
- *IT education* (training, management education)
- *IT R&D* (emerging technologies)

Technology infrastructure investments typically consume nearly 60 percent of IT expenditures. But this spending can rarely be directly associated with tangible benefits. The benefits arise from the applications that sit on top of IT infrastructure (or from avoiding losses from theft, disasters, and security violations). Executives must appreciate how investments in infrastructure enable the IT applications portfolio, and also how different infrastructures impose limits or create options for IT applications. For example, without a global networking capability, companies may not be able to develop knowledge management systems that allow professionals around the world to share experience and expertise.

ALIGN INFORMATION CAPITAL TO THE STRATEGY

Executives must ensure that their information capital applications portfolio aligns to the strategic internal processes on their organizations' strategy maps. Several organizations have achieved success by running a series of workshops after their initial strategy maps have been developed. In each workshop, participants develop an integrated information capital plan for a strategic theme on the strategy map, such as *provide rapid response* or *understand customer segments*. Workshop attendees come from line organization units, as well as from the HR and IT organizations. In this way, the expertise of the IT professionals, as well as that of other specialists, is brought to bear on the information capital required for each component of the strategy. The results from these workshops are communicated back to the various organizations that have to implement the plan.

Recall that Consumer Bank, introduced in Chapter 7 (see Figure 7-4), was pursuing a customer solutions strategy based on building personal relationships between its customers and its financial planners (see Figure 9-5). For the *cross-sell* process in the customer management theme, the workshop team identified a customer portfolio self-management system as a transformational application that would enable customers to analyze and manipulate their own financial plans. The workshop team identified an analytic application for cross-selling—a customer profitability system—and a transaction application—an integrated customer file. The *understand customer segments* process shared a need for a customer profitability system, as well as a separate customer feedback system for direct market research. The workshop could not identify any transformational application for this process.

The *shift to appropriate channel* process required a strong foundation of transaction systems, including a packaged CRM software suite, with modules for lead management, order management, and sales force automation. For the *provide rapid response* process in the operations management theme, participants identified a transformational application, customer self-help, and an analytic application, a best-practice community knowledge management system for sharing successful sales techniques among telemarketers. The *minimize problems* process required an analytic application service quality analysis to identify problems; and two related transaction level systems, an incident tracking system and a problem management system.

This portfolio of applications required several components of IT infrastructure. Several of the applications were add-on modules to an integrated CRM software package. The workshop designated the IT

Figure 9-5 Strategic Information Capital Portfolio: Consumer Bank

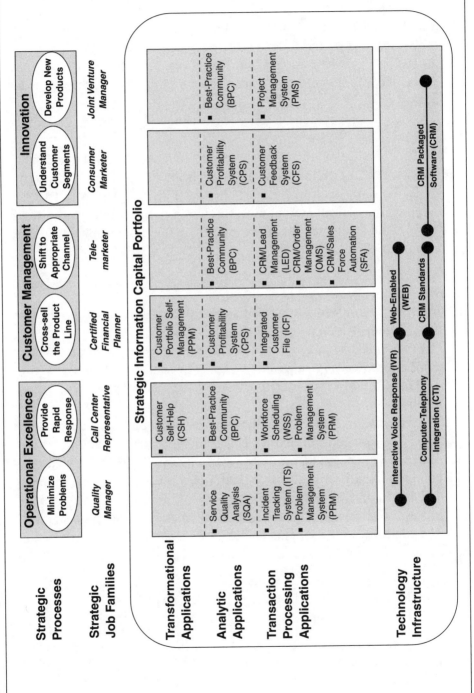

organization as responsible for acquiring, installing, and maintaining the vendor package. The IT organization would also be responsible for Web-enabling several of the applications and integrating these applications into the bank's overall Web site architecture. A new interactive voice response technology, requiring an internal R&D project, was required for the customer self-help application. The IT organization was again identified as the lead organization responsible for ensuring that the new technology would be successfully assimilated. The IT organization would also lead the implementation of computer-telephony integration, a relatively new technology for the bank.

Thus, the IC strategic planning process conducted by the bank defined an IC portfolio with fourteen unique applications and five IT infrastructure projects. By selecting this portfolio of applications and infrastructure based on the critical internal processes in the entity's strategy map, executives could be assured that the company's information capital would be aligned to its strategy.

Allocating Resources for Strategic IC Investments

Investment in information technology has been increasing steadily for more than thirty years. Yet 90 percent of the sizeable annual expenditures in a typical IT budget are locked into operating and maintaining existing applications. Only 10 percent is typically available for discretionary investment. But it is this discretionary IT investment that creates strategic alignment.

In Figure 9-5, we identified the set of information capital applications and IT infrastructure projects needed to support the strategy at Consumer Bank. The list of projects is plausible and defensible, but each requires an explicit investment of money and people to acquire, develop, and install the software. The creativity of the IT strategic planning process must coexist with the realities of the organization's economics. The guidelines for developing an information capital investment strategy, illustrated in Figure 9-6, must address:

- The overall level of investment in new information capital projects
- The desired mix of investment by strategic process
- The desired mix of investment by information capital category

Recent benchmarking studies indicate that the typical organization spends approximately 4 percent of its revenue on information capital–related activities.[4] This number varies considerably by industry; financial services companies spend 7.0 percent, manufacturing companies

Figure 9-6 Developing the Information Capital Investment Strategy

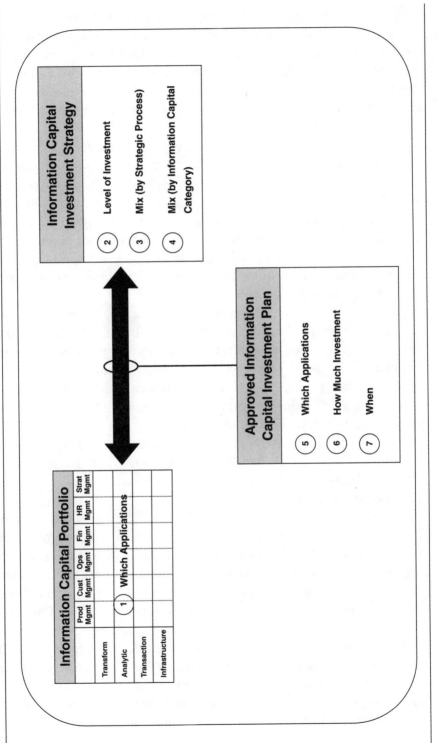

spend 1.7 percent, and retailing companies spend 1.0 percent of sales on information capital. Of this total amount, we have already noted that approximately 90 percent is not discretionary, since it must support the operation and maintenance of applications and infrastructure installed in the past. Companies should, however, be vigilant to improve the efficiency of existing systems and to remove applications that have become obsolete.

Discretionary spending supports the new information capital applications and projects that are required for the strategy. Companies can certainly spend too little on information capital and put the organization at risk. Advances in information technology are still the driving force behind the new economy. With the cost of producing chips continuing to drop by 50 percent about every twenty-one months, new applications and uses continue to emerge.[5] For example, technology breakthroughs in mobile and wireless computing will likely have a major impact on all sectors of the economy in the near future.

At the other extreme, organizations can also spend too much on information capital applications and projects. To capture the full potential benefits, each software investment must be accompanied by significant organizational change and development of new human capital competencies. Since organizations can absorb only a limited amount of change in a given period of time, attempting to develop too much new informational capital quickly will cause much of the new investments to be wasted. Surveys show that 70 percent of organizations that introduce expensive, comprehensive CRM software packages cannot show results, primarily because the software investments were not linked to change management initiatives.[6]

Spending on new information capital applications reflects two underlying phenomena: the replacement of obsolete systems with state-of-the-art technology (such as ERP systems), and the application of totally new technology to new applications (such as e-commerce). Both replacement and new applications will continue in the foreseeable future, so companies need strategic top-down guidelines for their investments in new information capital applications. By way of analogy, investors often evaluate an enterprise's innovation capabilities by comparing R&D investment levels to peer-group benchmarks. Companies such as Intel, in rapidly changing, technology-driven industries, spend 12 percent to 15 percent of their sales each year on R&D, whereas traditional manufacturing companies, such as Ingersoll-Rand, in more stable, slower moving industries, spend only 2 percent of sales on R&D. Our experience with information capital investments in new applications suggests that spending less than 5 percent (of total information capital spending) on R&D is probably below the critical mass, and 15 percent is at the upper limit that can be absorbed by the organization. Thus, new information capital investments should represent between 5 percent and 15 percent of total information capital spending.

The second guideline for information capital investment planning determines the investment mix between technology infrastructure and information capital applications. Figure 9-7 identifies the benchmarks developed by Weill and Broadbent in their multicompany research. The average firm commits 58 percent of its information capital spending to IT infrastructure with roughly equal percentages (12 percent, 16 percent, and 14 percent) in the three application categories. An organization focused on a *cost-reduction strategy* will invest considerably less in infrastructure (42 percent), considerably more in transaction processing applications (40 percent), and less in transformational applications (5 percent). An organization pursuing a strategy that requires *flexibility and agility*—to accelerate bringing new products to the market or to promote cross-selling—shifts funding from transaction processing applications (11 percent) to infrastructure (58 percent). Overall, agility-focused companies spend above the industry average on information capital, while cost-reduction motivated companies, not surprisingly, spend 10 percent to 20 percent below industry averages on information capital. These benchmarks provide reference points for developing an investment strategy for information capital.

As an illustrative example, let's return to Consumer Bank's desired information capital portfolio as shown in Figure 9-8, part A (see Figure 9-5 for the full description of the three-letter acronyms in this figure). Funding all potential projects in the portfolio would consume 20 percent of total information capital spending, above the high side of the recommended investment range. The investment table (Figure 9-8, part B) reviews three alternatives: low investment (5 percent of total information capital spending), moderate investment (10 percent), and high investment (15 percent). The moderate investment requires cutting the proposed application list in half, with the remaining half deferred to a subsequent year. In this case, the spending constraint enforces a discipline to conservatively manage the rate of change. The moderate investment scenario has a heavy investment in transaction processing applications (50 percent) and infrastructure (30 percent), reflecting an emphasis on building

Figure 9-7 Benchmark Economics of the Information Capital Portfolio: The Weill/Broadbent Research

Information Capital	Typical Source of Value	Typical Budget Mix	Cost Reduction Focused	Balanced Cost and Agility	Flexibility and Agility Focused
Transformational Applications	Improved speed to market or premium pricing results in higher revenue per employee	14%	5%	15%	17%
Analytical Applications	Provides information to manage the enterprise. Particularly important in information-intense industries (customer information, product quality)	16%	13%	20%	14%
Transaction Processing Applications	Primary focus is on cost reduction	12%	40%	15%	11%
IT Infrastructure	Creates business flexibility and integration, fosters cross-selling, new product introduction	58%	42%	50%	58%
Total Information Capital Spending	Level of Spending (IT/Revenue) All Industries 4.1% Financial 7.0% Manufacturing 1.7% Retail 1.0%		Total Information Capital Spending 10–20% Below Industry Average	At Industry Average	Total Information Capital Spending 10–25% Above Industry Average

Source: P. Weill and M. Broadbent, *Leveraging the New Infrastructure* (Boston: Harvard Business School Press, 2000), 64.

Figure 9-8 Consumer Bank Information Capital Portfolio/Investment Strategy

A. Information Capital Investment Portfolio (Candidates)

Category	Strategic Information Capital Portfolio						Total Information Capital Investment
	Product Management	Customer Management	Operations Management	Financial Management	HR Management	Strategy Management	
Transformational Applications		PPM	CSH	SVA	HCR	BSC	$WWW
Analytic Applications	CPS BPC	CPS BPC	SQA BPC			ABC	$XXX
Transaction Processing Applications	CRM/CFS PMS	CRM/ICF CRM/LED CRM/SFA CRM/OMS	ITS WSS PRM				$YYY
IT Infrastructure	Physical • CRM • WEB • CTI		Management • IVR (R & D) • CRM Standards				$ZZZ

Total Investment in New Information Capital — $XYZ

New Information Capital Investment (% of Total) — 20%

Total Spend (Information Capital/Revenue) — 6.6%

B. Information Capital Investment Strategy

Category	Low Investment	Moderate Investment	High Investment	Benchmark (Spending Mix)
Transformational Applications	–	10%	+	14%
Analytic Applications	–	10%	+	16%
Transaction Processing Applications	–	50%	+	12%
IT Infrastructure	–	30%	+	58%
Total Investment in New Information Capital	.25XYZ	.5XYZ	.75XYZ	
New Information Capital Investment (% of Total)	5%	10%	15%	
Total Spend (Information Capital/Revenue)	5.7%	6.0%	6.3%	6.0%

out the suite of CRM applications. Many of the strategic processes require different modules of the CRM software. If more funds were available, more investment would be made in the transformational and analytic applications. Though no absolute guidelines or benchmarks exist, the interplay between the information capital investment strategy and the information capital portfolio allow executives to examine the cost/benefits tradeoffs, eventually allowing an economically viable strategy for information capital investments to emerge.

MEASURE INFORMATION CAPITAL READINESS

The strategic readiness of the information capital applications and infrastructure is the most meaningful measure of the value of the organization's information capital. As with human capital strategic readiness, information capital strategic readiness measures the degree of preparedness of the organization's information capital to support the enterprise's strategy.

One can contemplate a spectrum of measurement approaches for the information capital portfolio. The easiest and most frequently used approach is a simple numerical indicator that identifies the status of each application. Figure 9-9 illustrates a six-level scheme. Levels 1 and 2 are considered normal and operational. Levels 3 and 4 represent new applications that have been identified and funded, and on which action is under way. The capability does not yet exist, but development programs are active to close the gap. Levels 5 and 6 represent the problem areas. Applications are needed to support the strategy, but no action has yet been taken to create and deliver the capability.

Managers responsible for the information capital development programs provide the subjective judgments for the simple measurement system illustrated in Figure 9-9. The CIO maintains ultimate responsibility for the integrity of the reported numbers. The measurement system focuses attention on the development process to ensure that the best efforts are being made to create strategic readiness. Figure 9-10 shows how the readiness measures of individual applications and infrastructure programs at Consumer Bank get aggregated into a portfolio status report. Managers viewing such a report can determine, at a glance, the strategic readiness of the organization's information capital, as well as the areas in which more focus is needed. The report provides an excellent tool for monitoring a portfolio of information capital development programs.

Figure 9-9 Measuring the Strategic Readiness of Information Capital

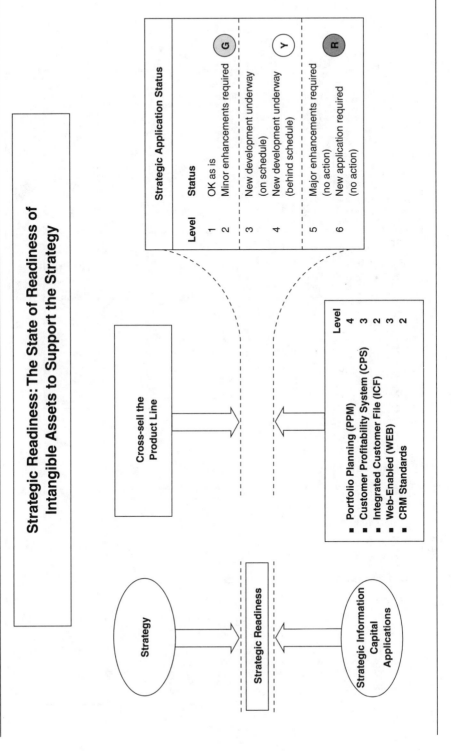

Strategic Readiness: The State of Readiness of Intangible Assets to Support the Strategy

Figure 9-10 Information Capital Readiness at Consumer Bank

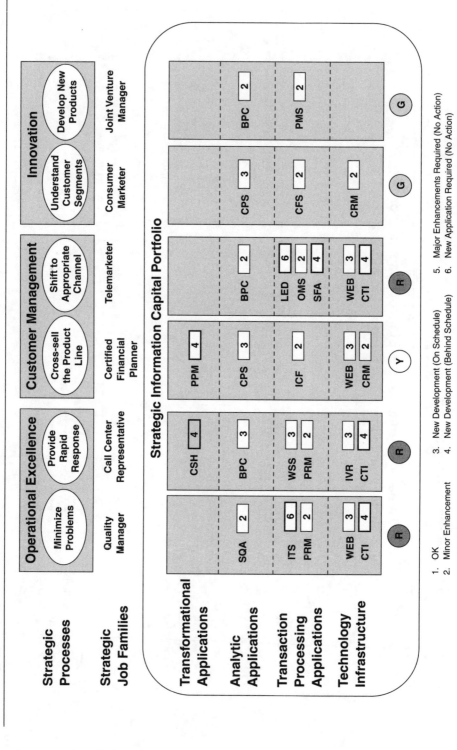

1. OK
2. Minor Enhancement
3. New Development (On Schedule)
4. New Development (Behind Schedule)
5. Major Enhancements Required (No Action)
6. New Application Required (No Action)

At the other end of the spectrum, many sophisticated IT organizations use more quantitative, objective assessments of their application portfolios. They might survey users to assess their satisfaction with each application. They can perform financial analysis to determine the operating and maintenance costs of each application. Some conduct technical audits to assess the underlying quality of the code, and the operability, documentation, and frequency of failure of each application. From this profile, an organization can build strategies for managing the portfolio of existing information capital assets, just as one would manage a portfolio of physical assets such as machinery or automobiles. For example, applications with high levels of maintenance can be streamlined, applications with high operating costs can be optimized, and applications with high levels of user dissatisfaction can be replaced. This more comprehensive approach is particularly effective for managing a portfolio of applications that are already operational.

SUMMARY

The measurement approaches proposed in this chapter create a new mindset for managing the development and deployment of information capital. The focus shifts from evaluating information capital performance by cost and reliability statistics to evaluation based on strategic alignment: measuring how information capital contributes to the organization's strategic objectives, particularly the critical, differentiating processes identified in the internal perspective of the organization's strategy map. Information capital must be managed like an asset, with its value measured by how it contributes to the organization's strategy for creating competitive advantage. The portfolio alignment techniques described in this chapter provide a practical approach for aligning information capital assets to the enterprise's strategic objectives.

The case study following this chapter describes the strategy map for the information technology group of the T. Rowe Price asset management company. The project team used the strategy map to align the company's IT strategy for delivering enhanced capabilities to the line organization.

NOTES

1. For an overview of useful information technology taxonomies, see "Using Measurements to Demonstrate the Business Value of IT" (Stamford, CT: Gartner Group, 2000), ESR #5610.

2. Regulatory and social processes, not illustrated here, also require information capital to drive their performance.

3. Peter Weill and Marianne Broadbent, *Leveraging the New Infrastructure: How Market Leaders Capitalize on the New Information Technology* (Boston: Harvard Business School Press, 2000).

4. Ibid., 38.

5. B. Schendler, "Intel's $10 Billion Gamble," *Fortune*, 11 November 2002, 98.

6. Scott Nelson, "Seven Reasons Why CRM Fails," Gartner Group Report 0702-0117-103570; D. Rigby, F. Reichheld, and P. Schefter, "Avoid the Four Perils of CRM," *Harvard Business Review* (February 2002).

CASE STUDY

T. ROWE PRICE

Background

T. Rowe Price (TRPA), a Baltimore-based asset management firm, is a leading provider of investment services for individual investors and corporate retirement programs, with $156.3 billion total assets under management at the close of 2001. TRPA serves as investment adviser for more than eight million institutional and individual accounts in the T. Rowe Price family of no-load mutual funds and other investment portfolios. With more than 600 employees and contractors and annual expenditures exceeding $100 million, T. Rowe Price Investment Technologies, Inc. (TRPIT), a wholly owned subsidiary of TRPA, provides mission-critical information and technology management services to business units in the T. Rowe Price enterprise.

The Situation

In late 2000, TRPA articulated an enterprise-wide goal of delivering "world-class service." Although TRPA had a long history of outstanding fund performance, the increasingly crowded market for individual and institutional fund management demanded more. Such giant players as Fidelity Investments and Vanguard reaped huge market share by delivering a constellation of fund choices and technology-powered high-function customer service. TRPA management was determined to defend and grow its market share.

In addition to supporting this enterprise goal, TRPIT faced challenges often seen in enterprise-wide IT organizations: to both deliver and demonstrate the value of technology to its customers, the business units, and to effectively and efficiently prioritize and apply scarce IT resources across the enterprise. In response to these conflicting pressures, senior TRPIT management engaged in an effort to improve the processes by which its own performance measures were selected, consolidated, communicated to stakeholders, and used to inform business decisions. The Balanced Scorecard management framework was selected.

The Strategy

A team of BSC facilitators worked with a small group of leaders inside TRPIT to develop and agree to a list of strategic objectives:

- Demonstrate value to business units
- Gain a shared understanding of TRPIT's strategy at all levels
- Ensure faster, more complete strategy alignment and execution, both within and across business units
- Assess performance and communicate results on a regular basis
- Establish greater accountability
- Evaluate and prioritize initiatives more quickly and effectively
- Enable world-class service

These objectives were communicated often to stakeholders to explain the effort as the TRPIT BSC took form. To develop an understanding of its implicit strategy, the facilitators interviewed key leaders inside TRPIT, as well as in the business units. The list of key shifts necessary for TRPIT's success became the basis for developing the strategy map.

TRPIT Change Agenda

	From	To
T. Rowe Price value proposition	Fund performance	Fund performance *and* customer service
TRPIT role	Tactical support	Strategic partner
TRPIT strategy	Implicit	Explicitly communicated
TRPIT knowledge	Technical competence	Technical competence *and* business knowledge
Sourcing emphasis	TRPIT as primary source	TRPIT as solutions broker
IT cost emphasis	TRPIT recovers costs	TRPIT demonstrates business value
TRPIT culture	Problem analysis and discussion	Solution identification and execution

| Project management | Missed estimates and targets | Shared risk and implications with business unit |
| Workload management | Too many projects | Strategic priorities and resource allocation |

The Strategy Map

Although TRPIT is only one of several contributors to TRPA's overall *financial performance,* enterprise earnings (EBITDA) is shown as TRPIT's primary financial objective on its strategy map (see Figure 9-11). Managing IT expenditures helps to manage fund performance, which is partially the result of fund expenses. Maximizing business unit value creation runs the gamut from attracting fund assets through superior customer service to enabling better investment performance by providing timely information to fund managers.

The four *customer,* or *partner, objectives,* written in the imagined voice of TRPIT's customers (business unit managers), expresses their need for TRPIT to manage and meet expectations for performance on cost and quality of services before the TRPIT organization is seen as a credible partner in using technology in innovative ways to achieve business unit strategy.

The *internal process objectives* organize delivery on the customer objectives around three themes: *operational excellence, business unit alliance, and solutions leadership.* The objective to provide reliable and functional systems is supported by the continuing challenge to develop and manage solutions using a centrally defined set of application and data architectures, hardware platforms, and business processes. Another key objective articulates the fundamental shift from TRPIT's role as the preferred provider to that of an objective broker, seamless integrator, and manager of internally and externally sourced solutions. Increasing TRPIT's understanding of business unit operations is the key foundation for managing relations with business units and contributing to their success. With this understanding, TRPIT is better able to deliver new functionality on schedule, and identify and implement business value-creating solutions, using technology in innovative ways to deliver superior customer service.

Innovation is an undercurrent of TRPIT's three learning and growth objectives. TRPIT's talented people are encouraged to innovate when the culture shifts from valuing problem analysis to recognizing and rewarding solution identification. Another important objective is TRPIT's commitment to create an environment that encourages, empowers, and expects all employees to communicate and lead as appropriate regardless of formal authority and responsibility. Finally, the three learning and growth objectives address the necessity of talented people enabled by leadership and communication in a contribution-oriented culture.

Figure 9-11 T. Rowe Price Investment Technologies Global Business Strategy Map

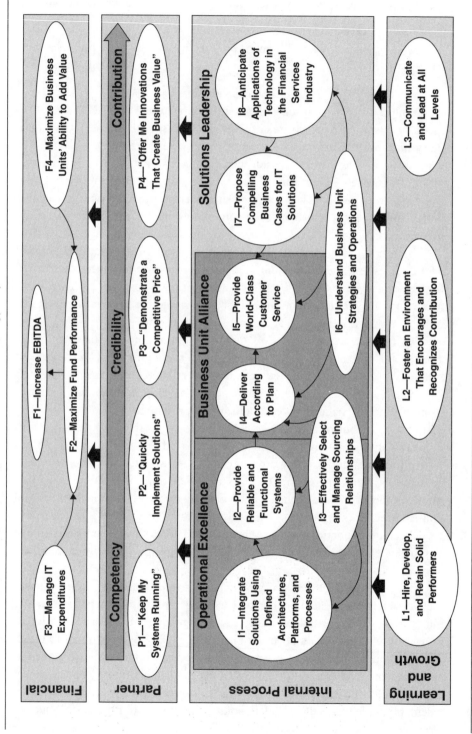

Following development of the strategy map, TRPIT quickly began collecting data and communicating results. In an all-day meeting attended by about forty senior and midlevel managers, TRPIT senior leaders and the enterprise CEO launched a carefully structured communication program that ensured that every member of TRPIT understood the strategy map and how his or her contributions fit into the big picture.

Anecdotes

Using an Excel spreadsheet linked to a PowerPoint presentation, TRPIT quickly developed an interactive quarterly report that enables managers and staff alike to click through each objective to see performance measures, targets, and analysis text. Although the September 11th attacks caused the organization to skip one edition of the report, it has become an important part of the strategic management process in TRPIT. A formal process for evaluating and prioritizing strategic initiatives was instituted, and the BSC resulted in a heightened focus on cost-benefit analysis, standards compliance, accountability for project management, and the contributions of the TRPIT organization. Customer satisfaction surveys were undertaken as part of the scorecard effort, and they provide managers with periodic feedback on TRPIT's progress in enabling business unit performance.

To fulfill the spirit of the P4 objective, "Offer me innovations that create business value," TRPIT's customer advocacy group undertook an effort to work with such TRPA staff organizations as finance, legal, and human resources to identify and map key business processes, understand and prioritize improvement opportunities, and develop technology solutions.

Finally, a tool and discipline for cost-benefit analysis developed by TRPIT in support of its BSC has been adopted and sponsored by the enterprise CFO and has become integral to the initiative budgeting process.

Case prepared by Robert S. Gold of Balanced Scorecard Collaborative and Pam McGinnis of T. Rowe Price. Our thanks to Pam McGinnis and her colleagues for sharing the T. Rowe Price experience.

CHAPTER TEN

ORGANIZATION CAPITAL READINESS

THE PREVIOUS CHAPTERS discussed the development and alignment of two vital intangible assets—human capital and information capital—to strategic internal processes. To complement this alignment of competencies and technologies, executives must also develop organization capital (see Figure 10-1), defined as the *ability of the organization to mobilize and sustain the process of change required to execute the strategy*. Organization capital provides the capability for integration so that individual intangible human and information capital assets, as well as tangible physical and financial assets, are not only aligned to the strategy, but are all integrated and working together to achieve the organization's strategic objectives. An enterprise with high organization capital has a shared understanding of vision, mission, values, and strategy, is strongly led, has created a performance culture around the strategy, and shares knowledge up, down, and across the organization so that everyone works together and in the same direction. Conversely, an enterprise with low organization capital has not succeeded in communicating its priorities and establishing the new culture. The ability to create positive organization capital is one of the best predictors of successful strategy execution.

Most organizations in our research database of strategy maps and Balanced Scorecards identify three to five organization capital objectives in their learning and growth perspective. Typical objectives are "build leaders," "align the workforce," "share knowledge," and "focus on the customer." But setting these objectives is usually an ad hoc and intuitive

Figure 10-1 Framework for Describing Organization Readiness

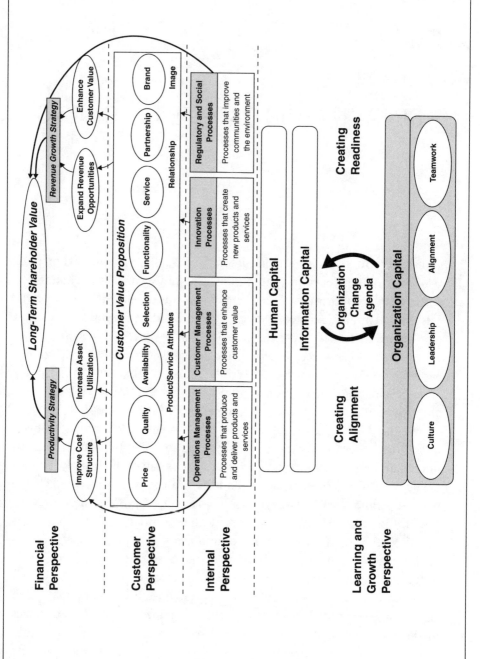

effort. Executives do not have a general framework to focus their thinking on organizational culture and climate, and, in particular, to align it to the strategy. Yet despite lacking such a framework and the considerable diversity taken in their individual approaches, we have identified important common elements used by most. We have synthesized these elements into a new, but still exploratory, framework for describing and measuring organization capital.

Organization capital is typically built upon four components:

1. *Culture:* Awareness and internalization of the mission, vision, and core values needed to execute the strategy
2. *Leadership:* Availability of qualified leaders at all levels to mobilize the organization toward its strategy
3. *Alignment:* Individual, team, and departmental goals and incentives linked to attainment of strategic objectives
4. *Teamwork:* Knowledge with strategic potential shared throughout the organization

The strategy map describes the changes required by a strategy, such as new products, new processes, or new customers. These changes, in turn, define *new behaviors and values* that are required within the workforce. The first step in developing an organization capital strategy is to define the *change agenda* implied by the broader strategy. This change agenda identifies the shifts in organization climate required by the strategy. Figure 10-2 summarizes the change agenda that emerges from the organizations in our database. The objectives fall into two categories: the behavioral changes required to create value for customers and shareholders, and the behavioral changes required to execute the strategy. Three different kinds of behavior changes are consistently highlighted for *value creation*:

1. Focus on the customer
2. Be creative and innovative
3. Deliver results

Four additional behavior changes are associated with *executing strategy:*

1. Understand the mission, strategy, and values
2. Create accountability
3. Communicate openly
4. Work as a team

Figure 10-2 The Organization Change Agenda

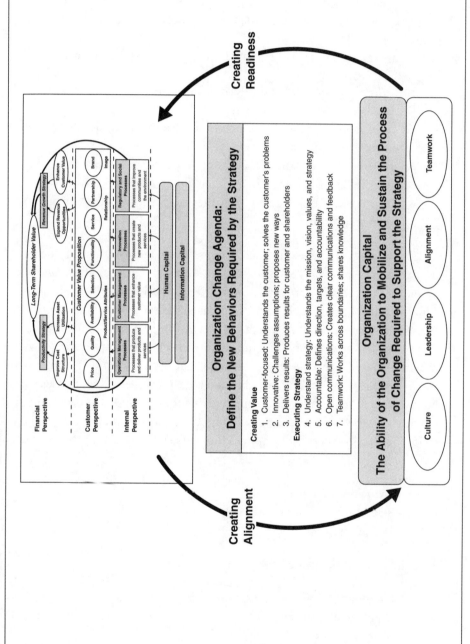

No one organization identifies all seven as its change agenda. Typically, a single organization will identify two to four of these changes for its scorecard. For example, companies in deregulated industries such as utilities or telecommunications place a heavy emphasis on becoming customer-focused and innovative, because these are totally new behaviors for them. Previously their culture was to operate efficiently, avoid risks, and negotiate effectively with regulators so that revenues from their monopoly position would cover their costs. Pharmaceutical companies, long driven by functional and disciplinary capabilities that supported their innovation strategies, now focus on becoming more customer-focused and creating teamwork to share knowledge across the organization. The change agenda should identify the three or four most important behavioral changes required for the new strategy to be implemented.

In Figure 10-3 we present the organization capital objectives of three enterprises. Crown Castle International (CCI) had grown rapidly through acquisitions. Its new strategy was to shift to internally generated growth by enhancing the delivery of value to customers. This shift required extensive change throughout the organization. CCI used all four organization capital objectives:

- Communicate new strategies to employees (Culture)
- Develop leadership and accountability (Leadership)
- Link pay to performance (Alignment)
- Improve global knowledge management (Teamwork)

Ingersoll-Rand (IR), a diversified industrial manufacturer with a broad spectrum of products and brands, wanted to create a new "one-company" culture that would leverage the power of its individual brands to create synergy across the organization. Its overall organization capital goal was expressed as: "leverage the power of our enterprise through dual citizenship." The "dual citizenship" referred to maintaining loyalty both to the individual brand and to IR as a company. The goal would be made operational through three organization capital objectives:

- Exemplify IR guiding principles (Culture)
- Leverage cross-business synergies (Alignment)
- Share best practices (Teamwork)

Media General, a multimedia communications company, introduced a strategy to achieve synergy in its regional (southeastern United States)

Figure 10-3 Profiles of Typical Organization Capital Strategies

Crown Castle

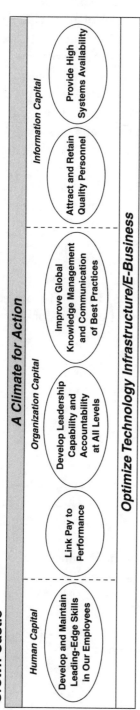

A Climate for Action

Human Capital

Develop and Maintain Leading-Edge Skills in Our Employees

Organization Capital

Link Pay to Performance

Develop Leadership Capability and Accountability at All Levels

Improve Global Knowledge Management and Communication of Best Practices

Information Capital

Attract and Retain Quality Personnel

Provide High Systems Availability

Optimize Technology Infrastructure/E-Business

Ingersoll-Rand

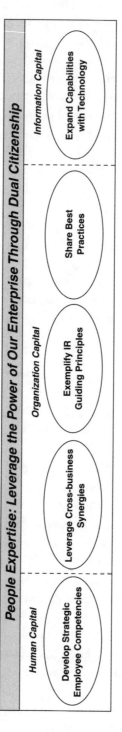

People Expertise: Leverage the Power of Our Enterprise Through Dual Citizenship

Human Capital

Develop Strategic Employee Competencies

Organization Capital

Leverage Cross-business Synergies

Exemplify IR Guiding Principles

Share Best Practices

Information Capital

Expand Capabilities with Technology

Media General

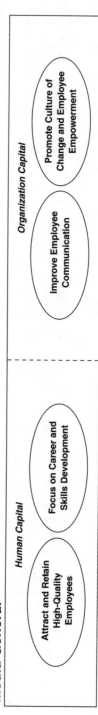

Human Capital

Attract and Retain High-Quality Employees

Focus on Career and Skills Development

Organization Capital

Improve Employee Communication

Promote Culture of Change and Employee Empowerment

market through managing the convergence of print, television, and online media. It expressed the role for organization capital with two objectives:

- Promote a culture of change and empowerment (Culture)
- Improve employee communication (Alignment)

With this framework for organization capital, and examples of its application in practice, we can now examine the four components—culture, leadership, alignment, and teamwork—in more detail.

CULTURE

Culture reflects the predominant attitudes and behaviors that characterize the functioning of a group or organization. "Shaping the culture" is the most often-cited priority in the learning and growth section of our Balanced Scorecard database. Executives generally believe that (1) strategy requires basic changes in the way of conducting business, (2) strategy must be executed through individuals at all levels of the organization and, hence, (3) new attitudes and behaviors—culture—will be required throughout the workforce as a prerequisite for these changes.

Culture can be a barrier or an enabler. Studies have shown that a large percentage of mergers and acquisitions fail to deliver synergies,[1] with a prime reason being "cultural incompatibility."[2] Yet a company such as Cisco is renowned for its ability to integrate newly acquired companies into its culture. IBM Services and EDS have built large, successful outsourcing businesses, while assimilating the staff of outsourced units into their culture. Does culture dictate strategy, or does strategy dictate culture? We believe the latter. In the case of companies such as IBM, EDS, and Cisco, the ability to assimilate new organizations into the company culture is clearly an asset for their growth strategies. Most strategies, however, are not about assimilating newly acquired organizations into an existing culture. They require dramatic changes in a company's existing culture. The leadership team must introduce new attitudes and behaviors in all employees for the new strategy to be successful.

Consider the experience of Information Management Services (IMS), the internal IT department of a major telecommunications company in the early 1990s. With the telecom industry undergoing deregulation, the parent company had converted IMS from a cost center to a profit center. IMS would now have to compete for both internal and external customers. Overnight IMS had to transform itself from a captive supplier of a monopoly customer in a regulated industry—in which cost increases could be recovered in higher rates—to a freestanding unit that would be customer-focused and market-competitive. Years of culture, values, and management approaches had just become obsolete. This radical cultural transformation had to occur in the midst of a technological disruption as well, one that had shifted the platform for information technology from centralized, mainframe-based services to distributed, mobile client-server computing. And customers had changed too; they were now looking to their IT supplier for solutions, not new technology.

Figure 10-4 shows a summary of the business model changes faced by IMS. In the past, IMS could recover its costs through overhead allocations imposed by the corporate parent on operating divisions. Now IMS had to earn profits and acquire business based on competitive fees, responsiveness, and services that added value to customers. A new culture of results delivery had to be established. The implications for cultural change were obvious and dramatic. The new IMS could no longer view its customers as "captives." It had to compete against companies such as EDS, Accenture, and IBM by convincing customers, internal and external, that it was the preferred knowledgeable partner. IMS personnel had to shift from measuring success by delivering system enhancements on-budget and on-schedule to becoming action-oriented, entrepreneurial, and knowledgeable partners with their customers, helping them get bottom-line benefits from IT solutions. These new attitudes and behaviors were fundamental to the success of the strategy. IMS would have to introduce many changes to make this strategy happen. New technologies, new processes, and new skills were required. But unless these changes could be complemented by the cultural shifts from captive supplier to profit-seeking entrepreneur, the strategy was doomed to fail.

We have seen many organizations embark on a cultural shift as dramatic as that faced by IMS. Figure 10-5 provides a cross-section of the most common cultural change objectives these organizations adopted. *Customer focus* was the most frequently identified change, especially in many service companies—such as in the telecommunications, financial, health-care, transportation, energy, and utilities industries—that were now competing in deregulated environments. Employees had to learn that customers created value, not regulators. Organization A, a regional health plan, attempted to create a customer-centric culture for executives by emphasizing "time spent by leadership with customers." Frontline em-

Figure 10-4 Changes Required by the IMS Strategy

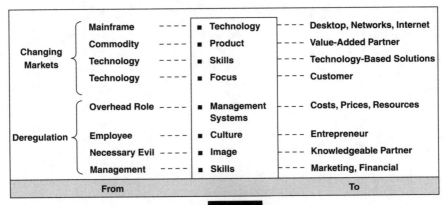

IMS Organization Change Agenda

1. **Customer-Focused:**
   Be viewed by the customer as a knowledgeable partner who understands technology and the customer's business.

2. **Innovative/Risk-Taking:**
   Be an entrepreneur who proposes new ways to the customer and is capable of acting fast.

3. **Deliver Results:**
   Deliver solutions to the customer's problems that create high value at competitive prices.

ployees were already close to customers, but executives also needed to spend time with customers if they were to become more effective leaders. Organization B, a regional bank, wanted its employees to become solutions-oriented, not transactions-oriented, so that they could build closer consulting relations with targeted customers.

While customer focus would seem most appropriate for companies shifting to a total customer solutions strategy, we have also seen objectives that relate to other strategies. For example, companies competing on consistency and reliability will likely want to establish a culture of *quality* and *continuous improvement*. A culture of *continuous cost reduction* would be relevant for companies competing on low total cost, especially with nondifferentiated products. And companies striving to maintain product leadership want to establish a culture of *creativity* and *product innovation*. Even with these alternative cultures, though, employees must still remain

Figure 10-5 Defining and Measuring Cultural Values: Some Examples

Organization Change Agenda	Strategic Objective	Strategic Measure	Organization
Creating Value			
1. Customer-Driven	(A) Create customer-centric culture	■ Employee survey ■ Customer perception survey ■ Time spent by leadership with customers	Health care
	(B) Build an empowered, solutions-focused, community-oriented culture	■ Employee survey	Regional bank
	(C) Foster customer-centric behavior	■ Employee ratings (corporate shopper)	Insurance
2. Innovative/Risk-Taking	(D) Foster a culture of continuous improvement, innovation, and creativity	■ Change readiness survey	Utility
	(E) Promote entrepreneurial culture	■ New service delivery training (percent of staff)	Utility
	(F) Promote risk taking while ensuring responsibility and accountability	■ Number of published "shared learnings"	Pharmaceuticals
3. Delivering Results	(G) Create a climate for results	■ Climate survey (leadership component)	Chemicals
	(H) Produce results	■ Achievement of BSC objectives	Utility
Executing Strategy			
4. Understanding of Mission, Vision, and Values	(I) Ensure that all employees know our strategic direction	■ Employee survey	Health care
	(J) Understand our unique business model and our distinct contributions	■ Strategic awareness (survey)	Professional services
	(K) Clearly define expectations and accountabilities aligned with strategic priorities	■ Percent of employees who can identify the organization's focus areas	Health care
5. Accountability	(L) Create high performance through accountability and encourage risk matched to reward	■ Number of employees in "President's Club"	Manufacturing
	(M) Create a values-driven, high-achievement culture	■ Employee survey	Services
6. Open Communications	(N) Create aligned thinking through two-way communication and education	■ Number of employees with cross-business focus	Pharmaceutical
	(O) Create a committed workforce as a result of constant two-way communication	■ Climate survey (communication)	Bank
7. Teamwork	(P) Leverage the power of our enterprise through dual citizenship	■ Amount of best-practice sharing	Manufacturing
	(Q) One team—one dream	■ Percent of people rotated	Services

focused on customers and how the value propositions they create and deliver adds value to targeted customers.

Innovation and risk-taking objectives send a message to the workforce that it is OK to challenge the status quo. Organizations D and E, both deregulated utilities, used words like "entrepreneur," "innovation," and "creativity" to stress the behaviors required in their new world. Organizations introducing shareholder value programs want a culture *focused on results*. Organization G, a chemicals company, wanted to shift its employees from an engineering culture to one that could apply technology to deliver financial results. Organization H, another newly deregulated utility, used the phrase "produce results" to signal that the measure of success had changed.

Understanding mission and strategy is important to organizations of functional specialists who must strike a balance between maintaining excellence within their silos while simultaneously integrating with other parts of the enterprise. Organization I, a health plan, wanted to improve performance by more closely integrating the medical staff with the administrative staff. Organization J, a professional service firm, had its technology group introduce innovative Web-based consulting services that appeared, on the surface, to threaten the company's consultants, who had grown accustomed to delivering results only through face-to-face interactions with clients.

Accountability plays an important role in organizations that historically were internally focused or highly regulated and now had to become customer- and market-focused. Organization L was a manufacturing company with international customers and a global network of manufacturing plants and suppliers. Formerly, L defined responsibility by function and used cost-based transfer prices to measure success for manufacturing units along the supply chain. No one was accountable for end-to-end profitability and performance. L's new strategy simplified the organization, provided more sourcing and buying discretion, and measured the performance of each unit with market-based prices for inputs and outputs.

Open communications is important for strategies that require high degrees of integration. Organization N, a pharmaceutical company, was attempting to accelerate knowledge and marketplace experience from its commercial division to its product development group. *Teamwork* is important on the change agenda when a strategy redefines the role of different units. Organization P, a multidivisional manufacturing company with many stand-alone brands, wanted to create synergy among these brands through more marketplace integration. *Dual citizenship* communicates the simultaneous role for a distinct brand to also be part of a corporate image. Company Q used the mantra "one team, one dream" to show how different branch offices, with somewhat different local objectives, still contributed to the success of the global corporate strategy.

Measuring Culture

Measurement of cultural values relies heavily on employee surveys. The beauty but also the complexity of the Balanced Scorecard is that the act of measurement forces somewhat vague and ambiguous concepts such as culture and climate to be defined more precisely. While often used interchangeably, scholars believe these two concepts are quite different. The concept of *climate* has its roots in social psychology. Chris Argyris, in a study of climate in a bank, defined it as "the formal organization policies and employee needs, values, and personalities that operate in a self-perpetuating system of living complexity."[3]

The concept of climate continued to evolve in the 1960s and is now generally understood to be the organizational influences on employees' motivation and behavior. It includes dimensions such as the organization's structure, the system of rewards, and the perceived warmth and support of superiors and peers. Climate is the shared *perception* of organizational policies, practices, and procedures, both formal and informal. Climate includes the clarity of organizational goals and the means used to attain these goals.

A recent book identifies twelve questions that describe a productive work environment.[4]

1. Do I know what is expected of me at work?
2. Do I have the materials and equipment I need to do my work right?
3. At work, do I have the opportunity to do what I do best every day?
4. In the last seven days, have I received recognition or praise for doing good work?
5. Does my supervisor, or someone at work, seem to care about me as a person?
6. Is there someone at work who encourages my development?
7. At work, do my opinions seem to count?
8. Does the mission/purpose of my company make me feel my job is important?

9. Are my coworkers committed to doing quality work?
10. Do I have a best friend at work?
11. In the last six months, has someone at work talked to me about my progress?
12. This last year, have I had opportunities at work to learn and grow?

Responses to these questions can provide a measurement of a healthy organizational climate.[5]

Culture arose from anthropology. It identifies the symbolism, myths, stories, and rituals embedded in the organizational consciousness (or subconsciousness).[6] Culture attempts to capture the systems of shared meanings, assumptions, and values in an organization. Culture is generally descriptive, while climate is typically a construct—based on an instrument developed by psychologists—to explain why some organizations are more effective than others. While the two concepts are clearly related, climate refers more to the organization's policies and routines as perceived by employees, whereas culture is about the common set of shared meanings among employees about goals, problems, and practices. Some believe that climate is the observable manifestation of culture but others maintain that culture is a somewhat deeper, less consciously held set of meanings.[7] As one example, culture may refer to assumptions held in the organization about what drives employee motivation, whereas climate would include the actual performance and reward systems used in the organization.

Anthropologists, who developed the concept of culture, make it operational through extensive description and storytelling. Clearly, storytelling is too general for the measurements and targets on a Balanced Scorecard. Organizational behavior scholars, however, are now attempting to measure culture. But before measuring, organizations should distinguish between values and norms. Values are the beliefs espoused by senior executives, such as communication, respect, integrity, and excellence.[8] Culture is reflected in the norms people share, which may or may not be linked to the values. This distinction forces executives to go one level deeper in deciding what the culture should be. It requires them to be clear about specific attitudes and behaviors that are needed to execute the strategy. Values by themselves are too vague to reveal what employees truly believe about the organization and how they should behave. Employees may all agree that integrity or customer service is important, but not know what these values mean to them in their everyday behavior. It is preferable to attempt to measure and manage specific attitudes and behaviors rather than values.[9]

Charles O'Reilly and colleagues have developed a measurement instrument, the Organizational Culture Profile (OCP), that contains a set of
statements that describe possible values of an organization.[10] Employees
are asked to rank fifty-four value statements about their perceived importance and relevance in the organization. The rankings of the fifty-four
value statements enable an organization's culture to be mapped, with an
acceptable degree of reliability and validity, into eight independent factors:

1. Innovation and risk taking
2. Attention to detail
3. Results-focused
4. Aggressiveness and competitiveness
5. Supportiveness
6. Growth and rewards
7. Collaboration and teamwork
8. Decisiveness

The OCP statements are based on norms, people's expectations about
specific attitudes and behaviors. They ask people to respond to questions
such as, "What does it really take to get ahead?" and "What are the un-
written rules around here?" A consensus within a unit or organization on
the responses represents the culture of the unit. The organization can assess whether the culture is consistent with its strategy. A lack of consensus reflects a lack of a common culture.

Different cultures may be required in different parts of the organization. An R&D group should have a different culture from a manufacturing unit; an emergent business unit should be different from a mature
one. Thus, an organization should want some variations in norms dependent on function and business strategy. But executives likely will want
organization-wide agreement around values such as integrity, respect,
and treatment of employee colleagues. These are the markers of the
corporate-wide culture.

The existence of an instrument like the OCP indicates that culture
has now become a measurable construct. But instruments like the OCP
have been influenced by a psychology literature that stresses constructs
such as motivation and climate. Since the strategy literature has not
perceived culture as essential for effective implementation, existing instruments to measure culture do not capture individuals' beliefs and understanding of the strategy. To align the culture dimension more closely

to an organization's strategy, rather than just its way of conducting its day-to-day business, the value statements in an OCP-type instrument should be modified to allow employees to evaluate a company on the dimensions identified in this chapter, including the value proposition underlying the strategy. We have suggested possibilities such as whether the culture is primarily about continuous improvement and quality programs, or creativity and innovation, or deep understanding of individual customers' preferences and needs. Developing improved instruments for measuring culture along dimensions relevant to the strategy is clearly an opportunity for further work.[11] Alternatively, organizations will have to develop and rely on ad hoc questionnaires of their own to measure this important dimension.

LEADERSHIP

Leadership, particularly leadership to manage transformational change, is a core requirement for becoming a strategy-focused organization. The mobilization and focusing of the entire workforce is essential to successful change. A cadre of effective leaders energizes and sustains the transformational program.

We have seen organizations use two approaches to define the role for leadership: a *process* for developing leaders, and a leadership *competency model,* which defines leader characteristics. As examples of the first approach, Figure 10-6 describes the strategic objectives and measures used by several organizations to manage their *leadership development process.* Company A, a regional bank, focused on its leadership succession program. Company B, a manufacturing company in a rapid growth mode, monitored its ability to attract good managers from outside the company to supplement its internal growth of managers. Company C, a military health-care organization, already had a highly structured leadership development program, so it monitored the penetration and adherence to this program throughout the organization. Company D, a pharmaceuticals company, wanted to develop leaders at lower levels of the organization and therefore focused on the establishment of self-directed work teams. These examples, as well as the others in Figure 10-6, describe objectives and measures related to the process of developing leaders.

The second approach, the *leadership competency model,* focuses on the specific competencies desired from leaders. Instead of monitoring *how* leaders are developed, this approach attempts to describe *what* a leader is. It identifies the traits that leaders should exhibit to contribute

Figure 10-6 Leadership Model: Process Focus

Strategic Objective	Strategic Measure	Organization
(A) Develop leadership depth	■ Percent of key positions without identified successor ■ Progress versus leadership development plan	Regional bank
(B) Develop our unique leadership profile	■ Internal versus external management hires	Manufacturing
(C) Develop leaders	■ Percent of personnel adherence to leader development life cycle	Military health care
(D) Make leadership a participative process	■ Number of projects run by self-directed work teams	Pharmaceuticals
(E) Develop effective leadership	■ Vacancy rate ■ Employee survey	Health care
(F) Foster an environment of leadership at every level	■ Number of approvals needed for decisions	Health care
(G) Increase senior management leadership skills	■ Percent of favorable leadership score on staff survey	Telecomm
(H) Take ownership and execute strategy	■ Leadership development rating (360° feedback)	Regional bank

to superior performance. From our Balanced Scorecard database, we can classify the desired competencies into three general categories (see Figure 10-7):

- *Creates value:* The leader delivers bottom-line results
- *Executes strategy:* The leader mobilizes and guides the process of change
- *Develops human capital:* The leader builds competencies and sets high standards for the organization

The leader who creates value and executes strategy, the first two categories, enhances organization capital by reinforcing the agenda for cultural change just discussed. The third role, developing human capital, supports objectives that enhance the organization's capabilities and reinforce its values. We illustrate the application of these three sets of leadership objectives with examples of leadership profiles developed by three [disguised] companies: Hi-Tek, a manufacturing and services company (see Figure 10-8); Finco, a global financial services company (see Figure 10-9); and Risk Management, Inc., a property and casualty insurance company (see Figure 10-10).

Create Value

Almost all the leadership models in our database begin with a focus on the *customer*. Hi-Tek urges its leaders to look at the world through the eyes of its customers. Leaders spend time with customers so that they can anticipate customers' future needs and the opportunities for new solutions. Finco, in addition to delivering value to direct customers, wants its leaders to build relationships with other external groups that create new ways of adding value. These could include end-use customers (insurance purchasers) of Finco's customers' products, and companies that create new insurance products and services. Risk Management identifies the changing nature of its markets and the need for leaders to anticipate these changes.

Innovation and risk taking is another priority for creating value. Each company recognizes the importance of being open to change and to new ways of thinking. A third priority is a bottom-line orientation, to *deliver results*. Hi-Tek stresses working better, faster, and at lower cost. Finco strives to deliver superior results to all its stakeholders.

Figure 10-7 Leadership Model: Competency Focus

General Attributes	Description	Role
Creating Value ■ Customer-Focused ■ Innovation/Risk Taking ■ Delivering Results	■ Understands the customer; solves the customer's problems ■ Challenges assumptions; proposes new ways ■ Produces results for customers and shareholders	**Creates Organization Readiness**
Executing Strategy ■ Understanding Strategy ■ Accountability ■ Communications ■ Teamwork	■ Clearly defines mission, vision, values, and strategy ■ Sets direction, targets; establishes accountability ■ Communicates openly; provides feedback ■ Works across boundaries; shares knowledge	
Developing Human Capital ■ Learning ■ Coaching/Developing ■ Personal Contribution	■ Learns from others; learns from self ■ Invests time in the development of others ■ Leads by example; sets high personal standards	**Creates Human Capital Readiness**

Figure 10-8 Leadership Competency Profile: Hi-Tek (Manufacturing/Service Business)

General Attributes	Leadership Competencies at Hi-Tek
Creating Value ■ Customer-Focused ■ Innovation/Risk Taking ■ Delivering Results	■ **Customer Insight:** Outstanding leaders understand their customers. They place themselves in the minds of their customers and spend time with them to understand their current and future underlying needs and to anticipate solutions. ■ **Breakthrough Thinking:** Outstanding leaders challenge conventional thinking and focus on possibilities. They thrive on complexity, identify and develop new solutions, and foster creativity and innovation. ■ **Drive to Achieve:** Outstanding leaders look for ways to accomplish work faster, at lower costs, and with higher quality. They set challenging goals for themselves and others, and take calculated risks to improve performance.
Executing Strategy ■ Understanding Strategy ■ Accountability ■ Communications ■ Teamwork	■ **Team Leadership:** Outstanding leaders link their vision to the company. They lead change and create a sense of urgency to meet challenges and implement strategies. They set direction, establishing goals and maintaining accountability. ■ **Open Communications:** Outstanding leaders tell the truth. They openly share information with peers, managers, and subordinates and tell the "whole" story, not just their position. They are role models for doing what is right. ■ **Teamwork:** Outstanding leaders work collaboratively with their own teams and across organizational and geographic boundaries. They empower their teams to achieve excellence.
Developing Human Capital ■ Learning ■ Coaching/Developing ■ Personal Contribution	■ **Building Capabilities:** Outstanding leaders act to build the organization's long-term capability to produce and sustain excellent results. They focus on learning. ■ **Coaching/Developing Talent:** Outstanding leaders actively develop others to build a strong team now and for the future. They coach by expressing expectations, providing feedback, and seeking learning opportunities. ■ **Personal Dedication:** Outstanding leaders act in ways that support company goals and strategies. They align their personal needs with company needs and support tough decisions made for the overall benefit of the company. ■ **Decisiveness:** Outstanding leaders make and act on tough decisions with speed, a sense of urgency, and tenacity. They seek input to the decision-making process as needed to make excellent decisions. ■ **Passion for the Business:** Outstanding leaders are outwardly passionate about our business, winning in the marketplace, and what technologies and services can do for the world.

Figure 10-9 Leadership Competency Profile: Finco (Financial Services)

General Attributes	Leadership Competencies at Finco
Creating Value ■ **Customer-Focused** ■ **Innovation/Risk Taking** ■ **Delivering Results**	■ **Focusing on Client Value:** Delivers high-quality solutions that meet clients' business needs; maintains strong client relationships. ■ **Cultivating Key Relationships:** Builds and maintains relationships which promote Finco's market presence and impact. ■ **Driving Innovation:** Promotes innovations—is open to change ■ **Delivering Results:** Produces and delivers superior results to all stakeholders.
Executing Stragegy ■ **Understanding Strategy** ■ **Accountability** ■ **Communications** ■ **Teamwork**	■ **Global Vision:** Has a broad view of Finco's business environment and is up-to-date on global developments in own area of expertise. ■ **Shaping Strategy:** Understands how vision is implemented through function-related strategies and action plans that achieve sustainable competitive advantage. ■ **Inspiring and Building Commitment:** Communicates openly and effectively, gaining support of others to share and support Finco's vision and core values. ■ **Fostering Integration and Teamwork:** Is effective in teamwork across individuals, organizations, and cultures—demonstrates intercultural competency.
Developing Human Capital ■ **Learning** ■ **Coaching/Developing** ■ **Personal Contribution**	■ **Fostering Organizational Learning:** Ensures continuity of the business through knowledge transfer and increase of intellectual capital. ■ **Financial and Business Acumen:** Understands the factors underlying the financial performance of their own business area—focuses on creating value for Finco.

Figure 10-10 Leadership Competency Profile: Risk Management, Inc. (RMI) (Property and Casualty Insurance)

General Attributes	Leadership Competencies at RMI
Creating Value ■ Customer-Focused ■ Innovation/Risk Taking ■ Delivering Results	■ **Thinking Strategically in a Changing Marketplace:** Anticipates and recognizes opportunities and key marketplace trends that would contribute to RMI's business goals. Creates a future course of action, under conditions of uncertainty, that aligns with the organization's vision and goals. ■ **Challenging and Taking Risks:** Directly challenges assumptions and beliefs of people at all levels. Willing to take a stand that may create a conflict or be unpopular. Encourages these behaviors in others. ■ **Leading Change and Innovation:** Leads change in people, structures, and processes that moves the organization from where we are now to where we want to be. Anticipates and responds to opportunities created by change. Produces exceptional results by seeking, generating, and encouraging new ways of doing things.
Executing Strategy ■ Understanding Strategy ■ Accountability ■ Communications ■ Teamwork	■ **Establishing a High-Performance Environment:** Creates an environment where vision and mission are clearly defined, where targets for performance are aggressive, where feedback is expected and utilized to improve performance, and where rewards for high performers and consequences for low performers are visible and real. ■ **Holding Self and Others Accountable to Deliver on Commitments:** Steps up and takes responsibility for initiatives that have significant corporate impact. Makes specific commitments and follows through for full implementation. Ensures that direct reports deliver on commitments. Clarifies roles for self and others. ■ **Working Across Boundaries:** Establishes partnerships at all levels and across department and functional lines to achieve optimum business results.
Developing Human Capital ■ Learning ■ Coaching/Developing ■ Personal Contribution	■ **Benchmarking Internally and Externally:** Measures and compares products, services, strategies, and processes against other external organizations or units within RMI practices. ■ **Developing Self and Others:** Creates an environment that fosters and reinforces the importance of development and learning as a business priority. Is a role model for continuous self-assessment and improvement. Proactively seeks challenging opportunities to develop and grow. Supports direct reports in this process.

Execute Strategy

Leaders motivate and guide the efforts of others, using four characteristic behaviors. First, they must *clarify organizational mission, strategy, and values*. Leaders at Hi-Tek set direction, establish goals, and maintain accountability. Similarly, Risk Management's leaders establish a high-performance environment. Finco's leaders understand the dynamic context in which the company operates and adapt their units' operations and strategies to changes in the external environment.

Accountability and alignment link enterprise strategy to personal performance. At Risk Management, leaders hold themselves and others accountable to deliver results. They set stretch targets and provide feedback that rewards high achievers and penalizes low performers. Finco's leaders align functional excellence to effective strategy implementation.

Leaders effectively *communicate*. The message and tone established by leaders influence others to voluntarily make day-to-day decisions that enhance the organization's long-term value. Honest communication enables control through socialization, shared beliefs, norms, and values. Finco's leaders communicate vision and core values. Leaders at Hi-Tek tell the truth, "the whole story, not just their position; they are role models for doing what is right."

Leaders promote *teamwork*. Finco's leaders operate effectively in teams containing diverse individuals, organizations, and cultures. Leaders at Risk Management and Hi-Tek work across organizational, geographic, and functional boundaries.

Develop Human Capital

Many organizations in our database expect leaders to enhance the human capital of their organizations. They *coach and develop* employees' capabilities. Leaders at Hi-Tek and Risk Management create environments that generate developmental opportunities, supported by coaching and feedback. Leaders also create a *learning* environment. Finco focuses specifically on developing intellectual capital through knowledge sharing across the enterprise. Risk Management promotes internal and external benchmarking to facilitate learning about best practices.

Leaders also provide role models of *personal excellence*. Hi-Tek emphasizes the personal traits of dedication, decisiveness, and passion for the business. Finco identifies how subject matter expertise provides a valuable building block for creating shareholder value.

Measuring Leadership

Measuring the leadership development *process* is more straightforward than measuring leadership competencies. Figure 10-6 identified a set of typical measures for the leadership development process. Most of these measures are observable and verifiable indicators, such as the number of key positions without a successor, number of external hires, and percent of units adhering to a leader development cycle. The leadership competency model, in contrast, requires judgments on a broader range of soft issues, such as the quality of communications and the leader's ability to coach and encourage teamwork. Often, organizations measure these traits in their leaders through *employee surveys*. The three companies, illustrated in Figures 10-8, 10-9, and 10-10, use 360-degree feedback programs to quantify their competency profiles. A staff or external unit solicits information from subordinates, peers, and superiors about a leader's mastery of the critical competencies. While such personal feedback is used mainly for coaching and developing the individual, the unit also aggregates the detailed (and confidential) data from the individual reviews to create an organization-wide status report on the key leadership competencies.

The Bonneville Power Administration (BPA) provides an excellent example of the leadership measurement process (see Figure 10-11). BPA measures leadership along two dimensions:

a. Employees, customers, and constituents understand BPA's mission and goals
b. The leader produces desired results

The internal employee Organization Assessment Survey, or OAS, shows that employees generally understand the agency's mission. The responses exceed the high benchmark target established for this measure. The benchmarks for a second survey, "Great Place to Work" (GPTW) compare results to those from an identical survey administered to employees of leading-edge companies in North America. BPA is below the benchmark for this measure—to be in the top 100—but is rapidly closing the gap. BPA also administers a separate annual survey to customers and constituents, monitoring their understanding of BPA's mission and goals. Any shortfall in performance on this measure motivates BPA's leaders to increase their efforts to communicate more effectively with these important constituents. Finally, BPA measures its leaders' ability to produce

Figure 10-11 Leadership Competency Profile: Bonneville Power Administration (BPA)

Strategic Objectives: Leadership demands setting a clear direction, focusing employees' efforts, and modeling high-performance behaviors. Organizational success depends on leadership exhibited at all levels. BPA leaders must provide both strategic awareness and alignment so that BPA is well positioned for the future; BPA leaders link people with business strategy, both inside and outside the agency. BPA's leaders also are expected to produce agency and workgroup results.

Measurement Intent: Determine the extent to which customers, constituents, and employees understand the mission and direction of the agency. Determine the extent to which BPA's leaders are successful in producing needed business results.

Results:

OAS Leadership and Quality Index

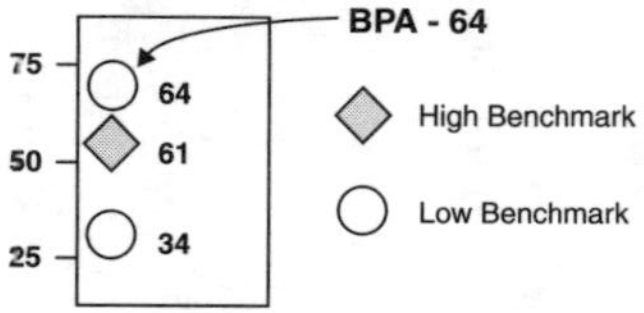

BPA - 64

75
64 ○ High Benchmark
61 ◇
50
34 ○ Low Benchmark
25

Key questions from the OAS survey:

- "Employees have an understanding of the organization's mission, vision, and values." *77% favorable*
- "Managers let employees know how their work contributes to the organization's mission and goals." *66% favorable*

Great Place to Work Survey

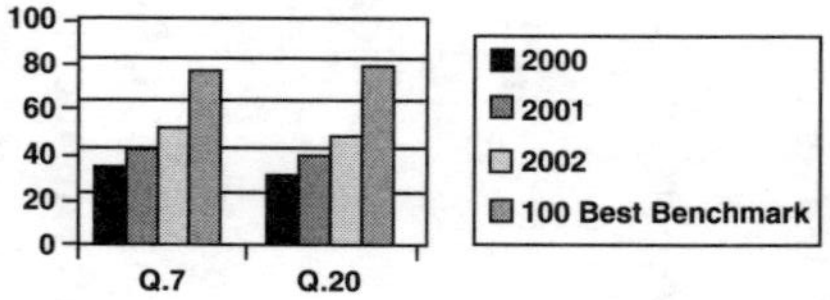

100
80
60
40
20
0
Q.7   Q.20

■ 2000
■ 2001
□ 2002
■ 100 Best Benchmark

Key questions from the GPTW survey (Agency Scores):

Q.7   "Management makes its expectations clear."
      52% favorable in 2002 (vs. 42% in 2001)

Q.20 "Management has a clear view of where the organization is going and how to get there."
      49% favorable in 2002 (vs. 41% in 2001)

Customer and Constituent Satisfaction Surveys

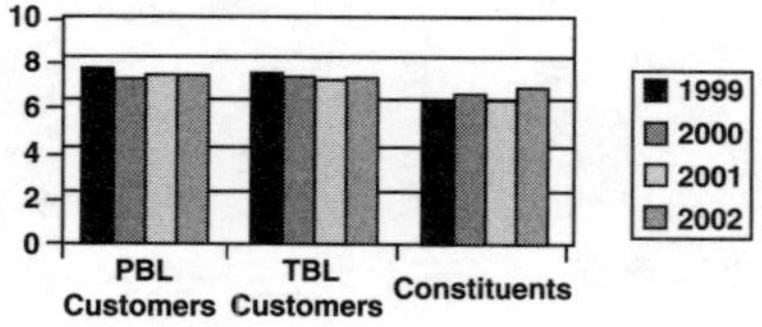

10
8
6
4
2
0
PBL   TBL   Constituents
Customers   Customers

■ 1999
■ 2000
□ 2001
■ 2002

Key questions from the annual customer and constituent surveys:

Q.5   "[The PBL/TBL] communicates with you in a forthright manner."
      7.5 PBL; 7.6 TBL in 2002

Q.8   "BPA clearly communicates its mission and policies."
      7.0 in 2002 vs. 6.5 in 2001

Accomplishment of Results:

Average accomplishment of Agency Success Share targets in 2001: *75%*

Average accomplishment of Team Share targets in 2001: *88% of base, 67% of stretch* desired results by monitoring their performance against Balanced Score-card targets. Both Success Share and Team Share (shown at the bottom of the figure) are group award programs that establish targets (usually six to ten) at the beginning of each year, based on the four dimensions of the Balanced Scorecard. Surpassing a threshold on those targets will result in a payout at year-end according to a preestablished formula. The payout for these team accomplishments is made in equal amounts to every member of the agency or workgroup team.

In summary, this section describes two leadership models used by organizations: the leadership development process model focuses on *how* leaders develop their requisite competencies; the leadership competency model depicts *what* an organization expects of its leaders. In practice, of course, each approach contains both the "what" and the "how." Companies focused on the development process must have a leadership competency model to guide the development process, and companies focused on leadership competencies must have leadership development programs.

ALIGNMENT

"Alignment is the necessary condition before empowering . . . the individual will empower the whole team."[12] Peter Senge, in *The Fifth Discipline*, stresses that broad-based organization change requires alignment, when all members of a team have a commonality of purpose, a shared vision, and an understanding of how their personal roles support the overall strategy. An aligned organization encourages employee empowerment, innovation, and risk taking because individual actions are directed at achieving high-level objectives. Encouraging and empowering individual initiative in an unaligned organization leads to chaos as the innovative risk takers pull the organizations in contradictory directions. The effect will be similar to the self-declared job description of a new business school dean: "taking sixty puppy dogs for a walk without a leash."

Alignment generally requires two sequential steps: (1) create awareness and (2) establish incentives. First, leaders must communicate the high-level strategic objectives in ways that all employees can understand. Second, leaders must ensure that individuals and teams have local objectives and rewards that, if achieved, contribute to achieving targets for high-level objectives. Leaders create *strategic awareness* through a multifaceted communications program involving a wide range of mechanisms: brochures, newsletters, town hall meetings, orientation and training programs, executive talks, company intranets, and bulletin boards.[13]

Organizations typically use employee surveys to determine whether employees are aware of and understand the high-level strategic objectives (see attribute 4, "Understanding of Mission, Vision, and Values," in Figure 10-5). Organizations achieve *strategic alignment* by linking personal objective setting and the compensation/reward system to business unit and corporate objectives.[14]

Figure 10-12 provides typical objectives and measures for strategic awareness and strategic alignment. Since these examples are drawn from organizations implementing the Balanced Scorecard, it is not surprising to see awareness and alignment defined around BSC objectives and measures. For example, the organizations defined alignment as "the percentage of staff with personal objectives tied to the Balanced Scorecard."

Figure 10-13 shows how one representative company, First Community Bank (FCB), describes its alignment strategy. FCB's learning and growth perspective has four objectives: two (L1 and L2) focus on developing human capital; one (L4) on information capital; and one (L3) on creating organization capital. FCB identifies "strategic alignment" as its primary organization capital objective. The company plans to cascade the corporate scorecard to the community group (CG), then to divisions within CG and, ultimately, to teams and individuals. The cascading program has three components:

- *Strategic understanding:* All individuals understand the key elements of the FCB, CG, and their division's strategy
- *Organization alignment:* The goals of FCB, CG, and the divisions are internally aligned
- *Personal alignment:* All individuals have goals aligned to CG and the division

The FCB implementation team designed an employee survey instrument to measure these three objectives. The team administered seventeen questions about organization alignment (shown in the three boxes at the bottom of Figure 10-13) to approximately 300 senior and middle managers. The team used the same instrument for periodic resurveys to check the status and progress of the strategic alignment program.

TEAMWORK AND KNOWLEDGE SHARING

There is no greater waste than a good idea used only once. No asset has greater potential for an organization than the collective knowledge

Figure 10-12 Defining and Measuring Strategic Awareness and Alignment

Attribute	Strategic Objective	Strategic Measure	Organization
Strategic Awareness	(A) Ensure that all employees understand the strategy	▪ Percent of employees who can identify organization's strategic priorities (survey)	Health care
Strategic Alignment	(A) Reinforce strategic direction and strengthen sense of urgency and purpose	▪ Percent of staff with objectives tied to BSC	Mutual funds
	(B) Align efforts through measurement and reward	▪ Percent of employees (director and above) with goals mapped to strategy	Health care
	(C) Create a motivated and prepared workforce	▪ Percent of staff with personal BSC	Process sector
	(D) Align personal goals	▪ Percent of staff with goals linked to BSC	National bank
	(E) Empower employees	▪ Percent of staff with training and development linked to BSC	City government (transportation)

Figure 10-13 Measuring Strategic Awareness and Alignment at First Community Bank (FCB)

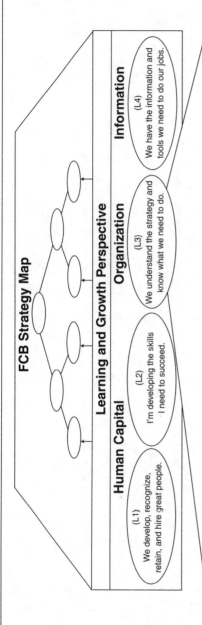

FCB Strategy Map

Learning and Growth Perspective

Human Capital

(L1)
We develop, recognize, retain, and hire great people.

(L2)
I'm developing the skills I need to succeed.

Organization

(L3)
We understand the strategy and know what we need to do.

Information

(L4)
We have the information and tools we need to do our jobs.

L3	We understand the strategy and what we need to do.	FCB will communicate its strategy through the Balanced Scorecard and cascade it to the appropriate levels within the organization over time. This will ensure that everyone knows what the FCB strategy is, how it relates to the big picture at FCB, and how it can be used to prioritize day-to-day activities. FCB leadership will work to make sure that strategic communications are open, clear, and consistent.

Measures

- **Strategic Understanding**
- **Organization Alignment**
- **Personal Alignment**

Strategic Understanding

- Q1 I understand the corporate strategy.
- Q2 I am regularly informed of the FCB strategy.
- Q3 I understand the FCB strategy.
- Q4 I understand the goals of my division.
- Q5 I understand how my division helps FCB achieve its strategy.

Organization Alignment

- Q6 The goals of FCB are well aligned with the corporate strategy.
- Q7 The goals of my division are well aligned with the FCB strategy.
- Q8 The goals of my division are well aligned with other FCB divisions.
- Q9 My division works effectively with other FCB divisions to meet customer needs.
- Q10 It's easy to get help from other FCB divisions to meet customer needs.
- Q11 Improving the degree of alignment and synergy between FCB divisions is a high priority.

Personal Alignment

- Q12 I understand how well corporate is doing in achieving its strategy.
- Q13 I understand how well FCB is doing in achieving its strategy.
- Q14 I understand how well my division is doing in achieving its strategy.
- Q15 I understand how my day-to-day job helps achieve the FCB strategy.
- Q16 I understand how my day-to-day job helps achieve the goals of my division.
- Q17 My personal goals are set with the FCB strategy and my divisional goals in mind.

possessed by all its employees. Many companies today use formal knowledge management systems to generate, organize, develop, and distribute knowledge throughout the organization.[15]

Generating Knowledge

Generating knowledge involves identifying content that could be relevant to others in the organization, and getting people to submit the relevant material to an electronic database. Most organizations have to go through a cultural change to shift from hoarding knowledge to sharing ideas. Steve Kerr, former chief learning officer at General Electric, has noted that a prime component of the Jack Welch management system was to break down barriers across the organization—vertical and horizontal—so that knowledge transfer could occur.[16] Welch would ask executives at annual reviews, "What ideas have you acquired from other GE units? What ideas have you contributed to other GE units?"

Organizing Knowledge

Information, to be accessible to users, must be organized so that it can be represented and retrieved electronically. Knowledge sharing systems—with knowledge bases, navigational devices such as search engines, user interfaces, and taxonomies—provide a systematic way to organize valuable information. The knowledge bases must be screened, distilled, filtered by subject matter experts, and continually maintained and refreshed so that it remains contemporary and relevant.

Developing Knowledge

Subject matter experts should screen and approve the information submitted by others. Such a review increases the validity of material that is published in the system, certifies that the knowledge is important and that it represents best practice, and recommends its use throughout the organization.

Distributing Knowledge

Knowledge management systems must provide easy access by users to the knowledge base. Organizations use two methods for distributing knowledge. The first, a "push system," catalogs the needs of users and selectively distributes information, often via e-mail, when it recognizes the potential use of information to a user. While this proactive approach is somewhat obtrusive, the designer of a push system recognizes that most users are too busy and preoccupied with their immediate tasks to take the time to use the second method, a "pull system," searching for existing information when it would be relevant and valuable to their immediate needs.

Knowledge management systems generally consist of:

- Database and database management systems that collect and store the knowledge base
- Communication and messaging systems that retrieve and transmit the knowledge material, independent of where the knowledge has been sourced from
- Secure browsing that allows employees to search databases remotely, even from public access facilities, yet protect against unauthorized use

The challenge is to find ways to motivate individuals to document their ideas and knowledge so that they are available to others. The simplicity of this thought is belied by its difficulty to implement. The difficulty, however, did not dissuade most organizations in our BSC database from identifying *teamwork and knowledge sharing* as a strategic priority in their learning and growth perspective. Figure 10-14 shows representative examples of the objectives and measures for best-practice knowledge sharing. Organization A, a chemical company, monitors the number of best-practice ideas that were identified and used. It also measures output per employee to assess the economic impact from the knowledge sharing. Organization B, an international insurance company, uses its corporate university to transfer knowledge. It measures the number of hours of training received by each individual. Financial service company C monitors the percent of employees who transfer knowledge in a work-out process, patterned after one popularized at General Electric. Pharmaceutical company D and software company E use formalized knowledge management systems to transfer knowledge and measure the level of system usage. Company E also monitors how up-to-date the material in its knowledge management system is. Financial services company F focuses on the comprehensiveness and currency of information in its performance databases.

All the organizations in Figure 10-14, with the exception of A, measure knowledge sharing with input or process measures, not the preferable

Figure 10-14 Defining and Measuring Teamwork and Knowledge Sharing

Attribute	Strategic Objective	Strategic Measure	Organization
	(A) Develop a learning organization	▪ Number of best practices identified ▪ Output per employee	Chemicals
	(B) Continually develop and transfer knowledge	▪ Hours of training per person	International insurance
	(C) Ensure communication of best-practice ideas	▪ Percent of employees participating in the workout process	Financial services
Knowledge Sharing	(D) Improve cross-company communication	▪ Percent of staff using knowledge-sharing channels	Pharmaceuticals
	(E) Create and utilize a common global system and process for sharing knowledge	▪ Currency of projects in knowledge bank (KB) ▪ Number of hits to KB	Software
	(F) Ensure availability of accurate, consistent information across the organization	▪ Percent of targeted measures, data, and statistics accessible across organization	Financial services
Organization Integration	(G) Integrate employees	▪ Number of cross-division movements	Manufacturing

outcome or output measures. Either they deem it too difficult to measure the outputs from knowledge sharing or knowledge management processes, or they believe that knowledge sharing is a process whose outputs show up in improved performance elsewhere on their strategy maps. It seems, however, that organizations can do better at measuring outputs, such as number of new ideas transferred or adopted or number of new ideas and practices shared with other teams and organizational units.

THE ORGANIZATION CAPITAL READINESS REPORT

At the beginning of the chapter, we defined organization capital as the ability of an organization to mobilize and sustain the process of change required to execute its strategy. We have discussed how every strategy map and Balanced Scorecard should contain objectives drawn from culture, leadership, alignment, and teamwork based on its change agenda. We illustrate the complete picture with a report on the strategic readiness of organization capital, as shown in Figure 10-15.

The leadership measure, in this example, draws from the leadership competency model and displays the percentage attainment of the key attributes for leadership. The report continues with two measures of culture. With customer focus as the dominant dimension, the report uses a survey to measure customers' understanding and alignment with the enterprise mission. A second measure of culture is derived from an employee survey of the enterprise's core values, including values such as "innovation," "risk taking," "accountability," and "teamwork." Alignment looks at two dimensions: employees understand the strategy, and employees' goals and incentives are aligned with the strategy. The first dimension, awareness, is measured by an employee survey that determines the percentage of staff that understands the strategy. The second dimension, strategic alignment, monitors the extent to which employees' personal goals and incentives are linked to the strategic objectives and measures on the Balanced Scorecard. Finally, teamwork is measured by the extent of use of the organization's knowledge management system for sharing best-practice information.

Not all of the strategy maps that we have developed or observed in practice—most of which were done prior to articulating the framework in this chapter—use measures of all four organization capital components. We believe that a strong case can be made for including at least one measure for *each* of them. Organization capital creates the climate for change that is required to implement the strategy. It's difficult to envision a com-

Figure 10-15 Organization Capital Readiness Report

Attribute	Strategic Objective	Strategic Measure	Target	Actual
Leadership	To develop the availability of leaders at all levels to mobilize the organization toward its strategy	■ *Leadership gap* (Percent of key attributes in competency model rated above threshold)	90%	92% G
Culture	To develop awareness and internalization of the mission, vision, and core values needed to execute the strategy	■ *Customer-focused* (Customer survey; percent who understand our mission)	80%	68% R
		■ *Other core values* (Employee change readiness survey)	80%	52% R
Alignment	To ensure alignment of goals and incentives with the strategy at all levels of the organization	■ *Strategic awareness* (Percent of staff who can identify organization's strategic priorities)	80%	75% R
		■ *Strategic alignment* (Percent of staff with objectives and incentives linked to Balanced Scorecard)	100%	60% R
Teamwork	To ensure the sharing of knowledge and staff assets with strategic potential	■ *Best-practice sharing* (Number of KMS hits/employee)	5.0	6.1 G

prehensive change program that does not rely on cultural values, effective leadership, an aligned workforce, and teamwork and knowledge sharing. What gets measured gets managed. What does not get measured gets forgotten or lost. Each of the organization capital components seems necessary to execute a strategy successfully.

The HR Role for Organization Capital

Once an organization capital readiness report has been articulated, the executive leadership team must establish targets for each of the measures. The targets, which should represent a significant improvement from existing performance, stimulate the discussion of the initiatives required to achieve targeted performance in each measure. The human resources organization will generally be responsible for the initiatives required to achieve the targets for organization capital measures. Typically, each functional group within HR (such as recruiting) will review the objectives, measures, and targets to determine specific initiatives. After accumulating the suggestions from the functional groups, the HR leadership team discusses with line executives the choices and tradeoffs in the plan, eventually determining the initiatives that will be most cost-effective in supporting the strategy. For example, to develop a specific attribute, the company can choose among training existing employees, recruiting new employees, or promoting knowledge sharing. The output from this activity is a comprehensive program for developing organization capital, as shown in Figure 10-16. The development program aligns HR organization investments to the enterprise strategy, and becomes the contract between the HR organization and the operating lines of business. The process also allows the various departments within the HR organization to understand their roles in supporting initiatives that help line operating units achieve the enterprise's strategic objectives. The alignment of HR with organizational strategic success has been long sought but rarely accomplished. In this chapter, we have introduced a new process that links the objectives and measures for the Balanced Scorecard's learning and growth perspective to organization success.

SUMMARY

The learning and growth perspective is the foundation of every organization's strategy. The measures in this perspective are the ultimate lead indicators. They represent the organization's intangible assets that create

Figure 10-16   A Strategic Program to Develop Organization Capital Readiness

Organization Capital Readiness Report		Organization Capital Development Program			
Attribute	**Measure of Strategic Readiness**	**Targets (Sample)**	**Strategic Initiatives**	**Lead Indicators**	**Strategic Program Budget**
Leadership	■ Leadership Gap (Key Attributes)	90%	■ Leadership Development ■ Succession Planning ■ Governance Process ■ Strategy Management	■ Percent of Internal Versus External Hires ■ Percent of Participation in Leadership Courses	$XXX
Culture	■ Customer-Focused ■ Core Values	80% 80%	■ Communications ■ Change Management ■ Leadership Development	■ Percent of Employees Regularly Surveyed ■ Culture Assessment	$XXX
Alignment	■ Strategic Awareness ■ Strategic Alignment	80% 100%	■ Performance Management ■ Total Compensation and Reward ■ Positive Work Environment	■ Personal Goals Linked to BSC (percent) ■ Percent Receiving Incentive Compensation	$XXX
Teamwork	■ Sharing Across Boundaries ■ Best Practices ■ Key People ■ Teams ■ Rewards	100% (versus plan)	■ Knowledgement Management ■ Organization Effectiveness ■ Staff Rotation	■ Percent Using Knowledge-Sharing Channels	$XXX

value by their alignment to the organization's strategy. That is why only the Balanced Scorecard, not financial measures, can quantify the value that intangible assets create. Human capital is enhanced when it is concentrated in the relatively few strategic job families implementing the processes most critical for the organization's strategy. Information capital is most valuable when it provides the vital infrastructure and strategic applications that complement the human capital for promoting outstanding performance on strategic internal processes. The even more intangible organizational factors—culture, leadership, alignment, and teamwork— also are vital for successful strategy implementation. Organizations introducing a new value proposition must create a culture of customer-centric values. The transformation to the new strategy requires exceptional leadership throughout the organization. The new directions for the organization require that communication and performance management systems be aligned to what the organization wants to accomplish. And the focus on outstanding performance on a critical few processes requires teamwork and learning.

Some shy away from measuring these intangible assets—human capital, information capital, and organization capital—because, by their very nature, the measures will be "softer," or more subjective, than the financial measures conventionally used to assess organizational performance. The Balanced Scorecard movement has encouraged organizations to address this measurement challenge. Companies can now measure what they want, rather than wanting only what they can currently measure. Organizations have learned that just the simple act of attempting to measure the capabilities of employees, knowledge systems, and organization capital, no matter the imprecision, communicates the importance of these drivers to value creation. The approaches described in the chapter illustrate how organizations have developed new ways to measure, and subsequently to create, their organization capital. The learning and growth measures stimulate the behavioral changes in the intangible assets that provide the necessary foundation to become a successful strategy-focused organization.

The following case study, Ingersoll-Rand, provides a strong example of the role of organization capital in business strategy.

NOTES

1. S. Chadturi and B. Tabrizi, "Capturing the Real Value in High-Tech Acquisitions," *Harvard Business Review* (September–October 1999).

2. Jeffrey A. Schmidt, *Making Mergers Work* (Alexandria, VA: Towers Perrin/ SHRM, 2002).
3. C. Argyris, "Some Problems in Conceptualizing Organizational Climate: A Case Study of a Bank," *Administrative Science Quarterly* 2 (1958): 501–520.
4. Marcus Buckingham and Curt Coffman, *First, Break All the Rules: What the World's Greatest Managers Do Differently* (New York: Simon & Schuster, 1999).
5. For further work on measuring a healthy organization climate, see D. Pratt, *The Healthy Scorecard: Delivering Breakthrough Results That Employees and Investors Will Love!* (Victoria, BC: Trafford Publishing, 2001).
6. This description of climate and culture is taken from Aaron Reichers and Ben Schneider, "Climate and Culture: An Evolution of Constructs," in *Organizational Climate and Culture*, ed. Ben Schneider (San Francisco: Jossey-Bass, 1990).
7. Edgar Schein, *Organizational Culture and Leadership : A Dynamic View* (San Francisco: Jossey-Bass, 1985).
8. These were the values actually espoused by the senior executives of Enron.
9. We are indebted to Charles O'Reilly of Stanford Graduate School of Business for this discussion on the distinction between values and norms.
10. C. O'Reilly, J. Chatman, and D. Caldwell, "People and Organizational Culture: A Profile Comparison to Assessing Person-Organization Fit," *Academy of Management Journal* (September 1991): 487–516.
11. For example, see the approaches available at Thinkshed, <http://www.thinkshed.com>, which draws upon the scholarly work of O'Reilly, Caldwell, and Chatman.
12. Peter Senge, *The Fifth Discipline: The Art and Practice of the Learning Organization* (New York: Doubleday, 1990), 235.
13. Communication methods are described in Chapter 8 of Robert S. Kaplan and David P. Norton, *The Strategy-Focused Organization: How Balanced Scorecard Companies Thrive in the New Business Environment* (Boston: Harvard Business School Press, 2001).
14. Details of linkages of strategy to personal objectives and rewards are described in Chapters 9 and 10 of *The Strategy-Focused Organization*.
15. The content on knowledge management processes has been drawn from D. Garvin and A. March, "A Note on Knowledge Management," Note 396-031, Harvard Business School, Boston, November 1997.
16. S. Kerr, "Transformational Leadership: Lessons in Mastering Change at General Electric," talk given at the Balanced Scorecard Collaborative North American Summit (October 2002).

CASE STUDY

INGERSOLL-RAND

Background

Ingersoll-Rand (IR) is a global, diversified manufacturer of industrial and commercial equipment, specializing in the major global markets of security and safety, climate control, industrial solutions, and infrastructure.

Ingersoll-Rand has a rich history dating back to 1871, with roots in the construction and mining industries. Over the years, the company built on that proud reputation, so that today's Ingersoll-Rand is a diverse array of multinational businesses with market-leading brands. Its product portfolio encompasses such brands as Schlage locks and security solutions, Thermo King transport temperature control equipment, Hussmann commercial and retail refrigeration equipment, Bobcat compact equipment, Club Car golf cars and utility vehicles, PowerWorks microturbines, and Ingersoll-Rand industrial and construction equipment. At present, IR is a $10 billion industrial enterprise with a workforce of 56,000 people and 130 manufacturing facilities throughout the world.

The Situation

By the mid-1990s, nearly two-thirds of Ingersoll-Rand's revenues came from outside its traditional business of manufacturing construction and mining equipment. But Wall Street had a different perspective. IR shares traded in lockstep with the likes of Caterpillar and John Deere, as the broader investment community remained uncertain how IR intended to leverage the vast assortment of unrelated brands it had acquired over the years.

In October 1999, Herb Henkel became the president and CEO of Ingersoll-Rand. He came to IR with a vision to make it a "global industrial enterprise." But Henkel realized that to achieve this vision, IR would have to be transformed from a product-driven holding company into a solutions-driven operating company, with synergistic businesses and an integrated portfolio of solutions.

The Strategy

Henkel introduced a common strategic planning process across the organization. The standardized planning process by itself did not produce the desired results. The fundamental new orientation toward "growth" and "solutions" was not taking hold fast enough, causing considerable frustration for the management team. An integrated strategic and performance management system was introduced to focus the organization on strategy execution. The strategy map and Balanced Scorecard became the key tools for articulating and communicating strategy across the enterprise.

The Strategy Map

Ingersoll-Rand's mission, to become "a global industrial enterprise with market-leading brands," is stated at the top of its corporate strategy map (see Figure 10-17). From a *financial performance* perspective, IR would drive increased shareholder value by achieving dramatic growth, fueled organically and through synergistic acquisitions, while continuously lowering the cost base. By aggressively managing the balance between revenue growth and productivity, IR seeks to improve asset utilization and drive cash flow generation.

Ingersoll-Rand would achieve its financial objectives by transforming itself from a product-focused manufacturer to a customer-focused solutions provider. From a *customer experience* perspective, IR's value proposition contains three themes: (1) provide the best solutions for customers by packaging innovative products with market-leading, value-added services; (2) develop true win-win partnerships with customers that enable IR to deliver the best total value by striking the right balance between price, performance, and service; and (3) create long-term customer loyalty through excellence in quality, service, and delivery and flawless execution, thereby deterring customers from considering taking their business elsewhere.

IR will enhance several *internal processes* to deliver this customer value proposition and thereby provide IR with a competitive advantage. The *process excellence* perspective is crafted around three primary strategic themes:

- *Drive operational excellence* by pursuing continuous improvement in all of IR's operations. This theme focuses on the core enabling processes for the IR enterprise. Embedded in this theme are key strategic objectives

Figure 10-17 Ingersoll-Rand Strategy Map

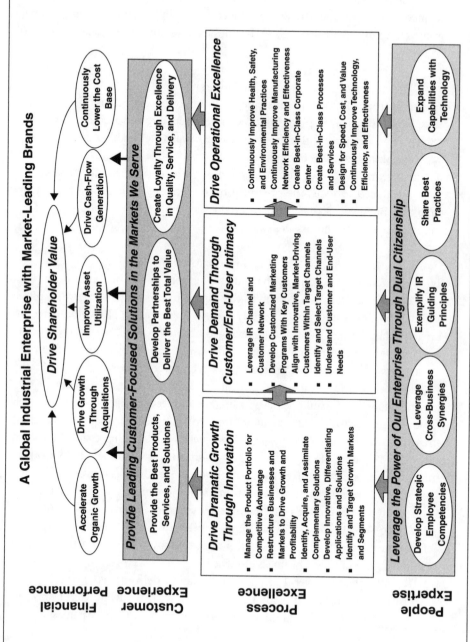

A Global Industrial Enterprise with Market-Leading Brands

Drive Shareholder Value

- Accelerate Organic Growth
- Drive Growth Through Acquisitions
- Improve Asset Utilization
- Drive Cash-Flow Generation
- Continuously Lower the Cost Base

Provide Leading Customer-Focused Solutions in the Markets We Serve

- Provide the Best Products, Services, and Solutions
- Develop Partnerships to Deliver the Best Total Value
- Create Loyalty Through Excellence in Quality, Service, and Delivery

Drive Dramatic Growth Through Innovation

- Manage the Product Portfolio for Competitive Advantage
- Restructure Businesses and Markets to Drive Growth and Profitability
- Identify, Acquire, and Assimilate Complementary Solutions
- Develop Innovative, Differentiating Applications and Solutions
- Identify and Target Growth Markets and Segments

Drive Demand Through Customer/End-User Intimacy

- Leverage IR Channel and Customer Network
- Develop Customized Marketing Programs With Key Customers
- Align with Innovative, Market-Driving Customers Within Target Channels
- Identify and Select Target Channels
- Understand Customer and End-User Needs

Drive Operational Excellence

- Continuously Improve Health, Safety, and Environmental Practices
- Continuously Improve Manufacturing Network Efficiency and Effectiveness
- Create Best-in-Class Corporate Center
- Create Best-in-Class Processes and Services
- Design for Speed, Cost, and Value
- Continuously Improve Technology, Efficiency, and Effectiveness

Leverage the Power of Our Enterprise Through Dual Citizenship

- Develop Strategic Employee Competencies
- Leverage Cross-Business Synergies
- Exemplify IR Guiding Principles
- Share Best Practices
- Expand Capabilities with Technology

Financial Performance

Customer Experience

Process Excellence

People Expertise

that could be considered basic "blocking and tackling." However, IR's leadership believes that these are critical elements to the overall strategy and cannot be ignored. The drive operational excellence theme highlights key business processes such as safety, health, environment, manufacturing, product development, IT, and enterprise-wide shared services.

- *Drive demand through customer/end-user intimacy* by partnering with key customers, managing the value chain, and expanding services. This theme focuses on market segmentation and targeting, channel management, and customer relationship management.
- *Drive dramatic growth through innovation* by focusing on innovative solutions for IR's customers. This theme develops and manages IR's products and services portfolio to enable long-term competitive advantage.

Supporting these internal process capabilities, IR designed a *people expertise* theme in its strategy map to clarify IR's cultural priorities, manage the critical people skills and competencies, and address the enabling infrastructure needs. From a people expertise perspective, IR will leverage the power of the enterprise through dual citizenship: the business unit and the corporation. Dual citizenship, bringing together the talents, energy, and enthusiasm of all IR people, will differentiate IR as a company, making the enterprise stronger because of the collective might of the individual businesses.

Anecdotes

IR did not just adopt the Balanced Scorecard; it developed and implemented an enterprise-wide Strategic Management System (SMS) that is now embedded in its corporate calendar. Ingersoll-Rand's "SMS" includes the following set of integrated management processes:

- Strategic planning
- Operations planning and budgeting
- Strategic initiative management
- Quarterly and monthly operating reviews
- Internal and external communications
- Performance management
- Career development planning
- Succession planning

As an example of an external communication, Ingersoll-Rand crafted much of its 2001 annual report around the primary elements of the Strategic Management System. Included in the annual report is an explanation of the Balanced

Scorecard framework and IR's strategy map. The following excerpts are taken from this report:

> IR's strategic management system consists of three primary components: the strategy map, the Balanced Scorecard, and the performance management process. Every IR business unit has created a strategy map unique to its business and every individual map is aligned with another in the organizational hierarchy to ensure that the enterprise moves in a coordinated fashion toward achieving our vision.

Case prepared by Michael A. Clark of Balanced Scorecard Collaborative and Don Rice, senior vice president of human resources of Ingersoll-Rand. Our thanks to Herb Henkel and his colleagues for sharing the IR experience.

PART FOUR

Building Strategies and Strategy Maps

CHAPTER ELEVEN

CUSTOMIZING YOUR STRATEGY MAP TO YOUR STRATEGY

WE HAVE NOW IDENTIFIED the full set of internal process and learning and growth objectives that are the foundation for any strategy. No organization can hope to excel at every single objective discussed in the earlier chapters. Also, the internal processes differ in priorities depending upon the strategy. For example, a company competing on product leadership should highlight innovation processes as the most important, while a company competing on low cost will emphasize operations management processes. But even beyond the relative emphasis on a particular set of internal processes for a particular strategy, all organizational processes should be aligned to deliver on the differentiating value proposition. Michael Porter argues that "the essence of strategy is in the activities—choosing to perform activities differently or to perform different activities than rivals."[1] He continues:

> *Strategic fit among many activities is fundamental not only to competitive advantage but also to the sustainability of that advantage. It is harder for a rival to match an array of interlocked activities than it is merely to imitate a particular sales-force approach, match a process technology, or replicate a set of product features. Positions built on systems of activities are far more sustainable than those built on individual activities.*[2]

Organizations' strategy maps should follow this prescription. The strategic objectives in the internal process and learning and growth perspectives cannot be individually optimized. They must be integrated and aligned to deliver the value proposition underlying the organization's strategy. In this chapter, we illustrate the process for several generic strategies. Of course, for any particular application, the organization must adapt and customize these generic strategy maps to its unique situation.

In his initial work, Porter articulated two basic sustainable strategies: low-cost or differentiation.[3] This classification has generally stood the test of time, though subsequent work has provided different subcategories of differentiation. Michael Treacy and Fred Wiersema proposed three generic types of strategies: operational excellence (their interpretation of Porter's "low-cost" strategy); and two differentiated strategies, customer intimacy and product leadership. We adopted and illustrated these three generic strategies in a previous book.[4] Arnoldo Hax and Dean Wilde have articulated a fourth generic strategy, "system lock-in," in which companies attract complementors—firms that deliver products and services that enhance the organization's own product and service offerings—to its standard.[5] The most obvious example of a company succeeding by system lock-in is Microsoft, though companies such as Intel, Visa, and eBay have also enjoyed competitive advantage from having many other organizations accept their standards. "Value innovation," introduced by W. Chan Kim and Renée Mauborgne, provides another perspective on strategy formulation.[6] Under value innovation, companies achieve superior and sustainable performance by outstanding performance along a selected set of attributes or service features that are especially preferred by large customer segments, while keeping costs and prices down for such superior performance by underdelivering on features not critical to customer satisfaction. For any of these strategic approaches, companies should develop customized strategy maps that represent their value propositions, as well as the alignment of their internal processes and learning and growth capabilities that will deliver superior financial performance.

In general, any strategy is an application of a fundamental principle illustrated in Figure 11-1. By looking across the entire value chain, upstream from suppliers, through the company, and downstream to customers, we can identify the value created: the maximum price that customers are willing to pay less the cost of products and services provided by suppliers (including employees). This total value creation can be split into three segments:

- *Value captured by suppliers:* The prices paid to employees and suppliers less their opportunity cost (actual expenses plus forgone mar-

Figure 11-1   Creating Value Across the Supply Chain

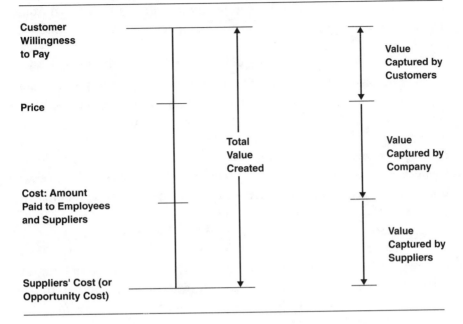

gins from sales to alternative customers) for providing products and services to the company

- *Value captured by company:* The net price received from customers less the prices paid to employees and suppliers for the products or services sold
- *Value captured by customers:* The difference between the maximum price they were willing to pay for the products or services and the actual prices they paid.

How much of the total value created is distributed among these three value chain participants depends on their relative strength and bargaining power. These dynamics are captured in Porter's famous "five forces" model.[7] For example, Microsoft and Intel, as suppliers to personal computer manufacturers, capture much of the value in the chain because of their near-monopoly position in operating systems and microprocessors, key components in PCs. PC customers also capture some of the value because of the fierce competition among the PC manufacturers who produce a mostly undifferentiated product. In retailing, Wal-Mart conducts tough negotiations so that vendors' products are supplied close to the vendors' opportunity costs. This enables Wal-Mart to offer customers prices that are lower than competitors (creating value for its customers), while still retaining an attractive margin between the prices received from its customers and the amount it pays its suppliers—employees, vendors, and real estate developers.

The various types of strategies—low cost, product leadership, customer solutions, system lock-in, or a unique combination of product and service attributes in a value-innovation strategy—are alternative ways of structuring a company's position in the value chain so that it can earn an attractive profit between the prices received by its customers and the cost of products and services acquired from its suppliers. If a company's offering is not unique relative to competitors, then power shifts to customers who earn much of the value created. The undifferentiated company operates with low margins between the net price it receives from customers and the amount it pays to suppliers and employees.

Ultimately, a successful business unit strategy positions a company in the competitive landscape so that it can capture a significant amount of value. Once this positioning has been identified, the company can translate this strategy into a strategy map and Balanced Scorecard. We illustrate the process with several of the generic strategies.

LOW TOTAL COST STRATEGY

Companies such as Southwest Airlines, Toyota, Dell Computer, Vanguard Mutual Funds, McDonald's, and Wal-Mart deliver a "low total cost" buying experience to their customers.[8] They offer highly competitive prices combined with consistent quality, ease and speed of purchase, and excellent, though not comprehensive, product selection. Competitive prices are an obvious feature of a low total cost strategy. But a low price alone is no longer sufficient for competitive success. The Yugo was the cheapest car available in the United States during the 1980s but went out of business because the quality was so poor that consumers were unwilling to buy the car at any price. A customer's total cost of acquiring and using a product and service includes the cost of failures and the costs of detecting and remedying defects. Companies following a low total cost strategy must deliver consistent quality to minimize the costs incurred by their customers to detect and remedy errors. Another component in the customer's cost is the time required to purchase and receive the product or service. Low total cost companies reduce the time required by their customers to order and acquire the product and service, and the time elapsed between ordering and receiving the product or service.

Finally, low total cost companies keep their own costs down by offering their customers a selection that is somewhat limited, but that meets the needs of most of its targeted customers. Wal-Mart offers fewer stock-keeping units (SKUs) than a full-service supermarket or department store. Southwest Airlines flies from a limited set of smaller cities in the United States, thereby avoiding the high cost and congestion of larger, more crowded airports. Toyota, in its rise to prominence, offered customers limited packages of options and colors. McDonald's sells only a few different types of hamburgers. By reducing the range of items and services offered, companies reduce their own production and service delivery costs, enabling them to offer an outstanding low total cost value proposition for their customers.[9]

Figure 11-2 shows a generic strategy map for a low total cost strategy. The key internal processes occur within the operations management cluster. Companies following a best total cost strategy, such as Wal-Mart, Costco, Toyota, and McDonald's, must have long-term relationships with excellent suppliers. In addition, these companies should have highly efficient operating processes that convert inputs from suppliers into outputs—products and services—for their customers. These conversion processes should not only be the lowest cost in the industry, they must also be consistent, high-quality, and highly responsive, with short cycle times to convert inputs, or customer requests, into outputs. The distribution processes to customers must also be low-cost, timely, and error-free. The companies manage their operating risk to maximize availability and minimize disruptions for customers.

The customer management processes for a low total cost strategy relate to providing convenience and ease of access for customers. Objectives include simple, accessible ordering processes such as Internet ordering and invoicing (for example, Dell and Amazon.com), and rapid check-in by airlines, hotels, and car rental agencies). Low total cost companies provide superb post-sales service on operational issues related to billing, delivery status, defects, and returns. Low total cost companies must also excel by understanding the most preferred range of products and services desired by the largest segments of customers. For example, Wal-Mart often stocks only the two leading brands in any category plus its own retailer-branded product. Dell gives a limited range of options (processors, keyboards, monitors) for each component in a computer. Toyota bundles options into broad packages and offers fewer car color options to reduce the diversity of cars it must produce and its dealers must stock. These companies excel at market research—understanding the limited set

Figure 11-2 Strategy Map Template: Low Total Cost

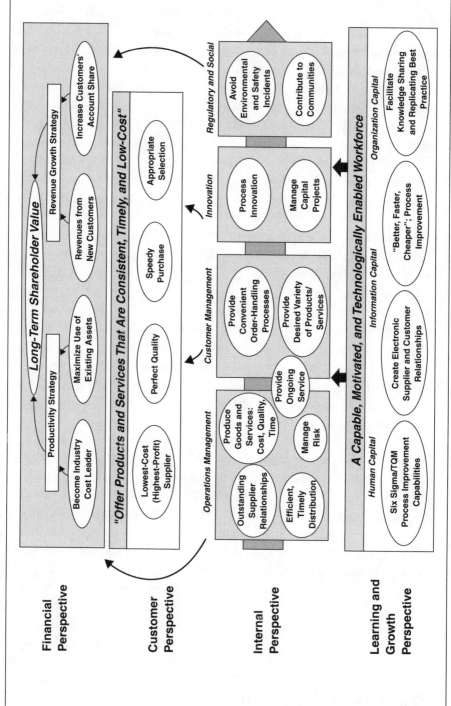

of products and options most desired by the largest customer segments—and keep their operating costs down by producing a limited product and service line.

Low total cost companies are product followers, not leaders. They don't invest a great deal in product and service *innovation*. They need capabilities for replicating the innovations done by product leaders so that their products and services do not become obsolete; eventually, consumers tired of having only black Model-T Fords even though these were cheaper than the newer, more colorful offerings from General Motors in the 1920s. When introducing new products, low total cost companies stress design-for-manufacturing choices so that they can profitably offer the new products at the lowest prices in the industry. The main focus on innovation will be for processes, not products. Companies continually search for process innovations that will lower the cost and improve the quality and responsiveness of their ordering, conversion, distribution, and customer management processes. As business expands, they also excel at adding capacity rapidly and efficiently to gain economies of scale in their purchasing, operating, and distribution processes.

Regulatory and social process performance is critical, not only to reduce hazards to employees and communities, but also to avoid accidents and environmental incidents that are highly costly to the company. Senior executives often look at accident rates as a leading indicator of future operating performance. They believe that "if employees are not looking out for themselves, they certainly aren't looking out for the company's equipment and processes."

Learning and growth processes, as discussed in Chapter 3, stress *employee competencies* for process improvement. These include knowledge of total quality management, six sigma, just-in-time, and activity-based management so that employees have the ability and knowledge to continually lower costs, reduce cycle times, and improve quality. The company's *information technology* objectives relate to enhancing the customers' buying experience (ease of ordering) and lowering the company's and its customers' costs of ordering and acquiring products and services. Electronic relationships with suppliers and customers are critical for such cost reduction. Electronic interchanges also make ordering and distribution processes error-free, accessible, convenient, and timely. An additional information technology objective relates to providing accurate and timely data to employees about the cost, quality, and cycle times of their processes and the company's customers. These data empower employees in their continuous improvement activities. The information systems should also perform internal benchmarking of processes so that managers can identify best practices and share these practices and process innovations across organizational boundaries.

The organization capital of low total cost organizations should stress local process learning and sharing of best practices around the organizations. The goal should not be to keep secret the practices that make one unit the most efficient within the company, but to have introduced the most process innovations and gained the greatest adoption of such innovations by other units. The culture should reinforce the company's strategic message of "better, faster, cheaper."[10]

PRODUCT LEADERSHIP STRATEGY

Companies such as Sony, Mercedes, and Intel emphasize product innovation and product leadership. Pharmaceutical companies also compete on superior product functionality by developing and obtaining rapid regulatory approval for new products that offer superior treatment for particular disease categories. The value proposition of product leadership companies emphasizes the particular features and functionality that leading-edge customers value and are willing to pay more to receive. The strategic objectives for this value proposition include outstanding performance, along dimensions such as speed, accuracy, size, or power consumption, that is superior to that offered by competitors' products.

Product leadership companies want to be first-to-market with their innovative or enhanced features and functionality. By being first, they can command high prices from early adopters who most value the unique functionality of the products, or else capture high market share in situations characterized by large switching costs or system lock-in that enable them to defend their early advantage without price cutting. And, as discussed in Chapter 5, product leadership companies also strive to extend the superior functionality of their products into multiple market segments.

Figure 11-3 shows a generic strategy map for product leadership companies. The key internal processes are in the *innovation* cluster. The companies must excel at anticipating customers' needs and discovering new opportunities for superior products and services. They must maintain an optimal balance among (1) fundamental research creating new scientific and technological breakthroughs, (2) introducing these breakthroughs through new product platforms, and (3) enhancing their existing platform products with incremental but still innovative derivative products. They

Figure 11-3 Strategy Map Template: Product Leadership

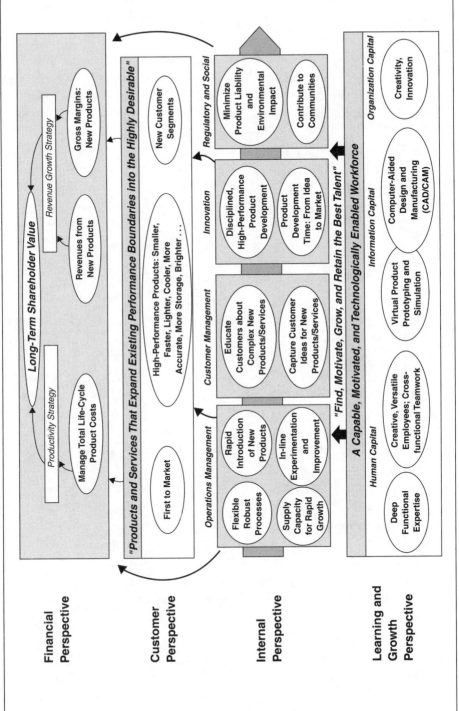

must have superb product development processes that bring new products to the market quickly. And they must provide protection to their innovative products through excellence in patenting, regulatory, and branding processes.

The *operations management* processes for product leadership companies are not the lowest cost in the industry. The operating processes must, however, be robust so that they can accommodate the continual introduction of new products. Product leadership companies want operating processes that can ramp up rapidly so that manufacturing capacity constraints do not inhibit market-share penetration. The operating processes must also be flexible to allow for minor changes in product characteristics based on feedback from the marketplace. They should also allow for in-line experimentation to reduce manufacturing costs once product characteristics have been stabilized. All these features indicate that flexibility and improvement of operating processes are more important to product leadership companies than low-cost production of highly stable products. The margins from the innovative features of innovative products more than cover their somewhat higher production costs. But inflexible operating processes that delay the introduction or production ramp-up of innovative new products will cost product leadership companies heavily through loss of high-margin revenues and market share.

Customer management objectives focus on two critical processes. First, product leadership companies want to identify their leading-edge customers and learn from them. These customers often have excellent ideas about which new features and functionality would be most valued. Companies that are close to their most demanding customers can generate many ideas for new capabilities to bring to the market. But existing customers are not always the best source for new ideas. Often, innovative product capabilities are so new and different from existing ones that even the most advanced customers cannot appreciate the benefits from enhanced functionality. So product leadership companies also need to be able to educate customers about the benefits from improved functionality. Customer representatives must be able to demonstrate how customers can capture the value from new product characteristics being offered. Objectives that capture changes in customers' own processes may indicate the success from new product functionality.

Companies that continually introduce radically new products must be vigilant at managing regulatory and social processes associated with their new products. Without much experience in the production or customers' usage of the new products, product leadership companies must strive to avoid adverse side effects from their introductions. The companies should have objectives relating to improving product safety, employee and customer health, and environmental impacts from their short-run production of these new products. Since the products of these innovation-based companies will typically have short life cycles, these companies must be highly sensitive to the total environmental costs, including product takeback, over the life cycle of their products. And the companies must have excellent government relations so that new products and services receive any necessary regulatory approval, and that delays associated with regulatory approval are minimized.

Product leadership companies' learning and growth objectives for *employee capital*, *information capital,* and *organization capital* have been covered in Chapter 5. These are summarized at the bottom of Figure 11-3.

COMPLETE CUSTOMER SOLUTIONS

A third type of value proposition stresses building long-lasting relationships with customers. With this value proposition, customers feel that the company understands their business or personal issues, and they trust the company to develop customized solutions tailored to them. Consider IBM from 1960 to 1980, when it dominated the computer industry. The company did not offer the lowest prices, nor did it often deliver its new products on time. Nor were IBM's products the most advanced technologically, the most powerful, or the fastest. But IBM offered its customer, the company's head of information technology services, complete solutions—hardware, software, installation, field service, training, education, and consulting—that were personalized to the company's individual needs. This bonding with the customer enabled IBM to earn exceptional returns over an extended period of time until technology changes, which it was slow to respond to, eroded this competitive advantage.

Other companies that excel at bonding with their customers include Goldman Sachs in financial services and Mobil in the United States, with its superior buying experience, involving large stations with many gasoline pumps for rapid access; Speedpass for convenient, rapid payment; outstanding convenience stores; clean and safe restrooms; well-lit stations; and friendly employees.

Companies offering such a "customer solutions" value proposition stress objectives relating to the completeness of the solution (selling multiple, bundled products and services), exceptional service (both before and after the sale), and the quality of the relationship. Often acquiring new customers is expensive and accomplished through a single, entry-level product. After the expensive acquisition of a new customer, companies must retain the customer (annual retention costs are typically far lower than the cost of acquiring entirely new customers), deepen the relationship with the customer, and broaden the relationship to encompass the sale of multiple, related products and services. The profits from customers in their year of acquisition could be negative, because of high acquisition costs. The objective, however, is to capture and retain customers to produce high lifetime profitability.

Figure 11-4 shows a generic strategy map for companies following a customer solutions strategy. The key internal processes are in the customer management cluster. Companies develop deep understanding about what their customers value, build strong, trusted relationships with their customers, bundle existing products and solutions into individually customized solutions, and help their customers achieve success. The operations management processes support the customer management processes by offering customers a broad product and service line. This often involves bundling products and services of suppliers, along with the company's own products and services, and delivering these to customers through seamless distribution channels. As with the product leadership strategy, a company following a customer solution strategy may have operating processes that are not the lowest cost in the industry, as long as the higher cost processes contribute to enhancing the customers' experience in buying and using the company's products and services. The company's innovation processes focus on finding new ways to create value for customers. Research is directed more at understanding customers' future needs and preferences than at fundamental product innovation. The research may also be directed at finding new ways for customers to access and use the company's products and services.

The *regulatory and social* processes for companies following a complete customer solution strategy may focus on gaining regulatory approval to offer services that cut across traditional industry barriers. Many service-sector industries, such as electric and gas utilities and telecommunications, financial, health-care, and transport companies that have been deregulated in the past twenty-five years, want to expand their service offerings with unregulated products and services. With vestiges of regulations still remaining, the companies may need regulatory approval to offer or bundle new services to customers. These companies may also want to use their excellent service capabilities to create improved social value in the communities where they operate.

Figure 11-4 Strategy Map Template: Complete Customer Solutions

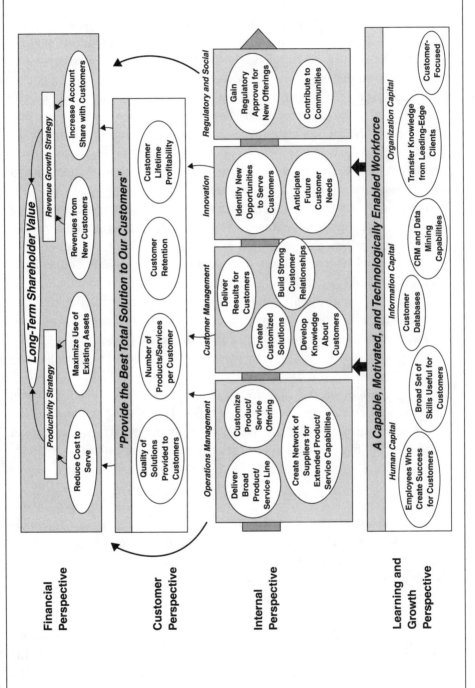

Employee competencies focus on skills and knowledge about the diverse products and services the company offers to its targeted customer segments. The employees must also have excellent knowledge about and be highly sensitive to targeted customers and their preferences. Employees should have a broad base of skills so that customers requesting or receiving service can be handled by a single company representative, not shuttled from one employee to another.

Information technology focuses on data about customers and analytic capabilities to learn more about customer preferences and buying patterns. Extensive, preferably proprietary, customer databases can provide a sustainable source of competitive advantage for customer-focused companies. CRM software enables the company to have an integrated and comprehensive view of all the transactions each customer has with the company. By combining CRM software with an activity-based costing system, companies can measure customer profitability accurately for each individual customer, gaining valuable information that enables companies to transform unprofitable relationships into profitable ones. Data mining capabilities give companies unique insights into constructing customer segments and marketing to customers based on their individual preferences and buying behavior. Knowledge management systems can focus on transferring knowledge gained from leading-edge clients both to develop new product and service offerings and to better serve other customers.

Organization capital objectives feature fostering a customer-centric climate and culture among employees. Employees must understand the primacy of customers and the value the company gains from developing and maintaining long-standing relationships with customers.

LOCK-IN STRATEGIES

During the 1990s, the increased importance of "new economy" information-based industries, such as software, computer hardware, the Internet, and telecommunications, led to the popularity of *lock-in*, a fourth type of generic strategy. [11] Under a lock-in strategy, companies generate long-term sustainable value by creating high switching costs for their customers. The switching costs can arise in different ways. Customers who contemplate switching from a Microsoft Windows-compatible computer to, say, an Apple Macintosh lose access to many application programs that run only on a Windows operating system. Customers who choose to buy or sell products on an auction service other than eBay lose access to the large community of buyers and sellers who use only the eBay auction site. A customer with extensive databases that run on a software package available only on an IBM computer faces high costs and considerable uncertainty if it contemplates purchasing a computer from another manufacturer with a different database software system. And a customer who wants to use a different credit card from the dominant Visa or Master-Card brands faces the risk of not being able to charge purchases at many merchants he or she may wish to buy from. All these are examples where companies have created a high barrier for their customers to switch from their product to a competitor's.

Lock-in strategies may not be feasible in all circumstances. Generally, opportunities for lock-in arise only at certain times and in certain segments of an industry. But companies should be alert to when such a strategy might be feasible since the rewards from a successful lock-in strategy can be enormous. Microsoft and Cisco enjoy stock market capitalizations that are hundreds of billions of dollars higher than the book value of their tangible assets, largely because their complex software and hardware have become standards for the industry, are difficult for rivals to replicate, and are costly for customers to switch from.

Lock-in strategies, of course, arose long before the invention of the personal computer or the Internet. Gillette, for decades, has sold its razors at low prices so that consumers would continually purchase its razor blades, which worked best with the patented Gillette razor. Polaroid made money on recurring sales of its film, not the camera that was the consumer's initial purchase. Elevator, telecommunication, and medical equipment manufacturers usually make more money from sale of repair, maintenance, and post-sale software services than from the initial equipment sale. The value of such lock-in strategies requires that patents, licensing agreements, or specialized knowledge preclude competitors from offering the post-sale products and services that provide the manufacturer with large, continuing profits. For this type of lock-in strategy to be most successful, the manufacturing company should be an exclusive provider of the follow-up products and services.

Hax and Wilde, in their work on the Delta strategy model, describe a powerful form of lock-in, which they call "system lock-in," that gets created when a company's core, proprietary product becomes the industry standard.[12] Hax and Wilde provide examples of the Windows operating system and Cisco's networking standard as exemplars of the system lock-in strategy. System lock-in occurs when customers make significant investments in capabilities and resources that are specific to the company's product. For example, customers may develop application programs and create large, complex databases that run only on a specific software operating system. As another example, telecommunication companies may develop, purchase, and install software that is compatible only with the analog and digital switches of a single manufacturer. In these cases, customers remain with their original vendor, and keep purchasing maintenance services and product upgrades, to avoid the service disruptions, delays, and out-of-pocket costs that would arise were they to switch to an alternative vendor for their basic hardware or software.

System lock-in requires that competitors cannot imitate the core product because of legal protection or through secrecy of its complex construction and continual upgrades of the core product. System lock-in through a proprietary standard creates value that increases nonlinearly with increased participation by customers. It is an example of "winner-take-all" competition, in which the winner enjoys increasing returns and protection from competitors.

Hax and Wilde, building on the work of Adam Brandenburger and Barry Nalebuff, feature the activities of *complementors* to reinforce system lock-in strategies.[13] Complementors are neither suppliers nor customers of the company, but they create great value through their selling of compatible and valuable products to the company's customers, or through their purchase of additional services from the company's existing suppliers. For example, the more than 20,000 companies and five million programmers that write application programs for the Microsoft operating system are complementors of Microsoft. Other examples are companies that enhance the capabilities of the Palm operating system by producing programs and capabilities that become available to owners of Palm devices; and the producers of hardware and software products that build on the Intel Pentium processing platform. United Airlines and American Airlines, while highly competitive for their airline passenger customers, are actually complementors for suppliers, such as Boeing. By coordinating their purchase commitments, they enable Boeing to achieve a scale economy sufficient to develop a new generation of aircraft.

Complementors, such as the millions of programmers who write application programs compatible with the Microsoft operating systems, maximize their own profits and also create system lock-in when they want to write programs for the operating system used by the largest number of customers. And customers prefer an operating system for which the largest numbers of complementors are continually writing new application programs. So the equilibrium solution has a single operating system becoming dominant and difficult to dislodge. Of course, competition is eventually possible if innovative competitors can find creative ways to lower customers' and complementors' switching costs. For example, Linux has become a credible competitor to Microsoft by providing an open source operating system that attracts its own army of entrepreneurial programmers who enhance and develop applications for Linux.

Another form of system lock-in arises when a company provides a dominant exchange for transactions between buyers and sellers. The company then becomes a sole-source clearinghouse for the transfer of information, money, or physical goods. The familiar example from the Internet is the success of eBay. People who buy items in an auction want to come to an exchange that has the largest number of sellers. Similarly, people who offer their goods for sale will come to the exchange with the largest number of potential buyers. For credit cards, consumers want a card that will be accepted in the largest number of stores, and merchants want to accept the few cards that are held by the largest number of consumers. The equilibrium has only a very few credit cards (such as Visa and MasterCard) surviving. For the telephone Yellow Pages, despite competition in the deregulated telecommunications era, merchants want to advertise in the phone book used most by consumers, and consumers will search in the book that lists the largest number of local merchants.

An event like the annual conference of the World Economic Forum in Davos, Switzerland, is another example of the winner-take-all nature from becoming the dominant exchange. Businesspeople, politicians, and journalists want to go to one international conference a year, and will choose the event where they expect the most opportunity for exchanging information with the most important and influential people. Once a critical mass of targeted people starts to attend the Davos conference, many more people want to participate in that conference to the exclusion of others.

The dominance of English as a second language is another example of providing a dominant exchange. As business in the world globalizes, Finns need to speak to Chinese, Japanese need to speak to Dutch, and Swedes need to speak to Swiss. Many non-native English-speaking businesspeople had already decided to learn English so that they could converse with the large number of single-language speaking Americans. This critical mass then made it more useful for others to use English as the default language when conversing with people from other lands, even if they were not American. As everyone, de facto, came to regard English as their second language, then even without Americans or British in attendance, English had become the natural language for discourse. In all these circumstances, one exchange (or one standard) will typically emerge as the winner.

A key success factor in becoming a dominant exchange is to exploit early-mover advantages by signing up a critical mass of buyers and sellers faster than competitors. In that way, the next buyer or seller finds the incremental benefit much higher to transact on your exchange (to access the already large embedded base of buyers and sellers) than to use an alternative exchange that has only a few buyers and sellers. The value of the exchange increases nonlinearly with participation and use. To maintain the first-mover advantages and ward off competition, the exchange provider should strive to continually improve the ease and value of use, in effect to make switching costs higher and higher. For if the exchange provider does not continue to enhance its offering, a rival has the opportunity to offer a superior exchange whose ease and value of use is sufficiently better to overcome the users' costs for consumers of switching to the smaller exchange.

With this background on lock-in strategies, we can define the objectives and measures for a *lock-in strategy map* (see Figure 11-5).

Financial

In the financial perspective, a lock-in strategy emphasizes revenue growth more than productivity. The opportunities for high margins and market share from implementing a successful lock-in strategy far outweigh the benefits from a cost-reduction focus. But since one of the success elements is to build market share rapidly, companies use low prices to attract customers and complementors. Thus lock-in companies have a productivity objective to lower the cost of supplying the entry-level product. Revenue growth objectives feature:

- Revenues from newly acquired customers
- High-margin revenues from selling secondary products and services (such as razor blades) to users of the basic product
- Revenues from providing third parties with access to the company's large and loyal customer base

Customer

All companies following lock-in strategies will have similar customer outcome objectives related to customer acquisition, retention, and deepening

Figure 11-5 Lock-in Strategy Map Template

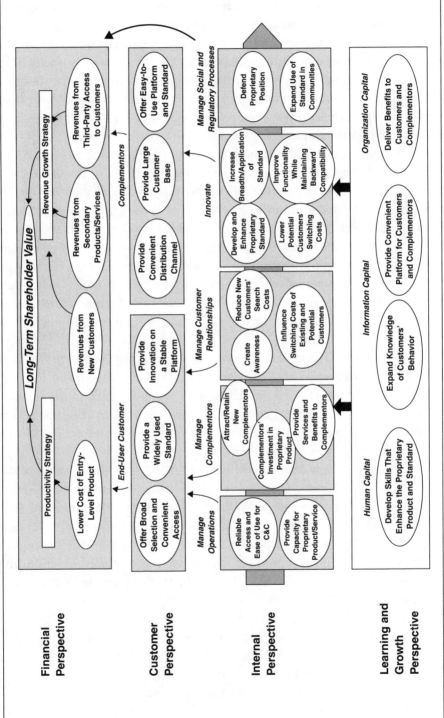

Financial Perspective

Long-Term Shareholder Value

Productivity Strategy

Revenue Growth Strategy

Lower Cost of Entry-Level Product

Revenues from New Customers

Revenues from Secondary Products/Services

Revenues from Third-Party Access to Customers

Customer Perspective

End-User Customer

Offer Broad Selection and Convenient Access

Provide a Widely Used Standard

Provide Innovation on a Stable Platform

Complementors

Provide Convenient Distribution Channel

Provide Large Customer Base

Offer Easy-to-Use Platform and Standard

Internal Perspective

Manage Operations

Reliable Access and Ease of Use for C&C

Provide Capacity for Proprietary Product/Service

Manage Complementors

Attract/Retain New Complementors

Complementors' Investment in Proprietary Product

Provide Services and Benefits to Complementors

Manage Customer Relationships

Create Awareness

Reduce New Customers' Search Costs

Influence Switching Costs of Existing and Potential Customers

Innovate

Develop and Enhance Proprietary Standard

Lower Potential Customers' Switching Costs

Increase Breadth/Application of Standard

Improve Functionality While Maintaining Backward Compatibility

Manage Social and Regulatory Processes

Defend Proprietary Position

Expand Use of Standard in Communities

Learning and Growth Perspective

Human Capital

Develop Skills That Enhance the Proprietary Product and Standard

Information Capital

Expand Knowledge of Customers' Behavior

Provide Convenient Platform for Customers and Complementors

Organization Capital

Deliver Benefits to Customers and Complementors

relationships. Rapid customer acquisition builds and sustains lock-in advantages. Companies can measure the percentage and the increase in number of customers who use its proprietary product or standard. In addition to measuring the number of new customers or percentage increase in the customer base, the company should strive to measure the lifetime net present value of newly acquired customers. Customer acquisition can be expensive, and a company pursuing a profitable lock-in strategy should strive to acquire customers at a cost below the value it can earn over the expected life of the relationship with the customer.

A second customer outcome objective, to enhance the lock-in, strives to retain and extend the company's reach with existing customers. A company can increase its share of customers' business by establishing loyalty programs that grant rewards based on large, cumulative purchases. Measures could include percentage of customers in loyalty programs, sales to customers enrolled in loyalty programs, and the percentage of customers who have qualified for elite status in such programs. Other measures are the average number of products per customer, and revenues per customers from the company's secondary products and services. Customers' account share—the percentage of a customer's total spending in a given category captured by the company—is another powerful measure of entrenchment. To ensure that the company is capturing the benefits from its installed customer base, it can compare its share from sales of new services to its share of the installed base. If its share from supplementary products and services is below its installed share, then competitors are capturing more of the benefits and the company is not exploiting the advantages from its installed base.

Customer retention occurs when companies raise the switching costs of existing customers. A company can measure the number (or percentage) of customer employees who are trained in the company's products and services. It can measure the extent of investment that customers have made in complementary assets, such as databases and software, using the company's proprietary product. By measuring customer attrition and customer churn (percent of customers lost), the company learns about customers for whom the switching costs were not high enough.

In addition to these common customer outcome objectives, the company must identify the value proposition that attracts and retains customers to the proprietary standard. First, the standard must be easy to use and easily accessible by customers. Second, customers must believe that the standard is widely used by others, so they have the opportunity to exchange files (for a software standard) or encounter others using the same standard (such as buying or selling on eBay, attending the annual World Economic Forum, or speaking English). And for a proprietary standard, customers will often expect continual innovations that enhance its power or ease of use, while still expecting backward compatibility with previous versions so that their existing investment in the proprietary standard is not made obsolete.

Companies should also treat their complementors as customers. As with end-use customers, companies can measure their acquisition, retention, and depth of relationship with complementors. The value proposition for complementors is also similar to that for customers. Complementors value a large, installed base of end-use customers who are potential customers for them as well. They want a convenient distribution channel for reaching these end-use customers, and they value a widely used standard platform that is easy for them to use to develop and distribute their products.

Internal Perspective

Innovation Processes

Lock-in strategies require powerful innovation processes. The company must first develop the proprietary product or protected standard that serves as the basis for the lock-in. The company must provide an interface for the product or service that can be used easily by complementors and by the company's own follow-up products. The goal is to provide an interface that facilitates powerful interactions among customers and complementors, but that does not impose high burdens on the work of the customers and complementors. Once the company has established its product or service as a proprietary standard or dominant exchange, its innovation process should continue to enhance the functionality of the core product—to keep delivering value and raising customer switching costs—while still maintaining backward compatibility with earlier product generations so that customers' considerable investment in their people and complementary assets are not destroyed as they purchase new versions of the product. Otherwise customers' switching costs would be low, and subject to competition, each time a new generation is introduced.

The innovation process also should search for ways to broaden the application of the core product in ways that attract more complementors and customers and preempt competitors. For example, Real Player started with a product that could play audio streams over the Internet, but it soon enhanced the functionality with a product that also played digital video streams. Innovation should strive to develop features that lower the switching costs of customers currently using competitive products, such as allowing customers to access the company's core product without scrapping their previous investments in a competitive product. For example, Microsoft Word finally triumphed over WordPerfect not only by embedding Word in the broader suite of Microsoft Office products, but by allowing WordPerfect users to continue to access their old files and to use familiar WordPerfect commands while working within and learning Word.

Finally, especially for software, the innovation process must find ways to prevent unauthorized use of the product by customers or complementors who do not pay for it. While legal protection, discussed under regulatory and social processes, may give the company access to the judicial system to reduce unauthorized use, such actions are expensive and rarely completely effective. Far better would be to develop methods by which the company can completely restrict the use of its product to authorized users only. Measures such as piracy losses and estimates of unauthorized and unreimbursed usage provide indicators of the company's lack of success along this dimension.

Manage Complementors

Complementors provide a key source of sustainability for system lock-in strategies by providing valuable products and services that require customers to use the company's proprietary product or standard. Measures such as number of complementors and sales of complementors' products and services to customers quantify this objective. To succeed with a system lock-in strategy, companies must develop a capability to influence people who are not employees and assets that it does not own.

A driver of complementor retention is the extent of investment that complementors have made in the company's proprietary product or technology. The investment could include the training and skills of complementors' employees in the proprietary technology, as well as specific complementor investments in software, equipment, and research and development. Drivers to attract and retain complementors are services and benefits the company provides. An example would be the revenues earned by complementors from using the company's core product and technology; consider, for Visa card adoption, the revenues and interest income a bank receives from its credit card receivables, or the complementor software revenues from products built on Microsoft's proprietary operating system.

Manage Customers

The lock-in company wants to attract new customers by lowering their switching costs. It also wants to create high switching costs for its existing customer base. To lower the switching costs for potential customers, a customer management objective would be to lower search costs and create awareness about the company's product. Measures such as number of citations, number of Internet hits, and rankings on popular Internet search engines provide indications of the ease of access and "buzz" about the company's product. The company should strive to attract highly visible and influential customers to provide credibility and additional awareness of the proprietary product and technology. Companies such as Apple Computer, as well as Digital Equipment Corporation in the 1960s and 1970s, generated awareness and initial sales of their proprietary products by offering computers to colleges and elementary schools. Young people, who would be most comfortable with the new technology, became familiar with the company's products and then selected them for use in their jobs after graduation. Lest the company overinvest in acquiring new customers (for example, AOL's carpet bombing of driveways in the 1990s with free diskettes containing AOL software and an introductory offer of free AOL Internet service for thirty days), a measure of customer acquisition cost could be worth including in the customer management internal process.

The company raises switching costs by training existing customers' employees in the proprietary product and technology, or subsidizing the customers' own investments in specific human resource knowledge and skills. The number of customers' employees trained in the company's proprietary technology indicates the extent of customers' specific investment with the company.

Manage Operations

The high margins from a successful lock-in strategy put less pressure on operating processes to be the most efficient in the industry. It is more important that operating processes have the *capacity* to produce the proprietary product or service without having to subcontract the core technology to suppliers. Once the proprietary technology is released to suppliers, it becomes vulnerable to imitation or appropriation by competitors. Coca-Cola locks in its extensive network of bottlers and distributors by being the sole-source provider of the secret Coke formula. Could the secrecy and inimitability of this product have been sustained for a century if bottlers also produced the syrup under contract to Coca-Cola?

Operations should also provide a product or service platform that is easy to use and access by customers and complementors. If the company's product is difficult to access or use, then customers and complementors incur high costs working with the company, which lowers their costs to switch to a competitor. For example, a major computer system outage for companies such as eBay and AOL could be fatal to customer loyalty. These companies must respond rapidly and massively to any degradation in customer access and use, lest customers become vulnerable to switching to rival suppliers. System reliability, waiting times, and speed of access provide valuable measures of ease of access. Finally, the company wants to continually attract new customers with its core product or service, so continuous improvements of quality and cost enable the company to keep entry prices low (that is, lowering the switching costs for potential customers) while still being profitable, or at least limiting the losses from initial sales to new customers.

Manage Regulatory and Social Processes

A company pursuing a lock-in strategy has two critical regulatory objectives. First, it must protect its proprietary product from imitation and use by competitors, and from unauthorized use by customers, complementors, and suppliers. This requires strong legal protection to prevent competitors from copying the product or core technology, and customers from using the product without paying for it, such as has been seen in the piracy and copying problems faced by many software companies. The company must vigorously protect and enforce the uniqueness it offers so that it can continue to enjoy the benefits from a successful lock-in strategy. The company must enforce contracts and penalize violators to ensure that customers, suppliers, and complementors do not deviate from or violate the proprietary standard or rules of exchange.

Second, the winner-take-all aspect of successful system lock-in strategies leads to high market shares that will inevitably attract the attention of antitrust enforcers in government agencies and entrepreneurial trial lawyers in civil litigation. It is not illegal to have a high market share, but a company with a high market share must be extra cautious about its business practices. It must strive for "Goldilocks" pricing of its core product: Prices that are too high could be perceived as exploiting consumers with its monopoly position (that is, eliminating all the value captured by consumers in Figure 11-1); and prices that are too low could be perceived as predatory to competitors. Prices must be "just right." The company must avoid illegal forced bundling of products and services to customers, and, in general, practices that violate a country's antitrust laws. As Microsoft discovered in the 1990s, and IBM and AT&T in the 1970s and 1980s, antitrust litigation is extremely expensive, damaging to the company's reputation, and distracting from the company's efforts to maintain and enhance its system lock-in advantages. High market share companies have to be diligent in signaling to all employees the business practices that make the company vulnerable to antitrust litigation. Measures of incidents that make the company vulnerable to antitrust actions should be developed in conjunction with the company's legal staff. Such measures, of *potential litigation incidents,* would be analogous to the environmental and safety incident measures used by many companies.

On managing social processes, the company should direct its community investments to activities that support the company's proprietary technology. We have already mentioned in this chapter how Apple donates computers to primary schools, and how Cisco uses "context-specific" philanthropy to establish the Cisco Networking Academy for training computer network administrators (see Chapter 6). Such investment in communities generates attractive job opportunities for urban high school graduates while at the same time alleviating a shortage of qualified employees for managing and maintaining complex networks that, by the way, happen to be built with Cisco routers. Companies can measure the extent of their social investment that reinforces its lock-in business model. The target for such context-specific philanthropy does not have to be 100 percent, but it is unlikely that the desired target for companies' context-specific philanthropic spending is zero.

Learning and Growth

Human Capital
The human capital requirement for a lock-in strategy, as for any strategy, must be aligned with the critical internal processes of that strategy. For innovation, the company needs scientists and engineers who are leaders in the proprietary technology. For managing customers and complementors, the company needs employees who have knowledge of these stakeholders' businesses and needs so that they can devise and deliver attractive services to them. For managing operations, employees must be intensely customer-focused, providing superb service and responsiveness that enhance loyalty among customers and complementors. Such actions keep perceived switching costs high among these critical stakeholders.

For managing regulatory processes, employees of high market share, successful lock-in companies must be knowledgeable about actions that can lead to litigation and governmental restraints. They must be committed to always staying within the law in their actions with customers and complementors. Even low-level employees can take actions or make statements in e-mails that will prove extremely damaging if disclosed during legal and regulatory proceedings.

Information Capital

Information capital is often the heart of a system lock-in strategy. The information resource provides the platform used by customers, complementors, and competitors. Ideally the information platform should be complex so that competitors cannot easily imitate it, but customers and complementors find it easy to access and use. Providing a complex information resource with an easy-to-use interface is a challenge for a company's information technology.

System lock-in advantages are reinforced when the company has extensive knowledge of customers' and complementors' behavior. Customer relationship management systems and customer databases, which also track the activities of complementors, are valuable assets for lock-in companies.

Organization Capital

The culture of a lock-in company should be highly customer- and complementor-centric. A key to success is providing exceptional service and responsiveness so that customers and complementors always perceive that a switch to an alternative provider would be fraught with uncertainty about whether they would continue to receive comparable excellent service from a rival. The entire organization must stay focused on raising the switching costs away from the company, and lowering the switching costs for potential customers and complementors. This culture should be pervasive for all employees, since it affects innovation, customer and complementor management processes, operating processes, and the regulatory and social processes.

SUMMARY

A well-constructed strategy map should show the interrelationships among the organization's internal processes and intangible assets that create sustainable competitive advantage. A strategy, as articulated by

Michael Porter, will be most successful when the collection of integrated and aligned activities enable the company to offer a value proposition—whether low total cost, product leadership, complete customer solutions, or system lock-in—better than competitors. In this chapter we have shown how the value proposition in the customer perspective, the critical internal processes, and the intangible assets in the learning and growth perspective of a strategy map will be completely different for companies following different strategies. This chapter makes operational our statement that an organization's strategy map and Balanced Scorecard should tell the story of its strategy, a story that differentiates the organization from competitors.

The case studies following this chapter show examples of four companies following quite different strategies. Tata Auto Plastics follows a low total cost strategy, though with the interesting twist of striving to excel at managing its product development process so that it can offer a complete life-cycle solution to its automotive customers. MDS is a diversified health and life sciences company whose strategy features innovation and growth in new markets. Boise Office Solutions wants to compete not on low-cost provision of standard office products but by a CRM strategy that would consolidate and integrate its business units and leverage a core distribution network to provide customers with seamless access to all products and services. Thomson Financial offers integrated information and solutions to its key customers in the financial industry through a desktop interface that gives customers complete and ready access to the large array of Thomson's financial products and services.

NOTES

1. Michael Porter, "What Is Strategy?" *Harvard Business Review* (November–December 1996): 64.
2. Ibid., 73.
3. Michael Porter, *Competitive Advantage: Creating and Sustaining Superior Performance* (New York: Free Press, 1985).
4. Michael Treacy and Fred Wiersema, *The Discipline of Market Leaders* (Reading, MA: Addison-Wesley, 1995); Robert S. Kaplan and David P. Norton, *The Strategy-Focused Organization: How Balanced Scorecard Companies Thrive in the New Business Environment* (Boston: Harvard Business School Press, 2001), Chapter 3, especially 83–99.
5. A. Hax and D. Wilde, *The Delta Project: Discovering New Sources of Profitability in a Networked Economy* (New York: Palgrave, 2001), 81–104.
6. W. C. Kim and R. A. Mauborgne, "Value Innovation: The Strategic Logic of High Growth," *Harvard Business Review* (January 1997): 103–112; "Creating Market Space," *Harvard Business Review* (January 1999): 83–93; and "Strategy,

Value Innovation, and the Knowledge Economy," *Sloan Management Review* (Spring 1999): 41–53.

7. M. Porter, *Competitive Strategy: Techniques for Analyzing Industries and Competitors* (New York: Free Press, 1980).

8. Treacy and Wiersema referred to this strategy as "operational excellence." We now agree with Porter that operational excellence is not a strategy. Any organization has to be operationally excellent for implementing its particular strategy. The value proposition must represent what the organization offers its customers, not how the organization manages its internal processes. We now reinterpret or relabel the Treacy and Wiersema "operationally excellent" strategy as a *low total cost* strategy.

9. Activity-based costing accurately reveals the cost of excess variety, a cost that many organizations fail to recognize because of distortions introduced by their traditional costing systems. See Robert S. Kaplan and Robin Cooper, *Cost & Effect: Using Integrated Cost Systems to Drive Profitability and Performance* (Boston: Harvard Business School Press, 1998).

10. "Better" in this message refers to higher quality (conformance to specifications), not "better" in the sense of the higher performance offered by product leadership companies or in the sense of more customized to an individual customer's needs.

11. Lock-in strategies are described in Chapters 5 and 6 of Carl Shapiro and Hal Varian, *Information Rules: A Strategic Guide to the Network Economy* (Boston: Harvard Business School Press, 1999).

12. Hax and Wilde, *The Delta Project*, particularly Chapter 5.

13. Barry Nalebuff and Adam Brandenburger, *Co-Opetition: A Revolutionary Mindset That Combines Competition and Co-Operation: The Game Theory Strategy That's Changing the Game of Business* (New York: Doubleday, 1996).

CASE STUDIES

TATA AUTO PLASTIC SYSTEMS

Background

The Tata Group of India is a leader in a diverse set of industries, both manu-facturing (materials, energy, engineering, chemicals, and consumer products) and service (telecommunications, computing, communications, financial ser-vices, and hospitality). Tata Auto Plastic Systems (TAPS), an operating sub-sidiary of the Tata Group, was set up in collaboration with the Faurecia Group of France and the Foggini Group of Italy. TAPS's customers include the major auto companies of the world such as Ford, Faurecia, MG Rover, and, in India, companies such as Tata Engineering, Fiat India, General Motors, and Bajaj Auto.

TAPS offers world-class interior and exterior products including dash-boards, door pads, air vents, bumpers, and trims with European styling and fin-ishes. Its customers demand high, consistent levels of quality, just-in-time delivery, and year-on-year cost reductions. TAPS adopted a strategy of total cost leadership.

Strategy Map and Balanced Scorecard

TAPS's financial perspective is straightforward, encompassing a high-level ob-jective to increase its *return-on-capital-employed* (ROCE) beyond the com-pany's weighted average cost of capital (WACC). It supports this high-level objective with an objective to increase business (earning above WACC) with ex-isting and new customers, and to expand export business for revenue growth and profitability. The productivity component emphasizes industry cost leader-ship and maximizing asset utilization (see Figure 11-6).

Figure 11-6 Tata Auto Plastic Systems Strategy Map

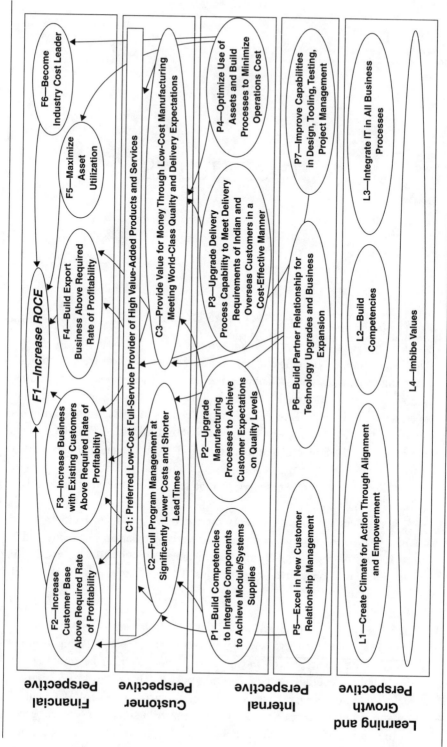

The customer perspective identifies how TAPS must meet customer expectations on quality, cost, and delivery to realize its revenue, growth, and profitability objectives. TAPS has objectives to retain its current position as a significant Tier I supplier in India and to become a Tier II supplier in the global market. The focus in the customer perspective is on low-cost full service, from product concept through product development, engineering, and delivery. TAPS strives to take full product responsibility for its customers, providing them with high value for their money through world-class quality, cost, and delivery of products and services.

The objectives in the internal perspective focus on creating processes and acquiring competencies necessary to support the customer objectives. Its internal competencies build around two strategic themes: cost leadership to penetrate Indian and global customer markets; and innovation to build design and engineering competencies that meet global standards so that it could move up the value chain in future years.

The learning and growth perspective supports the creation of a climate to achieve the objectives in the other perspectives, building competencies and integrating information technology in all processes.

The actual objectives and measures for the Tata Auto Plastic's strategy map are shown in Figure 11-7. Of the company's thirty-five measures, eleven were existing measures (all in the financial and internal perspectives), and twenty-four were entirely new to the company.

Perspective	Existing Measures	New Measures
Financial	7	2
Customer	0	6
Internal	4	10
Learning and growth	0	6

TAPS's existing measures had focused narrowly on financial and short-term operational objectives. Its new strategic measures focused on opportunities for revenue growth through forging new relationships with customers by not only excelling at cost, quality, and lead time but also building new relationships, excelling at product development and project management, and enhancing the capabilities of employees, systems, and organizational alignment processes.

Results

TAPS executives are using the Balanced Scorecard to balance expectations among its various stakeholders (see Figure 11-7). The strategy map and Scorecard have brought clarity and alignment so that the organization is now fo-

Figure 11-7 Tata Auto Plastic Systems Balanced Scorecard

	Objectives	Measures
Financial Perspective	F1: Increase ROCE F2: Increase customer base F3: Increase business with existing customers F4: Build export business F5: Maximize asset utilization F6: Become industry cost leader	■ Return on capital employed ■ Number of new OEMs ■ Sales from new OEMs ■ Sales (turnover) from existing OEMs ■ Sales of new products with existing OEMs ■ Sales from export business ■ Asset turnover ■ Operating cost/sales ■ Cost reduction achieved over standard cost, by product family
Customer Perspective	C1: Preferred low-cost full-service supplier of high value-added (HVA) products and services C2: Full program management at significantly lower costs and shorter lead times C3: Provide value for money through low-cost manufacturing that meets world-class quality and delivery expectations	■ Value of request for quotes (RFQs) received as full-service supplier (FSS) of modules and systems ■ Value of orders as FSS ■ Value of RFQs obtained for full program ■ Value of orders obtained for full program ■ Customer satisfaction index ■ Number of quality issues raised in J.D. Power report
Internal Perspective	P1: Build competencies to integrate components to achieve module/system supplies P2: Upgrade manufacturing processes to achieve customer expectations on quality levels P3: Upgrade delivery processes' capability to meet delivery requirements of Indian and overseas customers in a cost-effective manner P4: Optimize use of assets and build processes to minimize operations costs P5: Excel in customer relationship management P6: Build partner relationships to upgrade technology and expand business P7: Improve capabilities in design tooling, testing, and project management	■ Capability index ■ Part-per-million (PPM) customer rejects ■ Percent delivery compliance—on time, in full ■ Capability index ■ Reduction in logistics cost compared to standard cost ■ Overall equipment effectiveness ■ Material cost against standard cost ■ Energy cost as percent of sales ■ Direct labor cost as percent of sales ■ Relationship index ■ Number of new technologies acquired through relationships ■ Growth in turnover through partner relationships ■ Capability index ■ Year-to-year reduction in lead time for product development
Learning and Growth Perspective	L1: Create climate for action through alignment and empowerment L2: Build competencies L3: Integrate IT in all business processes	■ Number of employees whose key performace appraisals are linked to strategic objectives ■ Empowerment index ■ Number of key business processes empowered to lower levels ■ Strategic skill coverage ratio ■ Percent of processes covered by IT ■ IT effectiveness satisfaction survey

cused on key strategic performance areas. Various initiatives linked to scorecard objectives have become more focused and have resulted in teams achieving much better results. Two examples are presented below:

1. TAPS's industry cost leadership objective in the financial perspective has helped it identify various measures to control cost, such as the ratio of operations cost to sales and cost reduction achieved over standard cost. A focused review of the performance on these measures on a monthly basis has identified areas for improvement. Various initiatives, such as six sigma projects to reduce power and material consumption, reduction in material wastage, and improvement in IT systems for better information management, have been undertaken. Apart from the significant tangible benefits delivered by these initiatives, the focus has created cost ownership at departmental and functional levels.

2. The objective of *building competencies* in the learning and growth perspective led to identifying knowledge and skill gaps in key functional areas. The company has developed a road map to bridge the gaps.

We thank Rajiv Bakshi of Tata Auto Plastics and Muhamed Muneer, CEO of Innovative Media, for their assistance and support in developing the TAPS case.

MDS

Background

Headquartered in Toronto, MDS is an international health and life sciences company that provides products and services for the prevention, diagnosis, and treatment of disease. MDS is a publicly traded company listed on both the New York and Toronto Stock Exchanges. With locations in twenty-three countries, MDS employs more than 10,000 people and had fiscal 2002 revenues of CAN $1.8 billion. MDS is a diversified company operating through three major business sectors: MDS Isotopes supplies imaging agents for nuclear medicine, material for sterilization systems, and therapy systems for planning and delivery of cancer treatment; MDS Diagnostics provides laboratory information and services to prevent, diagnose, and treat illness; and MDS Drug Discovery and Development provides contract research services to the pharmaceutical industry, develops analytical instruments to assist in bringing new drugs to market, and pioneers the development of functional proteomics in finding completely new ways to discover drugs.

MDS had a long history of consistent growth in both earnings and revenues. Executive management felt, however, that the company needed to become much better at executing strategy. For MDS, success at executing strategy meant two things: First, it had to deliver financial success, defined by achieving a compounded annual growth rate (CAGR) of earnings of 15 percent on a rolling five-year basis, while sustaining its historic CAGR of 15 percent in revenues. Second, MDS had to transform itself. MDS executives believed that their markets and their position in those markets provided an enormous opportunity to shift from being a very good company to (in the words of Jim Collins) being a truly great company. Becoming a great company would require MDS to become sharply focused on what was strategically important, to unplug a number of activities, and to be more clearly aligned—from top to bottom—as an organization.

Strategy Map

As a multibusiness management company, each MDS business unit had a different customer value proposition and a different way of creating value for those customers. Therefore, MDS had a collection of strategies (customer intimacy, operational excellence, innovation) depending on the business unit and its customer base. Its enterprise strategy map was purposefully broad because it represented a portfolio of strategies. The components of the strategy map in rectangles—the core values and shared strategic destination—were common and unchanging (see Figure 11-8). The map communicated an equal balance between shareholder value and a passionate culture. Whereas each MDS business unit had a different path for creating value, the corporate strategy ensured that the financial, customer, internal process, and people perspective priorities would be collectively advanced.

Build an enduring global health and life sciences company: The overarching MDS vision was to build a great global health and life sciences company. To become global required expanding well beyond its historic Canadian and North American base.

Passionate about the kind of company we are building together: The professional passion shared by MDS employees would make the company distinct and competitively vital. Sustaining passion would build superior shareholder value and advance the goal of building an enduring company.

Build superior shareholder value: MDS would build superior shareholder value over the long term by achieving a compounded average annual EPS growth rate of 15 percent on a rolling five-year basis.

F1: Grow revenues: Revenue growth was a key objective of financial success for driving shareholder value. MDS targeted a compounded average annual revenue growth rate of 15 percent on a rolling five-year basis.

Figure 11-8 MDS Strategy Map

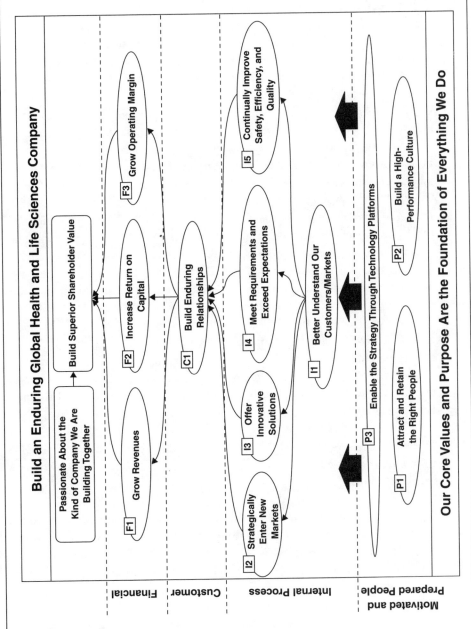

F2: Increase return on capital: Since MDS was becoming a much more capital-intensive business, it had to become more disciplined and rigorous in its allocation of capital. It would exit unproductive businesses and leverage technology to generate higher returns.

F3: Grow operating margin: MDS would manage operating expenses while remaining prepared to spend if expenditures could advance revenues. Elimination of inefficient, non-value-added activities was a priority.

C1: Build enduring relationships: All business units, despite different customers and value propositions, would focus on attracting, growing, and retaining customer relationships. Business units would deliver on customer value propositions that emphasized intimate customer relationships, innovative solutions, and superior service delivery.

I1: Better understand our customers and markets: In-depth customer and marketplace knowledge would drive all MDS processes. The marketplace included competitors, suppliers, regulators, current customers, and prospective customers. Armed with this knowledge, MDS would be better able to enter new markets, offer innovative solutions, meet expectations, and continually improve.

I2: Strategically enter new markets: This objective was the key for future growth potential as MDS brought valuable capital, knowledge, and networks to new market opportunities. The timing for entering new markets was important and needed to balance the effects of dilution with the life cycle of the market opportunity.

I3: Offer innovative solutions: Through internal efforts and partnerships, MDS would integrate science, research, and technology to deliver value-added innovative solutions.

I4: Meet requirements and exceed expectations: Follow-through on customer commitments was essential for building enduring relationships. MDS would meet customer requirements for specifications and performance agreements, and always aim to provide customers with an experience that exceeded their expectations.

I5: Continually improve safety, efficiency, and quality: To become a great company, MDS must find ways to continuously improve the safety, productivity, and quality of its operations.

P1: Attract and retain the right people: The key to MDS's continued success was the ability to grow and develop its talent pipeline. The "right people" would have the competencies and values consistent with MDS's culture and strategic objectives.

P2: Build a high-performance culture: Vital to the future of MDS was fostering a values-driven, high-achievement, and team-oriented culture in which people could fulfill their potential.

P3: Enable the strategy through technology platforms: Technology was essential for enabling the strategy. The right technology platforms would improve return on capital and allow greater focus on building enduring relationships.

Our core values and purpose are the foundation of everything we do: MDS's core values were common and shared across the firm. Everything MDS did would be aligned with the core values and the strategy.

Results

In 1998, having just achieved $1 billion in revenue, MDS set a goal to reach $2 billion by 2003. MDS launched the BSC in August 2001. Results for 2002 show that major financial indicators, including cash flow from operations and core earnings per share, were the strongest in the past five years. MDS was on target to achieve its 2003 $2 billion revenue target. Executive management attributed some of this success to the Balanced Scorecard, noting, "There is huge strategic value in using the strategy map and Balanced Scorecard to clarify the role of a corporate strategy and to describe the strategy and performance expectations of business units," and "Each of 10,000 employees is now linked to the strategy through individual or team Balanced Scorecards."

Case prepared by Mike Nagel and Jay Weiser of Balanced Scorecard Collaborative. Our thanks to Bob Harris, John Rogers, and their colleagues for sharing the MDS experience.

BOISE OFFICE SOLUTIONS

Background

Boise Office Solutions, a $3.5 billion distributor of office and technology products, office furniture, and paper products, had grown through acquisitions. This legacy led to its various lines of business operating independently. Its customers viewed office products as commodities to be acquired at the lowest prices.

The Strategy

Boise adopted a new CRM strategy that would consolidate and integrate its business units and leverage a core distribution network to provide customers with seamless access to all products and services. It set an objective to increase profitability by creating a clear distinction between high-value customer service—procurement process management—and limited customer value, a focus on per-item pricing. It would enhance value to customers through use of one-to-one marketing approaches that would create personalized experiences independent of the channel used by the customers and would anticipate customers' individual needs and preferences to provide customized offers. Boise would also reduce operating expenses through process improvements and reducing duplication across business units. For the new strategy to succeed, Boise would need to invest in customer-centric information technology and to realign, refocus, and retool the workforce around the new customer solutions business model.

The Strategy Map

Boise produced its strategy map to represent its new customer solution strategy (see Figure 11-9). The financial perspective reflected the normal combination of revenue growth and operating efficiency objectives. It highlighted the importance of customer segmentation by measuring growth, profit contribution, and cost-to-serve by individual customer segment. Figure 11-10 shows the measures for each objective in the strategy map.

In the customer perspective, Boise measured the value proposition with a customer satisfaction survey on relationship, service, and ease-of-access; these were the core elements in Boise's new customer value and service orientation. The second customer objective, to create distinctive customer value, was measured by success in acquiring new customers in targeted segments, retaining customers in the targeted segments, and estimates of lifetime customer value, to determine the company's success in breaking the downward spiral of commodity pricing.

Boise's internal process objectives were organized into three themes:

- *Operational excellence:* Rationalize operations
- *Customer management:* Leverage customer service
- *Innovation:* Redefine customer value expectations

For rationalizing operations, Boise wanted to move more of its customers to an e-commerce channel that would provide more convenient customer access, increase the customer's contact efficiency, and lower Boise's operational costs associated with customer contacts. Success for this objective would be measured by the percentage of business in targeted segments that used the

Figure 11-9 Boise Office Solutions Strategy Map

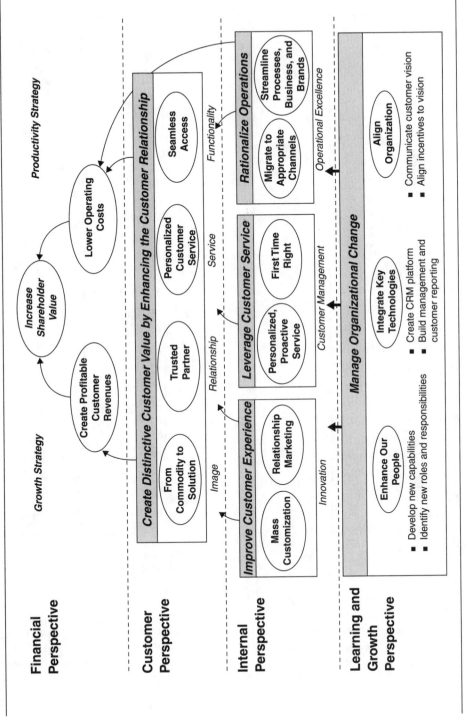

Figure 11-10 Boise Cascade Office Division CRM Balanced Scorecard

	Objectives	Measures
Financial Perspective	F1: Profitable growth	▪ Economic Value Added ▪ Earnings Before Interest and Taxes
	F2: Grow organically	▪ Growth by value segment ▪ Contribution profit/value impact by segment
	F3: Lower costs	▪ Cost to serve by value segment ▪ Cost to serve by channel
Customer Perspective	C1: Value proposition	▪ Customer survey (via sales representatives) ▪ Acquisition by segment
	C2: Creating distinction	▪ Retention by segment ▪ Lifetime customer value
Internal Perspective	*Improve customer experience* I1: Mass customization I2: One-to-one marketing	▪ Response rate to campaigns ▪ Number of customers using PIN
	Leverage customer service I3: Done-in-one I4: Personalized, proactive service	▪ Reduced number of customer cases ▪ Response to nonpromotional campaigns
	Rationalize operations I5: Optimized channel mix (orders, services, problems) I6: Streamline processes	▪ Channel mix ▪ Percent interactive channels by value segment ▪ Percent interactive channels by need segment ▪ Percent redundancies eliminated ▪ Savings
Learning and Growth Perspective	L1: Enhance our people's capabilities	▪ Percent trained in "one Boise" skills ▪ Percent "one Boise" new jobs filled
	L2: Align organization around "one Boise" vision	▪ "One Vision" staff survey—engagement with strategy ▪ Percent staff with incentives aligned with strategy
	L3: Integrate key technologies	▪ CRM technologies versus plan (R1, R2, R3, etc.) ▪ Percent "one Boise" reporting implemented ▪ Percent "one Boise" reporting implemented with customer ▪ Percent "one Boise" reporting implemented for management

e-commerce channel. Boise measured the objective of reducing operational costs not only in dollars of savings but also in the number of redundant operations eliminated through contact consolidation.

For leveraging customer service, Boise wanted to personalize the ordering experience, reduce the number of total interactions, and make interactions easier overall. It measured this objective with "done-in-one" rates (the ability to fulfill the complete range of customer needs in a single call), on-time delivery, and service performance, and by the number of open customer issues or concerns. It also took into consideration anecdotal customer responses to marketing and sales campaigns promoting higher service levels (not based on price or promotions) to determine that it was becoming a trusted, value-added supplier.

For innovation, Boise wanted to reset customer value expectations by demonstrating how its customers could achieve greater overall management control of its spending on office supplies. Doing this entailed finding new ways for effective mass customization and one-to-one marketing. Boise measured the number and percent of customer locations participating in contract purchase plans as well as overall customer purchase patterns annually against the customer's industry and against national averages, and evaluated purchase patterns by individuals within the customer organization.

For learning and growth, the capabilities had to focus on the new customer-centric strategy. Employee capabilities were measured by the percentage of people trained in the skills for the new strategy (an internal "One Boise" communication campaign) and the ability to translate understanding of the strategy into customer contacts and value propositions. The technology for the new strategy required implementing comprehensive CRM software capabilities across the company. One measure was milestone reporting on implementing this major IT initiative. IT capabilities were also measured by percentage of reporting that had been implemented in three critical locations: with the sales force in the field; in customer locations; and for Boise management. Organizational alignment would be measured by the percentage of staff with incentives aligned to the new strategy and a staff survey that would measure employees' awareness and engagement with the "One Boise" strategy.

Anecdote

Dave Goudge, senior vice president of marketing, reported that general managers and sales managers at Boise Office Solutions had rapidly embraced the One Boise customer-focused strategy. They could now offer even their price-sensitive customers an integrated office products solution that would deliver greater value than that offered by low-priced competitors. The strategy provided justification for an internal information technology initiative that enhanced the selling process by providing sales representatives with better customer information. Goudge used the BSC to measure and communicate the returns from the One Boise strategy for senior corporate executives.

Randy Russell of Balanced Scorecard Collaborative prepared this case. Our thanks to Dave Goudge, Scott Williams, and their colleagues for sharing the Boise Office Solutions experience.

THOMSON FINANCIAL

Background

Thomson Financial (TF) is one of four major market groups that comprise the Thomson Corporation. With 44,000 employees and operations in fifty-three countries, the Thomson Corporation is a leading global provider of integrated information solutions to business and professional customers with 2002 revenues of more than U.S. $7.8 billion. Thomson provides critical information, with supporting technology and applications that help its customers make better decisions faster. Thomson serves more than 20 million information users in the fields of law, tax, accounting, higher education, reference information, corporate training and assessment, financial services, scientific research, and health care.

By the end of 2001, Thomson CEO Dick Harrington had completed some major transformational activities throughout Thomson. He had divested 90 percent of the print-based businesses to complete his transformation strategy to be 80 percent electronic by 2005; acquired major content and technology-based assets such as Harcourt to gain scale for each of the market groups; and was now seeking a framework to add rigor to Thomson's operating system in order to drive organic growth, while pursuing operating efficiency. It was this final, corporate-driven push that presented the need for a consistent and proven strategy execution framework offered by the Balanced Scorecard. In late 2001, Thomson decided to implement the Scorecard throughout the organization as a corporate-sponsored program.

As a $1.5 billion provider of integrated information and solutions to the worldwide financial industry, TF's customers consist primarily of investment banks, money management firms, corporate investor relations divisions, and other firms, small and large, requiring real-time financial information to support buying and selling decisions. Historically a product-focused organization, competing against companies such as Reuters and Bloomberg, TF until recently had been better known in the marketplace by its leading brand names, such as ILX, Securities Data, First Call Analyst, and AutEx. This was the obvious result of Thomson having aggressively acquired numerous successful niche-based, technology-intensive businesses throughout the 1980s and 1990s.

At the end of 2002, TF had approximately 9,200 employees worldwide with operations in twenty-five countries.

The Situation

TF was already responding to a number of burning platforms at the time of initial BSC adoption in early 2002. The marketplace was experiencing technological changes (increasing use of Internet-based technologies), regulatory changes, and economic changes (the bursting of the stock market bubble in March 2000 and the attacks of September 11). The industry was suffering: Fewer and fewer financial deals were being announced and most companies were downsizing headcount and spending. TF customers who historically had been willing to pay a premium for TF's content-rich subscription-based services were now looking to consolidate accounts and reduce their costs. Thomson Financial, recognizing the need to deliver greater value more efficiently, was in the process of reorganizing both its technology infrastructure and organizational structure to be more customer-facing. Indeed, the ability to satisfy the customer's enterprise needs by establishing a strategy of "One TF" was already under way by the time the BSC program began.

Dave Shaffer, CEO of Thomson Financial, has numerous roles and responsibilities across Thomson, including executive vice president and chief operating officer of Thomson Corporation. As COO, he was a strong proponent of better leveraging all Thomson assets, and led the efforts early on at TF to transform this collection of businesses to "One TF."

The Strategy

TF's new strategic direction was partially an extension of its reorganization into strategic customer-facing units (SCUs) at the end of 2001. SCUs included the investment management group, banking and brokerage group, corporate group, and a global sales and account management team to target the top fifty worldwide accounts. TF's approach also involved mapping out the customer's workflow within and across these three customer segments, leveraging appropriate assets, and developing enterprise-wide solutions that spanned the value chain. If and when a gap became apparent, TF planned to partner strategically with both the customer and other suppliers to complete and deliver an integrated information solution. This would make TF a strategic partner with its customers as opposed to a product seller in what was becoming an increasingly commoditized marketplace. As Sharon Rowlands, TF's COO, pointed out in a midyear 2002 memo to employees, "A positive impact of the current business environment is that customers are continuing to move to partnering with single providers like TF and purchasing high-value integrated solutions in order to better manage their costs."

The Strategy Map

Since TF's business units traditionally had the primary role in executing the strategy, TF adopted a single strategy map that would serve the purpose of uniting them to a common strategy around *providing tailored desktop technology bundled with workflow applications and integrated "must-have" information* (see Figure 11-11). The "One TF" map therefore contained a set of objectives that could be applied across the entire organization:

a. *Financial:* Grow revenue through expanded markets—that is, increase both geographical and product presence and increase market share. On the productivity side, improve return on invested capital (ROIC) by growing EBITDA, managing receivables, and capital spending.

b. *Customer:* Provide customers with the right information and technology solutions at the right time so they can make better decisions faster and get a demonstrated benefit (ROIC). Develop strategic relationships with major clients and promote the Thomson Financial brand as leading, global, innovative, and authoritative.

c. *Internal Themes:*
Markets and Customers: Understand customer workflow through value chain analysis to inform product development, cross-selling potential, and partnership opportunities.
Solutions: Rationalize technology by consolidating platforms, components, and tools.
Operations: Improve systems reliability and consistency of service.

d. *People:* Develop leaders, attract and retain high performers—especially those with industry experience—and broaden sales skills (including product knowledge). Finally, create and reinforce a common strategy-focused culture.

Anecdotes

Since change management initiatives tend to come and go, the Balanced Scorecard was initially greeted with some skepticism and a management mind-set that the BSC is a metrics program. Several key managers at TF had also experienced use of a scorecard at their previous companies and generally described those programs as ineffective.

According to CFO David Turner:

When I arrived in 2001, TF was a decentralized organization where basic, centralized processes were lacking and independent strategies and measurements existed. The introduction of the Balanced Scorecard underscored not only the cost of decentralization but the benefits to change as well as a clear road map to guide our transformation. It essentially

Figure 11-11 Thomson Financial Strategy Map

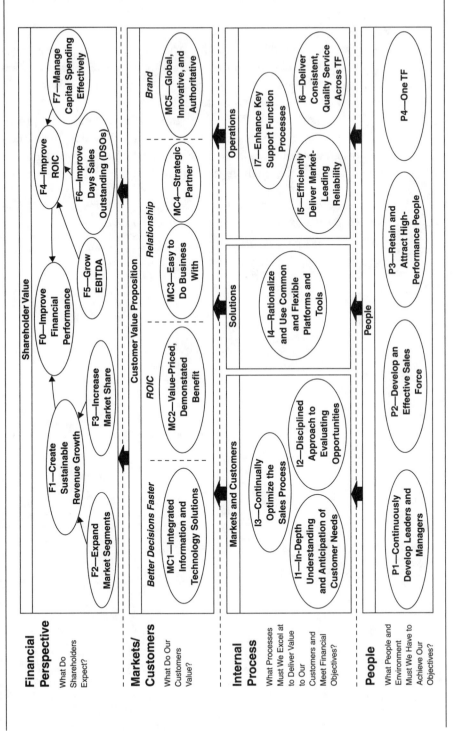

provided a discipline and incentive to get our strategy, people, and processes aligned.

TF has also instituted and aligned monthly operational business unit-level reports on key measures and major initiatives that drive quarterly scorecard results. These are consistent across business units, with only a few minor differences based on the uniqueness of the unit.

A close-knit community of scorecard program managers and other practitioners now meets quarterly to share best practices. TF will be able to continually leverage progress made elsewhere in the organization and evolve their use of the scorecard to extract even more value in the future.

Case prepared by Barnaby Donlon and Rondo Moses of the Balanced Scorecard Collaborative and Ro Pavlick of Thomson. Our thanks to Dick Harrington and Dave Shaffer for sharing the Thomson experience.

CHAPTER TWELVE

PLANNING THE CAMPAIGN

IN PREVIOUS CHAPTERS, we described the building blocks of strategy and value creation. We showed how internal processes create and deliver the differentiating value proposition to targeted customers. We demonstrated how to align intangible assets—human, information, and organization capital—to these critical internal processes so that the value proposition can be continually improved. These connections, however, represent only a static model of value creation. In this chapter, we introduce the value creation dynamics.

Three ingredients must be added to the strategy map to create the dynamics of strategy.

1. *Quantify:* Establish targets and validate the cause-and-effect relationships in the strategy map
2. *Define the time line:* Determine how strategic themes will create value in short-, medium-, and long-term horizons to create balanced and sustained value creation
3. *Select initiatives*: Choose the strategic investments and action programs that will enable the organization to achieve its targeted performance in the stated time frames

Without quantifying, a strategic objective is simply a passive statement of intent. "Reduce the product development cycle," for example, signals that product development is one of the critical few processes to improve if the strategy is to succeed. "Reduce the product development cycle from three years to nine months" signals that radical, outside-the-box thinking is required to achieve such a breakthrough. "Reduce the product development cycle from three years to nine months by year $(t_0 + 4)$" signals that this is a long-term project; the ultimate achievement of the objective will take place four years from now. For the organization to achieve this objective within the specified time period, it will require specific action programs; for example, the product development process must be reengineered, and new skills and new technologies must be acquired. Figure 12-1 identifies specific initiatives and the associated budget that are required to achieve the overall objective for a strategic theme of enhancing internal product development at Hi-Tek Manufacturing.

Setting targets is part of any planning exercise, but the usual approach is fragmented and not cumulative. For example, the engineering department sets targets to reduce the product development cycle while the HR department sets targets for retaining key staff members. The strategy map allows an organization to take a holistic perspective. The organization, by clarifying the complete value-creating logic of a strategic theme, now has a framework that integrates the various processes for implementing the strategy: setting targets, defining and selecting initiatives to achieve the targeted performance, and authorizing the budgets for the initiatives. The collection of linked objectives, targets, initiatives, and budgets for a strategic theme, such as that shown in Figure 12-1, provides a complete, stand-alone business case for that piece of the strategy.

The strategic theme is the building block of strategy. It creates a *microeconomic model* of *one* dimension of the strategy. But strategy requires that several such value-creating themes be managed simultaneously. The strategy map of Hi-Tek Manufacturing, shown in Figure 12-2, identifies seven complementary and simultaneous themes, each creating value at a different point in time. The *innovation* themes create value over a three- to five-year period. The "internal product" *development* theme (just described) and the "technology partnership" theme both ensure the flow of new products that will sustain growth in the future. The *customer management* themes—"solution selling" and "relationship management"— will take one to three years to change the interface with the customer. The *operations management themes*—"just-in-time" operations and "flexible manufacturing"—will create value quickly through cost reductions and productivity improvements. The *responsible citizen* theme—"build the community"—shapes long-term success by ensuring availability of a quality workforce. Each of these themes has its own microeconomic action plan.

Figure 12-1 Quantifying the Strategy at Hi-Tek Manufacturing

Strategic Theme: Internal Product Development

Strategy Map		Balanced Scorecard			Action Plan	
	Objective	Measure	Target	Initiative	Budget
Financial Perspective — Revenue Growth	Grow Revenue from New Products	■ Annual Revenue Growth ■ Percent Revenues from New Products	+25% 30%	■ XX ■ XX	 $AAA
Customer Perspective — Innovative Products	Satisfy Customer Needs for State-of-the-Art Capabilities	■ Customer Retention ■ Share of Account	80% 40%	■ Relationship Management ■ Gain Sharing Program	$BBB
Internal Perspective — World-Class Internal Product Development	Accelerate New Product Development	■ First to Market ■ Time to Market	75% 9 months	■ Annual Industry Show Program ■ Development Cycle Time Reengineering	$CCC $DDD
Learning and Growth Perspective — Stable High-Talent Workforce	Acquire, Develop, and Retain Strategic Skills	■ Specialized Competency Availability ■ Key Staff Retention	100% 95%	■ Competency Model ■ New Hiring Program ■ Supervisory Training ■ Benefits Program	$EEE $FFF $GGG
				Total Budget	**$HHH**

Strategy Map arrow: Internal Product Development → Stable High-Talent Workforce → World-Class Internal Product Development → Innovative Products → Revenue Growth

Figure 12-2 The Hi-Tek Manufacturing Strategy Map

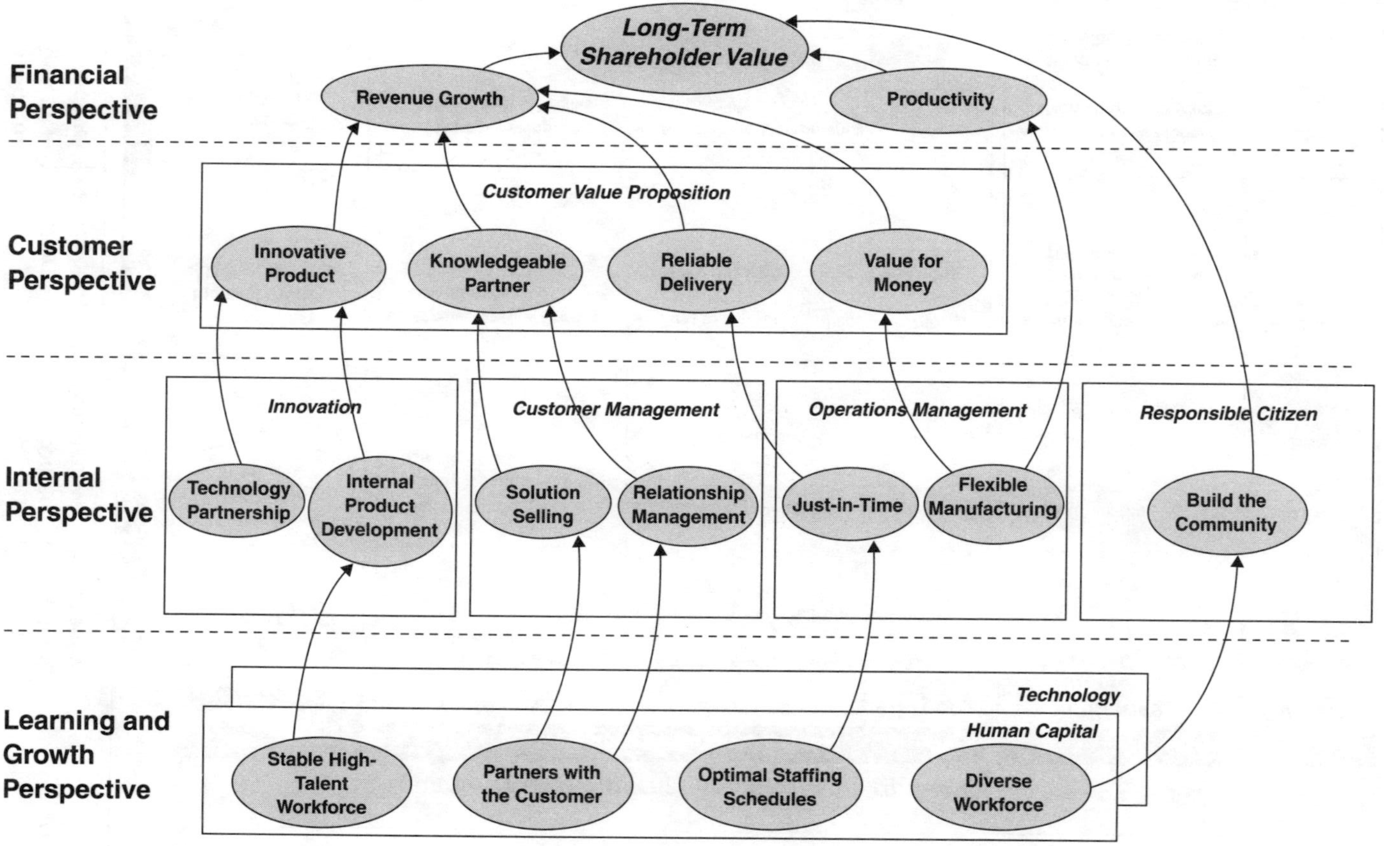

Using a military metaphor, each strategic theme is analogous to a battle; the strategy includes a "battle" to improve solution selling, and a "battle" to reduce the product development cycle. Battles are the building blocks of a military campaign, but unless battles are organized into a broader strategic logic, one can win several battles, and still lose the war. The same is true for our model of enterprise strategy—managers can successfully execute one theme, one piece of the strategy, but not achieve desired performance. They lose the war, in effect, because they have not executed or coordinated other strategic themes.

The strategy map of the enterprise provides the *macroeconomic model* for planning the overall campaign. The same principles of quantifying targets and establishing time lines for accomplishment that we applied to strategic themes also apply to the overall strategy map.

The Cigna case, introduced in our earlier work, provides an excellent example of the dynamic management of parallel strategic themes.[1] Gerry Isom accepted the presidency of Cigna Property & Casualty in 1993 when the division was on the brink of failure. Business losses had mounted and the division was nearly bankrupt. By 1998, Isom and his management team had transformed the division into a high-profit performer, with many business units producing top-quartile profit performance. Isom launched this remarkable turnaround by creating a clear picture of what Cigna P&C could become over the next five years. He used the term *specialist* to define the basic change in strategy that could create success; the division would, in the future, write policies only when its specific knowledge of an underwriting risk exceeded that of the industry. *Top quartile* defined a target for success that, while difficult to comprehend when the organization was on the brink of bankruptcy, reenergized employees' pride that they worked for a high-performing organization. The five-year goal gave a realistic window of time for achieving the top-quartile stretch target.

The vision created the picture of the destination. The strategy defined the logic of how this vision would be achieved. Vision and strategy are essential complements. At Cigna, Isom's vision was appealing, but it would lack credibility unless managers could develop a strategy to show how the vision would be realized. Isom used a simple but clever technique when he "quantified" his vision. The insurance industry uses the combined ratio measure as a surrogate for profitability. The ratio divides the expenses of the organization—claims paid plus operating expenses—by its revenues from premium income. In an ideal world, with operating revenues exceeding expenses, the combined ratio should be less than one. But because the cash from premiums received is invested until it is required for claims, top-quartile performers can have combined ratios of 103 by depending on returns from investments to provide the additional income source to achieve profitability.

In 1993, Cigna P&C's combined ratio was nearly 140. Isom's high-level strategy to achieve a top-quartile combined ratio, shown in Figure 12-3, had four themes:

1. Improve agents' productivity
2. Focus on target markets
3. Align the underwriting and claims processes
4. Upgrade the underwriting process

Isom established a time line and an approximate target for reducing the combined ratio for each theme of the strategy. In this way, he broke a seemingly impossible goal of a thirty-seven-point reduction in the combined ratio into more manageable and realistic components, each with a specific target and time frame. Instead of one giant, impossible leap to the top quartile, the vision had become translated into a strategy consisting of a series of smaller, time-phased steps. The organization could now see a feasible path for achieving Isom's vision. He reported, "The structure of the scorecard helped us clarify our strategy and keep the organization *focused* on making our vision a reality."

USING STRATEGY MAPS TO PLAN THE CAMPAIGN

Strategy maps provide a static snapshot of the enterprise strategy. Quantifying targets, establishing time lines for accomplishment, and planning and authorizing initiatives allow the strategy map to become a dynamic representation of value creation over time. We have developed a six-step process, called *planning the campaign*, based on the cause-and-effect logic of a strategy map, to conduct scenario planning exercises while the map is being built. Figure 12-4 describes the six steps:

1. *Define the shareholder/stakeholder value gap:*
   Set the stretch targets and the value gap that must be closed
2. *Reconcile the customer value proposition:*
   Identify the target customer segments and value propositions that provide new sources of customer value
3. *Establish the time line for sustained results:*
   Show how the value gap will be closed over the planning horizon

Figure 12-3 Planning the Campaign at Cigna Property & Casualty

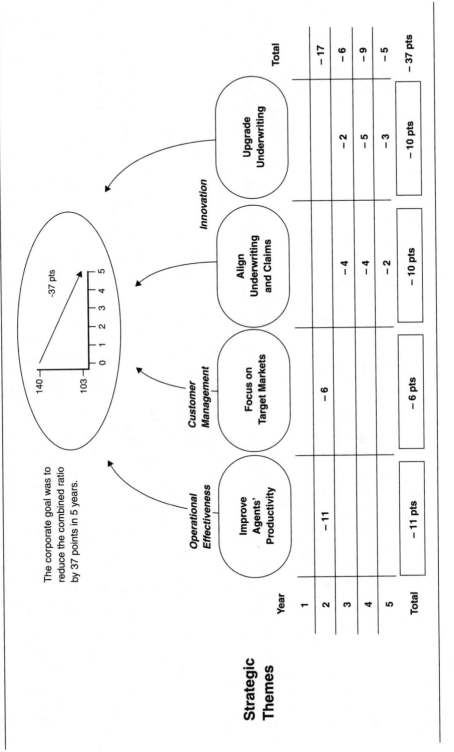

Figure 12-4 Using Strategy Maps to Plan the Campaign

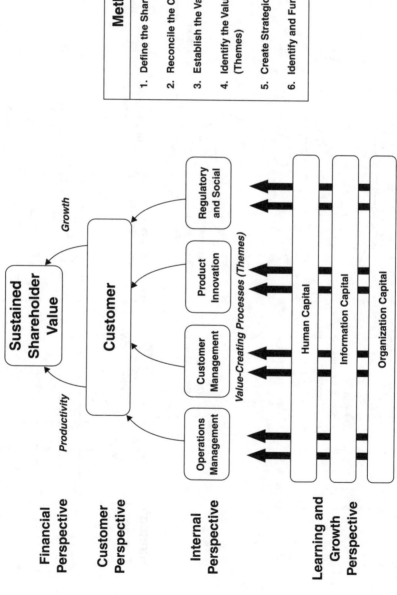

Methodology

1. Define the Shareholder Value Gap
2. Reconcile the Customer Value Proposition
3. Establish the Value Time Line
4. Identify the Value-Creating Processes (Themes)
5. Create Strategic Asset Readiness
6. Identify and Fund the Strategic Initiatives

Financial Perspective

Sustained Shareholder Value

Productivity   *Growth*

Customer Perspective

Customer

Internal Perspective

Operations Management | Customer Management | Product Innovation | Regulatory and Social

Value-Creating Processes (Themes)

Learning and Growth Perspective

Human Capital

Information Capital

Organization Capital

4. *Identify the strategic themes (critical few processes):*
   Allocate the value gap to strategic themes
5. *Identify and align intangible assets:*
   Define the readiness gap in human, information, and organization capital
6. *Identify and fund the strategic initiatives required to execute the strategy:*
   Fund the strategy

The process yields a set of action plans including targets, initiatives, and resources for each piece of the strategy in the organization's strategy map and Balanced Scorecard. We illustrate the six-step approach with the Consumer Bank case study, discussed in chapters 7 and 9.

Step 1: Define the Shareholder Value Gap

a. Define the overarching financial (or mission) objectives and measures
b. Define the targets and value gap
c. Allocate the value gap to growth and productivity goals

Strategy maps start, in the financial perspective, with objectives for creating shareholder value through two financial objectives: a long-term revenue growth component, and a short-term component from productivity improvements. Figure 12-5 shows the financial objectives at Consumer Bank. The overarching shareholder objective was to "dramatically increase earnings per share." The stretch target for this overarching objective was to "increase net income by $100 million in five years." The stretch target creates a *value gap*—the difference between future aspiration and current reality. The value gap communicates to the organization that dramatic change is required since the stretch target should not be achievable solely by continuous improvements.

Establishing the size of the value gap is an art. Executives must balance the benefits from challenging the organization to achieve dramatic improvements in shareholder value with the realities of what can possibly be achieved. A stretch target viewed as impossible to achieve will not only fail to motivate employees; it could actually demotivate them and cause them to believe the executive's head is in the clouds, not in the reality of conducting business day by day.

Figure 12-5   Case Study: Defining the Value Gap at Consumer Bank

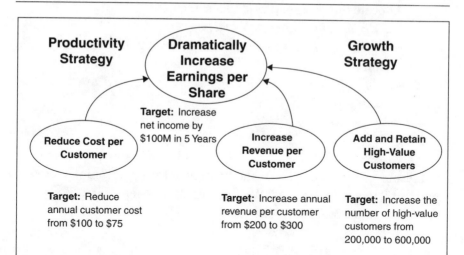

The first test of feasibility occurs when the executive team allocates the overall value gap to the different financial sub-objectives. Consumer Bank set three sub-objectives to support the high-level objective of income growth: (1) a productivity sub-objective to "reduce cost per customer," (2) one growth sub-objective to "increase revenue per customer," and (3) a second growth sub-objective to "add and retain high-value customers." The targets for the three financial sub-objectives were:

1. Reduce annual customer cost from $100 to $75
2. Increase revenue per customer from $200 to $300
3. Increase the number of high-value customers from 200,000 to 600,000

If Consumer Bank could achieve the targets for these three financial sub-objectives over the next five years, then it could achieve its overarching goal to "increase net income by $100 million." While this high-level assignment provides some breakdown of the overall stretch target, few in the organization will yet understand how or even whether the three financial sub-objective targets can be achieved. That is the role for targets in the remaining three perspectives of the strategy map. The high-level financial targets shape how the remainder of the strategy is defined. After working through the objectives and targets in the other three perspectives, management may conclude that the financial targets are not achievable and need to be revised. Thus, the breakdown of the high-level shareholder value target may require several iterations. On the other hand, setting stretch targets for the organization stimulates innovative thinking at lower levels of the organization that could lead to performance levels dramatically better than any seen in the past. Creating a value gap for financial performance stimulates managers and employees to brainstorm about how to radically enhance customer relationships, internal processes, and employee, information, and organization capital to produce the desired performance level.

Step 2: Reconcile the Customer Value Proposition

a. Clarify target customer segments
b. Clarify the customer value proposition
c. Select the measures
d. Reconcile customer objectives with financial growth goals

Cost and productivity improvements are relatively easy to target and plan for. After all, the amounts currently being spent are visible in the organization and can be benchmarked against the cost of processes operated by other organizations. So the opportunities for cost and productivity improvements should be tangible. Much harder is articulating how revenue growth targets will be achieved. Revenue growth requires explicit attention to targeted customer groups, including selling more to existing customers and also selling to entirely new customers. Such growth is unlikely to happen automatically or just because the organization has approved a financial plan based on a spreadsheet that assumes 11 percent annual revenue growth. The company must identify the value proposition it will offer customers in targeted groups that will lead to the desired revenue growth.

Figure 12-6 illustrates the shift in the marketplace that Consumer Bank was attempting. To achieve the target for increased revenue per customer, the bank planned for its employees to become trusted financial advisers, capable of helping customers develop and implement long-term financial plans. In building these relationships, the bank would proactively introduce a tailored package of integrated services to the customer, instead of the past approach of waiting for customers to request individual products and services. The past strategy of the bank appealed to "transaction" (segment A) customers who used only a small subset of the

Figure 12-6 Case Study: Reconciling the Customer Value Proposition at Consumer Bank

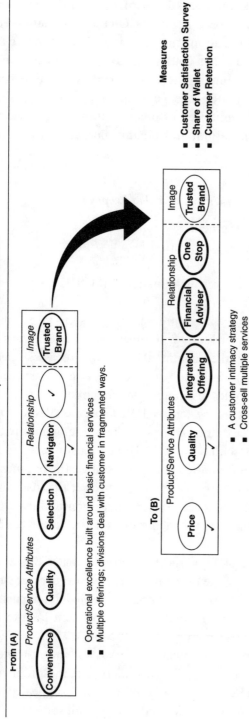

From (A)

Product/Service Attributes

| Convenience | Quality | Selection | *Relationship* | Navigator | ✓ | *Image* | Trusted Brand |

- Operational excellence built around basic financial services
- Multiple offerings; divisions deal with customer in fragmented ways.

To (B)

Product/Service Attributes

Price | Quality | Integrated Offering | Relationship | Financial Adviser | One Stop | Image | Trusted Brand

- A customer intimacy strategy
- Cross-sell multiple services
- Trusted adviser

Measures

- **Customer Satisfaction Survey**
- **Share of Wallet**
- **Customer Retention**

Customer Segmentation		
Segment	Now	+ 5 Years
(A) "Transaction"	70% (140K)	30% (180K)
(B) "Relationship"	30% (60K)	70% (420K)

bank's services, as needed. Most customers (about 70 percent) used other financial service providers for their credit cards, mortgages, investments, retirement planning, and insurance. By cross-selling multiple, integrated services to "relationship" (segment B) customers, the bank would increase its revenue per customer. The bank established a target that within five years, 70 percent of its customers would be based on the relationship value proposition. The customer perspective, with its definition of the new targeted customer segment, the value proposition that would enable cross-selling to be both credible and effective, and the targets for customer retention and cross-selling, became the focus for objectives, targets, and initiatives in the internal and learning and growth perspectives of the strategy.

Step 3: Establish the Value Time Line

a. Establish the time line for results
b. Allocate the value gap to different themes

Figure 12-7 illustrates Consumer Bank's value time line—how value will be created over time by different internal processes. The overall time horizon for the strategy was five years. *Operations management* processes would reduce cost per customer. The major impact of this strategy would be felt in the first two years as cost per customer dropped from $100 to $80 per year. If this target were achieved, the company's net income would double in the first two years, from $20 million to $47 million. *Customer management processes* would increase the number of relationship (Segment B) customers. Although progress would be made in each year, the major growth would come in year three, helping to boost net income in that year to $96 million, from $47 million in year two. *Innovation* processes would introduce new products and services that would eventually increase revenue per customer from $200 to $300 per year. Developing new products typically took two to three years, so the impact from the innovation processes would be felt mostly in years three, four, and five. By year five, each component of the strategy would have been established, enabling Consumer Bank to achieve and even exceed what initially had been seen as a highly aggressive stretch target of net income growth exceeding $100 million. The allocation of this stretch target to the separate internal process clusters enabled everyone to see that the target was achievable and the increases in new income expected during each of the five years in the planning horizon.

Figure 12-7 Case Study: Establishing the Value Time Line at Consumer Bank

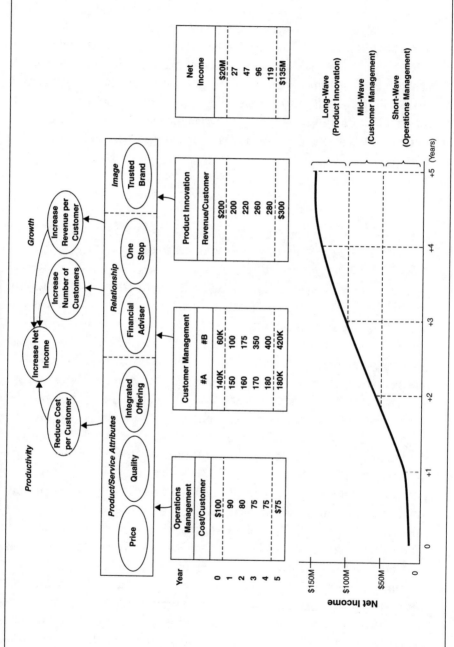

The breakdown of the high-level financial targets into targets for specific internal processes allows feasibility testing to take place at lower levels of detail. The organization can now assess whether the high-level targets in the financial perspective (stakeholder perspective, for nonprofit and public-sector organizations) are achievable or whether they need to be lowered. In our experience, seemingly impossible financial targets can often be realized through the compounding of targets at the internal process level. When a financial goal is first announced to "double shareholder value" or "increase net income by a factor of six," everyone in the organization is skeptical. Such levels of performance may never have been achieved in the past; why should the future be different? Financial targets by themselves are difficult to internalize and inspire. Only when financial targets get broken down into targets for internal processes and strategic themes, and with specific time frames attached, can everyone in the organization get comfortable with the feasibility of the overall target.

Step 4: Identify Strategic Themes

a. Identify the critical few processes (strategic themes) that have the greatest impact
b. Establish measures and targets

The customer value proposition defines how the enterprise creates value for its customers and, hence, its shareholders. The value time line describes how this value will be generated over the planning horizon by processes in the four internal clusters. In Part II of the book, we identified sixteen value-creating processes in these four clusters. Whereas most organizations must perform each of these processes, not all are decisive for the success of a particular strategy. Step 4 identifies the critical few value-creating processes expected to have the greatest impact on the customer value proposition and the financial productivity objectives. This step aligns the critical internal processes (the drivers) to achieving the targets for the organization's financial and customer objectives (the outcomes).

Figure 12-8 summarizes the value-creating processes selected at Consumer Bank. The bank selected two operations management processes for satisfying existing customers and delivering desired productivity gains for the financial perspective. "Provide rapid response" (measured by request fulfillment time) allowed the bank to shift more of its support to Web-based self-help technology. "Minimize problems" reduced the incidence and cost of errors while increasing customer satisfaction.

Figure 12-8 Case Study: Identifying the Value-Creating Processes at Consumer Bank

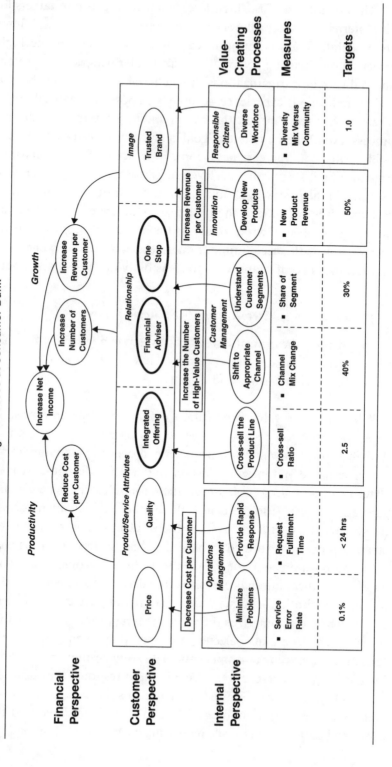

Customer management processes would shift the customer base from transaction/convenience shoppers (segment A) to high-value relationship customers (segment B). The bank identified three critical processes: "Understand customer segments" (customer selection) focused on clarifying the customer value proposition, segmenting the market, and communicating the message to potential customers in the targeted segments. The bank selected "shift to appropriate channel" (customer acquisition) as the second critical customer management process. A telemarketing campaign would migrate customers from old-fashioned "bricks-and-mortar" banking to a more cost-effective "bricks-and-clicks" approach. The third process, "cross-sell the product line" (customer growth), measured by the number of products per customer, focused on relationship management that would introduce a broader range of services to the customer.

The target for the innovation process, to increase revenue per customer by 50 percent, required that the bank create additional services that its representatives could sell to targeted (relationship) customers. The bank selected the innovation process, "develop new products," which would be measured by "new product revenue." Finally, the bank identified an important regulatory and social process objective, to build a diverse workforce that would reflect the demographic mix of the communities in which it operated.

Thus, Step 4 showed how the strategy of the bank to increase net income by $100 million could be broken down into seven value-creating processes. The bank performed its feasibility test at this point by establishing targets for each of the seven process measures that, in the opinion of the participants, would be adequate to achieve the targets defined in the value time line. For example, a segment share of 30 percent, a cross-sell ratio of 2.5 products per customer, and a 40 percent change in channel mix would yield the desired growth in target customers, as well as the revenue per customer target. Creating the linked objectives, measures, and targets in the strategy map enabled Consumer Bank to define and test the linkages between its high-level financial target (increase operating income by $100 million in five years) and a set of targets for nonfinancial measures that would deliver the desired financial performance.

Step 5: Create Strategic Asset Readiness

a. Identify the human, information, and organization capital required to support the strategic processes
b. Assess the readiness of these assets to support the strategy
c. Establish measures and targets

In the fifth step, the organization sets targets for the learning and growth objectives that align and create readiness for human, information, and organization capital, the intangible assets. Figure 12-9 describes the learning and growth objectives for Consumer Bank. For each of the seven value-creating internal processes identified in Step 4, the management team asked two questions: (1) "Which job families are critical to managing this process?" and (2) "Which information systems are critical for improving this process?" The answers to these questions established the priorities for developing and aligning human and information capital to the strategy.

Continuing our example, the executive team identified quality managers as the strategic job family for the operations management process to "minimize problems." Similarly, it identified an incident tracking system as the strategic IT application for this critical process. For the "shift to appropriate channel" objective within the customer management processes, the executive team identified telemarketers as the strategic job family and the CRM/lead management system as the strategic information system. For the "develop new products" objective within the innovation processes, the strategic job family was the joint venture manager, who would seek partners for new product development, and the critical information system was a project management system.

For organization capital—culture, leadership, alignment, and teamwork—Consumer Bank featured two *culture* objectives: a focus on the customer, and a dedication to the bank's core values. The *leadership* priorities were to align the bank's leadership competency model to the strategy. The *personal alignment* objective focused on two aspects: strategic awareness—the degree to which each individual understood the strategy, and the extent to which personal goals were aligned to the Balanced Scorecard. Finally, the *teamwork* objective was to share best practices across the organization.

Setting targets for the learning and growth objectives requires a different approach than that used for the objectives in the three other perspectives. The learning and growth objectives must be brought to a high state of readiness to facilitate the improvement in the critical internal processes. Figure 12-10 shows the measures selected at Consumer Bank. For human capital, the target was to achieve 100 percent readiness for the portfolio of selected strategic job families (Figure 12-9). Similarly, a target of 100 percent readiness was established for the portfolio of strategic IT applications (Figure 12-9). Consumer Bank measured its "customer-focused culture" through a direct survey of customers. The goal was to

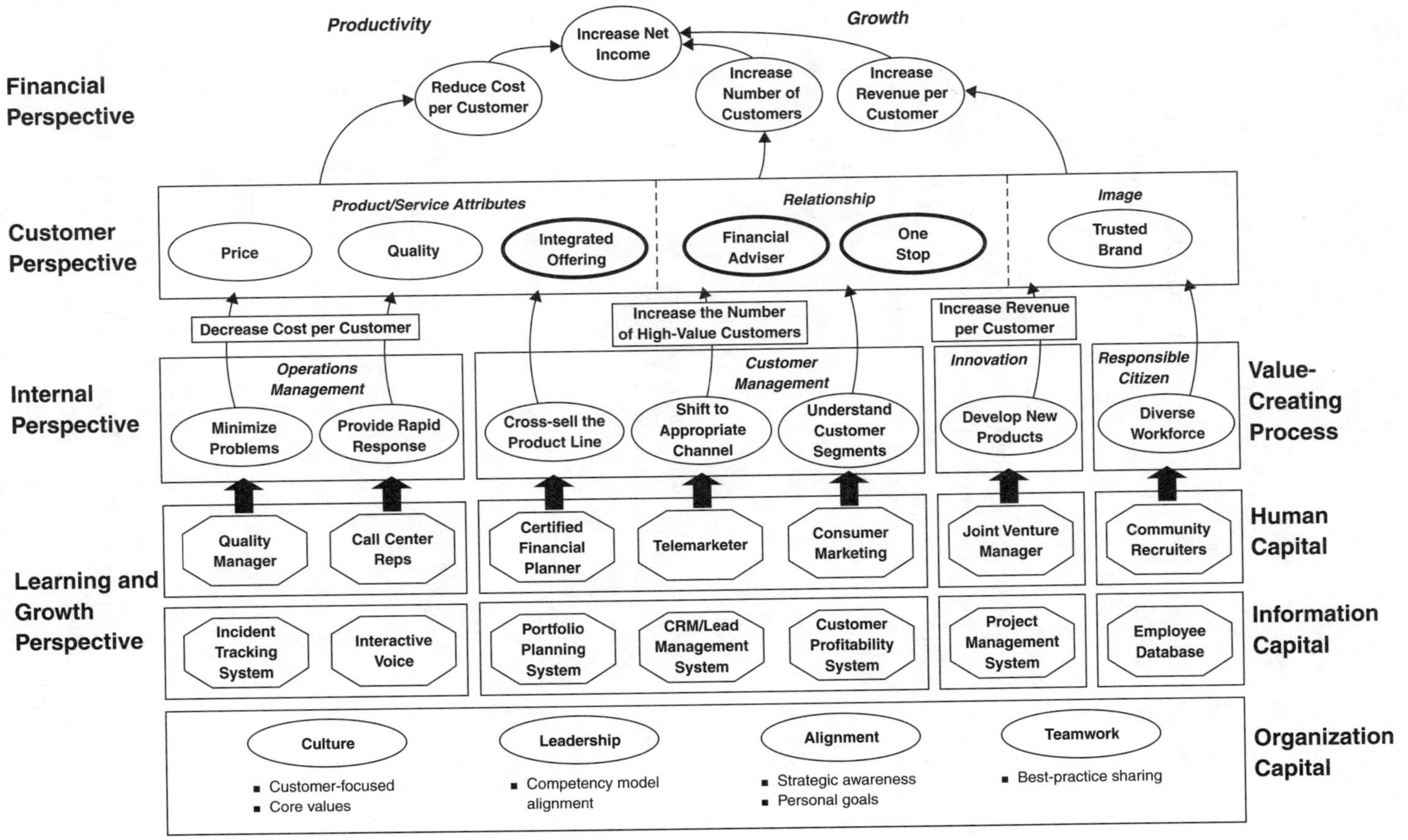

Figure 12-9 Case Study: Defining Strategic Asset Readiness at Consumer Bank

have 100 percent of its customers believe that Consumer Bank's employees were customer-focused. The bank used an employee survey to determine how well its leaders met their competency profiles. It used the same survey to measure employees' "strategic awareness." Targets of 70 percent and 90 percent were set for these two objectives. A personal goal-setting process would align the staff with the strategy. The goal was to have 100 percent of the workforce with personal goals linked to the Balanced Scorecard. Finally, Consumer Bank sought to improve best-practice sharing through the introduction of a knowledge management system (KMS). It set a target that every member of the relevant organization would be an active user and contributor to KMS.

Figure 12-9 represents the full strategy map for Consumer Bank. Figure 12-10 describes the Balanced Scorecard that complements this map. By extending the logic of the strategy map into targets for specific human, information, and organization capital, the bank creates an organization that is completely aligned to the strategy. The strategy is both understandable and actionable. As one executive stated at the completion of this process:

> We always had strategic objectives to upgrade the skills of our people and to invest more in information technology that would enhance the customer experience. But when the pressure for short-term earnings hit, these were the first programs to be cut. Now we all understand that we must start investing today in our people, systems, and culture if we are to have any chance of achieving our five-year financial targets.

Step 6: Identify and Fund the Strategic Initiatives

a. Define the specific initiatives required to support the processes and to develop the intangible assets
b. Clarify and secure the funding

The strategy map describes the logic of the strategy, showing clearly the set of critical processes that create value as well as the intangible assets required to support them. The Balanced Scorecard identifies measures and targets for each objective in the strategy map. But objectives and targets are not achieved simply because they have been identified. For each measure on the Balanced Scorecard, managers must identify the strategic initiatives needed to achieve the target. And they must supply the resources—people, funding, and capacity—required to successfully

Figure 12-10 The Balanced Scorecard for Consumer Bank

Perspective	Strategic Objectives	Strategic Measures	Targets
Financial Perspective	F1: Increase earnings per share F2: Add and retain high-value customers F3: Increase revenue per customer F4: Reduce cost per customer	▪ Net income (versus plan) ▪ Revenue mix (by target segment) ▪ Revenue per customer ▪ Cost per customer	+$100M 30% (A); 70% (B) $300 $75
Customer Perspective	C1: Become a trusted financial adviser C2: Provide superior service	▪ Customer satisfaction (survey) ▪ Share of wallet ▪ Target customer retention	90% 50% 90%
Internal Perspective — *Customer Management*	I1: Understand customer segments I2: Shift to appropriate channel I3: Cross-sell the product line	▪ Share of segment ▪ Channel mix change ▪ Cross-sell ratio	30% 40% 2.5
Product Innovation	I4: Develop new products	▪ Revenue from new products (percent)	50%
Operations Management	I5: Minimize problems I6: Provide rapid response	▪ Service error rate ▪ Request fulfillment time	0.1% <24hrs
Responsible Citizen	I7: Build diversity reflecting community	▪ Diversity mix versus community	1.0
Learning and Growth Perspective — *Human Capital*	L1: Ensure readiness of strategic jobs	▪ Strategic job readiness	100%
Information Capital	L2: Ensure availability of strategic information	▪ Information portfolio readiness	100%
Organization Capital	L3: Create a customer-focused culture L4: Build cadre of leaders L5: Align the organization L6: Best-practice sharing	▪ Customer survey ▪ 360° survey (leadership model) ▪ Strategic awareness survey ▪ Personal goals aligned to BSC (percent) ▪ KMS utilization/currency	100% 70% 90% 100% 100%

complete each initiative. The initiatives create the results; they are the basis for successful strategy execution.

Consumer Bank, for example, was currently experiencing a 3 percent service failure rate that was leading to the loss of many important customers. It set a target to reduce the service error rate to 0.1 percent. It identified two strategic initiatives to accomplish this defect reduction: Install a new problem tracking system, and redesign the front end of several processes. By identifying and managing these initiatives, the bank soon achieved its 0.1 percent error rate target. The defect rate reduction stemmed the customer losses, and thereby successfully delivered that component of the strategy.

The action plans that define and provide resources for the strategic initiatives must be *aligned* around the strategic themes (see Figure 12-9), and must be viewed as an *integrated* bundle of investments, not as a group of stand-alone projects. Each strategic theme should represent a self-contained business case around which the organization aligns and integrates processes and initiatives. Figure 12-11 illustrates the action planning for *one* of Consumer Bank's themes—"Shift the Customer to the Appropriate Channel." This theme requires a telemarketing program to attract new customers to the bank and to shift their usage to technology-supported services. This theme affects one component of the customer value proposition—specifically, the relationship with a personal adviser and one-stop shopping. The primary financial impact of this theme is the acquisition of new customers in the target segment. For the telemarketing process in this theme to be successful, the bank must upgrade the skills of the relevant job family, the telemarketers, provide them with the appropriate information systems, and reshape the organization climate. Figure 12-11 shows the partial set of Balanced Scorecard measures and targets needed to execute the plan. Each measure has at least one strategic initiative needed to achieve its targeted value. And the bank specifies, for each initiative, the funding and staffing required and the individual (the initiative owner) who has primary responsibility for managing the initiative and delivering the results.

Consider the process, "shift customers to appropriate channels." Its target, to achieve a 40 percent shift in channel mix, requires three strategic initiatives: (1) a telemarketing campaign, (2) the acquisition of prospect lists, and (3) a direct-mail support program. The theme also requires a training program to develop specific marketing skills, several new information systems, and a new survey instrument to solicit customer feedback.

Figure 12-11 Case Study: A Strategic Action Plan at Consumer Bank

Strategic Theme: "Shift to Appropriate Channel"

Strategy Map	Balanced Scorecard		Action Plan	
	Measure	Target	Initiative	Budget
	▪ Net Income Growth (Volume Contribution)	+$100M	▪ Customer Profitability Database	$AAA
	▪ Revenue Mix (Relationship Customer)	+$67M 70%		
	▪ Customer Satisfaction	90%	▪ Segmentation Initiative	$BBB
	▪ Share of Wallet	50%	▪ Improved Customer Surveys	$CCC
	▪ Channel Mix Change	40%	▪ Telemarketing Campaign	$DDD
			▪ List Purchase	$EEE
			▪ Direct-Mail Support	$FFF
	▪ Strategic Job Readiness	100%	▪ Telemarketer Skills Training Program	$GGG
	▪ Information System Availability	100%	▪ CRM System Rollout	$HHH
	▪ Customer-Focused Culture	100%	▪ Internal Education	$III
	▪ Leadership Survey	70%	▪ Leadership Development Program	$JJJ
	▪ Strategic Awareness	90%	▪ Employee Community	$KKK
	▪ Best-Practice Sharing	100%	▪ Weekly Team Meetings	$LLL
			Total Budget	**$MMM**

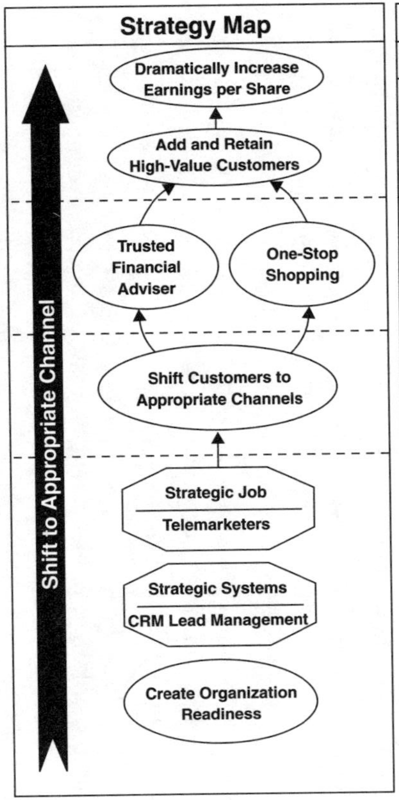

Strategy Map elements:

- Dramatically Increase Earnings per Share
- Add and Retain High-Value Customers
- One-Stop Shopping
- Trusted Financial Adviser
- Shift Customers to Appropriate Channels
- Strategic Job — Telemarketers
- Strategic Systems — CRM Lead Management
- Create Organization Readiness

Shift to Appropriate Channel

Each of the initiatives is essential for overall success. The resources supplied for the collection of initiatives must be viewed as a bundled investment, not as stand-alone improvement programs. Many organizations today screen investments and initiatives in isolation and by function. Investments in IT are reviewed separately from investments in HR, and both are reviewed separately from marketing and physical capacity investments. This piecemeal approach cannot succeed for successful strategy implementation; each of the strategic initiatives is but one component in a complex recipe whose success depends on all the ingredients being present simultaneously. This is another reason why attempting to attribute overall value creation to individual HR or IT investments is futile. Value is created by an integrated set of processes, each supported by an integrated set of several initiatives. The channel mix theme at Consumer Bank has a target to increase the customer base from 200,000 to 600,000 in five years. This growth in the customer base contributes about $67 million per year, approximately two-thirds of the overall financial objective. Relating the tangible financial outcome to the required investment ($MMM in Figure 12-11) in the entire bundle of initiatives that enhance critical internal processes and support intangible assets creates the financial business case. The cause-and-effect logic of the strategy map makes this linkage clear.

SUMMARY

The strategy map, by providing a clear and comprehensive description of an organization's strategy, gives executives an enhanced ability to execute their strategies. People can't manage what they can't measure, and they can't measure what they can't describe. The strategy map solves this problem by providing a framework for a simple, one-page representation of the cause-and-effect linkages among the objectives for both the outcomes and the drivers of the strategy. The word statements of objectives in a strategy map are, in turn, converted into a Balanced Scorecard of measures, targets, and initiatives. The strategy map and Balanced Scorecard enable everyone in the organization to have a common understanding of the strategy. For the many organizations referenced in this book, the strategy map has facilitated performance breakthroughs by allowing them to link their management processes to a clearly defined strategy.

The strategy map by itself, however, is but a *static* representation of the strategy. It identifies the outcomes and the drivers of value creation. This chapter describes how the strategy map can be used as a *dynamic* management tool. Setting targets adds the dimensions of time and speed to the strategy. Targets identify the performance gaps that must be closed, and the time scale over which the change must occur. Setting targets, and defining the drivers of their success in a strategy map, allows the feasibility of the strategy to be tested.

Strategic initiatives are the actions required to close the performance gaps between targeted and current performance. Initiatives are the ultimate drivers of change. A performance objective will not be met simply by measuring it. Executing strategy requires that initiatives be actively managed. Integrating the strategy map's measures, targets, and initiatives provides a complete description of how value is created—that is, a complete description of the organization's strategy and its successful execution.

The U.S. Army case study following this chapter illustrates the challenges of capturing the conflicting, simultaneous dimensions of strategy, maintaining readiness for missions in the short run, while simultaneously transforming to new capabilities required for future threats and commitments.

NOTES

1. Robert S. Kaplan and David P. Norton, *The Strategy-Focused Organization: How Balanced Scorecard Companies Thrive in the New Business Environment* (Boston: Harvard Business School Press, 2001), 73–75.

CASE STUDY

THE UNITED STATES ARMY

There are moments in history when events suddenly allow us to see the challenges ahead with a clarity previously unimaginable. The events of this past year have created one of those rare opportunities. Now we see clearly the challenges facing us—and we are confronting them.

—Thomas E. White
18th Secretary of the Army
Army Green Book 2002–2003

Background

The attacks of September 11, the global war on terrorism, and the ongoing transformation of the army to a lighter, more mobile force provided the backdrop for the introduction of the Balanced Scorecard at the U.S. Army. The army was just a few years into its complex long-term effort to transform the operational force and institutional base into the *objective force*—the full-spectrum force of the future that could leverage technological advances and organizational flexibility. Simultaneously, the army was supporting the global war on terrorism—a new kind of war that required deployment of active forces, reserves, and National Guard, and integration with joint forces and coalition partners. The need to maintain the well-being of the troops and their families remained a constant priority for the army.

The army had been using the same information system since 1963 to report and monitor the readiness of the force. The system did not provide a complete picture of army status, and it relied on lagging indicators and often outdated data. The rapidly changing needs of the national military strategy and the evolving role of the ground combat force made it essential for the army to have a new approach for reporting readiness. The challenge was to create a complete view of *strategic* readiness that would inform the leadership about the army's ability to meet the needs of today *and* the future. The army decided to create a new readiness reporting system, called the Strategic Readiness System (SRS), with the Balanced Scorecard at its foundation.

Strategic Architecture of the Army Scorecard

The project team modified the generic strategy map to reflect the army's mission-driven organization. It placed the mission at the top of the strategy map, and the financial perspective at the bottom as the driver or enabler that made attainment of the mission possible (see Figure 12-12). The customer, internal, and learning and growth perspectives remained, but under slightly different names; for example, customers became stakeholders.

While the multiple perspectives provided the framework for the army scorecard, the themes on the strategy map captured the strategic priorities of the army. Army leadership, both in interviews and in Congressional testimony, continually articulated *people, readiness, and transformation* as clear priorities. *People* were the cornerstone of the Army—the well-being of the troops and their families was paramount to attainment of the mission. Current *readiness* was essential for the Army to meet the immediate needs of the national defense strategy. And *transformation* was the change effort that would secure the preeminence of the U.S. Army in the new security environment. The theme of *sound business practices* communicated the standard of practice to ensure efficiency and optimal use of resources in all processes. *Core competencies* outlined the capabilities that the Army must maintain to fulfill national military responsibilities whatever they should be. Finally, *secure resources* emphasized the acquisition and use of the resources required to execute all of the above.

The Strategy Map

Stakeholder Perspective

The American people, the president, secretary of defense, Congress, and combatant commanders were all considered critical stakeholders or customers. What did they want from the army? Given the uncertain nature of future defense requirements, this was a difficult question to answer. The stakeholders expected trained and ready forces. Yet major questions persisted: Trained and ready for what? What level of readiness? For what type of combat?

Ultimately, leadership reaffirmed a set of core competencies in which the army must be proficient to meet any requirement of the stakeholders. These competencies had previously been identified in an army strategy document, the

Figure 12-12 Army Mission Map

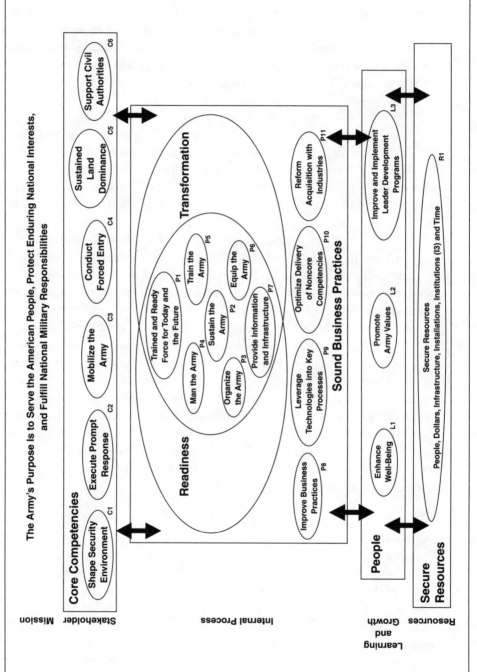

The Army's Purpose Is to Serve the American People, Protect Enduring National Interests, and Fulfill National Military Responsibilities

Army Planning & Program Guidance. The requirements of a major theater war, multitheater demands, peacekeeping support, cooperation with allies, and response to a domestic disaster could all be met if the army maintained a level of performance in each of these competencies.

Internal Process Perspective

The challenge of strategy execution is embodied in the internal perspective, which articulates the relationship between current readiness and future readiness defined by the long-term *transformation campaign plan*. The ultimate goal is to transform into the Future Objective Force, but this objective has to be balanced with the priority to maintain a current readiness to support the global war on terrorism. The strategic challenge for the army leadership is to monitor the strategic trade-offs between these two priorities. The Balanced Scorecard helps to monitor the tension between delaying transformation so that current readiness requirements could be met, and the compromises for today's readiness to ensure continual progress toward achieving the transformation campaign plan. The two themes of readiness and transformation are depicted as interlocking circles. The U.S. Army must maintain the appropriate tension and balance between them to ensure that trained and ready forces are available for both today's and the future's missions, providing core competencies as needed.

Execution of sound business practices supports the internal perspective by increasing the overall effectiveness of the army, both in readiness and transformation.

Learning and Growth Perspective

The key theme in the learning and growth perspective is *people and their well-being*. Soldiers are the centerpiece of the army. The army has an imperative to create an environment in which soldiers and their families can thrive. Army values must penetrate life in the army, and a focus on leadership development must be present at all levels of the enterprise.

Resources Perspective

The theme to secure resources provides the foundation for the strategy map. Attaining the resources required to achieve the mission and satisfy the stakeholders is a critical driver of success. Resources are defined more broadly than just financial. They include people, dollars, infrastructure, installations, institutions, and time to utilize the resources. Each of these must be provided to the army and invested wisely for its mission to be achieved.

Impact

General John M. Keane, the twenty-ninth vice chief of staff of the U.S. Army, outlined the benefits of SRS in a statement before the Subcommittee on Readiness of the U.S. House of Representatives Armed Services Committee on March 18, 2003:

> *The Army's Strategic Readiness System was implemented in October 2002 as a comprehensive strategic management and readiness assessment tool. It provides Army leadership with accurate, objective, predictive, and actionable readiness information to dramatically enhance strategic resource management. For the first time we have an Army enterprise management system that integrates readiness information from both the Active and Reserve Components—enabling the Army to improve support to Combatant Commanders, invest in Soldiers and their families, identify and adopt sound business practices, and Transform the Army to the Objective Force. This reporting system markedly improves how we measure readiness by gathering timely information with precision and expands the scope of the data considered. We are further addressing issues that affect readiness before they become problems.*

This case was prepared by Laura Downing and Patricia Bush of Balanced Scorecard Collaborative with the assistance of numerous colleagues at the U.S. Army.

PART FIVE

The Case Files

CHAPTER THIRTEEN

PRIVATE-SECTOR ORGANIZATIONS

IN THIS CHAPTER, we document three case studies of strategy maps in private-sector service companies. Two of them—Northwestern Mutual and Media General—adopted the scorecard as they introduced radically new strategies. Northwestern Mutual was shifting from a more than century-old strategy of offering superior insurance products through its career sales force to a strategy focused on offering comprehensive financial security to its end-use customers. Media General had expanded from its traditional base as a newspaper publisher into a regional media powerhouse with multiple publishing, broadcast, and electronic media outlets. The company wanted to gain synergies from its diverse media businesses by a strategy it called "convergence," coordinating the different media in a given market so that they could provide quality information in the way each does best, but delivered from a comprehensive and unified perspective. Both companies used strategy maps to clarify, communicate, and align their organizations to their new strategies.

Volvofinans used the strategy map to solve a serious management problem: the lack of understanding by employees about the company's strategy and a consequent decline in employee satisfaction and commitment. The clarity offered by the strategy map led quickly to substantial improvements in employee morale, which subsequently translated into heightened customer and financial performance.

NORTHWESTERN MUTUAL

Background

Northwestern Mutual is one of the oldest and most respected companies in the United States. Headquartered in Milwaukee, the company, with its subsidiaries and affiliates, offers insurance, investment products, and advisory services to address the needs of policy owners and clients for financial protection, capital accumulation, estate preservation, and asset distribution. Since its founding in 1857, the company has been driven by a strong value system and culture of integrity with one core premise: doing what's best for its policy owners. As a mutual company, Northwestern Mutual has no shareholders. It focuses solely and directly on its three million members. The company's approach to mutuality, including its long-term investment strategy and intense attention to operating fundamentals, helps it maintain the highest financial strength ratings from all four of the country's major rating agencies. In 2003, Northwestern Mutual expects to remain the leading U.S. individual life insurance company paying dividends to policy owners.

The Situation

Traditionally, Northwestern Mutual's business model was premised on providing superior life insurance and a few ancillary products, all through a single, career sales force of financial representatives. Although the company had sold investment products for several decades, its primary focus remained on selling risk-based insurance products. But the world had changed. In the mid- to late 1990s the company broadened its focus in response to evolving needs of policy owners and clients, more fluid investment markets, and finally, in 1999, enactment of the Gramm-Leach-Bliley Act that formalized direct competition between insurance companies, banks, and other financial institutions. Northwestern Mutual was now pursuing a strategy that emphasized helping clients achieve financial security by offering integrated solutions containing both insurance and investment products. In 2001, Ed Zore became the company's new CEO. He had an extensive background in investments and a firm belief that employee engagement and measurement would be critical to the future success of the company.

The Strategy

Northwestern Mutual adopted a strategy that focused on enhancing its core insurance business and expanding its investment product business to meet more diverse policy owner and client needs. The company's vision was to leverage its traditional strengths—building enduring relationships, providing expert advice, and offering strong product value—to become the premier company helping clients achieve lifelong financial security. The company would build out its "network of specialists," a joint work model that enabled its traditional life insurance sales force to draw upon product and investment experts, as needed, to address clients' increasingly complex financial security needs. This strategy required the company to balance its desire to expand capabilities to address more policy owner and client needs while continuing to maintain focus on the fundamentals that had allowed it to become the premier life insurance company.

Northwestern Mutual viewed the Balanced Scorecard as a tool to communicate and monitor the success of its broader strategy. The Scorecard framework also served to further Zore's goals of enhancing employee engagement and moving the company to a performance and measurement-based culture.

The Strategy Map

As a mutual company focused on doing what's best for its policy owners and clients, Northwestern Mutual's overarching *financial objective* is to deliver strong product value to policy owners and customers in the form of dividend-paying capacity and exceptional financial strength (see Figure 13-1). This primary financial objective is supported by four others: two dealing with insurance and investment product revenue growth, and two reemphasizing the company's commitment to aggressively managing its operating fundamentals, such as mortality and morbidity, operating expenses, and investment results.

From the *customer perspective,* Northwestern Mutual's strategy map describes how to achieve differentiation from its converging competition. The company has an objective that policy owners and clients continue to view it as a world-class provider of leading products and relationship-based services. It also emphasizes the expert advice and needs-based planning required to address clients' broad array of financial needs. Deb Beck, executive vice president of planning and technology, commented, "Our field force has a long history of conducting needs-based analysis and planning. Our strategy seeks to leverage this strength so we can address more of our clients' insurance and investment needs through a robust, integrated planning approach."

Northwestern Mutual's *internal process perspective* centers around two primary themes. The first focuses on the processes needed to help the company expand its "network of specialists." For example, to make its "network" more robust, the company will continue to expand its exclusive sales force through better recruiting and retention and enhanced financial representative productivity. These goals, in turn, will be furthered by a "network" objective, in the learning and growth perspective, to increase the capabilities of specialists and encourage joint work on complex client cases.

The other internal process theme emphasizes the internal home office processes that drive the company's operating fundamentals. The company wants its employees to find new and more efficient ways of working, and to manage company projects to deliver maximum benefits.

Figure 13-1 Northwestern Mutual Strategy Map

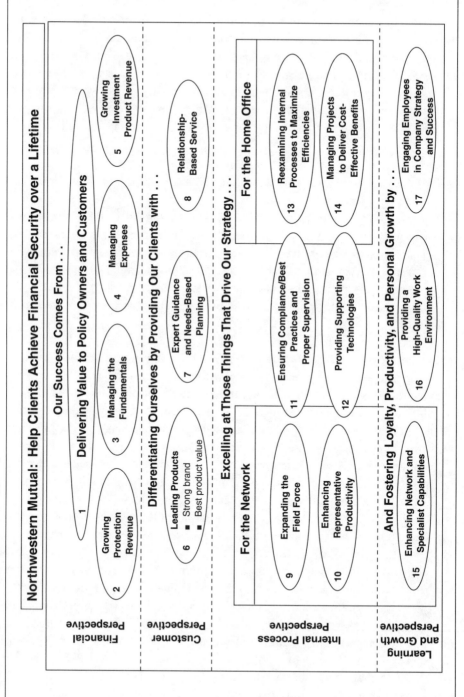

Northwestern Mutual: Help Clients Achieve Financial Security over a Lifetime

Financial Perspective
Our Success Comes From . . .
Delivering Value to Policy Owners and Customers

1
2 Growing Protection Revenue
3 Managing the Fundamentals
4 Managing Expenses
5 Growing Investment Product Revenue

Customer Perspective
Differentiating Ourselves by Providing Our Clients with . . .

6 Leading Products
■ Strong brand
■ Best product value
7 Expert Guidance and Needs-Based Planning
8 Relationship-Based Service

Internal Process Perspective
Excelling at Those Things That Drive Our Strategy . . .

For the Network
9 Expanding the Field Force
10 Enhancing Representative Productivity

11 Ensuring Compliance/Best Practices and Proper Supervision
12 Providing Supporting Technologies

For the Home Office
13 Reexamining Internal Processes to Maximize Efficiencies
14 Managing Projects to Deliver Cost-Effective Benefits

Learning and Growth Perspective
And Fostering Loyalty, Productivity, and Personal Growth by . . .

15 Enhancing Network and Specialist Capabilities
16 Providing a High-Quality Work Environment
17 Engaging Employees in Company Strategy and Success

The company has a regulatory process objective, shared both by the network and home office, to ensure that compliance remains a point of emphasis. Another dual objective for network and home office is to adopt new technology aligned to the strategy.

The company will foster employee loyalty, productivity, and personal growth by engaging employees in company success and strategy and by providing a high-quality work environment.

Anecdotes

Northwestern Mutual's senior management team is using the company Scorecard as a mechanism for facilitating regular, quarterly discussions about execution of the company strategy. According to Beck:

> *Part of the beauty of the tool is that it meshes well with our form of mutuality and value system. Unlike some companies, we've never focused solely upon short-term financial measures like stock valuation and quarterly results. Instead we've tended to frame our decisions with a longer-term horizon in mind and have focused upon both the financial and nonfinancial aspects of meeting policy owner and client needs. The Balanced Scorecard helps us to do this regularly with our company strategy in mind.*

The company has used the company Scorecard as an element in a broad campaign to educate employees about their tight connection to company strategy. Beck said:

> *When Ed Zore became our new CEO, he made employee engagement a top priority. We believe the Scorecard has helped us take engagement to another level, as employees have been better able to visualize how their roles further the company's strategic objectives.*

Northwestern Mutual has cascaded the Balanced Scorecard framework into its business units and support departments. The company appointed departmental Balanced Scorecard coordinators to help embed Scorecard concepts within each organization.

The Scorecard has also become a visible part of the company's annual planning cycle. All new project-funding proposals are now linked to the company's strategic objectives. And Northwestern Mutual has begun to see results. Within one year of aligning projects to the Scorecard, the company saw a 21 percent improvement in the number of projects meeting scope, schedule, and budget goals.

Last year, Northwestern Mutual began a series of employee surveys designed to measure, among other things, employee engagement and commitment. The most recent survey showed a dramatic improvement in the number of employees who felt that they "understood company business direction and saw a clear link between their jobs and company objectives." The Balanced Scorecard rollout was a principal reason for this improvement.

Case prepared by Arun Dhingra of Balanced Scorecard Collaborative and Deborah Beck of Northwestern Mutual. Our thanks to Ed Zore for sharing the Northwestern Mutual experience.

VOLVOFINANS

Background

Founded in 1959 and headquartered in Göteborg, Sweden, Volvofinans is the leading vehicle-financing company in Sweden, with total lending reaching 23.5 billion kroners ($2.7 billion) in 2001. This small but powerful lender employs about 190 people and has a highly focused mission: support sales of Volvo and Renault products in Sweden by financing products and sales. Ford Credit International owns 50 percent of the company. Swedish Volvo dealerships own the remaining 50 percent. Dealers are thus the firm's customers *and* its owners. Additional customers include fleets (firms operating more than fifty company cars) and individual consumers seeking attractive financing terms for their auto purchases.

The Situation

In 1996, Volvofinans's executives observed a troubling lack of shared vision throughout the company's workforce. Surveys revealed declining commitment, eroding satisfaction, and scanty knowledge of corporate goals throughout the ranks. The firm sought a tool that would enable employees to support the company's overall mission, to "promote the sales of Volvo and Renault vehicles in Sweden through competitive sales-financing solutions attractive to dealers, private customers, and companies." Intrigued by Swedish-based insurer Skandia Group's experience with the Balanced Scorecard and by *Harvard Business Review* articles on the subject, Volvofinans's then-managing director, along with business controller Marianne Söderberg, assembled a Scorecard team. The project produced a Scorecard that could be displayed using PowerPoint slides and Excel spreadsheets. But the project stalled because the Scorecard was difficult to circulate and use by more than one person at a time.

The project was idle until August 2000, when Björn Ingemanson became the new managing director. Determined to renew the effort, Ingemanson authorized the building of a new IT system that would facilitate easy BSC use and circulation on the company's intranet. Ingemanson and his team also decided to focus the revived initiative on the Strategy-Focused Organization principle of "making strategy everyone's job." The firm espoused having an open, decentralized culture in which employees felt free to speak their minds and challenge management's ideas. But few people outside the senior management team participated in discussions about strategy and the development of future business. Ingemanson believed it was time to mobilize the pool of intellectual capital for strategy implementation.

The Strategy Map

During a series of lively seminars attended by managers and employees from a cross-section of many functions and levels—up to one-third of the company's workforce—the Scorecard team began crafting Volvofinans's strategy map (see Figure 13-2). They called the document their *Vägvisaren,* or road map. Rank-and-file employees defined most of the map's objectives and measures—an effective first step in aligning everyone behind the strategy.

The company initially identified more than thirty-five objectives, then combined several to arrive at a manageable twenty-two. Executives also decided to emphasize product leadership and operational excellence as keys to implementing Volvofinans's strategy. Within the strategy map, themes such as *motivated and involved coworkers, win/win with Volvo dealers,* and *growth and efficiency strategy*—along with a value chain flowing from *product development* to *customer loyalty*—provided the framework for the map's cause-and-effect relationships. Although the Scorecard team included arrows indicating causal connections in the map, they decided to circulate an arrow-less version throughout the organization, because people found it easier to absorb visually. The team used the strategy map to communicate high-level strategy effectively and compellingly to all employees.

The highlights from the map included the following:

- *Coworkers/Learning perspective:* To fulfill its mission, Volvofinans needs a motivated, actively involved, and knowledgeable workforce. It now nurtures a culture of learning by encouraging everyone to participate in strategy discussions, leveraging the company's existing consensus-oriented culture. In contrast with the aborted initial Scorecard project, the team adopted objectives for "efficient IT support" and "high availability of information."
- *Process perspective:* In this perspective, the emphasis on product leadership and operational excellence come together. This section of the map outlines ways to improve product development, sales and marketing, risk handling, credit handling, and cultivation of customer loyalty. Objectives include developing innovative financing products, continually educating Volvo dealers on Volvofinans's offerings, serving customers

Figure 13-2 AB Volvofinans Strategy Map

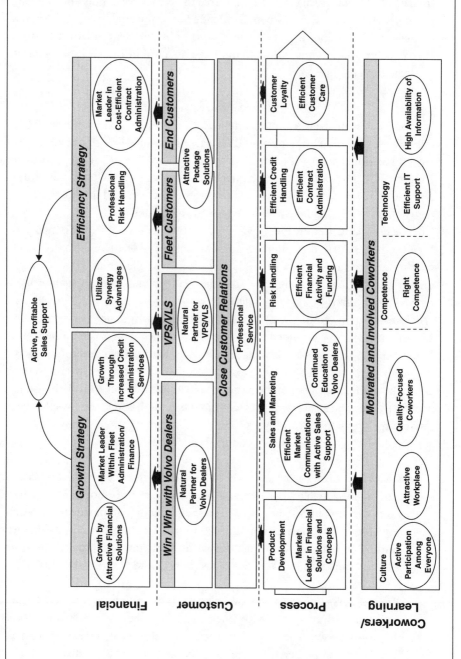

efficiently, and administering contracts quickly and accurately. The arrow flowing from left to right indicates the direction of the company's value chain.

• *Customer and financial perspectives:* The process objectives feed into objectives in the customer and financial perspectives. For instance, by meeting its process objective for "market leadership in financial solutions and concepts" (reflecting its emphasis on product leadership), Volvofinans expects to boost its ability to partner successfully with dealers. Successful partnering in turn supports growth through "attractive financial solutions" and "increased credit administration services." But dealers aren't Volvofinans's only customers. Market leadership in financial solutions and concepts also supports the objective for "attractive package solutions" for fleet and end-customers. Serving these customers in turn supports another objective under the *growth strategy* theme in the financial perspective: "market leader within fleet administration and finance." Another objective in the process perspective— "efficient contract administration"—links directly to the financial efficiency objective to be the "market leader in cost-efficient contract administration."

Anecdotes

Volvofinans's inclusive strategy map development process paid big dividends. Recent surveys revealed that employees now had a stronger grasp of department and company strategy. Morale and commitment to company goals have also soared, as has employees' mastery of industry dynamics. These improvements led to tangible outcomes. In 2001, the company's share of the new-car financing market through Volvo dealerships in Sweden expanded, leading to significant increases in lending amounts and the number of contracts in force.

Its emphasis on product leadership and operational excellence also yielded results. The company launched "Volvo Carloan," an insurance plan that pays customers' monthly auto-loan bills if they lose their jobs or develop a long-term illness. By mid-2002, more than 100,000 customers had signed up for the plan; Volvofinans's competitors have belatedly launched similar products. And the company boasts the lowest cost per administered contract in its market. Volvofinans is a member of the Balanced Scorecard Hall of Fame.

Case prepared by Carl-Frederik Helgegren of the Balanced Scorecard Collaborative, Sweden, and Lauren Keller Johnson, a contributor to the Balanced Scorecard Report. We thank Marianne Söderberg and Björn Ingemanson for sharing their Volvofinans experience.

MEDIA GENERAL, INC.

Background

From a small newspaper empire founded in the 1850s, Richmond, Virginia-based Media General has grown into the ninth largest publicly traded newspaper company in the United States, with divisions in publishing, broadcast, and electronic media. Concentrated in the Southeast, the firm publishes twenty-five daily newspapers that have a combined circulation of more than one million. Media General's twenty-six network-affiliated television stations reach more than 30 percent of U.S. households. The company also operates more than fifty online enterprises related to its print and broadcast properties. In 2002, it employed more than 8,000 people and generated revenues of $837 million.

The Situation

Over the decades, Media General had expanded somewhat haphazardly beyond the Southeast. When J. Stewart Bryan III became chairman and CEO in 1990, the company embarked on a massive transformation, shedding old businesses and acquiring others to fit with its new, regionally focused strategy. However, competitive pressures and the explosive growth of cable television and the Internet depressed the value of Media General's stock.

The Strategy

Media General's mission statement was "to be the leading provider of high-quality news, entertainment, and information in the Southeast by continually building on our position of strength in strategically located markets." But Bryan recognized that success lay in synergy—exploiting the individual and collective strengths of Media General's three divisions. The goal, he explains, was to "coordinate different media in a given market to provide quality information in the way each does best—but delivered from a comprehensive and unified perspective." This approach, known as "convergence," became the cornerstone of Media General's strategy.

Convergence required strong teamwork, communication, and cooperation—no small feat for traditionally autonomous, culturally disparate units that often competed with each other.

Strategy Map

Adopted in 2002, the Balanced Scorecard fostered the common vision that would make convergence a reality (see Figure 13-3).

Customer Perspective

Defining its customers and recognizing their different needs proved one of the most challenging tasks for the cross-functional BSC team. Articulating a common customer value proposition forced differences of opinion to surface. In

Figure 13-3 Media General Strategy Map

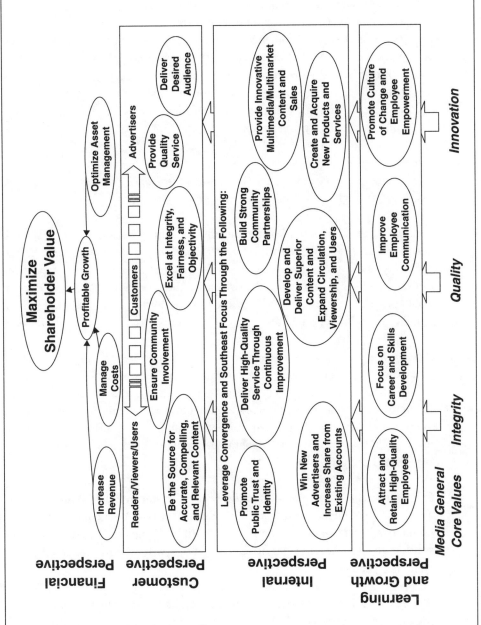

addition, for media organizations, the customer perspective represented the locus of a historical tension—between the editorial side, which served readers, and the publishing side, which served advertisers. These two customer bases competed for space and airtime. Finally, Media General division heads perceived more differences than commonalities among their respective readers and viewers—even though all audiences wanted quality news and information. "Accurate, compelling, and relevant content" thus represented Media General's goal to become the dominant source of information in each market. Across its diverse media, the company sought to provide its advertiser-customers "a desired *audience*," leveraging demographic and geographic reach with multimedia, multimarket advertising packages.

Internal (Process) Perspective

The internal perspective strategic theme was to *leverage convergence and Southeast focus* through several subthemes:

Promote public trust and identity: Beyond their inherent value, integrity and fairness fulfill core customer expectations. *Build strong community partnerships* supported the community involvement identified in the customer perspective. Brand image drove and would be driven by these objectives. Media General would promote its individual brands and link the corporate brand to individual brands, among all its stakeholders.

Develop and deliver superior content: The objective *deliver superior content* spoke directly to convergence. The common news desk exemplified this objective in action. Editors from newspapers, broadcast stations, and interactive media in a given market would work together and make daily decisions on how to cover a given story from their respective vantage points. By orchestrating coverage in this way, Media General believed it could increase readership, viewership, and users.

Create and acquire new products and services: Greater interaction among divisions, units, and departments (sharing new ideas, cross-referencing sister media) would help Media General's companies identify and exploit new growth opportunities. This subtheme would drive customer growth on both sides of the customer perspective.

Win new advertisers: By better understanding its advertising customers' businesses, Media General could better serve existing customers—and attract new ones—with, for example, creative multimarket and multimedia advertising packages that offered economies of scale. Increasing the percentage of multimedia advertisers and nurturing long-term relationships supported the financial perspective's objective to increase advertising revenue.

Deliver high-quality service: This operational excellence objective reinforced efficiencies and profitable growth in the financial perspective. Besides the standard efficiency gains achieved through process improvements, convergence encouraged units to leverage their purchasing power to reduce costs through coordinated procurement. Quality improvements included establishing guidelines on when to interrupt scheduled coverage with breaking news and fact-verification standards for online news (this objective also contributed to public trust).

Innovative content: "Innovative solutions" could include a lifestyle magazine, produced from leveraged content, that could be distributed throughout multiple markets.

Learning and Growth Perspective
Promote employee communication would facilitate heightened interaction for the critical internal process objectives. *Promote culture of change and employee empowerment* involved nurturing creativity and innovation, as well as fostering decision making among lower-level employees. These objectives had the greatest bearing on the two major sources of revenue growth.

Financial Perspective
Leveraging news content from multiple media sources would enable Media General to deliver new products and services. This, along with new acquisitions, represented the revenue growth objective for the reader and viewer customers. (Subscriptions are loss leaders in media.) Advertising revenues, bolstered by multimedia, multimarket advertising packages, would provide the other key revenue source. Operational excellence, boosting efficiencies, would improve cost and asset management.

Results
According to Bryan, the strategy map's first big accomplishment was to facilitate massive culture change. By providing a shared language and common ways to measure success, the map helped employees see the value in cooperating toward common goals. Media General also gained a much deeper understanding of its customers' needs. Its stock, already on the rebound, has performed well under the BSC; per-share earnings almost tripled in 2002 (taken before accounting rule adjustments). Company revenues grew 4 percent in 2002, a brutal year in the publishing industry. And convergence was working: Multimedia

advertising packages brought a stunning 42.5 percent revenue gain to Media General's interactive media division in 2002.

Case prepared by Patricia Bush and Janice Koch of Balanced Scorecard Collaborative. Our thanks to Stewart Bryan for sharing the Media General experience.

CHAPTER FOURTEEN

PUBLIC-SECTOR ORGANIZATIONS

IN THIS CHAPTER we present strategy map case studies of:

- Royal Canadian Mounted Police (RCMP)
- Economic Development Administration (EDA) of the U.S. Department of Commerce
- United Kingdom Ministry of Defence (MoD)
- Fulton County School System (FCSS)

The RCMP offers policing services to local municipalities, provinces, territories, and the Canadian nation. It developed a strategy map to coordinate and align its diverse initiatives, ranging from community policing to an internationally coordinated fight against terrorism. The strategy map made operational the RCMP mission of "safe homes and communities."

The EDA promotes economic activity in America's economically distressed communities. A new administrator developed a strategy map and Balanced Scorecard for EDA to revive a demoralized and underperforming government agency. The clarity and focus of the new strategy helped EDA become an efficient and effective government agency that now meets or exceeds targets for creating jobs and encouraging private-sector investment.

The U.K. Ministry of Defence, with a £25 billion ($40 billion) budget and more than 300,000 military and civilian personnel, is the fifth-largest military spender in the world. Its mission is to provide for the national defense, as well as to foster international peace and security. U.K. MoD developed a strategy map to facilitate a major modernization program that would transform the armed forces for the new security environment. In addition to realizing benefits from better internal communication, decision making, and teamwork, U.K. MoD uses its strategy map and Scorecard in its negotiations with the U.K. Treasury by demonstrating the impact of various funding scenarios on the MoD mission.

The Fulton County School System, in metropolitan Atlanta, Georgia, is perhaps the first school district to adopt the Balanced Scorecard. Building upon an existing and excellent quality initiative, the process of developing a strategy helped to align its various stakeholders—students, teachers, principals, parents, communities, and school district administrators—to specific outcome performance measures. FCSS has enjoyed substantial and recognized performance improvements with its new management system.

ROYAL CANADIAN MOUNTED POLICE

Background

The Royal Canadian Mounted Police (RCMP) is Canada's storied and historic national police organization. Created in 1873, and inspired by the Royal Irish Constabulary and the mounted rifle units of the U.S. Army, the Royal North West Mounted Police was created to bring law, order, and Canadian governance to the North-West Territories (present-day Alberta and Saskatchewan).

Today, the Royal Canadian Mounted Police is the Canadian national police service and an agency of the Ministry of the Solicitor General of Canada. The RCMP is unique in the world since it is, simultaneously, a national, federal, provincial, and municipal policing body. The organization provides a total federal policing service to all Canadians and policing services under contract to the three territories, eight provinces (all except Ontario and Quebec), approximately 200 municipalities, and up to sixty-five First Nations aboriginal communities. With more than 22,000 employees, approximately 750 local RCMP detachments across Canada, and a budget in excess of $2.6 billion (CAD), today's RCMP leads Canada's counterterrorism and anti–organized crime efforts, while demonstrating excellence at "on-the-ground" community-based policing across Canada.

The Strategy

In 2000, the RCMP undertook to develop a robust strategic performance management system to address three key issues:

1. Describe the vision and strategic direction of a newly-appointed Commissioner (G. Zaccardelli) who had a mandate to lead the organization into the twenty-first century with a new policing model, capable of meeting the challenges of the third millennium, and a passion for organizational excellence
2. Align the disparate elements of a national organization around a set of common strategic and operational priorities
3. Enhance credibility with funding agencies by successfully executing this strategy and achieving demonstrable, measurable results

The foundation of this passion for strategy execution was the unveiling of a new strategic framework—a document that expressed the RCMP's highest-order policing objectives. The strategic framework aligns the core strategic outcome of the RCMP—"Safe Homes and Communities" with the key organizational priorities that drive and influence this outcome.

At the heart of the strategy are five key strategic themes:

- Reduce the threat and impact of organized crime
- Reduce the threat of terrorist activity
- Reduce youth involvement in crime
- Maximize support of international operations and initiatives
- Facilitate safer and healthier aboriginal communities

The RCMP Leadership Team decided that the five themes represented the key "levers" of success. If RCMP could achieve success across the five themes, its core strategic outcome of "Safe Homes and Communities" would be realized.

The Strategy Map

The RCMP decided to adopt the Balanced Scorecard as the tool to manage the execution of the strategic framework. The Balanced Scorecard would enable the RCMP to accomplish the following:

- Translate the strategic framework into a series of coherent objectives, measures, and targets. In short, the BSC would describe and measure the RCMP strategy
- Make accountability for results against the strategic framework more open and transparent
- Ensure organizational alignment by cascading the scorecard into each of the divisions and functional areas of the organization

The Commissioner of the RCMP would manage the high-level Strategic Executive Council (SEC) strategy map (see Figure 14-1). This map provides

Figure 14-1 Royal Canadian Mounted Police Strategy Map

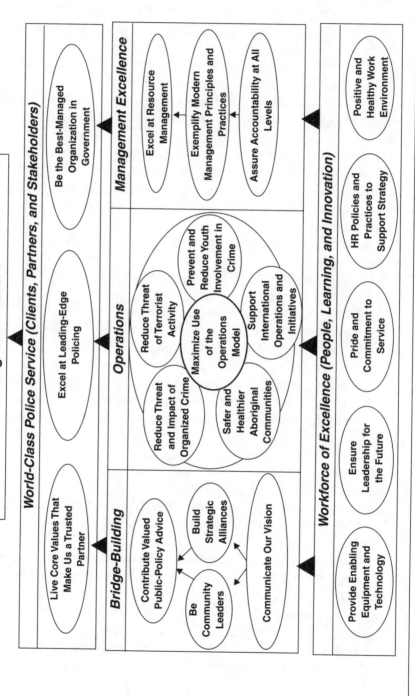

direction and clarity to each of the subsidiary strategy maps, and a clear line of sight between the police operations in a division or detachment, and the Commissioner's priorities.

The SEC strategy map adopts the traditional public-sector architecture for describing strategy. The "North Star" for the strategy is the Strategic Framework document that breathes life into the mission of the entire organization.

The *clients, partners, and stakeholders* perspective captures the RCMP value proposition to the core groups it serves: funding agencies, other levels of government (both domestic and international), and citizens in direct receipt of policing services. For example, the value proposition for *funding agencies* is for the RCMP to be "the best-managed organization in government," whereas the value proposition for *partners* is to "live core values that make us a trusted partner." Each of these objectives contributes to a primary objective to *excel at leading-edge policing*. In summary, the RCMP overall value proposition delivers world-class, leading-edge policing services, at a minimum cost, to partners, stakeholders, and citizens.

Internal process themes link to core group customer value propositions. For example, communication, partnership, and alliance processes in the *bridge-building* theme support the goal of becoming a trusted partner. Processes in the *operations* theme maximize the use of the operations model—an RCMP methodology for being intelligence-led in all activities and conducting investigations. This objective is placed at the heart of this theme, since excelling at the operations model will increase the quality of all the policing operations that support the strategic framework. Finally, processes in the *management excellence* theme support the requirements of the funding agencies.

The *people, learning, and innovation* perspective capture the importance the RCMP places on providing a dynamic and safe work environment for its employees.

Anecdotes

Using the SEC strategy map as a strategic guide, scorecards were developed in the remaining five business lines and four corporate headquarters functions, as well as for each of the fourteen operational divisions and four regional administrative centers across Canada.

This traditional approach to strategy maps was augmented by a significant breakthrough in how strategy maps are designed and used in large, matrixed public-sector institutions.

Embedded in the SEC strategy map is a reference to the five strategic priorities contained in the RCMP strategic framework (terrorism, organized crime, youth, aboriginal communities, and international policing). Understanding that each of these required national-level strategic coordination, the RCMP developed five "virtual" strategy maps for each of these priorities. These maps are accompanied by measures, targets, and the initiatives required to execute each of the five strategic priorities. Each strategic priority and virtual strategy map is owned by an RCMP executive. A panel of executives meets periodically to review progress against the strategic priorities.

To ensure alignment and consistent execution of these strategic priorities, each objective on the virtual strategy maps was assigned to a business line, or corporate service line, and placed on the relevant strategy map. The business lines similarly cascaded critical objectives, measures, targets, and initiatives to the divisional-level strategy maps. The end result was a set of linked and aligned strategies devoted to the execution of the five strategic priorities of the organization. The business lines and divisions also added objectives to their strategies that reflected the specific realities of the division and business line operations.

The final step in implementation of the Balanced Scorecard has been performance reporting. The RCMP has created a simple "dashboard"; for the short term an Excel spreadsheet has been developed to enable the reporting of progress against the objectives and their corresponding initiatives, measures, and targets identified in the Scorecard.

Beginning in September for the 2004–2005 fiscal year, the intent is to implement full strategy-focused business planning and the allocation of resources against strategically aligned priority initiatives at all levels in the organization. The Balanced Scorecard–based business plans will drive budget allocation, as resources are allocated to the priority-aligned initiatives identified in the objectives and Scorecards. Business planning will, in effect, focus on critical initiatives driving strategic priorities.

Case prepared by Andrew Pateman of Balanced Scorecard Collaborative and Geoff Gruson of the RCMP. Our thanks to Commissioner Zaccardelli for sharing the RCMP experience.

U.S. DEPARTMENT OF COMMERCE ECONOMIC DEVELOPMENT ADMINISTRATION (EDA)

Background

The U.S. Department of Commerce helps American businesses and communities achieve greater success both at home and abroad through the work of thirteen different bureaus reporting to the Secretary of Commerce.

Congress established one bureau, the Economic Development Administration (EDA), in 1965 during President Lyndon Johnson's War on Poverty. EDA's mission is to work with states, local governments, and nonprofit organizations to help bolster economic activity in America's economically distressed communities.

Whereas the basic role of the bureau has remained unchanged since its inception, support for EDA has ebbed and flowed dramatically over the years. President Reagan called for the abolishment of EDA during his first State of the Union Address. During his administration, the bureau was not an officially authorized federal program, meaning that neither the Congress nor the executive branch took the necessary steps to approve legislation to officially continue authorization of the bureau's activities.

An odd quirk in federal government practice allows for programs that can secure funding to operate even if they are not officially authorized. EDA was eventually reauthorized in 1998, but the many years of uncertainty had exacted a severe toll. Buffeted by reductions-in-force (the government term for layoffs), dwindling budgets, and an uncertain future, the organization had developed a "going-out-of-business" mentality, where survival was prized above all else.

The Situation

The arrival of President George W. Bush in 2001 presented EDA with an opportunity and a challenge. President Bush recognized the potential positive role that programs such as EDA could play in helping his administration achieve the goal of "leaving no geographic or demographic sector behind in the pursuit of the American dream." President Bush also brought the same results-oriented management style to Washington that he employed while governor of Texas. Drastic change would be needed if EDA were to survive.

President Bush selected David A. Sampson as his assistant secretary of commerce for economic development. Dr. Sampson came to EDA with an extensive economic development background in the private sector. Among his first acts was to update and reaffirm EDA's mission:

> The mission of EDA is to help our partners across the nation to create wealth and minimize poverty by promoting a favorable business environment to attract private capital investment and jobs through world-class capacity-building, planning, infrastructure research grants, and strategic initiatives.

Dr. Sampson also established a bold goal: to transform EDA into the premier agency for domestic economic development.

To fulfill its mission and achieve the goal established by the assistant secretary, EDA embarked on a comprehensive strategy to transform the bureau by focusing on three pillars of reform:

- Establish sound organizational management
- Develop outcome-based performance measures
- Enhance communication with key stakeholders

EDA Strategy Map

EDA exists to satisfy the needs of both *stakeholders* and *customers* (see Figure 14-2).

Stakeholders—the White House, Congress, Department of Commerce, and taxpayers—provide direction and oversight for EDA's work, play a critical role in EDA's funding, and serve as the guardians of the public interest. EDA would satisfy its stakeholders by becoming an effective, efficient, results-oriented agency.

EDA's customers are distressed communities, investment partners, and private-sector businesses that directly or indirectly receive assistance from EDA and reap the benefits from economic growth. EDA must improve distressed communities by being knowledgeable and responsive advisers on economic development. EDA must also make investments that promote growth and show visible results. Such accomplishments would advance the administration's domestic agenda.

EDA will meet its stakeholder objectives by satisfying the needs of its customers and achieving its *financial* goals.

In order to serve its customers, EDA must provide a transparent and responsive process that addresses the needs of the entities it serves. EDA, by providing information and technical assistance, will help its partners create large numbers of high-skill, high-wage jobs.

EDA must be fiscally responsible in accomplishing its customer objectives. It must streamline administrative processes. EDA must also leverage its limited resources by capitalizing on private-sector investment.

To meet expectations of shareholders and customers and achieve its financial objectives, EDA must execute on three strategic themes: *internal policy leadership, high-impact investment, and organizational excellence.*

Demonstrating policy leadership will allow EDA to serve as knowledgeable economic development advisers. In order to achieve policy leadership, EDA must first enhance research capabilities. Better information will strengthen EDA's ability to make superior decisions about its investment policy. Improved research capabilities will also give it the credibility needed to provide policy options to the highest levels of government.

The high-impact investments will increase EDA's ability to develop greater numbers of quality job opportunities. Enhanced research capabilities will support efforts to emphasize funding priorities. In turn, emphasizing funding priorities will enable EDA to expand deal flow by investing with new partners. A focus on enhanced due diligence will promote higher quality initial investment decisions and facilitate post-approval monitoring. The impact of these efforts will produce greater benefits for each taxpayer dollar spent.

Achievement of the first two themes will be assisted by a third strategic theme: *organizational excellence*. Organizational excellence refers to the internal processes necessary for EDA to become an efficient and effective organization.

Figure 14-2 Economic Development Agency (EDA), U.S. Department of Commerce, Strategy Map

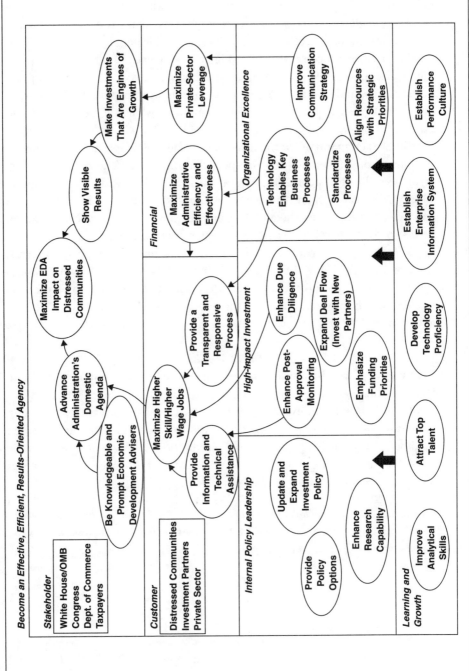

EDA must first align resources with strategic priorities by assigning the right people to the initiatives critical to EDA's strategy. Next, improving EDA's communication strategy and standardizing processes will create value by providing the *understanding* and the *means* to accomplish its goals. And EDA will maximize organizational effectiveness and efficiency by leveraging technology to enable key business processes to achieve high performance.

Finally, nothing at EDA would be accomplished without providing the skills, culture, and infrastructure necessary for its workforce to do the work required. EDA will help its people improve analytical skills and develop technology proficiency so that they can be successful. EDA will supplement current staff by attracting top talent to fill key posts. Talented people are not enough—the culture of EDA must foster a spirit that allows EDA to establish a performance culture. Information capital must be linked with human capital. EDA will establish an enterprise information system that will keep employees connected to each other, stakeholders, and customers and provide information necessary to do their jobs. These are the enablers for EDA success.

By focusing on its people and informational enablers to support its internal work processes, EDA will be better able to serve its customers, meet its financial goals, satisfy its stakeholders, and ultimately fulfill its goal "to become the premier standard-bearer for domestic economic development in the federal government."

EDA Results

EDA's results are already apparent. It has been singled out by the White House's Office of Management and Budget as an efficient and effective government agency meeting or exceeding its targets for creating jobs and encouraging private-sector investment. The White House rewarded EDA with an increased funding request for fiscal year 2004. Considering the President's focus on the critical needs of national and homeland security, EDA's achievement is a significant milestone in its thirty-eight-year history.

Case prepared by Mario Bognanno of Balanced Scorecard Collaborative and Sandy K. Baruah and Danette R. Koebele of EDA. Our thanks to Dr. David Sampson and his colleagues for sharing the EDA experience.

U.K. MINISTRY OF DEFENCE

Background

With a £25 billion ($40 billion) budget and more than 300,000 military and civilian personnel, the United Kingdom's Ministry of Defence (MoD) is among Great Britain's largest government departments—and is the fifth-largest military spender in the world. Comprising a navy, army, and air force, as well as eleven "top-level budgets" (akin to strategic business units), this immense organization has a broad mission: providing for the national defense, as well as fostering international peace and security. In recent years, the MoD has extended its personnel and influence worldwide to include humanitarian and peacekeeping missions in regions as far-flung as Kosovo, the Persian Gulf, and East Timor. At home, the ministry's activities range from search-and-rescue operations to agricultural epidemic management.

The Situation

The MoD decided to adopt the Balanced Scorecard after a late-1990s strategic defense review—a radical assessment of the strategic implications of national foreign policy objectives that spurred the modernizing of Britain's armed forces. As part of this review, the ministry also examined ways to contribute to a larger government-wide agenda centering on modernization. With the help of several strategic teams, the MoD's Defence Management Board (DMB) began exploring ideas for enhancing its performance management in response to the modernization initiative. The Scorecard model promised to enable the ministry to streamline its performance management, as well as distill and communicate its strategy throughout the organization.

The Strategy Map

The ministry began building its strategy map and Scorecard by first explicating its strategy: "generating battle-winning defence capability" (see Figure 14-3). It then identified two overarching themes for the map—*improved operational effectiveness* and *better use of resources*. Together, these themes would define a path to fulfillment of the MoD's strategy and achievement of its mission, as well as permeate every objective in the map's four perspectives.

In laying out the strategy map's perspectives, the MoD decided to forgo the traditional financial, customer, internal business process, and learning and growth perspectives. Instead, it defined its perspectives as

- Output deliverables: "Are we delivering what the government wants?" (Equivalent to the stakeholder perspective)
- Resource management: "Are we being good stewards of our personnel, reputation, defense infrastructure, and budget?" (Equivalent to financial perspective)
- Enabling processes: "What processes must we establish or improve to support our strategy?" (Similar to the internal processes perspective)
- Building for the future: "How can we invest in people, technology, and infrastructure to support our strategy?" (Reflecting the learning and growth perspective)

Figure 14-3   U.K. Ministry of Defence Strategy Map

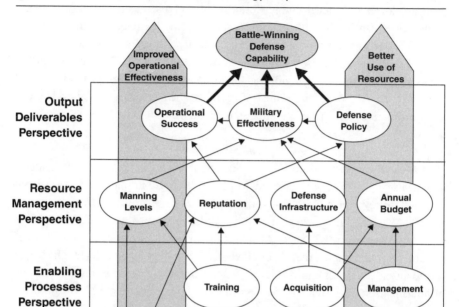

The MoD's map depicts numerous arrows connecting objectives. For this public-sector organization—in which resources are limited and investing in one resource means taking funds away from another—it is crucial to show the complex web of interactions and causality that the Scorecard team envisions. Here's a closer look at several lines of reasoning that thread their way up through the strategy map:

- *Building for the future perspective:* In the Scorecard team's thinking, the MoD's ability to fulfill its strategy and mission starts with investing in the right people, technology, and modernizing infrastructure. For instance, the "investing in people" objective signifies a specific train of thought: If the MoD ensures satisfactory living conditions for enlisted men and women, provides them with sufficient time to spend with their families, and takes care of them in other ways, their morale will increase. With higher morale, the ministry will see improvements in retention (which the

MoD's Scorecard includes as a metric). Better retention in turn will support the objectives "manning [staffing] levels" and "reputation" in the resource management perspective, as well as "training" in the enabling processes perspective. Effective training further contributes to a positive reputation and sufficient manning levels. Moreover, sufficient manning levels translate into "military effectiveness"—that central output deliverables objective contributing directly to the strategy.

- *Enabling processes, resource management, and output deliverables perspectives:* Success on the objectives in the building for the future perspective bubbles up into numerous objectives in the other perspectives. For example, if the ministry can boost retention rates, it will then be freer to spend less on retention incentives and recruiting initiatives. Reduced spending in these areas will in turn liberate funds for other important objectives, such as enhancing technology and equipment. With the right technology and equipment in hand, the MoD can fulfill its "acquisition" objective, which translates into improved "defense infrastructure" and "annual budget"—two objectives that further feed "military effectiveness."

Results

The ministry's use of its strategy map and Scorecard has improved communication and teamwork within the organization, enhancing decision making. Equally vital, communication with other government offices has also improved. For instance, the MoD now uses its map and Scorecard during funding negotiations with the Treasury—the body that authorizes appropriations for the ministry. By removing the emotion from funding discussions and enabling the MoD to dispassionately demonstrate the impact of various funding scenarios, the strategy map and Scorecard focus these crucial conversations on what matters: facts, and the MoD's and government's key priorities.

Case prepared by Lauren Keller Johnson, a contributor to the Balanced Scorecard Report, with generous assistance from Royal Navy Captain Mike Potter, Royal Air Force Wing Commander Des Cook, and Simon Howard of the Performance Management Team at the U.K. Ministry of Defence. Special thanks to Sir Kevin Tebbit, Permanent Under Secretary, U.K. Ministry of Defence, for sharing the MoD experience.

FULTON COUNTY SCHOOL SYSTEM

Background

The Fulton County School System encompasses seventy-seven public schools in two subdistricts, north and south of the city of Atlanta. The district has 70,000 students and a $560 million annual budget (2001 data). The district had a history of excellent planning and management. In 1998, Dr. Stephen

Dolinger, the FCSS superintendent, launched a Model of Excellence quality program guided by Malcolm Baldrige educational criteria. The criteria assigned up to 1,000 points based upon performance in seven categories: leadership; strategic planning; student, stakeholder, and market focus; information and analysis; faculty and staff focus; process management; and organizational performance results. Administrators felt that the Model of Excellence helped with local tactical activities and implementation but lacked alignment between strategy, performance measurement, and performance improvement.

FCSS hired Martha Taylor-Greenway in November 1999 as director of strategic planning with a primary emphasis on enhancing the performance management system. Taylor-Greenway had previously worked as vice president of organizational development at United Way of America, where she had been the project leader for the first Balanced Scorecard implementation at a nonprofit organization, in 1996–1997. She felt that the Balanced Scorecard could provide a strategic framework, a bigger picture, within which the Model of Excellence initiative could operate. Taylor-Greenway facilitated the development of a Balanced Scorecard for FCSS that organized objectives and performance measures in five categories: student achievement, stakeholders, instructional and administrative processes, staff learning and growth, and financial performance (see Figure 14-4).

Strategy Map

The high-level social impact objectives on the FCSS strategy map represent objectives for student achievement: to master curriculum and be nationally competitive. FCSS measured curriculum mastery through scores on curriculum-based tests and high school completion and graduation rates. It measured its students' national ranking through uniform exams, such as the Scholastic Aptitude Tests and Advanced Placement tests, as well as students' performance in their first two years after graduation, either in college or in employment.

The next level of the strategy map captured one set of driver objectives for student achievement, creating a *safe and enriching climate,* measured by attendance, extracurricular participation, and student and parent perceptions of safety. This level also contained objectives for two other FCSS stakeholders: *parents are involved and satisfied,* measured by a parent survey on quality, responsiveness, and communication; and *community is involved and has positive perception,* measured by number of volunteer hours; donations of money, service, and product; number of community and business organizations involved with FCSS; and a community survey of quality, community, and safety.

The internal process objectives related to delivering value to students and the community included *instructional effectiveness* (teacher training and use of technology), *transportation* (safety and on-time arrivals), *facilities and con-*

Figure 14-4 Fulton County School System Strategy Map

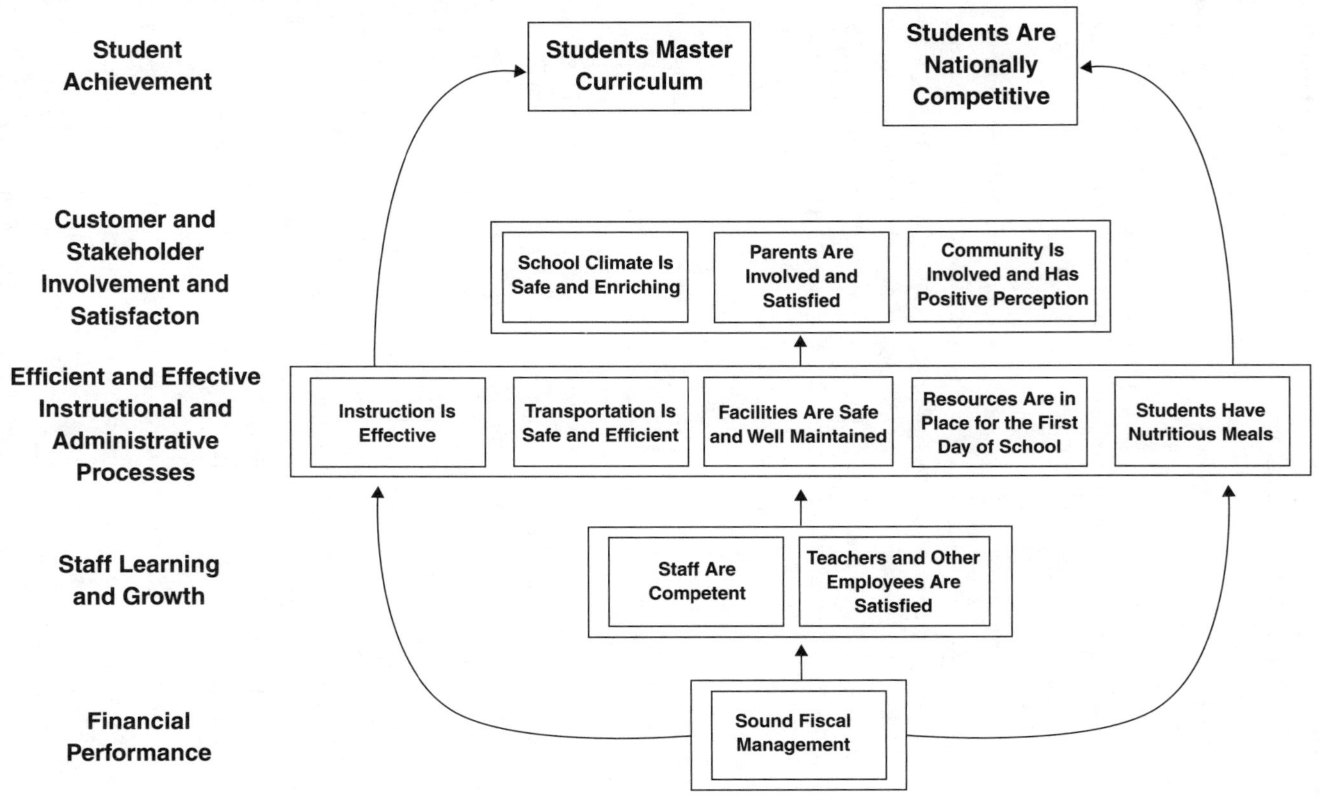

Student Achievement

Customer and Stakeholder Involvement and Satisfaction

Efficient and Effective Instructional and Administrative Processes

Staff Learning and Growth

Financial Performance

Students Are Nationally Competitive

Students Master Curriculum

Students Have Nutritious Meals

Community Is Involved and Has Positive Perception

Resources Are in Place for the First Day of School

Parents Are Involved and Satisfied

Facilities Are Safe and Well Maintained

School Climate Is Safe and Enriching

Transportation Is Safe and Efficient

Instruction Is Effective

Teachers and Other Employees Are Satisfied

Staff Are Competent

Sound Fiscal Management

struction (facility inspection report, backlogged maintenance requests), *readiness for start of school* (percentage of books and teachers available on the first day of school, accurate enrollment and cost forecasts), and *student nutrition* (student participation in meal program).

Learning and growth objectives related to *staff competency,* measured by teachers with at least seven years of experience, advanced degree, and national board certification; *employee satisfaction,* measured by staff attendance, attrition, and ratings of communication, teamwork, and morale. FCSS placed the financial perspective at the base of the strategy map with an objective for *sound fiscal management,* measured by expenditures on instruction support, fund balance, and budget variances.

The project team worked to ensure that valid data collection and reporting processes existed for each measure. It set systemwide performance targets for each measure based on historical trends and by benchmarking against other school districts. Local schools then developed initiatives aimed at contributing to meeting the designated targets. By the end of 2001, all FCSS schools were using the Balanced Scorecard to develop their strategic plans and to guide resource allocation.

Results

Among the short-term reactions and impact from the FCSS Balanced Scorecard were the following:

- There was a 22 percent improvement (from 66 percent to 88 percent) in one year in students passing a standardized mathematics test.
- A principal developed a tool for tracking student and teacher progress during the year rather than waiting for end-of-year results.
- A high school principal declared, "I want 90 percent of my students to pass every standard. That's what I put into the plan."
- An assistant superintendent of an administrative department noted, "The plan has forced us to ask hard questions on why budget items exist. Why are we doing X if X doesn't help us reach our goals?"
- An elementary school principal stated, "The Balanced Scorecard tells me which priorities are important to help the system perform better."

In 2001, the Fulton County School Board approved a pay-for-performance plan for the superintendent and school district cabinet members based on achieving BSC systemwide targets. Even more significant, the board approved a financial incentive plan for teachers that could award up to $2,000 to employees who contributed to meeting the targets within their local school's strategic plan. Individual schools set their own benchmarks and targets for this plan, guided by the central targets and approved by the central administration. The new incentive program changed the focus at local schools from performance measurement to performance rewards.

An article in the February 7, 2003 *Citizen* reported on the annual state-of-the-system address given by Dr. Thomas M. Payne, interim superintendent of FCSS. He noted:

> *The school system has made steady, deliberate progress to improve student achievement and organizational performance. We have consistently moved upward with no sudden peaks or slumps. . . . We have turned our organization around using a combination of best practices from education and business. We operate like a big business whose business is education.*

Among the gains during the past two years noted by Dr. Payne were:

- The percentage of students meeting and/or exceeding state-level reading and math performance expectations had typically increased by about 5 percentage points.
- High school students earning college credit prior to graduation increased from 10 percent to 16 percent.
- 76 percent of students taking Advanced Placement exams earned a score of 3 or higher (a 39 percent increase from two years earlier and 17 percent higher than the regional average).
- The number of students taking the SAT exam increased from 1,837 to 3,192 over eight years; the average test score increased from 992 to 1039 during this period. At FCSS, 88 percent of high school seniors now took the SAT exam, compared to the national average of 45 percent.
- Only 7 percent of FCSS parents expressed a safety concern, compared to 31 percent nationally.
- Volunteer hours increased by more than 87,000; 98,000 volunteers now were supporting FCSS schools .
- 82 percent of parents expressed satisfaction with their childrens' schools, compared to the national average of 68 percent.
- New schools opened on time and under budget.
- The first day of school began with textbooks, equipment, and supplies in place at all schools.
- Final budget was within 1 percent of projected revenue and expenses.

Dr. Payne used the Aesop fable of "The Tortoise and The Hare" to remind his constituents that perseverance, not speed, is most important when working toward a goal. FCSS will use its Balanced Scorecard performance management system for continuous improvement and to uphold its reputation as one of the premier school systems in Georgia and the nation.

We appreciate the active support of Martha Taylor-Greenway for providing access and documentation for the Fulton County School System story.

CHAPTER FIFTEEN

NONPROFIT ORGANIZATIONS

APPLYING THE BALANCED SCORECARD to nonprofit organizations has been one of the most gratifying extensions of the original concept. These organizations strive to deliver mission outcomes, not superior financial performance. So even more than for-profit companies, these organizations need a comprehensive system of nonfinancial and financial measures to motivate and evaluate their performance.

The Boston Lyric Opera (BLO) strategy map demonstrates how organizational performance can be measured even when the output is as intangible as beautiful music and an aesthetic experience. The BLO adopted the Balanced Scorecard after a period of rapid growth and success so that it could have a clear strategy for the future that would be easily understood and supported by its staff, board of directors, and artistic directors. The BLO strategy map represents desired outcomes and performance drivers for its three core constituents—loyal and generous donors, the national and international opera community, and Boston-area residents. The strategy map has led to mission-related initiatives bubbling up from frontline employees, better alignment of management and board processes, and support for a major community opera event in Boston.

Teach for America (TFA) recruits a national teacher corps drawn from talented, highly motivated graduating college seniors who commit two years to teach in urban and rural public schools. TFA developed its strategy map to represent the objectives and drivers for its two core themes for social change by corps members. First, corps members would enhance the educational experience of existing students through their two-year teaching positions. Second, they would influence future and fundamental educational reform through subsequent career decisions and voluntary participation activities. TFA has used its strategy map to engage a new generation of funders in its mission, to align recruiting for its teaching corps, staff, and board members, and to focus more intensively on activities that support alumni initiatives.

BOSTON LYRIC OPERA

Background

The Boston Lyric Opera (BLO) features world-class emerging singers, conductors, directors, and designers. Its mission is to produce high-quality professional opera productions, develop future opera talent, and promote opera appreciation through educational and community outreach. This three-pronged mission statement was enough to sustain the BLO through its early growth. Between 1995 and 2000, subscribers more than doubled, and the number of performances increased by 50 percent, making it the fastest-growing opera company in North America.

The Situation

In 2000, the company faced the challenge of what it should become. Even with the higher audience base, revenues from ticket sales remained less than 40 percent of operating expenses. The BLO needed to convert more subscribers to donors and attract significant funding from its supporters. A key board member felt that the BLO's kitchen cabinet-style governance structure was no longer sufficient and that a formal strategic planning process was essential to grow to the next stage. An active participant in several arts organizations, this board member had seen organizations fail because leaders had not actively involved the board in strategy and planning deliberations.

Janice Del Sesto, general director, formed a project team of senior BLO executives and key board members, to develop an explicit strategy that could be described with a Balanced Scorecard strategy map. The team included the board chairman, the chairman of the planning committee, and senior administrative staff, including Del Sesto and deputy general director Sue Dahling-Sullivan. Ellen Kaplan, a board member with extensive experience implementing the BSC in nonprofit organizations, served as the internal consultant and facilitator.

The Strategy Map

The team organized its strategy map by three high-level strategic themes, each relating to a key customer group (see Figure 15-1):

1. *Loyal and generous supporters:* Ticket sale revenues, even from selling out every performance, covered less than 35 percent of annual expenses. Subscribers who were willing to pay amounts over and above the high ticket prices (opera is the most expensive performing art to produce) were critical for long-term success. The BLO needed extensive, ongoing support from donors, foundations, and the community. Customer objectives for this strategic theme included attracting new donors, increasing support from existing donors, and recruiting new board members who could help the BLO accomplish its strategic objectives.

2. *National and international opera scene:* BLO could not hope to compete with the world's great opera houses, but wanted to differentiate itself from the many regional companies in North America. The BLO knew that attracting wealthy opera neophytes by offering a steady diet of Mozart, Puccini, and Verdi would not be adequate for meeting other elements of its mission. It wanted to have an impact on the national and international opera scene through artistically interesting and innovative productions.

   The customer objectives for this second strategic theme included attracting the best young talent who become future performers with the world's most prestigious opera companies, and developing a unique BLO style: crisp, simple, and elegant productions of popular, lesser known, and contemporary works.

3. *Community:* To attract new generations of audiences, the BLO would build support for opera in the greater Boston community and develop opera education programs for children, their families, and their schools.

With the customer objectives defined for the three high-level constituents, the project team could drill down to defining objectives for the three strategic themes. *Enhancing customer relationships* largely drove customer objectives for loyal and generous supporters, processes in the *operational excellence* theme largely drove the production of innovative, quality performances that would be recognized nationally and internationally, and innovation or increase brand awareness theme pointed at enhanced education, awareness, and support in the broader Boston-area community. The three strategic themes enabled tight linkages between the internal and customer perspectives on the BLO strategy map.

Learning and growth objectives related to human capital development, organizational alignment, and technology deployment that would enhance the performance of its critical internal processes. And the *financial perspective,*

Figure 15-1 Boston Lyric Opera Strategy Map

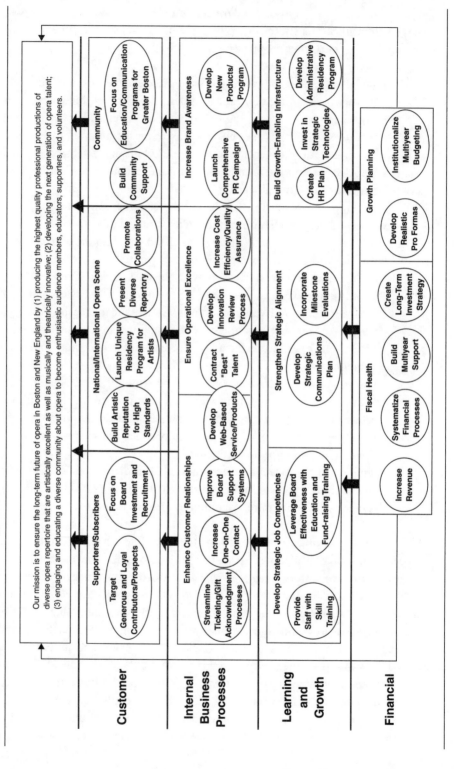

Our mission is to ensure the long-term future of opera in Boston and New England by (1) producing the highest quality professional productions of diverse opera repertoire that are artistically excellent as well as musically and theatrically innovative; (2) developing the next generation of opera talent; (3) engaging and educating a diverse community about opera to become enthusiastic audience members, educators, supporters, and volunteers.

Customer

Supporters/Subscribers
- Target Generous and Loyal Contributors/Prospects
- Focus on Board Investment and Recruitment

National/International Opera Scene
- Build Artistic Reputation for High Standards
- Launch Unique Residency Program for Artists
- Present Diverse Repertory
- Promote Collaborations

Community
- Build Community Support
- Focus on Education/Communication Programs for Greater Boston

Internal Business Processes

Enhance Customer Relationships
- Streamline Ticketing/Gift Acknowledgment Processes
- Increase One-on-One Contact
- Improve Board Support Systems
- Develop Web-Based Service/Products

Ensure Operational Excellence
- Contract "Best" Talent
- Develop Innovation Review Process
- Increase Cost Efficiency/Quality Assurance

Increase Brand Awareness
- Launch Comprehensive PR Campaign
- Develop New Products/Program

Learning and Growth

Develop Strategic Job Competencies
- Provide Staff with Skill Training
- Leverage Board Effectiveness with Education and Fund-raising Training

Strengthen Strategic Alignment
- Develop Strategic Communications Plan
- Incorporate Milestone Evaluations

Build Growth-Enabling Infrastructure
- Create HR Plan
- Invest in Strategic Technologies
- Develop Administrative Residency Program

Financial

Fiscal Health
- Increase Revenue
- Systematize Financial Processes
- Build Multiyear Support
- Create Long-Term Investment Strategy

Growth Planning
- Develop Realistic Pro Formas
- Institutionalize Multiyear Budgeting

with objectives for fiscal health and growth planning, anchored the foundation of the BLO strategy map.

Anecdotes and Results

The BLO project team cascaded the Scorecard down to individual departments within the opera company, including the artistic leaders. The process fostered a unity and integrity of purpose that had not existed before. The board became much more knowledgeable and aware of the three priorities for the opera company, and did not deflect it into marginal initiatives with little chance of payoff along one of the three strategic themes. All the company's constituents had become aligned and focused on BLO's strategy.

Jan Del Sesto, general director, wrote the three themes on the top of the whiteboard in the conference room before every staff meeting, saying, "I want our conversations to relate only to activities that support the themes. That way, we will stay focused on our objectives." Pre-BSC, Del Sesto noted, the company's fund-raising and subscriber events had few measures of success and little linkage to strategy. Post-BSC, the development office set priorities for its work and positioned its day-to-day activities to focus on "loyal and generous donors." These departments did not, as in the past, dissipate their scarce resources on programs that would not yield substantial payoffs. Young artistically trained staff understood for the first time how their day-to-day work affected BLO's business and the accomplishment of the BLO mission. The staff began to focus on initiatives and events that were likely to have the highest impact on organizational objectives. Cross-departmental initiatives arose: One junior staff person designed a new database application that streamlined donor information and increased the success of solicitation activities. The development department began to work more closely with the marketing/box office department on VIP seating and donor education initiatives. Many suggestions emanated from employees. A junior production staffer created a backstage tour for board members and prospective large donors to show how the magic in *The Magic Flute* was produced. For its community objectives, the company delivered a major new program, "Carmen on the Common," two evenings of opera performed free to more than 130,000 people in a downtown Boston park in September 2002. For many, this was their first opera experience.

The BSC had become a management tool for setting priorities among initiatives, motivating employees, aligning the board, and soliciting external support for the BLO's production and community outreach activities.

Our thanks to the leadership of Janice Mancini Del Sesto (general director), Sue Dahling-Sullivan (deputy general director), and BLO board members Sherif Nada (chairman), Ken Freed (planning committee), and Ellen Kaplan (BSC project consultant).

TEACH FOR AMERICA

Background

Wendy Kopp founded Teach for America (TFA) in 1989, based on her under-graduate honors thesis at Princeton.[1] Her vision was to ensure that one day all children in this nation would have the opportunity to attain an excellent education. TFA recruits a national teacher corps drawn from talented, highly motivated graduating college seniors who commit two years to teach in urban and rural public schools. TFA was one of the most successful nonprofit start-ups in recent years. By 2002, more than 8,000 young people had served as corps members, reaching more than one million students in sixteen urban and rural areas.

Strategy

TFA's strategy was based on an explicit model of social change in which corps members played two roles. First, they would improve the education experience and life experiences of existing students through their two-year teaching positions. Second, they would influence fundamental educational reform throughout their lives through their careers and voluntary participation activities.

Even before developing a Balanced Scorecard, Teach for America had established five key organizational priorities and started to measure performance for each priority. The priorities were:

1. Ensure corps members experience real success in closing the achievement gap between their students and students in more privileged areas.
2. Foster the leadership of alumni in pursuing the systemic changes needed to realize our vision.
3. Ensure our movement is as large and ethnically and racially diverse as possible.
4. Develop a sustainable funding base to support our efforts.
5. Build a thriving, diverse organization capable of consistently producing outstanding results over time.

Specific initiatives had been launched to drive improved performance for each priority.

The Strategy Map

With this excellent background in strategy formulation and performance measurement, it was a natural evolution to represent both the priorities and the measures within a strategy map framework. TFA's senior staff translated its high-level vision, mission, and organizational priorities into a Balanced Scorecard strategy map of linked strategic objectives (see Figure 15-2).

The social impact perspective, at the top, explicitly recognized two high-level objectives: improving the educational performance of today's students, and enhancing the educational opportunities for tomorrow's students. The first objective was difficult to measure because of the lack of standardized, high-quality metrics in the myriad of schools, regions, subject areas, and grades taught by corps members. TFA chose to use a subjective metric based on staff members "knowing it when they see it." TFA staff, in end-of-year one-on-one meetings, would ask corps members where their students started the year academically, where they finished the year, and how they knew it. Corps members who could supply reasonable evidence of dramatic gains (as defined more specifically by an internal standard) by their students would count toward this metric.

The second high-level objective, to create social change, would use several new metrics:

- Number of alumni (former corps members) in high-impact, visible positions effecting social change
- Number of alumni engaged in special initiatives
- Results of one-time studies

TFA would review annually the career paths of alumni to determine how many were currently engaged in important positions that could effect social change. TFA executives highlighted, in its special initiatives measures, four specific paths in which to encourage alumni: running for public office or working in public policy, entering school or district leadership, being truly outstanding classroom teachers, and publishing pieces about education and low-income communities. The third measure would be based on ad hoc studies such as those done by Surdna and Stanford on the impact of the Teach for America experience on its alumni.

The social impact measures helped further communicate to staff, resource providers, and especially the corps members themselves that success was not confined to their two-year teaching experiences. To achieve TFA's vision, corps members had to become lifetime agents for educational change and innovation.

TFA organized its internal operations key levers perspective through three strategic themes tied to their existing organizational priorities:

- Grow size and diversity of corps members
- Enhance corps member effectiveness
- Catalyze alumni movement

The organizational capacity perspective contained several typical learning and growth objectives relating to enhancing the talent and diversity of the employee base, deploying enhanced technology, and establishing alignment of employee goals to the strategy. One new objective would focus on building increased capabilities for its national board of directors.

Figure 15-2 Teach for America Strategy Map

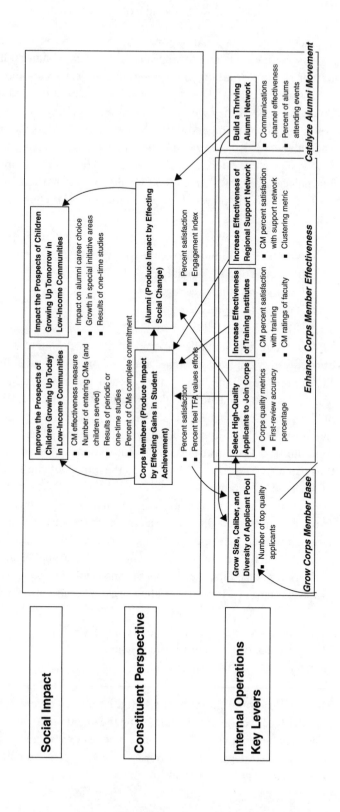

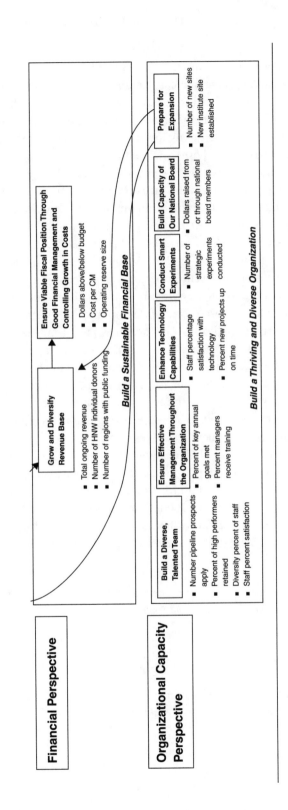

Financial Perspective

Organizational Capacity Perspective

Grow and Diversify Revenue Base

- Total ongoing revenue
- Number of HNW individual donors
- Number of regions with public funding

Ensure Viable Fiscal Position Through Good Financial Management and Controlling Growth in Costs

- Dollars above/below budget
- Cost per CM
- Operating reserve size

Build a Sustainable Financial Base

Build a Diverse, Talented Team

- Number pipeline prospects apply
- Percent of high performers retained
- Diversity percent of staff
- Staff percent satisfaction

Ensure Effective Management Throughout the Organization

- Percent of key annual goals met
- Percent managers receive training

Enhance Technology Capabilities

- Staff percentage satisfaction with technology
- Percent new projects up on time

Conduct Smart Experiments

- Number of strategic experiments conducted

Build Capacity of Our National Board

- Dollars raised from or through national board members

Prepare for Expansion

- Number of new sites
- New institute site established

Build a Thriving and Diverse Organization

Results

Teach for America has used its strategy map and Balanced Scorecard in a variety of settings to help communicate its direction and illuminate future challenges. For instance, at a major meeting of "investors" who had contributed large amounts of money to help it grow, a presentation of the strategy map and Scorecard led to a robust discussion of how to measure the impact of its alumni. That discussion and others led, ultimately, to improving the new measure of alumni impact to which all stakeholders agreed. Another discussion of the strategy map strengthened the focus on a key internal process. Previously, senior leaders had tended to think of and manage the process of placing corps members in school districts as one part of their broader efforts to train and support corps members. After articulating "placement" as a separate key lever, the organization focused high-level energy on doing everything possible to ensure the placement process went smoothly.

Over the past few years, despite a broadly challenging environment of reduced funding and increased scrutiny for nonprofits, Teach for America has continued to thrive. Applications to the corps grew from just under 5,000 in 2001 to 13,800 in 2002 and close to 16,000 in 2003. This has enabled an increase in the size of the incoming corps from just over 900 to close to 1,900 (nearly achieving, one year early, the 2004 target for an incoming corps size of 2,000). The objective to gauge the effectiveness of corps members led them to revamp the training curriculum and to strengthen the regional support network still further. The alumni movement continues to gain traction, such as through the new and widely used Office of Career and Civic Opportunities. While senior executives are cautious, they expect to continue their 30 percent annual growth in fund-raising and hit their 2003 target of close to $28 million in ongoing revenues, up from $12 million in 2000. And the organization has continued to build its capacity for the future by adding to its technology infrastructure, bringing on strong new staff members and acquiring prominent new national board members.

We appreciate the support of Jerry Hauser, chief operating officer of Teach for America, for sharing the organization's experience.

NOTES

1. Wendy Kopp, *One Day All Children . . . :The Unlikely Triumph of Teach for America and What I Learned Along the Way* (New York: Public Affairs, 2001).

INDEX

ABOUT THE AUTHORS

ROBERT S. KAPLAN is the Marvin Bower Professor of Leadership Development at Harvard Business School. Formerly he was on the faculty of the Graduate School of Industrial Administration, Carnegie-Mellon University, where he also served as Dean from 1977 to 1983. He is the creator of the Harvard Business School video series *Measuring Corporate Performance* and the author or coauthor of thirteen *Harvard Business Review* articles, more than 100 other papers, and eleven books, including three with David Norton. His research, teaching, consulting, and speaking focus on new performance and cost management systems, primarily the Balanced Scorecard and Activity-Based Costing. He has received numerous honors, including the Outstanding Educator Award from the American Accounting Association and the Chartered Institute of Management Accountants (UK) Award for "Outstanding Contributions to the Accountancy Profession." Dr. Kaplan is Chairman of the Balanced Scorecard Collaborative. He can be reached at rkaplan@hbs.edu.

DAVID P. NORTON is President of Balanced Scorecard Collaborative, Inc., a professional services firm that facilitates the worldwide awareness, use, enhancement, and integrity of the Balanced Scorecard. Previously he was the President of Renaissance Solutions, Inc., a consulting firm he cofounded in 1992, and of Nolan, Norton & Company, where he spent seventeen years as President. Dr. Norton is a management consultant, researcher, and speaker in the field of strategic performance management. With Robert Kaplan, he is the cocreator of the Balanced Scorecard concept, coauthor of four *Harvard Business Review* articles, and coauthor of *The Balanced Scorecard: Translating Strategy into Action* and *The Strategy-Focused Organization: How Balanced Scorecard Companies Thrive in the New Business Environment*. He is a Trustee of Worcester Polytechnic Institute and a former Director of ACME (the Association of Consulting and Management Engineers). He can be reached at dnorton@bscol.com.